ELEMENTARY CURRICULUM

By

Prof. Marlow Ediger
Truman State University
201 W, 22nd, Box 417
North Newton KS 67117
United States of America

Editor

Dr. Digumarti Bhaskara Rao
R.V.R. College of Education
1-22-10, Srinivasa Nagar
Guntur—522 006
A.P., India

DISCOVERY PUBLISHING HOUSE
NEW DELHI-110002

First Published-2003
Reprint 2005
Reprinted-2006
Reprinted-2007
Reprinted: 2013
ISBN 81-7141-658-6

Published by
DISCOVERY PUBLISHING HOUSE
4831/24, Ansari Road, Prahlad Street,
Darya Ganj, New Delhi-110002 (India)
Phone: 3279245 • Fax: 91-11-3253475
E-mail:dphtemp@indiatimes.com

Printed at: Dynamic printers, Delhi

Preface

The curriculum is the soul of the educational process, the heart of educational institution and the mind of the academic programme. It is the tool in the hands of the teachers to mould his students according to the goals of the education, and aims and objectives of the course. Any course cannot be conducted without a prescribed curriculum. More particularly, a definite as well as flexible curriculum at elementary level is needed as it is a combination of various subjects, skills, abilities, aptitudes and understandings.

The present book on elementary curriculum is intended to guide preservice and inservice teachers to teach effectively, to provide insights to the curriculum designers to develop a suitable curriculum, to the writers to suggest suitable learning experiences, and to the parents to cooperate to realise the potentialities of their children.

This book is touching all the important issues of curriculum, curriculum development, language arts, social studies, science, mathematics, assessment and evaluation.

The curriculum designers, textbooks writers and practicising teachers may utilize the views and opinions presented in this book for the quality improvement of elementary education.

Prof. Marlow Ediger
Dr. D. Bhaskara Rao

Contents

1

The Curriculum

Curriculum is the soul of the process of education. It is the heart of the educational institution and mind of the course and all that only goes with it. Identifying the place of curriculum in educational process Cunningham once said that "Curriculum is the tool in the hands of the artist (the teacher) to mound his material (the pupils) according to his ideals (aims and objectives) in his studies (the school)."

The word curriculum is derived from a Latin word 'currere' which means 'to run'. So, "the curriculum means a course to be run for reaching a certain goal". This meaning does not inform enough specifically and intelligently. In fact, the term curriculum has a rich past which in itself is an interesting subject of study. An important definition of curriculum states the role and characteristics of a curriculum.

'The requisite content of knowledge arranged systematically for progressive acquisition; the total living of the child so far as the school can influence it or should take responsibility for developing it; the specialised environment deliberately arranged for directing the interests and abilities of children toward effective participation in the life of the community and the nation; concerned with helping children, enrich their own lives and contribute to the improvement of the society through the acquisition of useful informations, skills and attitudes; the learning experiences which children and youth have under the direction of school; the sequence of potential experience set up in the school for the purpose of disciplining children and youth in group; ways of thinking and acting; the continuous activity of the individual interacting with the environmental factors about him, the learnings or changes in behaviour that occur in the chain of series of experiencing; the systematic arrangement of course designed to meet the needs of a pupil or a group of pupils; the complete school environment involving all the courses, activities, readings and associations furnished to the pupils in the guidance of the school; all the learning experiences provided by the school, class study, health recreation services and guidance services; social inheritance organised for its rapid assimilation by immature minds; the means to attain the aims of education, *viz.*, the complete manhood for the attainment of a full life; and all the experiences which take place under the sponsorship of the school.'

According to the Secondary Education Commission's Report, 'Curriculum is much more than the boundaries by the academic subjects taught traditionally'. It should include totality of experiences that pupil receives through the manifold activities that go on in the school, in the classroom, library, laboratory, workshop, playgrounds and in the numerous informal contacts between teachers and pupils. In this sense, the whole life of the school becomes the curriculum .... and helps in the evaluation of balanced personality.'

These explanations rule out the possibility of a nation-wide curriculum for all pupils of all people if one considers the individual differences among pupils not only at various age levels but also at the same as well. In a report, Half Our Future: A Report of the Central Advisory Council for Education, on the education of average pupils in England says:

> We should neither draw up a fixed table of information, subject by subject, what all pupils should master, nor even prescribed beyond the minimum essentials set out in the preceding paragraph a set list of subjects which all should study. A universal subjects curriculum ought to be ruled out if only because of the wide range both of capacity and of taste among the pupils with whom we are concerned. At the bottom end of the scale, it is a matter of finding a very few things in which the pupils show interest and can make progress and working outwards from them. Near the top of our terms of reference, half-way up of the whole scale of ability, it is a matter of selecting from, fairly large number of possibilities those that are likely to be more valuable to the individual pupils. The selection will vary from group to group. On the pupil's side, a prime consideration will often be relevance to what they are going to do when they leave school; on the school's side, the selection is bound to be affected by the strengths and weaknesses of the staff. An historian turned reluctant geographer, or vice versa, is not likely to inspire pupils who take a great deal of rousing at the best of times. Both subjects can, as we shall see later, offer many of the same values. If the head decides that the cobbler had better stick to his last, we shall neither be surprised nor unduly distressed.

We can say that the curriculum is an evolving concept. It is always in the making, being more in the nature of the process than a finished product. It informs us what to teach before we can consider methods and approaches to teaching and the age at which the various ideas are to be introduced (Vaidya). It is futile to talk 'how' and 'when' to teach without first deciding 'what' to teach.

There are four significant dimensions essentially to be considered when one talks of curriculum development. They are the determination of educational directions, the choice of principles and procedures for selecting and ordering the potential experiences comprising the instructional programme, the selection of a pattern of curriculum organisation and the determination of principles and procedures by which changes in the curriculum can be made (Smith, Stanely and Shores).

Variables of Curriculum

A curriculum does not exist in isolation. It comes about as a resultant of many variables having varying degrees of mutual interaction which impinge on it. Some of the most important variables are teacher, pupil examination and evaluation, instructional and illustrative material and research (Vaidya).

Purpose of Curriculum

The curriculum serves of the following purposes since it is the source of all activities of the institution.

(i) To provide pupils continuous as well as sequential experiences right from the very beginning of the school onward, that is, through the secondary school on into the college;

(ii) To approach science conceptually rather than factually as well as with somewhat less emphasis on the technical application of science;

(iii) To use those methods of instruction which familiarize students not only with the nature of scientific enterprise but also with various processes of science (measuring and counting precisely, hypothesizing, setting up control experiments, recognising assumptions, testing and evaluating evidence, generalising and applying concepts and principles) which lie at the heart of scientific method;

(iv) To provide deeper insights into the schema of the structure of science, that is, its philosophy, history and methods of inquiry;

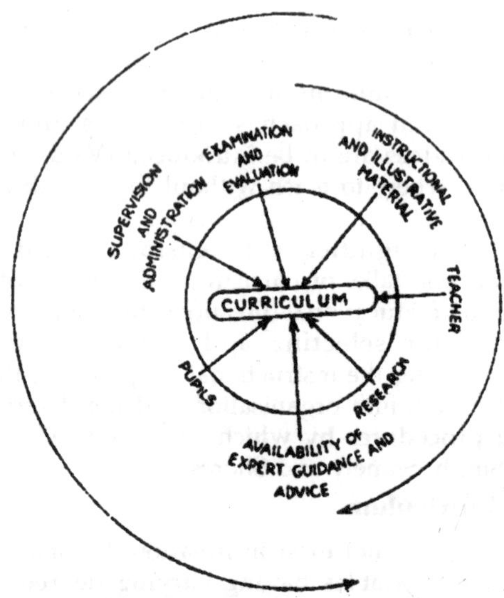

(v) To provide effectively for dividual differences, ability, needs and interests;

(vi) To make maximum use of local skills and resources; and lastly

(vii) To provide for built in mechanisms which provide for its continuous and critical re-evaluation.

Curricular Requirements for Exceptional Children

Usually, the curriculum will be developed considering the class children as average. But, in any class one can see gifted as well as backward children. The existing curricula do not at all take into consideration their felt needs, interest, capacities, capabilities, aspirations, etc. We now mention below the significant considerations of the educational programmes (Vaidya).

Characteristics of the Curriculum

The curriculum considers many aspects such as course objectives, institutional facilities, individual needs, societal requirements and so on. Hence it possess certain characteristics.

Smith, Stanely and Shores have felt the need of a progressive curriculum. The main characteristics of it are:

1. It must be mostly based upon the first hand experiences of the pupils from all the significant areas of human living. These experiences are characterized by newness, novelty, challenge,

	Significant considerations	Gifted	Backward	Remarks
1.	Individual instruction	It should be adapted to their potentialities. There should be, then, increasing emphasis on self-education	They respond better when taught individually in small groups of two, three or four	Backward pupils need continuous individualised attention throughout the the school period
2.	Education based upon immediate experience	It should only be in the beginning. This, then becomes their take-off point	Their education should centre on concrete experience They can thus check their thoughts against experience	—
3.	Emphasis on subject matter and the development of personal curriculum	Subject matter should receive increasing emphasis	Subject matter is of secondary importance Development of personality is of paramount importance	—
4.	Utilitarian type of work	Not essential	Essential	—
5.	School as 'home base'	Not necessarily	It strengthens their self-confidence and reinforces self-respect	—

(Contd...)

	Significant considerations	Gifted	Backward	Remarks
6.	Teacher strong in one of the disciplines	Essential	Broad based and trained in psychology and guidance	—
7.	Elastic time-table	It is highly desirable	It is highly desirable	—
8.	Use of psychological tools for identification purposes	Their use is highly desirable. Their problems can be easily identified and relevant steps taken in advance. Teacher can also plan their instructional and educational programmes on secure grounds in the light of their potentialities	Their use is highly desirable. Their problems can be, thus, easily determined and the corresponding measures can be easily applied	—
9.	Rapport between teacher and pupil	Even less rapport at a later stage can work without suffering any loss in efficiency. If teacher is a researcher, then first class rapport between the teacher and pupil is a must, Generally speaking, the goal should be: pupils should depend less and less on the teacher as they go up the school ladder.	More highly desirable. In fact, the same teacher should work with them throughout the school.	—

Significant considerations	Gifted	Backward	Remarks
10. Motivation	It is desirable in the beginning but, later on, they can motivate themselves.	They require more of it. Motivation needs to be reinforced quite frequently.	—
11. Methods of teaching	Expository discourse and techniques of explanation. Teaching techniques largely based upon language activities, lecture, method and question-answer method, etc.	Their teaching needs to be approached through concrete methods of teaching. They respond very effectively to methods involving self-activity.	—
12. Deliberate social direction	It is desirable but not essential.	It is highly desirable and essential.	—
13. Examination	Choice of subjects should be theirs but the examination standards should be highly exacting and demanding.	It should be optional for them. Focus should be on the development of wholesome personality.	—

(Contd...)

	Significant considerations	Gifted	Backward	Remarks
14.	Immediate opportunities for success	Immediate opportunities for experiencing success are not essential. High standards can be fixed for them.	They need immediate success experiences otherwise they lose interest in their work.	—
15.	Individual and group work	It is highly desirable.	It is essential. They hardly benefit from ordinary classroom teaching.	—
16.	Role of the teacher	They demand high standards from the teacher.	They demand emotional understanding and dedication from them. from them.	Teacher should enjoy more professional freedom in his local situations.
17.	Emphasis on environmental studies.	These should receive general emphasis. Productive thinking and theory-building need to be increasingly stressed.	Their curriculum should be organised around their centres of interest. Environmental studies vitalize their learning.	—

	Significant considerations	Gifted	Backward	Remarks
18.	Field trips	Field trips are essential as these vitalize their subject matter knowledge and, thus, lead to the deeper understanding of facts, concepts and principles.	They play a significant part in their lives. These should be dovetailed with their vocational plans.	—
19.	Repetition and drill	It should only be to a limited extent.	They need more of it.	—
20.	Education for life, more of the basic education variety	It is highly desirable but of secondary importance. They are expected to dig more and more of new knowledge and develop highly sophisticated skills. They will be our future pace-setters in national affairs.	It is essential.	—

stimulation and creativity. Content receives increasing emphasis as the children move to the higher grades.

2. It should emphasize intellectual structure; and conceptual themes.
3. It should provide sufficient scope for observation, experimentation, independent work, drawing of inferences and criticism of experimental results obtained in the laboratory. Further, it should provide pupils sufficient experiences in formulating problems not only pinpointedly but more and more productively as well. Pupils will thus gain practice in the use of scientific method indirectly at their level of development.
4. It should provide sufficient scope for the cultivation of skills, interest, attitudes and appreciations.
5. It should be psychologically sound. It should take into account the theories of learning relevant to science teaching (Gestalt psychology, Geneva School and the work of those psychologists and educators which relates to the Acceleration of Mental Development in particular). Further, children's capacities and capabilities, if taken into account, will lead to the development of differentiated curriculum (for meeting individual differences). Incorporating geographical difference in it will be another innovation.
6. It should aim at bringing about an intelligent and effective adjustment with the environment itself. Further, it should enable pupils to acquire relevant scientific information of subsequent use in the significant areas of human living.
7. It should foster the growth or development of attitude and skills required for manipulating a planned social order of democratic type. To put more concretely, it should contribute towards democratic living.
8. It is tested and improved through research.
9. Lastly, it should not be narrowly conceived, should not be static but dynamic and forward looking; sample adequately both the scientific content and the abilities of the pupils to be developed, should cater to the right use of leisure later on and should be related to the environment in which the children live. Consequently, it will then become exciting, real and imaginative.

Sharma wants the following reorientation to the curriculum.

(i) The content chosen should be in conformity with the aims and objectives of teaching science.

(ii) It should be related to the interests of different age groups and everyday life and the needs of the community. It should bear direct significance to life's problems and activities. There should be a wide range of scientific subjects which will emphasis the unity of scientific approach to meaningful and socially significant human problems. They should not be meaningless disconnected fragments but should be sought for social understanding and develop desirable social behaviour and are learnt through child's experience.

(iii) Mastery of the subject-matter should not be made an end in itself. Teaching pupils 'how to think' is more important than teaching them 'what to think'.

(iv) It should consist of a variety of physical and mental activities that will lead to those knowledge, skills, interests and attitudes which are necessary for proper adjustment to the social and physical environments.

(v) The content that is used in giving pupils experiences in scientific, thinking must be interesting, informative and free from inaccuracies of superficialities.

(vi) Opportunities should be provided for first hand experience and for application of scientific method, acquired knowledge, skills, and attitudes to life situations, but various experiences that are educative should not be neglected.

(vii) It should be flexible and should suit the varying needs of the children and the community.

(viii) It should also include the material which helps in the appreciation of the work and sacrifice of great scientists in their search for truth.

(ix) It should be such as can be adequately dealt with under stipulated conditions, such as available time, staff, equipment etc.

(x) The learning activities should be organised in order to difficulty so that the pupils through reasonable effort may gain the satisfactions of accomplishment. This will afford opportunity for the exercise of creative abilities of pupils which in turn will make the students self-confident, self-reliant and independent. He will pursue science as a hobby and not something forced upon him.

(xi) The course should be divided into units, each should contain essentially a major problem of everyday life. Each unit should again be divided into subordinate problems

to facilitate learning by the pupils. These units or topics should be organised in such a way that the succeeding units will call for the understanding of larger and larger relationships and conceptions. Though for the sake of convenience the topics may be listed under different branches of science but it should always be borne in mind that topics should not be dealt as isolated items but should be so inter-related and integrated that their independence and their usefulness to mankind may be stressed thoughout.

(xii) Provision should be made for science societies, visits to places of scientific interests and projects, etc.

Since curriculum development is a dynamic process and must never be static, the curriculum should always be in a process of revision leading to modernisation, refinement and enrichment.

REFERENCES

Bhaskara Rao, D (1993). *Vignanasashtra Bhodhana (Teaching of Science)*. Guntur: Nagarjuna Publishers.

Bhaskara Rao, D. and K. Vijaya (1995). *A Text Book Evaluation*. Ambala Cantt: The Associated Publishers.

Ediger, Marlow and D. Bhaskara Rao (1996). *Science Curriculum*. New Delhi, India: Discovery Publishing House.

Sharma, R.C. (1995). *Modern Science Teaching*. Delhi: Dhanpat Rai and Sons.

Smith, Stanely and Shores (1957). *Fundamentals of Curriculum Development*. New York: Harcourt, Brace and World, Inc.

Vaidya, Narendra (1971). *The Impact Science Teaching*. New Delhi: Oxford and IBH Publishing Co.

2

Curriculum Development

The prime aim of education has shifted to totality of experiences from acquisition of knowledge. As education is regarded as a dynamic process so the aims and objectives have changed. In order to justify the aims and objectives of a subject as well as a course it is essential to know what to teach? So vast is the field of science that it is no small problem to decide what facts should be taught? Since curriculum is the totality of experiences of a child, and the experiences of each child are different from others, so the curriculum will be different for each pupil. It is, therefore, very essential to develop or prepare or construct or organise curriculum which should meet the requirement of each individual, necessities of the society and aims and objectives of the course. The curriculum is developed in different countries in different ways.

I. Styles of Curriculum Development

Three specific styles are followed, in the United States, namely instrumental, interactive and individualistic. The specific needs for more and better-prepared students led to the development of instrumental type of curriculum in 1950s. In mid-sixties, it is followed by interactive style as curriculum reform which extended to other aspects of the school programmes and other sections of the school community. By the end of 1960s, a third style called individualistic which aimed at the development of the individual. Each style has its own specific characteristic.

II. Approaches to Curriculum Development

The curriculum can be organised depending on the objectives to be achieved. Majority five approaches, *viz.*, Integrated or Disciplinary, Flexible or Structured, Conceptual or Factual, Process or Content, and Teacher-centred or Pupil-centred. Any one or a combination of these approaches can be used in developing the curriculum.

Styles of Curriculum Development

Styles	Instrumental	Interactive	Individualistic
Major Goals	Utilitarian Job/career oriented	Society oriented Social development.	Personal or individual development
Implicit values	People as things (competition)	People as social animals (Interaction and cooperation)	People as individuals (idioswncratic/ self-development)
Subject Domains	Disciplinary	Interdisciplinary (humanities, G. sciences, social studies)	Gross inter-disciplinary (Science and humanities mix)
Taxonomic Domains	Cognitive	Affective	Creative
Materials	Highly structured (Teachers handbooks, students workbooks, prescribed texts etc.)	Loosely structured (Students packages, teachers guides, multi-media etc.)	Unstructured (Modular based, resource banks, retrieval system).
Teacher's Role	As Director	As Manager	As Assistant
Teaching Techniques	Lecture, Discovery, Inductive, Inquiry	Group projects, Problems Solving, Discussions	Self-instructional techniques, practical tasks
Evaluation Techniques	Teacher evaluation—mainly objective (Pre-specified goals)	Teacher evaluation mainly Subjective	Self-evaluation (goals identified during the process of learning)

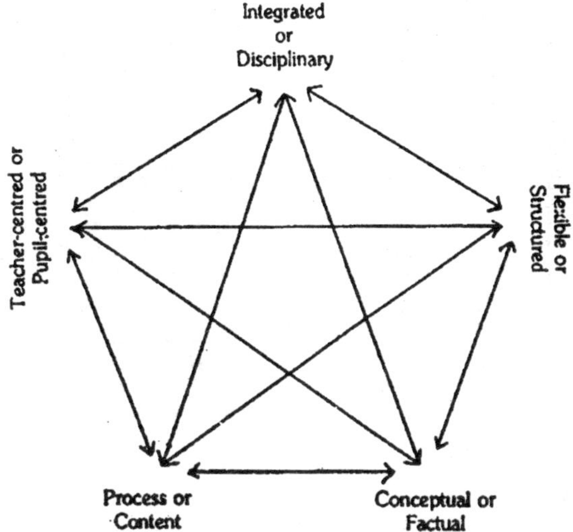

Approaches to Curriculum Development

III. Patterns of Curriculum Development

Curriculum can be organised by following different patterns, namely, Subject-centred, Activity-centred, and Core-centred. These patterns can be used independent of each other or can be mixed-up, depending on the content, subject and purpose.

IV. Trends in Curriculum Development

Many trends are followed in developing the curriculum. But, Individualised, Inter-disciplinary, and Social-issues Oriented trends and followed mainly at the time of curriculum organisation.

1. Individualised Trend

Individualised trend is widely supported by educationists as it allows the student to engage in activities or programmes or instruction uniquely appropriate to his own style and pace of learning. The instruction in this type promotes independence and provides opportunities for study beyond resources. This trend meets the individual requirements of each child at his peculiar level of ability, achievements and progression. But this trend consumes lots of resources and requires high quantities of manual and material facilities.

2. Interdisciplinary Trend

The trend has presently shifted from uni-disciplinary to inter-disciplinary as there is increasing co-relation among various

Characteristics	Patterns of Curriculum Organisation			
Distinctive Characteristics	Subject centred	Activity centred	Core centred	Additional remarks
1. Research scientists classify total knowledge into its different branches so as to master atleast one branch of knowledge. It is assumed that after schooling is over, one may continue mastering the rest.	Present	—	—	
2. Four kinds of exposition are used: Simple to complex, whole to part, chronological, and pre-requisite learnings.	Present	—	—	
Teaching techniques stressed are: lectures, discussions, questions and answers, written exercises, oral reports, term papers, only relevant laboratory work in science and activities, like painting, cartooning, modelling, designing and constructing (in broader sense) receive less emphasis.	Present	—	—	Emphasis is on the mastering of facts, principles and laws rather than for the evidence of growth in habits of thinking and social processes. Development of critical thinking is not ruled out, knowledge is not arranged to increase the practical intelligence and wisdom.

(Contd...)

Characteristics	Patterns of Curriculum Organisation			
Distinctive Characteristics	**Subject centred**	**Activity centred**	**Core centred**	**Additional remarks**
3. Solely depends upon interest and purposes of children what is taught and how it is approached depend upon the realisation of children's purposes.	—	Present	—	—
4. Common learnings result from the pursuit of common interests by particular groups of children. At its best, teacher does not hesitate to develop personal curriculum for each child.	—	May or may not be present	Present	—
5. Curriculum emphasizes social values	May or may not be present	May or may not be present	Present	It is woven around themes of social living, for example protection and conversion of life, property and natural resources, felt needs of the individual for social adjustment in a variety of circumstances. Further, it fosters social integration

(Contd…)

Characteristics		Patterns of Curriculum Organisation			
	Essential Characteristics	Subject centred	Activity centred	Core centred	Additional remarks
6.	Curriculum is planned in advance.	Present	—	Only minimum common learnings are insisted upon for all students regardless of their ability and socio-economic status.	In subject curriculum, help is sought from experts and some times teachers are co-opted. Individual differences are met through optional subjects and designing differentiated assignments.
7.	Mastery in one of the school subjects at a very advanced level is important.	Present	Present	Present	—
8.	Activities are planned co-operatively by students and teachers	—	Present	Present	—
9.	Problem-solving is employed as a dominant method of teaching. Teacher does not short circuit the learning process Project method is preferred.	—	Present	Present	—

(Contd...)

Characteristics	Patterns of Curriculum Organisation			
Essential Characteristics	Subject centred	Activity centred	Core centred	Additional remarks
10. Children's individual needs and interests are met within the programme—special pursuits or subjects provide for differentiated interests.	—	Present	Present	—
11. Teachers having broad general education with specialized training in child and adolescent psychology and guidance are required.	--	Present	Present	—
12. Availability of flexible teaching facilities in abundance for carrying out various types of activities (Individual, small group and class) is required.	—	Present	Present	—

(Contd...)

Characteristics	Patterns of Curriculum Organisation			
Essential Characteristics	**Subject centred**	**Activity centred**	**Core centred**	**Additional remarks**
13. Availability of equipment and materials consistent with children's interest and requirements at various age levels.	—	Present	Present	—
14. Availability of transport facilities.	Present	Present	Present	For enriching subject matter knowledge in case of subject curriculum and development of interest etc. in case of the other two.
15. Length of the period.	As necessary and then fixed	Flexible	Flexible	—
16. Grouping of students is allowed.	Rarely	Frequently	Frequently	—

subjects or branches of curriculum. The recent efforts to develop curricula in the areas of environmental and population education indicate a trend towards inter-disciplinary approach in curriculum construction. These areas are challenging in the sense that they require consideration in the context of biological, sociological, historical, economical and political realities. There are, however, certain problems to implement inter-disciplinary curriculum. We need expert teachers to co-relate different disciplines. Team teaching serves better in this trend. There must be inter-disciplinary training in teacher education.

3. Social-issues Oriented Trend

There is an increased trend in developing curriculum to emphasize in social implications. There are many social issues, norms or problems, which must be included in the curriculum. Because of this only, many subjects are having concepts on population, pollution, health, mental health, agriculture etc. This trend in constructing the curriculum would require an open classroom format for teaching. It emphasizes self-discipline, free choices of instructional materials and format by the pupils and social relevance. It will take teachers and taught some time to get comfortable in the less structured teaching and learning (Sharma). Teacher education programmes will have to be changed drastically to meet the challenge.

V. Principles of Curriculum Development

Curriculum development involves certain principles which need to be considered to fulfill the requirements of the individual and the society and to achieve the aims and objectives of the course and institution. Those principles are:

1. Principles of the Nature and Objective of the Course

As every course is started to achieve certain aims and objectives depending on its nature, the curriculum should be in confirmity of those goals.

2. Principle of the Duration of the Course

Every course will have its times duration. Depending on the availability of time the curriculum must be constructed.

3. Principle of the Availability of Resources

The curriculum implementation requires both manual and material resources. Hence the curriculum must be practical by considering the availability of teachers, laboratories, equipment, text books, evaluation tests, etc. If one aims highly, there will be a total failure.

4. Principle of the Totality of Experiences

The curriculum must be facilitator of total experiences needed for a child.

5. Principle of the Individual Interests

(a) ***Principle of Utility:*** The curriculum should meet the daily needs of the children. It should give practical knowledge so as to enjoy the life and to adjust to the changing conditions of life and society.

(b) ***Principle of Vocational Requirement:*** The curriculum should prepare the pupils for future life by providing information about their future vocational requirements, otherwise the schooling will result in a waste.

(c) ***Principle of Creativeness:*** Every child will have some creativity. The curriculum must provide opportunities to utilize and promote creativeness of the pupils.

(d) ***Principle of Development of Innate Powers:*** The innate powers of the children must be drawn out and sharpened by the curriculum. The pupils can be kept in place of a scientist so as develop their innate powers.

(e) ***Principle of Child Centredness:*** No two children will be alike in this universe as the knowledge, achievement, interests, abilities, attitudes, social status, and physical conditions change from individual to individual. Hence the curriculum should meet the individual requirements by having the characteristic of child-centredness.

(f) ***Principle of Elasticity and Variety:*** The curriculum shall create dis-interest in it if it is rigid and narrowly conceived. So it should balanced by giving emphasis to cultural values, interests, abilities and by permitting a variety of skills, habits, hobbies, etc.

(g) ***Principle of Leisure Time Pursuits:*** We are well aware of the proverb that 'an idle man's brain is a devil's workshop'. So the curriculum should provide work for the leisure time of the children. This can be achieved by nature study, collection and preservation of specimens, photography, gardening, socially useful productive work, and such other activities.

(h) ***Principle of Activity Centredness:*** Emphasis should be there in the curriculum on learning by doing. Elaborate provision should be there for laboratory activities and field experiences.

(i) ***Principle of Forward Looking:*** The curriculum should help a child in adjusting and preparing for a full and effective adult life.

(j) ***Principle of Moral Values:*** To live in the society as a successful citizen the curriculum should develop the social norms and mores.

6. Principle of the Society Interests

(a) ***Principle of Vocational Requirements:*** Society is a complex organisation. For its effective functioning agencies such as transport, communication, productivities, electricity, agriculture, health, water, etc., are required in a good way and to achieve these we need trained personnel. Hence the curriculum should have provisions to meet these vocational requirements.

(b) ***Principles of Progress of the Society:*** The progress of a society depends on its people who have scientific knowledge as the scientific knowledge develops a complete personality in a man. So the curriculum should be in a position to improve the scientific knowledge of the learners.

(c) ***Principle of Integrity of the Society:*** The existence of any society mainly depends on its integration. By providing opportunities of learning about the advantages derived by integration the curriculum can develop integrative attitude in the minds of pupils.

(d) ***Principle of Conservation:*** The curriculum should preserve and transmit the customs, traditions, standards of conduct, social norms, etc., on which the culture and civilization depend.

(e) ***Principle of International Consciousness:*** Though one belongs primarily to his birth nation, he is no more limited to one nation and he is indebted to the constitutions of many nations. So one must feel that he is first a man and a world citizen and hence this should be achieved by the curriculum. The knowledge about the contributions of scientists to mankind, the interdependence of nations, etc., can help the children in developing in them the international consciousness.

VI. Systems of Organising Curriculum

The content organisation in the curriculum needs a careful consideration depending on the objectives to be achieved and facilities that are available. The content can be organised in different ways.

1. Logical Order Method

In logical order method, the topics or lessons will be arranged in an orderly manner from simple to complex stages. The arrangement of lessons will be in the same class or it can be spread to some other classes of the course.

2. Concentric Method

The topics, in this method, will find a place in different classes of different years of a course in a progressive manner. The content will be included from simple to complex as the classes progress so as to make the pupils understand the content according to capabilities that present in chronological and mental ages. This method is useful in primary and secondary school levels.

3. Topic Method

In this method, the content selected will be explained in detail in the same class at the same point. Once completed, there will be no future learning about his at any stage. Usually, this method will be of use at higher stages of learning.

4. Psychological Method

The subject matter, in this method, will be selected basing on the psychological level of the pupils. Depending on the mental ages, the content will be chosen.

5. Historical Method

Arrangement of subject matter takes place as per its historical development. The content will be linked with contemporary issues, inventions, kingdoms, etc.

6. Seasonal Arrangement of Lessons Method

The lessons will be arranged in the curriculum according to availability of natural resources. It will be absurd to teach about rain in summer or about a frog's life history in non-seasons. Hence the arrangement or content follows the seasons.

VII. Modern Emerging Trends in Science Curriculum Development

Science education is now major concern all over the world as it is expanding beyond our imagination both quantitatively and qualitatively. It is gratifying the needs and desires of the human populations. Now, since the beginning the century, many new trends in the construction of science curriculum.

1. Establishment of State Institutes of Science Education

Many parts of the world, of course many parts of a nation too, are witnessing separate institutions of science education which are responsible the development of science curriculum, planning and implementation of science education in schools, and training the teachers of science.

2. Emphasis on Conceptual Learning

There is a shift to conceptual understanding of science from the traditional learning of facts. The curriculum is also so planned and implemented in many states.

3. Integrated Science

The present trend is toward unified or integrated approach to the organisation of content within various branches of science, rather than studying separate branches. In some countries, attempts are underway to integrated science with social sciences and humanities. In India, also, there are such subjects of learning at under-graduate level.

4. Decentralised Curriculum

The curriculum is developed centrally in the traditional systems. No doubt it helps in utilizing the resources of expenditure and ensuring qualitative and equal standards, but the class teachers are unable to teach effectively as the local needs and resources differ from place to place. So now the curriculum construction is decentralised and such curricula are developed including the local needs and interests.

5. Pupil-centred Instruction

Now, it is well recognised that first hand experiences are very effective in teaching-learning process, and it is only possible through active involvement of students in the learning process through discovery and inquiry approaches. Provisions are now made in curriculum for heuristic method, problem-solving method, project method, etc.

6. Self-learning Materials

In addition to the traditional instructional material, multi-media learning packages are developed. Self-learning kits, modules, programmed instruction/learning materials, computers, etc., are under use to a great extent.

7. Low-Cost Materials

There is great emphasis on developing low-cost or no-cost science materials rather than lying on expensive and sophisticated equipment. Certain centres are established to design and develop low-cost science materials. The teachers can also develop their own materials getting locally available material.

8. Non-formal Science Education

There is a trend towards providing non-formal science education to the people who are outside the reach of formal science education. There are many such programmes in many countries including India and the United States of America.

9. Indigenous Curriculum

Now many countries are developing their own curriculum rather than importing if from developed countries based on their past experiences. This indigenous curriculum is helping in meeting the local needs and interests utilizing local manual and material resources.

10. Teachers Involvement

In many occasions, the practising teachers are made part of curriculum development rather putting the so-called experts on the panel. The teacher, in turn, with their practical experiences, either way, contributing well to the development of quality curriculum.

REFERENCES

Bhaskara Rao, Digumarti (2002) *Effective Science Teaching*.

Bhaskara Rao, D. (author) and Marlow Ediger (editor (1995). *Scientific Attitude vis-a-vis Scientific Aptitude*. New Delhi: Discovery Publishing House.

Ediger, Marlow and D. Bhaskara Rao (1996). *Science Curriculum*. New Delhi, India: Discovery Publishing House.

Sharma, R.C. (1993). *Modern Science Teaching*. Delhi: Dhanpat Rai and Sons.

Vaidya, Narendra (1971). *The Impact Science Teaching*. New Delhi: Oxford and IBH Publishing House.

3

Scope and Sequence in the Curriculum

Teachers, supervisors, and principals must consider carefully the problems of scope and sequence in the curriculum. Scope pertains to the breadth of content taught in various units of study in the curriculum. Sequence pertains to when a unit is taught.

Jarolimek and Foster wrote the following on inductive sequencing:

> Inductive sequencing refers to the process of going from specific examples to a rule, a generalization, or a broad principle. For example, suppose in a social studies lesson the teacher wanted to develop the idea that "money (a medium of exchange) serves as a convenient way of exchanging goods and services". The idea as expressed here is a generalization. In inductive teaching it would come near the *end* of the teaching or presentation sequence. In other words, the teacher would engage the children in a series of activities and experiences that would provide them with a broad exposure to the exchange of goods and services.

For deductive sequencing, Jarolimek and Foster wrote:

> Deductive sequencing reverses the procedure just described. In this case, the teaching sequence moves from a rule, generalization, or principle to specific examples. Teaching is planned in a way that introduces learners directly to the rule, generalization, or principle. They are then expected to search for examples or instances of it. It can provide inquiry or discovery aspects if the given rule, generalization, or principle is accepted as a *working* hypothesis. Learners can then gather data to prove or disprove it.
>
> Deductive sequencing is a common form of teaching. It has been subjected to a fair amount of criticism in recent years because it is associated with traditional telling and recitation teaching procedures. An obvious limitation of deductive sequencing is that the learner

may commit the rule or generalization to memory and be able to reproduce it for examination purposes, yet have no familiarity with the basic concepts and supporting details that give depth of meaning to such statements. For example, a child may be able to recite "money is a convenient means of exchanging goods and services," but may not be able to support such a statement with examples and nonexamples.

Scope in the Curriculum

What should be the breadth of content comprising the curriculum? As an example, it is generally agreed that the social studies should consist of the following six social science disciplines as a minimum:

1. Geography—A study of the natural environment such as rivers, lakes, oceans, diverse land forms, and climatic factors as they affect human beings.
2. History—A study of the past as it relates to relevant, selected events and issues pertaining to human beings.
3. Political science—A study of involvement of people in government and governmental activities on the local, state, national, and international levels.
4. Economics—A study of goods and services produced in a society and how these are utilized in a given state, country, or area.
5. Anthropology—Among other branches, a study of culture and its effects upon human beings. Culture pertains to artifacts, values, beliefs, customs, and ways of living of a specific set of human beings.
6. Sociology—A study of the norms, values, and goals of a specific group of people and how sanctions are applied to attain these norms. Sociologists, among other areas, study urban living, rural living, overpopulation, crime, delinquency, the family, institutions in society, and race relations.

Various units of study then can be developed from these social science disciplines which provide content for the social studies.

The scope of social studies may also be perceived as consisting of the following activities of human beings:

1. Fulfilling recreational needs of humans.
2. Providing needed goods and services.
3. Meeting religious and spiritual needs of individuals.
4. Establishing rules and regulations in government—local, state, national and international levels.
5. Fulfilling educational needs of human beings.
6. Transporting people, materials, and objects.

7. Communicating with others in face to face situations as well as in using technology.
8. Providing for health needs of individuals.
9. Receiving recognition, status, and security in life.
10. Respecting institutions in society such as the home and family.
11. Determining a suitable vocation in life.

These endeavours or activities of human beings provide titles for, as well as content in, diverse units of study in the social studies. For example, in human endeavour number one stated above entitled "fulfilling recreational needs of humans," the teacher may select a unit on "Hobbies in Our Lives" as being relevant for pupils in teaching-learning situations. The teacher may at selected intervals in a given school year discuss with learners recreational interests which they have such as collecting stamps, coins, or rocks; playing baseball, basketball, and football; and reading library books.

The scope of the social studies curriculum may also relate to the interests and needs of pupils. These interests and needs may be determined in the following ways:

1. Discussing with pupils which units of study they wish to pursue.
2. Having pupils assist in determining which problem areas to pursue within a unit of study introduced by the teacher.
3. Listening to comments made by pupils as to what captures their interests; objectives, learning experiences, and evaluation procedures may be selected and evaluated based on student comments.
4. Learning centers may be developed cooperatively by pupils with teacher leadership. The learning activities contained at each center would then largely determine what pupils are to learn.

The scope of elementary school social studies may also be determined in the following ways:

1. Writers of social studies texts determine the scope of the social studies curriculum. Within each unit of study, writers of social studies textbooks stress selected facts, concepts, and generalizations that pupils are to achieve. Additional learning experiences selected by the teacher in ongoing units of study guide pupils in developing understanding in greater depth.
2. Programmers aid in determining the scope of the social studies curriculum. The content contained in programmed learning stresses selected ideas that pupils need to achieve. The programmer determines what pupils are to learn. The order or sequence of these learnings would also be decided by writers of programmed materials.

Sequence in the Curriculum

After determining scope in the social studies, teachers must decide sequence of units. Sequence in units of study should be based upon the following criteria:

1. Units of study need to be on the interest levels of learners.
2. Pupils must perceive purpose in ongoing units of study.
3. Individual differences should be provided for in ongoing units of study.
4. Pupils must develop adequate readiness to participate in the new social studies unit.
5. Leaners should be able to attach meaning pertaining to what is being studied. The expanding environment is one approach utilized in determined sequence in units of study. In the expanding environment approach in determining sequence in units of study, pupils study what is near to them in the early primary grade levels and gradually develop understandings pertaining to what is further removed in their environment. The following units of study stress what is close to a child on the kindergarten level; gradually the child's environment expands to units of study which may eventually be quite far removed from the local community:

Kindergarten and Grade one. Units on the home, school, pets, and holidays.

Grade two. Units on the local community, city, and neighborhood shopping center.

Grades three and four. Units on the local state, and areas in the United States such as the southern states or the midwestern states.

Grade five. Units on Canada, Mexico, and American History.

Grade six. Units on Western Europe, Eastern Europe, the Soviet Union, Japan, China, India, Antarctic area, the Middle East, South America, and Africa.

Thus, in determining sequence of social studies units, the expanding environment approach may be utilized. Pupils then study units pertaining to what is nearby on the early primary grade levels. Gradually, as pupils go through the elementary school years, units are taught which pertain to content farther removed from the learner in terms of distance.

A second approach in determining sequence in social studies units would pertain to teachers, principles, and supervisors selecting which units and in what order these units should be taught on each of the grade levels in the elementary school. The following sequence of units, as an example, may be selected based on careful thought:

Kindergarten: Living in the Home, Our School, Our Pets, Animals on the Farm, Our Community, Whether and How It Affects Us, and Units on Selected Holidays.

Grade one: Careers in Our Community, The Neighbourhood Shopping Center, Pollution and How It Affects Us, Homes Around the World, Living in Our City, and Living Safely in Our Environment.

Grade two: Cities Around the World, Buying Goods and Services, Culture and the Community, City Government, History of Our Community, and Maintaining a clean and Safe Environment.

Grade three: Important Careers in Our State and Nation, Minority Groups in the United States and Their Contributions, Living in Our State, Inflation-Recession and How They Affect Us, and Manufacturing Areas of the United States.

Grade four: Visiting Industrial Areas of the United States, Careers of the Future, Farming Around the World, Shopping Wisely, Culture and Human Beings, and Getting Along Well with Others.

Grade five: Visiting Mexico and Its Southern Neighbours, Canada-Our Neighbour to the North. The Age of Discovery and Colonization, A New Nation Begins, Division Between States, and Developing a Modern Nation.

Grade six: Visiting Japan, Thailand, and Indonesia; The Common Market Countries; India and Pakistan; The Middle East; Brazil and Its Neighbours; The Soviet Union; and China.

A third approach in determining sequence in social studies units would pertain to pupils being heavily involved in determining titles as well as order of units taught. Thus, intermediate grade pupils with teacher guidance may agree to pursue the following units of study:

1. Making friends.
2. Getting along with parents.
3. How to earn and use spending money.
4. Writing letters to friends.
5. Important jobs in the community.
6. Learning more about minority groups.
7. Ways of preventing wars.
8. The Middle East, Northern Ireland, and Southeast Asia.
9. The United States and the Soviet Union.
10. Political and economic systems in the world.

When pupils are involved in determining units of study and their sequence, these criteria may be followed:

1. The interests of learners are of utmost importance.

2. Learners must perceive purpose in ongoing units of study.
3. Pupils must have adequate background information to pursue new units of study.
4. Units of study must be relevant for learners.
5. It is possible to make provisions for each learner within the framework of the agreed upon units of study.
6. Pupils must perceive learnings as being sequential within, between, and among the diverse units of study.

A fourth way of selecting social studies units sequentially would pertain to selecting that which is important in current happenings on the face of the earth. Thus, units such as the following may be taught depending upon their relevancy in the current affairs:

1. Crisis in the Middle East.
2. East versus West in World Affairs.
3. Conflict in Southeast Asia.
4. Struggle for independence in Africa.
5. Common market countries of Europe.

Selecting units of study based on current affairs items should follow these criteria:

1. The current affairs items must be perceived by learners as being vital and salient.
2. Pupils should possess ample readiness to study units involving current affairs.
3. A variety of learning experiences should provide for each learner in the class setting.
4. A rich learning environment must be in evidence to capture pupil interest and purpose.

Content has been written about the schools without walls concept pertaining to teaching and learning. In emphasizing schools without walls, the community becomes very important in providing learning activities for pupils. Through teacher-pupil planning in the class setting, decisions are made as to which learning activities students may participate in. Thus, in studying the judicial system in the United States, pupils visit and see in operation an actual courtroom situation. Following the excursion, pupils with teacher guidance may discuss their observations. This involves using a variety of reference sources in the class setting to get needed information to answer questions and solve problems. An attorney may be invited to the class setting to answer and discuss questions identified by learners. Further excursions could involve visiting different kinds of types of courts in a life-like setting. Observations made need to be discussed and evaluated. Additional data needed to solve problems and answer questions come from several sources such as library and trade books, encyclopaedias, films and filmstrips, slides and pictures, objects and models, resource personnel, panel presentations, debates, interviews, and video discs.

Values inherent in utilizing the school without walls may be the following:

1. Experiences for pupils are real and life-like.
2. Learners with teacher guidance determine sequence of what is to be studied and learned.
3. Pupils are actively involved in problem-solving situations.
4. The concerns of pupils are important in determining sequential learnings.
5. Pupils' interests may serve as a valid criterion in determining what is to be learned and the order of these learnings.

In Summary

There are selected ways which teachers utilize in determining the scope of units in the elementary school. Among others, the following approaches may be used:

1. Adequate emphasis should be placed upon each major social science discipline becoming a relevant part of ongoing units of study in the social studies.
2. Major activities of human beings in society may also provide the framework for determining the scope of units in the social studies.
3. Interests and needs of learners should be thoroughly considered when deciding upon the scope of the curriculum.

Sequence in social studies pertains to when selected units of study are taught in the elementary school.

1. The expanding environment of the learner may assist in determining sequence in social studies units.
2. Teachers, principals, and supervisors may decide which units of study to teach in a sequential order.
3. Through teacher-pupil planning, sequence in social studies units may be determined. Thus, learners can be heavily involved in deciding upon sequential units of study.
4. Relevant current affairs items provide a framework for determining sequence in ongoing units of study.
5. Schools without walls in teaching-learning situations involve pupils' interests and purposes greatly when thinking about sequential units in the social studies.

REFERENCES

Beyer, Barry K. *Inquiry in the Social Studies Classroom: A Strategy for Teaching*. Columbus: Charles E. Merrill Publishing Company, 1971.

Goodlad, John I. *A Place Called School: Prospects for the Future*. New York: McGraw Hill Book Company, 1984.

Gulek, Gerald L. *Education and Schooling*. Englewood Cliffs, New Jersey: Prentice-Hall Inc, 1983.

Jarolimek, John, and Clifford D. Foster. *Teaching and Learning in the Elementary School*. Third Edition. New York: Macmillan Publishing Company, 1985.

Michaelis, John U. et. al. *New Designs for Elementary Curriculum and Instruction*. Second Edition. New York: McGraw Hill Book Company, 1975.

Miller, John P., and Wayne Seller. *Curriculum*. New York: Longman, Inc., 1985.

Ryan, Frank L. *Exemplars for the New Social Studies. Englewood Cliffs: Prentice-Hall, Inc., 1971.*

Skeel, Dorothy J. (Ed.). The Challenge of Teaching Social Studies in the Elementary School. Pacific Palisades: Goodyear Publishing Company, Inc., 1972.

Stanford, Gene, and Albert E. Roark. *Human Interaction in Education*. Boston: Allyn and Bacon, Inc., 1974.

4

Issues in the Curriculum

There are numerous issues in the curriculum which educators should consider and attempt to resolve. Each issue must be understood in terms of its strengths and weaknesses. Thus, teachers, principals, and supervisors may be able to eliminate or modify identified weaknesses within an issue. Objectives, learning experiences, and evaluation procedures utilized in teaching-learning situations should be grounded in recommended principles of learning and teaching as well as in a consistent, sound philosophy of education.

Use of Textbooks

Elementary school textbooks have, in selected situations, been greatly misused in classroom settings. Thus, for example, in a class of thirty pupils, all students have been studying and reading content from the same page at the same time. This violates providing for individual differences among learners in a class who differ much from each other in capacity, achievement, interest, motivation, and socio-economic levels.

Elementary school textbooks may be misused if the following methods of teaching are followed:

1. The content of the text is followed in sequence as written by the author with all learners being on the same page at the same time.
2. The teacher does not provide adequate readiness learning experiences for pupils prior to reading content from the basal textbook.
3. A lack of creativity is in evidence in teaching when the teacher utilizes teaching suggestions contained in the teacher's manual section only, related to the textbook used by learners.

4. Pupils not reading up to the level of achievement demanded by the series of textbooks being utilized hinder optimal achievement on the part of these learners.
5. Proficient readers reading well above the expectations of the content contained in the social studies texts may become bored and create discipline problems due to a lack of challenge in reading content.

Elementary school textbooks may be wisely used if the following teaching procedures are utilized:

1. Prior of reading content from a text, pupils should have ample opportunities to gain related background information. The ideas will sound more familiar to pupils when reading content if needed background information has been developed.
2. While background information is being developed through viewing related pictures, filmstrips, and films, along with other needed learning activities, pupils should see new words in print which they will meet later on in reading a given selection. Through the use of audio-visual aids, pupils may attach meaning to these terms.
3. Ultimately, pupils should have some questions in mind whereby they would read a selection from the text to get related information.
4. Following the reading of a given selection in the textbook, pupils may reveal understandings in satisfying ways such as the following:
   (a) Discussing the contents using higher levels of thinking.
   (b) Developing an illustration, frieze or diorama pertaining to content read.
   (c) Dramatizing selected parts of content comprehended.
   (d) Making models and objects related to information obtained from the textbook.
   (e) Reading related library books and presenting content to other learners within a committee.
   (f) Developing a mural within a committee setting.
   (g) Writing a summary or outline over content read.
   (h) Reporting to the class selected relevant main ideas gained from the reading activity.
   (i) Developing a movie set and putting in related content covering what has been read.
   (j) Letting pupils determine how they wish to reveal what has been gained in terms of content from the ongoing reading activity.

Inductive Versus Deductive Learning

Educators have rather recently stressed the importance of pupils achieving learning inductively. Thus, in inductive learning, the role of the teacher consists of

1. Guiding pupil achievement rather than serving as a lecturer or explainer of content.
2. Stimulating pupils in identifying problems and working toward desired solutions.
3. Being a good asker of questions rather than a dispenser of information. Questions need to be asked in proper sequence.
4. Helping pupils realize desired generalizations and main ideas as a result of interacting with a variety of learning experiences.
5. Developing positive attitudes within learners in wanting to discover facts, concepts, conclusions, and methods of working.
6. Helping pupils obtain needed materials and aids necessary in inductive learning.

Disadvantages given for inductive learning include the following:

1. It may take much time in helping pupils achieve learnings inductively as compared to deductively.
2. It may not be necessary for pupils to discover content which has been discovered and recorded by others.
3. Deductive learnings may be presented to pupils in a purposeful and interesting manner.
4. A skillful and responsible teacher can teach well using either the inductive or deductive approach.

Group Work Versus Individual Efforts

There are plans in education whereby pupils could learn on an individual basis only. This would be true of the following plans in teaching-learning situations:

1. Individualized reading. Here pupils individually select and read a library book of their own choosing. Following the reading of the library book, the teacher has a conference with the pupil to assess comprehension.
2. Individualized spelling. Pupils individually with teacher guidance would develop a set of spelling words to master. The set of words could come from an ongoing unit of study. Thus, in a unit on the Middle Ages, a specific learner may study the correct spelling of words such as manor, serf, nobleman, castle, knight, chivalry, crusaders, moat, drawbridge, and tournament.
3. Writing activities. At a writing center, a pupil would select a picture of his or her own choosing to write about. Thus, if

pupils are studying a unit on "Visiting a Farm," a learner may select from among the following a picture to write about; tractors with air-conditioned cabs and power steering; dairy cows in a barn and a pipeline milker; sileage being augered down from a silo to a herd of hungry beef cattle; and laying hens in cages receiving mash using automated procedures.

There are many other good learning activities which may be mentioned pertaining to pupils learning on an individual basis only. However, there are selected questions which need to be asked concerning learning experiences whereby pupils develop learnings on an individual basis as compared to pupils working in committees or large group instruction.

1. How can balance in the curriculum be developed and maintained which emphasizes individual as well as committee work by learners?
2. How much emphasis should be placed upon pupils developing well individually as well as socially?
3. Which criteria should the teacher follow in teaching-learning situations pertaining to having pupils develop well individually as well as socially?

General Versus Specific Objectives

How specific should educational objectives be stated? Advantages given for specific objectives in teaching-learning situations include the following:

1. Clearly stated objectives are necessary for good teaching to occur. Vague objectives indicate a lack of clarity as to what will be taught.
2. With clearly stated objectives, it can be measured if pupils have or have not achieved the desired ends.
3. Quality learning experiences can be selected only if the objectives are clearly stated. Thus, the learning experiences must relate directly to the desired ends.
4. Measurable objectives and related learning experiences make it possible to determine the degree to which pupils are making progress.

Disadvantages given for utilizing behaviourally stated objectives are the following:

1. Relevant behaviours that pupils are to achieve cannot be stated precisely such as pupils developing an adequate self-concept or developing feelings of respect toward others.
2. Trivia may be taught if measurable objectives alone are used in teaching-learning situations.

3. Major emphasis should be placed upon selecting learning experiences rather than objectives for pupils to achieve.

When focusing upon learning experiences as compared to educational objectives in teaching-learning situations, the following kinds of activities would be better to emphasize:

1. Those which require critical thinking, creative thinking, and problem solving.
2. Those which develop feelings of appreciation and respect toward others.
3. Those which aid pupils in developing a healthy self concept.

The Structure of Knowledge

Various educators have emphasized that pupils should achieve key structural ideas as identified by academicians. Social scientists from colleges and universities include historians, geographers, political scientists, anthropologists, sociologists, and economists. The methods that each of these social scientists utilize should also be used by elementary school children, according to selected social studies educators. Advantages given for using this approach in teaching in the elementary school would be the following:

1. Pupils would be achieving relevant concepts and generalizations.
2. Learners would be using appropriate methods of gathering data, such as using primary sources of information as historians do or using and making maps and globes to gather and summarize data as geographers do.
3. Teachers have more security in teaching of selected vocabulary terms, main ideas, generalizations, and structural ideas pertaining to each academic discipline. Statements of structural ideas would be available to public school teachers to implements in teaching-learning situations.

Disadvantages inherent in using the structure of knowledge concept in teaching would be the following:

1. Pupils may not be interested nor perceive purpose in gaining these structural ideas.
2. Methods that academicans use in gathering information may not harmonize with the needs and abilities of elementary school pupils.
3. Within each discipline, academicians may not be able to agree upon relevant structural ideas.
4. An adult-centered curriculum may be in evidence if pupils are to achieve structural ideas as identified by academicians in their area of speciality.

Newer Disciplines in the Curriculum

Older disciplines making up the elementary school social studies curriculum include history, geography, and political science. Newer disciplines incorporated into the social studies program include economics, anthropology, and sociology. Psychology and philosophy may also be included as newer disciplines in the curriculum. Reasons given for expanding the scope of the social studies include the following:

1. It was not adequate to study human beings from the point of view of history, geography, and political science only. Human beings should also be studied from the social science disciplines of economics, anthropology, and sociology, as well as psychology and philosophy.
2. Pupils should learn to utilize methods of gathering information that academicians utilize who specialize in the different social science disciplines mentioned in number one.
3. The curriculum becomes more relevant in the lives of pupils if additional social science disciplines are added to the social studies, namely economics, anthropology, and sociology.

There are selected questions which may be asked pertaining to the different social science disciplines which provide content in the social studies.

1. How can balance be maintained among history, geography, political science, anthropology, sociology, and economics in the social studies?
2. How can these different social science disciplines become a part of the integrated social studies curriculum?
3. Which of these disciplines, if any, should become the basis for unit planning?
4. Can the classroom teacher have knowledge of the diverse methods that social scientists in their area of speciality use?
5. Do public schools have the aids and materials for pupils to utilize in working and inquiring as social scientists do?
6. Can the scope of elementary social studies become too board when additional social science disciplines aid in providing content in the social studies curriculum.

The Child and the Teacher in Determining the Curriculum

An important issue in elementary school social studies that needs resolving pertains to who should select educational objectives, learning experiences, and evaluation procedures within teaching-learning situations. There are selected questions which need appropriate responses.

1. Who chiefly should determine what pupils are to learn? The teacher? the child? The teacher are the child? Should other individuals be involved in deciding what pupils are to learn such as principals, supervisors, parents, members of boards of education, and diverse societal organisations within the community?
2. Who should select learning activities to achieve these desired objectives or ends?
3. Who should sequence learning experiences for pupils? Should the teacher or the child, or both, be involved in determining sequence in learning for pupils? What role should the programmer have in sequencing learnings for pupils?
4. Who should be involved in assessing pupil achievement? What role should standarized achievement tests play in evaluating pupil achievement? Should pupil achievement be assessed in terms of specific or behaviourally stated objectives? To what degree should the learner and/or the teacher be involved in determining the achievement of pupils?

Programmed Learning

Programmed learning has contributed much toward thinking in education.

1. Pupils progress in very small steps thus generally insuring learner success in each step of learning.
2. Pupils basically know immediately if they are right or wrong in terms of responses given in programmed learning.
3. Learners individually may work at their own optimal achievement in programmed learning.
4. Programmers develop their materials so that pupils feel rewarded by being successful at each step of learning.
5. Pupils can become independent learners when pursuing sequential steps in programmed materials.

There are selected differences in programmed materials that are sold on the market. However, there are also many basic agreements in philosophy as to what should comprise content in programmed learning. For example, a programmed book or booklet may follow these criteria:

1. Pupils look at a small picture or pictures.
2. Content is read by learners below these pictures.
3. Pupils then respond to a completion item.
4. Learners check their own response.
5. If a pupil is right, he/she is rewarded. If wrong in the response, he/she now knows the correct answer.

6. The pupil then looks at the next picture, reads the related content, responds to an item, and then checks the response.
7. Again, if the pupil is right, he/she is rewarded. If the response given by the learner is incorrect, the pupil now knows the correct answer.
8. The same steps may be followed over and over again when programmed materials are utilized in the class setting.

Programmed learning has been criticized by selected educators. Reasons given for the criticism are the following:

1. Programmed materials may become monotonous for pupils in ongoing learning activities.
2. Selected learners can advance at a more rapid rate in learning as compared to the small steps arranged sequentially by the programmer.
3. Relevant content may not have been selected by the programmer in writing programmed materials.
4. The child individually is a better determiner of sequential learnings as compared to the programmer.
5. Achieving content in small steps may not meet the learning styles of selected learners.
6. Learning experiences need to be varied in the class setting.

Competition Versus Cooperation in the Class Setting

A very important issue that needs resolving in the elementary curriculum pertains to competitive versus cooperative efforts on the part of pupils in ongoing learning activities. Reasons given for pupils engaging in competitive experiences include the following:

1. Life in society demands that individuals excel in performance.
2. Achievements in the United States have come about due to rugged individualism in society.
3. Competition between and among learners brings out the best within individuals.
4. Individuals take pride only in personal achievements and not group or committee work.
5. The United States is in competition with other countries on the face of the earth for survival.
6. It is normal for individuals to be competitive.
7. Not all individuals can get to the "top" in achievement; thus survival of the fittest is important in school and society.

Disadvantages given for competition as a means of motivating learners in achieving include the following:

1. Human beings in groups can do a better job of solving problems as compared to the efforts of individuals.

2. Progress in society has come about due to cooperative efforts of inventors, scientists, other professionals, and non-professionals.
3. Human beings must be educated to take pride in group efforts since this is more effective in scope as compared to the attempts of an individual in improving happenings in society.
4. Much merit can be placed on the statement "in union there is strength". Thus, achievement in society comes about due to united efforts of individuals determined to improve society.

It does seem necessary to emphasize balance between the concepts of competition and cooperation in the social studies curriculum. Individual efforts in positive achievement need to be rewarded in teaching-learning situations. Human beings need to find fulfillment in accomplishments on an individual basis. They, however, also must feel successful in group endeavours. Needed changes in society can come about through individual as well as group efforts. In the study of American history, individuals and groups of individuals helped to change society from what it was to what exists presently. The following criteria are given to resolve controversies pertaining to individual and group efforts in achievement:

1. All individuals should feel successful in learning.
2. Individual achievement should definitely not be at the expense of others.
3. Respect for others is an important objective in the school curriculum.
4. Individuals working in committees and groups should feel rewarded in their efforts.
5. Good human relations should exist in group endeavours.

Pupil Involvement in the Community

Selected social studies educators have recommended that pupils' experiences in the school setting should involve participating in community activities. Thus pupils' social studies experiences could involve the following pertaining to working in the community:

1. Cleaning up the school and nearby environment when studying units on pollution.
2. Making recommendations to the mayor or city manager and council on ways to avoid pollution in a city area.
3. Participating in a mayor-council meeting by making specific recommendations on selected issues.

There are selected issues in having pupils become directly involved in community participation:

1. To what degree should pupils become involved in community affairs?
2. How much of the school day should be given in having pupils participate in community activities?
3. How relevant can these learnings be made for pupils?

There are advantages in having pupils participate in community affairs.

1. Learnings can be highly realistic for pupils.
2. Pupils become actively involved in learning.
3. School and society become integrated entities.
4. Learners have opportunities to practice good citizenship.

Disadvantages which may be listed for pupils becoming actively involved in community work include the following:

1. Mundane tasks may be performed by pupils.
2. The lay public may question the value involved in having pupils participate in community work.
3. There is a question, of course, pertaining to priorities in the public school curriculum.
4. The cost may be high in terms of money when having pupils participate in community affairs, such as transportation costs.

Camping Experiences

There are selected elementary schools which provide camping experiences for pupils away from the school setting. Boy Scouts, Girl Scouts, and 4-H Club organisations have provided camping experiences for young people over the years. Thus, camping experiences for pupils may have the following opportunities to offer in relationship to the public school curriculum:

1. Pupils have opportunities to learn from a completely different environment as compared to the school setting.
2. Learning activities provided for pupils can be more varied as compared to those provided in the school setting only.
3. More facets of everyday living can be stressed in camping experiences as compared to what is experienced during a regular school day.
4. Teachers may get to know pupils in an informal environment and under different conditions.

Disadvantages which may be listed in having pupils participate in camping experiences involve the following:

1. There are adequate opportunities for pupils to participate in camping experiences through organisations such as Boy Scouts and Girl Scouts.

2. The cost of providing camping experiences for pupils to participate in may be excessively high.
3. It is not necessary for pupils to attend a campsite area to have worthwhile educational experiences.
4. Excursions can be taken to the community to aid pupils in experiencing reality.
5. There are other ways of having pupils experience reality such as having resource personnel come to the class setting. Teachers and pupils may bring objects and models to the class setting; thus, reality in degrees is brought into the classroom.

Performance Contracting

A few years ago performance contracting was given considerable limelight. Performance contracting emphasized the following:

1. The company doing the contracting guaranteed a given school a certain level of gain in pupil achievement within a specified time.
2. Terms of the agreement were stated in a contrast.
3. The company was to receive no payment for those learners who did not achieve according to specified results in the contract.
4. Teachers were trained to use methods and procedures of teaching as emphasized by the company engaged in performance contracting.

Disadvantages given for performance contracting included:

1. No one in advance can predict needed pupil gains in a given school year.
2. It is difficult to determine which test should be utilized to measure pupil achievement in a pretest-postest situation.
3. No test can measure all relevant achievement that pupils need to make.
4. Methods and materials used in teaching as recommended by companies may stress lower level cognitive learnings.
5. Pupils' needs may not be met in the school setting.

Advantages which may be listed for selected schools participating in performance contracting are the following:

1. The methods and materials utilized in teaching may provide for individual differences among selected learners with unique learning styles.
2. Attempts are made in pinpointing pupil gains in a given schoo' year.
3. Parents may be more satisfied with the public school setting if learner achievement can be verified.

4. Payment for pupil achievement is made only if predetermined levels of achievement have been acquired.
5. Teacher skills may be updated with appropriate recommended methodology and materials if the company engaged in performance contracting emphasizes inservice education of teachers.

Criterion Referenced Supervision

With the use of specific behaviourally stated objectives, selected educators have recommended criterion-referenced approaches in supervision of instruction. Criterion-referenced supervision recommends utilizing the following criteria:

1. The supervisor assessing the quality of objectives with the teacher prior to observing teaching-learning situations.
2. Alternative objectives may be emphasized by the supervisor if the latter perceives this to be necessary.
3. The quality of teaching is evaluated in terms of how well pupils have achieved the desired objectives.
4. Harmful side effects on the part of pupils in teaching-learning situations are also evaluated by the criterion-referenced supervisor.
5. If pupils have not achieved stated objectives, the criterion-referenced supervisor may suggest alternative learning experiences.

Advantages given for using the criterion-referenced approach to supervising instruction include the following:

1. It can be an objective way of supervising instruction since teacher success is evaluated in terms of pupils' achieving agreed upon objectives.
2. Stated objectives written by the teacher are further assessed by the supervisor in attempts at having pupils achieve the best objectives possible.
3. The success of learning activities is evaluated only in terms of pupils achieving desired objectives.
4. Pupils achievement can be assessed in terms of having achieved stated specific objectives.

Disadvantages which may be given in question form in relation to using criterion-referenced supervision include the following:

1. How far in advance do supervisors need to study teachers' selection of objectives before the observational visit is made?
2. Is the achieving of specific objectives by pupils the only reasonable criteria to emphasize when evaluating teacher performance?
3. Are supervisors adequately knowledgeable to recommend alternative objectives in a limited amount of time, other than those stated in writing by teachers?

4. Are teachers and supervisors in the best position to specifically determine objectives that pupils are to achieve? Should pupils be involved in determining educational objectives which they are to achieve?
5. When observing teachers teach, can supervisors immediately notice harmful side effects on the part of learners in teaching-learning situations? (Detrimental learnings for pupils may be revealed more so over a longer period of time.)
6. Can all worthwhile objectives such as critical thinking, creative thinking and problem solving be stated behaviourally?

In Summary

There are selected issues which teachers and supervisors should study, evaluate, and attempt to achieve closure in. These issues include the following:

1. Use of elementary school social studies textbooks.
2. Inductive versus deductive learning on the part of the pupils.
3. Group versus individual efforts in learning.
4. General versus specific objectives in teaching.
5. The structure of knowledge.
6. Newer disciplines in the social studies.
7. The child and the teacher in determining the curriculum.
8. Programmed learning and the social studies.
9. Competition versus cooperation in the curriculum.
10. Pupil involvement in the community.
11. Camping experiences and the social studies.
12. Performance contracting.
13. Criterion-referenced supervision.

REFERENCES

Alcorn, Marvin D., and James Linley (Eds.). *Issues in Curriculum Development*. Yonkers-on-Hudson: World Book Company, 1959.

Doll, Ronald C. *Curriculum Improvement*. Sixth Edition. Boston: Allyn and Bacon, Inc., 1986.

Ediger, Marlow. *Issues in Developing the Relevant Elementary Curriculum*. Kirksville, Missouri: North-east Missouri State University Stenographic Office, 1974.

Kourilsky, Marilyn, and Loury Quaranta. *Effective Teaching*. Glenview, Illinois: Scott, Foreseman, and Company, 1987.

Menacker, Julius, and Erwin Pollack (Eds.). *Emerging Educational Issues*. Boston: Little, Brown and Company, 1974.

Nerbovig, Marcella H., and Herbert J. Klausmeier. *Teaching in the Elementary School*. Fourth Edition. New York: Harper and Row, Publishers, 1974.

O'Connell, April, et. al. *Choice and Change*. Second Edition. Englewood Cliffs, New Jersey, 1985.

5

Democracy and the Curriculum

Democracy as a way of life needs to be stressed as a philosophy of education in all curriculum areas. Tenants pertaining to democratic living would emphasize the following standards.

1. Pupils must develop attitudes of respect toward other human beings.
2. Each person is to be valued for his or own uniqueness as well as for sameness of traits inherent between and among individuals.
3. Each individual regardless of race, creed, or religion should have ample opportunities to develop to his or her own optimum.
4. Ample learning experiences must be provided whereby individuals are able to relate to each other in a positive way.
5. Democratic living is an ideal and each individual may continually move in the direction of realizing these and related objectives more fully.
6. Individuals differ from each other in degrees in terms of exhibiting democratic behaviour.
7. Pupils individually and in groups must have ample opportunities to engage in identifying and attempting to solve realistic lifelike problems.
8. Learners personally and in committees must develop a set of values which give direction and meaning to life.
9. Each pupil should be guided in developing an adequate self-concept. This is necessary so that each person may exhibit responsible behaviour in society.
10. Pupils individually and in groups must develop a system of values whereby problems and weaknesses in society are identified and attempts made at remedying these deficiencies.

11. A relaxed environment in the school and class setting is necessary so that pupils may be able to achieve at an optimal level in all facets of development.
12. Ample opportunities must be provided whereby pupils may engage in decision making practices as to what to learn as well as methods and procedures to utilize in achieving these learning.

Democracy as a way of life in the school and class setting must not be confused with the following:

1. Pupils doing as they please with little or not respect for the rights of others.
2. Little or no direction or guidance given by the teacher in teaching-learning situations.
3. Pupils alone determining objectives, learning experiences, and assessment procedures in the school curriculum.
4. A highly competitive environment where selected individuals are winners while others face numerous situations involving failure.
5. The teacher alone determining what pupils are to learn in a prescribed manner and making it appear as if democratic procedures are being used in the school setting.

A different extreme to be avoided in the school and class setting pertains to the educational thinking of the autocratic teacher. The autocratic teacher behaves according to methods and procedures in teaching such as the following:

1. Selects objectives, learning experiences, and evaluation techniques without regard for concerns and purposes of learners.
2. Believes strongly in teaching the basics only, such as reading, writing, and arithmetic.
3. Strongly emphasizes rote learning and memorization as important methods of teaching.
4. Does not stress the interests of pupils in ongoing experiences.
5. Has rigid rules of content for pupils to follow.
6. Expects pupils to sit quietly in neat rows during most of the school day.
7. Expects pupils to respond to teacher's questions with exact answers.
8. Does not like to raise questions which require critical and creative thinking since this wastes valuable time in learning.
9. Reprimands pupils in front of the class for minor misdeeds.
10. Feels that being strict in dealing with pupils is good teaching procedure.

11. Favors children from middle class homes more so than those that come from lower income homes.
12. Frowns at children who speak nonstandard English.
13. Feels that all pupils in a class must measure up to the desired standards of the teacher.
14. Disapproves of committee work as being too noisy and unproductive.
15. Believes strongly in failing pupils if they do not achieve well on any selected grade level.
16. Approves strongly in using textbooks and workbooks to provide most of the learning activities for pupils.

Moving Toward Democratic Schools

There is much that any school or entire school system an do to move in the direction of adopting democratic tenets in the class setting.

1. Faculty members of a school should be aided in perceiving purpose in studying democracy as a way of life in school.
2. Criteria should be developed as to the meaning of democratic living in the school setting.
3. Continuous revision of these standards is necessary as evidence warrants making these changes.
4. Objectives for pupils to achieve should be formulated based on a democratic philosophy of life.
5. Learning experiences should be provided for pupils to achieve these desired objectives.
6. Frequent assessment should be in evidence to determine if learners have realized stated goals pertaining to democratic living in the school setting.

Learning Experiences to Achieve Objectives

The teacher must select learning activities carefully to have pupils achieve objectives pertaining to democracy as a way of life in the school setting.

1. The teacher, for example, in a unit on The Middle East could have pupils select which committee to participate in such as in *(a)* developing a relief map pertaining to that area of the world, *(b)* writing a report on developments leading to the Arab-Israeli crisis and dilemma, *(c)* preparing a mural on related current affairs items, *(d)* planning a "newscast" on related current affairs items, *(e)* dramatizing a Security Council session and debate on the Arab-Israeli dilemma, and *(f)* developing a penal report on issues and events that led up to the present day Middle East situation. Pupils with teacher

guidance could set up appropriate criteria for learners working on committees of their own choosing. During and after committee work has been in operation, assessment procedures need to be utilized to determine if pupils have achieved objectives pertaining to democracy in the school curriculum.

2. After several learners have completed reading library books of their own choosing on the Middle East, they may in a small group discuss major ideas gained from the reading activity. Respect for the thinking of others is very important in small group activities such as these.
3. A resource person having excellent knowledge of the middle East area can come to the class setting. It would be excellent if the resource person has selected audio-visual aids to use in the presentation. During the presentation, pupils may ask questions as well as present related content as possible answers to these identified problems. Pupils with teacher guidance should assess learner behaviour in terms of criteria pertaining to democratic living.
4. Pupils with teacher leadership could formulate standards of conduct in the class setting. Frequent evaluation of pupil behaviour in terms of these standards would be important. The standards may need modification and revision as time goes on. New standards may need to be added as well as old standards deleted. Standards of conduct developed by pupils with teacher guidance may include *(a)* speaking politely to others, *(b)* respecting the rights of others, *(c)* helping pupils who need help, *(d)* sharing materials and equipment with others, *(e)* recognizing one's responsibilities in a social setting, *(f)* helping to keep the classroom neat and tidy, *(g)* developing skills of good human relations, *(h)* tolerating deeds and acts of others, *(i)* accepting the feelings of others, *(j)* aiding the less fortunate to receive their share of the good things in life, and *(k)* assisting the teacher in developing a good learning environment.

In Summary

It is important for the school and class setting to emphasize democratic tenets of living. Faculty members of an elementary school must continually engage in defining standards pertaining to democratic living in the school and class setting. Democracy as a way of life must be separated in definitions from autocratic as well as anarchic methods of instruction in the public school environment. Learning activities must be selected which will help pupils in achieving desirable objectives pertaining to democratic living. Frequent evaluation of pupil achievement in terms of having achieved objectives of democratic living must be in evidence.

Davis wrote:

> Some classroom disruptions are routine and minor, others are severe and intolerable. Disruptiveness may be caused by boredom, frustration, peer recognition for being a hero, or by deeper problems of poverty, alienation, low ability, irrelevant curriculum, impersonal schools, or peer traditions of defiance. A few students will have severe problems, including psychosis.
>
> The best solution to disruptiveness lies in preventing trouble before it happens, which is precisely what classroom management is about. Good management will include reasonable rules, positive expectations, accountability, planning for interest and variety, smooth transitions between activities, continual surveillance, control of stimuli which trigger clowning or other disruptiveness, and using threats carefully.

REFERENCES

Ediger, Marlow. *The Curriculum in the School Setting* (A Collection of Essays). Kirksville, Missouri: Stenographic Office, Northeast Missouri State University, 1987.

Ediger, Marlow. *School Administration and the Curriculum* (A Collection of Essays). Kirksville, Missouri: Stenographic Office, Northest Missouri State University, 1987.

Kaltsounis, Theodore. *Teaching Elementary Social Studies*. West Nyack, New York: Parker Publishing Company, Inc., 1969.

Ord, John E. *Elementary School Social Studies for Today's Children*. New York: Harper and Row, 1972.

Ragan, William B., et. al. *Teaching in the Elementary School*. New York: Holt, Rinehart and Winston, Inc., 1972.

Wehlage, Gary, and Eugene M. Anderson, *Social Studies Curriculum in Perspective*. Englewood-Cliffs: Prentice-Hall, Inc., 1972.

6

Human Relations in the Curriculum

Good human relations are important in the elementary school. The curriculum must definitely make its contribution in order to help pupils to get along well with others. The teacher can reveal positive attitudes toward pupils in the following ways:

1. Accept each child as an important individual.
2. Reward each child with praise or through nonverbal communication (gestures and facial expressions) if a learner is doing better than previously.
3. Use a pleasant speaking voice with proper volume, stress, pitch, and juncture.
4. Help pupils individually to be accepted in a positive manner by other learners.
5. Guide each pupil in achieving to his or her optimum.
6. Provide learning experiences which capture pupils' interests and purpose.
7. Do not embarrass or ridicule a learner.
8. Give each pupil ample opportunities to participate actively in ongoing learning experiences.
9. Help pupils to feel positively about themselves.
10. Emphasize "getting along well with others" in ongoing teaching-learning situations.

Beane, Toepfer, and Alessi state the following:

> In developing goals and curriculum plans, educators must consider both contemporary society and the future in which young people will live their lives. Attention must be paid to such issues as technology, family structure, work, lifestyles, and other aspects of society. At the same time, thought must be given to how the school, an institution that developed in the industrial age, will respond to the growing diversity of the emerging postindustrial society.

Whatever the outcome of these deliberations, sociology presents a challenging and exciting field for curriculum planners.

Committee Work and the Learner

The teacher should guide pupils to become proficient in working within a committee framework. Thus, criteria such as the following should be stressed in committee work for pupils:

1. All pupils should contribute to their optimal achievement in ongoing learning activities.
2. Content presented by pupils should be presented to all committee members and not to one or two individuals only.
3. Respect toward the thinking of others is important in committee work.
4. Ideas presented within a committee should circulate among members and not between the chairperson and the individual presenting content.
5. Each committee member should have ample opportunities to choose desired learning experiences; no member then is left with performing routine tasks only.
6. Chairpersons within a committee should encourage members to become actively involved to group work.
7. Concepts, generalizations, and tasks which lack meaning should be clarified in the committee setting.
8. Critical thinking, creative thinking, and problem solving are to be encouraged within each committee.

Self-discipline and responsibility are important objectives for pupils to achieve.

Initiating Committee Work

The teacher must think of methods to use which will encourage pupil participation in committee work. Thus, factors such as the following are important to consider when pupils are to participate in working together with others:

1. Obtaining the interests of learners.
2. Pupils perceiving purpose in learning.
3. Learners understanding what is to be done in terms of achieving objectives.
4. Pupils realizing that they are to assume responsibility in completing tasks.
5. Individual differences being provided for in the committee setting.

The teacher then must select with great care those learning experiences which will initiate a unit properly and help pupils individually to desire to work within a committee framework. A learning experience such as the following may be desirable in stimulating pupil interest in committee work:

Showing a filmstrip pertaining to the unit being studied. If pupils are studying a unit on Brazil, the related filmstrip may contain content on *(a)* coffee production, *(b)* the Amazon River, *(c)* jungle lands. *(d)* Rio de Janeiro and Sao Paulo, *(e)* animal life, and *(f)* farming in Brazil.

Following a discussion of the contents of the filmstrip, pupils with teacher guidance may decide upon specific committee they would wish to work on. A set of four pupils may wish to learn more about the Amazon River in Brazil. A second set of three to five classmates may wish to gather more data on coffee production in Brazil. Other pupils in the class setting may desire to work on committees such as finding more content on large cities, agriculture, jungle climate and plant forms, as well as native animals in Brazil.

Each committee with teacher guidance may decide upon the following pertaining to duties and responsibilities in committee work:

1. What pupils wish to learn about the Amazon River.
2. Which reference sources are available to use in getting the needed information such as using audio-visual materials, reading materials, and resource personnel.
3. How to present findings on content gained such as writing summaries and conclusions, developing drawings, dramatizing information obtained, presenting oral reports to the class, and making related objects and models.

Evaluating Committee Work

Pupils with teacher leadership should assess the quality of work done in committee settings. Adequate emphasis must be placed upon the following processes when assessing learner achievement in committee work:

1. Each pupil contributing to his optimum in ongoing learning experiences.
2. Pupils working on meaningful projects until completion.
3. Learners respecting contributions of others.
4. Pupils aiding others to do their best in committee work.
5. Learners being interested in and perceiving purpose in learning.

Pupils' products need also to be evaluated in terms of standards:

1. Does the finished product show effort in producing it?

2. Is each pupil doing better now than formerly in terms of optimal achievement?
3. Are the interests of all learners reflected in the finished product of a specific committee?
4. Did each pupil in a committee do his or her best work possible?

Dick and Carey stated the following:

> The area of motivation is both broad and complex. What seems to be motivating to one person is not to another. However, one often useful technique is to show learners what they will be able to do when they finish the instruction. This is more than a statement of the objective of the instruction, which is the next component of the instructional strategy. It is the instructor's demonstration, written description, or illustration of what the learner will be able to do. The initial part of the instruction may also consist of some historical background or interesting fact about what is to be learned. It is important to note that there is no objective for this information, so it will not be tested. It is simply a means of attracting the student to the instruction.

Teacher Attitude and Committee Work

It is important for teachers to accept a philosophy of education which harmonizes with pupils' working on committees in the class setting. Standards such as the following must be accepted by the teacher in order that committee work may progress well in the school setting:

1. Busy pupils working on diverse projects and activities will make some noise. Absence or presence of noise is not the major consideration when evaluating pupil achievement in committee work. The most important factor in the quiet-noisy classroom continuum is that pupils are achieving worthwhile objectives.
2. Differences in capacity and achievement of individual learners is to be desired rather than frowned upon. Since, each pupil differs in degrees from other learners in interests, capacity, motivation, and achievement, the teacher should capitalize on these differences and invite unique contributions in committee work based on each learner's strengths.
3. The teacher is neither in the center of the stage nor in the limelight in teaching-learning situations involving committee work on the part of pupils. The teacher rather becomes a stimulator or guide in motivating pupils to achieve desirable ends.
4. Flexibility is a key concept for teachers to accept when pupils work in committee. Time allotments to committee work on a

daily basis, topics pursued by learners in committee work, contributions from each participant in the group, and quality as well as quantity of each committee's findings and products must be considered in a flexible manner when making comparisons with desirable standards or norms.

5. The textbook and workbook approach in teaching situations must give way to the use of varied reference sources to be utilized in problem solving activities.
6. A relaxed learning environment is important in that pupils may achieve to their optimum without fear of being embarrassed or punished for unique ideas and products presented in the class setting.

The Principal or Supervisor and Committee Work

Principals and supervisors have important roles to play pertaining to teachers emphasizing committee work.

1. Principals and supervisors need to give emotional support to teachers who are introducing and using committee work in the school setting.
2. Administrators need to show interest in small group work in the class setting.
3. Additional teaching aids and materials will be needed in the class setting to guide learners to solve problems within a committee. Principals and supervisors should become aware of classroom needs in terms of resources needed with the intent of attempting to fulfill these needs.
4. Principals and supervisors should attempt to meet needs of teachers in the area of inservice education. Workshops and faculty meetings may be conducted to help teachers use committees more effectively in the class setting.

Workshops and Faculty Meetings

An adequate number of workshops and faculty meetings should be held within a given school year to upgrade teaching skills and methodology. Supervisors and principals need to avoid an excessive amount of time devoted to inservice education for faculty members. Balance must be maintained in providing inservice education for faculty members between nothing being done in this area to overdoing this important facet of the total growth of teachers, principals, and supervisors.

Criteria to follow in conducting workshops include the following:

1. All involved faculty members should have a voice in determining the central theme of a workshop.

2. A general session should be conducted to determine relevant problem areas for study in the workshop.
3. Participants may then volunteer to select a committee in which to participate when working to solve problems.
4. Adequate opportunities need to be given to participants to work on an individual project of their own choosing.
5. Needed resources should be available to individuals to aid in the solving of problems.
6. Consultant services should be available at the workshop.
7. Individuals as well as committees should be able to share findings with other individuals, committees, or with participants in the general session.
8. Relevant processes must be emphasized during the time the workshop is in operation such as participants respecting the thinking of others, everyone contributing to their optimum but not dominating any facet of interaction, and individuals working in the direction of achieving worthwhile objectives.

Faculty meetings may also make their important contributions in improving the curriculum. Relevant standards must be adhered to in order to implement faculty meetings which directly influence teaching-learning situations.

1. Any faculty member should feel free to suggest items for an agenda pertaining to a future faculty meeting.
2. An agenda committee should select and arrange items in terms of perceived importance for a faculty meeting.
3. Membership should rotate on the agenda committee so that all faculty members may become actively involved in inservice education programs involving the use of faculty meetings.
4. The planned agenda should be in the hands of participants, approximately, two days before the faculty meeting will be held. Participants need ample time to think about possible solutions to items listed on the agenda.
5. Committees may be formed which can work in the direction of attempting to solve short-range as well as long-range problems.
6. Resources, such as professional reading materials as well as audio-visual aids, should be available to faculty members engaged in problem-solving activities.
7. Consultant service should be available when requested by faculty members in a public school engaged in the solving of problems as identified at faculty meetings.
8. Items on the agenda may be modified or changed as indicated by participants at the faculty meeting.

9. Conclusions realized by committee members as well as the larger faculty should be implemented in the school setting if evidence warrants doing this.
10. Faculty members in the school setting should attempt to continually identify and solve problems in the school setting.

Innovations in the Curriculum and the Lay Public

The lay public, parents in particular, should definitely be informed and helped to accept innovations in the curriculum prior to implementation. The following approaches may be utilized to inform parents and interested lay persons on new programs in education:

1. Talk informally with parents about worthwhile innovative ideas in teaching.
2. At parent-teacher conferences, discuss new practices in education which benefit pupils on an individual basis.
3. Have selected faculty members speak on innovations in teaching and learning at parent-teacher meetings.
4. Provide programs at selected intervals on radio and television on needed changes in the curriculum.
5. Write articles for the local newspaper on relevant innovations in teaching.

With these approaches in informing the lay public about curricular changes, hopefully lay citizens will become interested in and wish to seen implemented necessary changes in the curriculum.

In Summary

It is important to have pupils experience positive work in committee settings. Thus, pupils may learn to respect others better and in return receive more respect. A more wholesome self-concept should become an end result.

To guide learners in becoming effective members within a committee, the following criteria may be followed:

1. The teacher must react to pupils in a positive manner.
2. Pupils should have knowledge of and implement needed criteria when working in committees.
3. Effective procedures must be utilized by teachers when introducing committee work to pupils.
4. A stimulating learning environment should aid pupils in identifying selected problems area for which possible solutions are necessary.
5. Pupils need to have knowledge of and be able to utilize appropriate reference materials in problem-solving activities.

6. Contributions made within a committee need to be assessed in terms of desirable criteria.
7. Teachers must develop a relevant philosophy of teaching and learning which harmonizes with doing desirable committee work.

Approaches must be found in having parents and interested lay persons become knowledgeable and acceptable of innovative approaches in teaching prior to their implementation. Thus, various means of communication must be utilized to inform the lay public of recommendable procedures to use in teaching-learning situations in the school setting. This would include conducting conferences, giving speeches, talking informally with others, presenting school programs, providing radio and television programs, and writing articles for local newspapers on innovative procedures in teaching.

REFERENCES

Bhaskara Rao, Digumarti, editor. *International Encyclopaedia of Human Rights*, 7 volumes in 13 parts. New Delhi, India: Discovery Publishing House.

Beane, James A., Toepfer, Contad F. Jr. and Alessi, Samuel J. Jr. *Curriculum Planning and Development*. New York: Allyn and Bacon, Inc., 1986.

Collier, Calhoun C., et. al. *Modern Elementary Education: Teaching and Learning*. New York: Macmillan Publishing Co., Inc., 1976.

Dick, Wlater and Carey, Lou. *The Systematic Design of Instruction*. Second edition. Glenview, Illinois: Scott, Foresman and Company, 1985.

Ediger, Marlow. "Preparing Quality School Administrators," *The Hoosier* Schoolmaster, Spring, 1987.

Ediger, Marlow. "Staff Development and Curriculum," *The Bulletin*, Alabama Association of Secondary School Principals, 1987.

Eliot, John (Ed.). *Human Development and Cognitive Process*. New York: Holt, Rinehart and Winston, Inc., 1971.

Gall, M.D. *Handbook for Teaching and Evaluating Curriculum Materials*. Boston: Allyn and Bacon, Inc., 1971.

Glatthorn, A.A. *Differentiated Supervision*. Alexandria, Virginia: Association for Supervision and Curriculum Development, 1984.

Simon, Sidney B. et. al. *Values Clarification*. New York: Hart Publishing Company, Inc., 1972.

Stephens, Lillian S. *The Teachers Guide to Open Education*. New York: Holt, Rinehart and Winston, Inc., 1974.

7

Resource Units, Teaching Units, Lesson Plans

Teachers must carefully plan the objectives, learning experiences, and evaluation techniques in teaching a given set of learners.

There should be rational balance among educational objectives selected from the following sources:

1. Objectives which arise from a study of learner interests and needs.
2. Objectives which result from studying society as it now exists and as it should be.
3. Objectives which pertain to recommended structural ideas as identified by academicians in their academic areas of speciality such as anthropologists, sociologists, economists, historians, geographers, and political scientists.

There also needs to be rational balance among the following categories of objectives:

1. Understandings. This category of objectives pertains to facts, concepts, main ideas, conclusions, and generalizations that pupils might gain in an ongoing unit of study.
2. Skills. Skills objectives pertain to doing something such as listening, speaking, reading, writing, observing, classifying content, interring, and predicting.
3. Attitudes. These objectives relate directly to feelings, values, beliefs, ideals, and the effective dimension of the individual.

A diff-rent classification scheme may be used to analyze and select objectives in attempting to provide balance among different categories of goals within teaching-learning situations.

1. Cognitive objectives. These objectives pertain to the use of the intellect primarily.

2. Psychomotor objectives. These purposes relate directly to the use of the muscles predominantly.
3. Affective objectives. Affective objectives emphasize the feeling, valuing, or attitudinal dimension of the human being.

Learning activities to achieve selected objectives should be varied and provide for individual differences. Learning activities should, among others, include the following:

1. Reading for enjoyment or to gather data in problem-solving activities.
2. Viewing audio-visual aids to obtain needed information.
3. Listening to tapes, cassettes, records, reports, and video discs.
4. Writing reports, summaries, conclusions, main ideas, generalizations, and factual information.
5. Drawing pictures developing friezes, murals, and using finger paints.
6. Constructing models, replicas, scenery, and objects.
7. Performing folk dances and engaging in singing activities.
8. Participating in speaking activities such as presenting oral reports, discussing, interviewing, and conversing.

Evaluating pupil achievement could involve the use of procedures such as the following:

1. Using true-false, essay, multiple choice, matching, and completion items.
2. Utilizing checklists and rating scales to obtain data on learner performance.
3. Using valid standardized achievement, personality, and IQ test results to assess pupil achievement.
4. Using teacher observation to notice progress on the part of each pupil.
5. Conducting conferences with pupils individually in groups to assess achievement.
6. Guiding pupils to evaluate their own progress.

The Resource Unit

Teachers individually and in committees may develop resource units to aid in improving the curriculum. Resource units should follow these guidelines in their preparation:

1. They are general in nature and can be used for many classrooms of pupils in teaching-learning situations, usually on a specific grade level. Selected resource units have been developed which may be utilized in teaching-learning situations for more than one grade level.
2. They contain more objectives, learning experiences, and assessment procedures than is possible to use in teaching a

specific class of pupils. The teacher may select from among many objectives, learning experiences, and assessment procedures when planning to teach a specific set of learners. Provision may then be made for individual differences.

3. Units are recognized around related major problem areas.
4. The interests, needs, and purposes of pupils are important to consider when developing resource units.

There are diverse formats available in developing resource units. However, there is considerable agreement as to major parts that go into the development of the resource unit.

1. The title of the unit and grade level. Units of study should have descriptive appealing titles. Instead of teaching a unit on "Japan," the unit may have more appeal with the title "Visiting Japan". The selected unit of study must be interesting, meaningful, purposeful, and on the maturity level of the individual learner.
2. Justification for teaching the unit. This section of a resource unit is of utmost importance. If units of instruction in the social studies cannot be justified in the curriculum, they definitely should not be taught. The explosion of knowledge is with us presently and will, no doubt, increase in rate as the years progress. Knowledge appears to double at least every ten years. It behooves teachers, supervisors, and principals to select relevant units for pupils.
3. The objectives of the unit. There should be rational balance among understandings, skills, and attitudinal objectives. These objectives must be relevant for pupils to achieve. Objectives should be comprehensive in emphasizing the total development of the learner. The intellectual, social, emotional, and physical facets of pupils need to be developed to the optimum. Only attainable objectives for pupils should be stressed in teaching-learning situations. Input for selecting important objectives should come not only from teachers but also from parents, learners themselves, principals, and supervisors.
4. Problems for pupils to solve. Developing problem-solving skills is important for all learners. Each individual engages rather continuously in the solving of problems. It is important for pupils to develop proficiency in the area of problem solving. In a resource unit it is relevant to have a section listing possible problems for learners to solve. The problem section of a resource unit relates directly to objectives discussed above.
5. Learning experiences for pupils. The experiences should guide pupils in achieving desired objectives.

(a) Introductory experiences need to stimulate pupil interest in learning. Thus, learners in a stimulating learning environment may identify relevant questions and problems to solve. The introductory learning activities could include, among other centers, a picture center, a filmstrip center, a dramatization center, a speaking center, a puppet center, and an art center. Each of these learning centers must be appropriately introduced to pupils so that an inward desire to learn will be in evidence.

(b) Developmental activities should aid learners in developing concepts and generalizations in greater depth as compared to what is possible in the introductory activities. In the introductory learning activities, pupils should have gotten an over-view of the entire unit. In the developmental activities, pupils achieve understandings objectives pertaining to diverse topics in depth in an ongoing unit of study. Skills objectives being stressed in teaching-learning situations emphasize development in depth pertaining to listening, speaking, writing, reading, outlining content, using the table of contents as well as the index and glossary, using the dictionary, making careful observations, predicting consequences, and doing cause and effect thinking. Out of these learning activities, hopefully, learners will develop desirable attitudes.

(c) Culminating activities should help pupils perceive that knowledge is related. Learners should have ample opportunities to relate previous learnings by experiencing a variety of interesting and purposeful learning activities. Students need to have further opportunities to identify new questions and problems. In culminating a unit, there are further opportunities for pupils to explore and discover new learnings.

6. The evaluation section of a resource unit should contain a list of suggested techniques to assess learner achievement. The assessment procedures evaluate pupil growth in intellectual, social, emotional, and physical development.
7. The bibliography section of a resource unit lists entries pertaining to materials that the teacher and pupils will be using in teaching-learning situations. It is significant that films, filmstrips, textbooks, library books, and other reference materials be listed in the bibliography section of a resource unit.

The Teaching Unit

Teaching units are specific and may generally be utilized in teaching a specific class of pupils only. Resource units provide information in developing teaching units.

1. Objectives in a teaching unit in teaching a specific class of pupils should come from the objectives section of a resource unit. The objectives must be attainable for a specific set of learners.
2. There needs to be a pretest to determine where learners are presently in achieving prior to teaching a new unit. The pretest could pertain to relevant test items written by the teacher on a teacher-prepared test. There, no doubt, are better means to preassess learners prior to teaching a new unit other than utilizing paper-pencil test items. Approaches in pretesting pupils include discussions, pupils presenting content for an experience chart, learners engaging in dramatizing, and pupils in committees developing oral or written summaries relating to previous learnings developed pertaining to the new unit of study.
3. Learning activities to achieve the desired objectives may be selected from the resource unit. The learning experiences should be interesting, meaningful, purposeful, and provide for individual differences within a specific set of pupils. Proper sequence of the activities is very important.
4. During the time a unit is taught, pupils with teacher guidance assess learner achievement in terms of realizing desired ends. Evaluation of pupil achievement should not occur at the end of a specific unit of study only. The teacher must assess pupil achievement continuously to determine if relevant ends are achieved by pupils. It is important to have an adequate number of assessment procedures available to evaluate learner achievement continuously during the time a selected unit is being studied. Techniques of assessment should promote and not destroy interest in learning.
5. Ultimately, it is important to evaluate pupil achievement as the unit draws to a close. Assessment techniques which may be used here can be selected from the evaluation section of the resource unit. The teacher may then evaluate his or her own achievement in teaching a specific unit by noticing learner progress.

The Daily Lesson Plan

Teachers must carefully plan of objectives, learning experiences, and assessment procedures for each day of teaching.

Careful planning by the teacher for each day of teaching can aid teaching-learning situations in the following ways:

1. It provides security for teachers in ongoing learning experiences.
2. It gives direction in identifying relevant learnings for pupils.
3. Sequential learnings on the part of pupils may be identified prior to teaching.

A lesson plan carefully planned and developed prior to teaching should be utilized in a flexible way. Feedback from pupils during ongoing learning experiences may indicate that the original lesson plan must be changed in terms of objectives, learning experiences, and assessment procedures.

Educators have recommended diverse formats to follow in writing daily lesson plans. There are, however, selected parts which may be inherent in the written plan pertaining to a specific lesson on a particular school day.

1. Objectives. Relevant objectives for a daily lesson plan should be selected from the teaching unit. The objectives are attainable by learners individually in the class setting. There must be national balance among understandings, skills, and attitudinal objectives. Comprehensive objectives must be stressed in ongoing learning experiences. Thus, the intellectual, social, emotional, and physical development of learners is continually being emphasized in teaching-learning situations. Objectives for teaching should come from a study of pupils themselves. The interests, needs, and purposes of learners are important when planning objectives, learning experiences, and assessment procedures. Input from parents is also important when planning teaching-learning situations. Further input in determining educational objectives should come from studying relevant happenings and trends in society. The structure of knowledge as identified by academicians from the college and university levels of instruction should also be considered as being very important when selecting ends for pupils to achieve.
2. Learning experiences to achieve objectives. Learning activities should guide learners in achieving desired objectives. These activities may come from the teaching unit and should provide adequately for all learners in the class setting. Learning activities must provide for diverse learning styles of pupils. Thus, pupils with teacher guidance choose a variety of activities in providing for diverse styles of learning. Dramatizations, pictures, slides, transparencies, art work, construction, activities, music experiences, records, tapes,

filmstrips, films, excursions, video discs, among others, should aid in providing for individual differences within a given set of learners.

3. Assessing to notice if ends have been achieved by pupils. A variety of assessment procedures needs to be utilized to evaluate pupil progress. Teacher-made tests, discussions, conferences, rating scales, checklists, teacher observation, sociometric devices, logs, and diary entries will be utilized in assessing pupil achievement. All facets of a child's development must be assessed. These facets would include subject matter learnings, skills in diverse types and kinds of thinking, general and specific attitudes of pupils, approaches in locating and organising data, and physical as well as mental health of pupils. Evaluation techniques utilized to assess pupil achievement should be assessed in terms of validity, reliability, and relevance.

In Summary

Teachers, administrators, and supervisors need to develop appropriate rationale in selecting relevant parts that make up the format of resource units, teaching units, and lesson plans. Resource units may be effectively developed by containing the following parts:

1. The title of the unit and intended grade level or levels.
2. Justification or relevance for teaching the unit.
3. The objectives of the unit in terms of understandings, skills, and attitudinal intents.
4. A section devoted to problems which pupils may solve.
5. Learning experiences to initiate, develop, and culminate the involved unit of study.
6. An evaluation section containing diverse vital techniques to assess pupil achievement.
7. A bibliography section containing entries related to learning activities for pupils.

The teaching unit may contain the following parts or sections:

1. Objectives for pupils to attain.
2. A relevant pretest to ascertain present achievement levels of pupils.
3. Learning activities which guide pupils individually in achieving desirable objectives.
4. Assessing pupils achievement during the time the involved unit is being taught.
5. A section devoted to diverse evaluation techniques to be used in assessing pupil achievement toward the close of the unit.

A daily lesson plan should contain:

1. An objectives section.
2. A learning experiences section.
3. An assessment section to determine pupils achievement.

Maxim wrote the following on effective teaching:

Effective teachers of elementary school social studies are good decision makers. They examine the recommendations of experts in the field, weigh the consequences of each, and settle on a program that is compatible with their philosophies and the group or individual needs of the children. Nothing is as exciting and rewarding as watching children react positively to a dynamic program that grows and develops under your guidance. Every paycheck or outstanding evaluation from your supervisor pales in comparison to the feeling on the last day of the school year when a tearful group of youngsters says to you "We don't want to leave. School was so much fun this year!"

REFERENCES

Bhat, K.S., and S. Ravishankar. *Administration of Education*. New Delhi, India: Seema Publications, 1985.

Ediger, Marlow. "Goals in the Mathematics Curriculum," *Journal of Mathematics*, Volume XIX, 1986.

Ediger, Marlow, "Philosophy and Morality," *New Frontiers in Education*, March, 1987.

Ediger, Marlow. "The Reading Curriculum: Issues and Design," *The Teaching of English*, May, 1986.

Firth, Gerald R., and Richard D. Kimpston, *The Curricular Continuum in Perspective*, Itasca, Illinois: F.E. Peacock Publishers, Inc., 1973.

Hanna, Lavone A., Gladys L. Potter and Robert W. Reynolds. *Dynamic Elementary Social Studies, Unit Teaching*. Third Edition. New York: Holt, Rinehart and Winston, Inc., 1973.

Lavatelli, Celia Stendler, et. al. *Elementary School Curriculum*. New York: Holt, Rinehart and Winston, Inc., 1972.

Maxim, George W. *Social Studies and the Elementary School Child*. Third Edition. Columbus, Ohio: Merrill Publishing Co., 1987.

Michaelis, John U. *Social Studies for Children in a Democracy*. Seventh Edition. Englewood Cliffs: Prentice-Hall, Inc., 1986. Chapter two.

Wesley, Edgar Bruce, and William H. Cartwright. *Teaching Social Studies in Elementary Schools*. Third Edition. Boston: D.C. Heath and Company, 1968.

8

Assessing Pupil Achievement

It is important for teachers, principals, and supervisors to utilize a variety of techniques to assess pupil achievement. This is true for a variety of reasons:

1. Not all techniques of assessment evaluate the same facet of achievement. For example, teacher-made tests generally evaluate academic learnings and not social development of children.
2. Pupils do not respond equally well to diverse means utilized to assess pupil achievement. For example, pupils on the intermediate grade levels not possessing a good writing vocabulary may do rather poorly on an essay test.
3. Selected pupils do not read well. Thus, achievement in true-false, multiple choice, completion, essay, and matching items may not be optimal for learners who have difficulty in reading.

Writing Teacher-made Test Items

There are selected criteria that educators should follow when writing teacher-made test items.

1. Test items should be written on the understanding level of pupils.
2. Meaningful test items, valid and reliable, should be written.
3. Ambiguity in written test items should be eliminated.

Examples will be given and discussed pertaining to different kinds of test times which teachers may write to assess pupil achievement. The following are examples of true-false items:

1. Paris is the capital of France.
2. Major farm crops of the midwestern part of the United States include corn, soybeans, and hay.
3. Spain and Mexico contain areas of land which are classified as desert.

The first true-false item above represents recall of information which is the lowest level of cognition. The pupil merely recalls if Paris is or is not the capital city of France. The second objective may also represent the recall level of cognition in that pupils respond to a memory item as to the main crops of the midwest area of the United States. It could also represent a higher level of thinking if the child relates climate and soil to the kinds of crops that could be grown. The third objective might be recall of information by pupils if they have learned previously that both Mexico and Spain have desert regions. True-false items written by the teacher to assess pupil achievement in ongoing units of study in the social studies should reflect learner achievement in analyzing and synthesizing information as well as in problem solving.

Multiple-choice items written by the teacher may also be utilized to assess pupil achievement in terms of stated objectives in ongoing units of study.

London is the capital of

(a) Great Britain *(b)* France
(c) Spain *(d)* West Germany

In writing the above stated multiple-choice item, the following criteria were followed:

1. The stem together with each of the responses makes a complete sentence.
2. No clues are given in the stem as to which is correct response.
3. Each of the responses may be considered as being plausible since countries of Europe represent distracters in this test item.
4. Responses are somewhat similar in length.

The multiple-choice item discussed previously is limited in content coverage and pertains to recall of content by pupils. The following multiple-choice item pertains to a higher level of thinking as compared to the recall level depending upon the learner's present level of achievement:

Which of the following does NOT belong?

(a) Great Britain is noted for its achievement in manufacturing products.
(b) Great Britain procedures more farm products than it can use.
(c) Great Britain is located in Western Europe.
(d) Great Britain is a part of continental Europe.

In the above multiple choice item, the learner needs to analyze which statements are true about Great Britain and which generalization does not apply. If the student has been taught each of these generalizations directly, recall of information is all that is necessary to respond correctly to the test item.

Completion test items may be written to assess pupil achievement. These test items should emphasize, among others, criteria such as the following:

1. The items relate to stated objectives in teaching-learning situations.
2. Adequate information is given in each item so that pupils know what is wanted in terms of correct responses.
3. If more than one response is correct in the completion item, the teacher must give proper credit for the answer or answers.

Completion items, such as the following, may be written to assess learner progress:

______________ is the capital city of Japan.

The major manufactured products of Japan are ______________, ______________, and ______________

Major farm crops grown in Japan consist of ______________, ______________, and ______________.

In the above completion items, factual responses are required of students. If pupils are asked to recall facts, relevancy of content is very important.

Essay items can measure pupil achievement in terms of relevant objectives if the following criteria are followed in writing the test items:

1. The essay items must be properly delimited. "Discuss present day United States" would be too broadly stated. Volumes of content could be written on that topic. "Discuss the concept of recession and how it affects most workers" would be a more delimited relevant essay item.
2. Pupils must have an adequately developed writing vocabulary so that meaningful content can be written in response to essay items.
3. Responses of pupils to essay items should be assessed in terms of adequacy of ideas presented rather than the mechanics of writing (spelling, punctuation, usage, capitalization, and handwriting).

Matching tests may also be utilized in evaluating pupil progress. The matching test should pertain to one topic only (homogeneous content). Other criteria to follow in writing matching test items may include the following:

1. There are more responses in one column as compared to the second column so that the process of elimination may not be used excessively in completing a matching test.
2. Items for one column, to be matched with the second column, should contain important concepts or phrases only and not lengthy sentences. It is difficult to match column one with column two if lengthy sentences were inherent in each column.

3. The number of items in each column should be adjusted to what pupils can reasonably master. Too many items in each column of a matching test could be excessively difficult for learners when matching entries in column one with column two.

The following is given, as an example, of a matching test pertaining to a homogeneous set of items on colonization in the New World:

—— *(a)*	Massachusetts Bay Colony	1. Roger Williams
—— *(b)*	Plymouth Rock	2. William Penn
—— *(c)*	Georgia	3. Puritans
—— *(d)*	Connecticut	4. James Oglethorpe
—— *e)*	Rhode Island	5. Pilgrims
—— *(f)*	Pennsylvania	6. Thomas Hooker
—— *(g)*	New Netherlands	7. William Bradford
		8. Peter Stuyvesant

Using Standarized Achievement Tests

Standarized achievement tests may be utilized to assesses pupil progress.

1. The tests must be recommended by specialists in the area of the testing and measurement.
2. Tests used in the school must be reliable and valid.
3. The tests must guide in determining if pupils have achieved relevant objectives of the school such as problem solving, critical thinking, and creative thinking.
4. Items on standardized achievement tests and methods of administering need to be in harmony with child growth and development characteristics.
5. Teachers should have ample opportunities to assess items missed by pupils on standarized tests to determine if these selected items need to become relevant objectives in teaching-learning situations.

Using Checklists

Carefully developed checklists may be utilized to diagnose pupil difficulty in learning. Values to be obtained in using checklists in the class setting are the following:

1. The teacher may forget relevant facets of each child's achievement unless progress is recorded for learners on an individual basis.
2. Specific errors and weaknesses exhibited by pupils may be diagnosed, recorded, and remedial work given to remedy perceived deficiencies.

The following is an example of a checklist which may be utilized to diagnose pupil progress in selected facets:

Name ____________________ Date ____________________

1. The child actively participates in discussions.
2. The learner respects ideas presented by others.
3. The pupil stays on the topic being discussed.
4. The learner evaluates ideas critically.
5. Creative solutions are sought by the learner in the discussion.

In devising a checklist to assess pupil behaviour, the teacher must

1. Select important behaviours relating to ongoing units of study.
2. State behaviours as specifically as possible and still not sacrifice worthy objectives which are difficult to write with precision.
3. Realize that his/her feelings will vary from one assessment situation to the next when checklists are utilized to evaluate pupil progress.

Developing a Behavioural Journal

It is important for the teacher to systematically record representative behaviour of each child in the class setting. This is true for a variety of reasons.

1. Behaviour of individual pupils may be forgotten unless it is recorded.
2. A pattern of behaviour may be noticed for a pupil if the teacher records typical reactions of children on a regular basis.

There are several cautions to notice when writing behaviour representative of a child.

1. Do not use vague, loaded terms such as "a child is a potential delinquent and trouble maker."
2. Record what is truly a random sample of a pupil's behaviour. Do not record only negative behaviour, but attempt to record representative reactions of any specific child.
3. Be aware of negative feelings that the teacher may have toward the learner.

Using Sociometric Devices

Sociometric devices are used to assess pupil progress in social and emotional development. This technique of evaluating pupil progress does not assess achievement in academic learnings. The teacher may ask pupils to write on paper responses to the following:

1. If you worked on a problem-solving activity with another person in the social studies, who would be your first choice, second choice, and third choice?

2. If you could play a game in social studies with three other children, who would be your first, second, and third choices?

There are selected criteria to follow when using the sociometric devices to assess pupil growth in social development.

1. Keep the results obtained from pupil's response to questions strictly confidential.
2. Use responses from pupil's answers to selected questions to determine committee membership in the social studies as well as in other curriculum areas.
3. Use the sociometric device at selected intervals to determine success in getting isolates and fringe area students to become accepted more so by others than was formerly true.
4. Do not force pupils to respond to selected items if resentment on the part of individual students is in evidence.

Using Discussions

Pupils certainly reveal much of previous learnings obtained through participating in discussions. Selected criteria must be followed when pupils participate in discussion groups:

1. Each learner should contribute, but no one should dominate the discussion.
2. Learners should not digress from the topic being discussed.
3. Each member of the discussion group should attempt to present ideas clearly.
4. Ideas in the group setting should be discussed; this involves the use of critical and creative thinking as well as problem-solving skills.

The teacher of social studies may assess the following when learners participate in discussions:

1. Levels of understanding that individual pupils have pertaining to relevant facts, concepts, main ideas, and generalizations.
2. Skills that pupils possess which make a discussion truly effective.
3. Attitudes that pupils have toward each other and the problem areas being discussed.
4. Interest and enthusiasm that pupils in ongoing learning experiences.

Using Diary Entries and Logs

Diary entries may be written by a committee of learners pertaining to content gained for each specific day of a school week. A different committee may record learnings gained on a daily basis for the next school week. Thus, committee membership changes as to who records daily diary entries in the social studies. This can prevent monotonous learning experiences on the part of pupils.

After diary entries have been written by pupils, the teacher may evaluate learner achievement in terms of having gained relevant concepts, generalizations, and main ideas.

Pupils in the class setting can refer back to the diary entries as purposes, needs, and interests dictate. By reviewing diary entries, pupils can have ample opportunities to review what has been learned previously.

Logs are quite similar to diary entries. A committee of pupils may record what has been learned from an ongoing unit of study at the end of a week. Committee membership in recording content acquired from a specific unit of study for each week should be changed. Variation in learning experiences is important for pupils. Logs may be used by pupils to review what has been learned previously.

The use of diaries and logs may be helpful to pupils in ongoing units of studies if the following criteria are followed:

1. Have pupils in their respective committee thoroughly appraise what has been learned before it is recorded.
2. Let learners decide which facts, concepts, generalizations, and main ideas to record.
3. Guide pupils in the direction of being responsible individuals when participating in committee work.
4. Evaluate with the involved committee as to the relevancy and importance of content recorded in diary or log entries.

Additional Methods to Use in Assessing Achievement

There are many other techniques available to assess pupil achievement.

1. Pupils may construct models and objects related to a unit of study in the curriculum. For example, in a unit on the Westward Movement, pupils in a committee may construct a model stockade. The teacher may then evaluate the quality, accuracy, and thoroughness of the completed model.
2. Pupils may dramatize selected scenes and situations pertaining to the previously mentioned unit on the Westward Movement. Thus, the teacher may evaluate pupil's knowledge, understandings, skills, and attitudes pertaining to this unit of study.
3. Business letters, friendly letters, reports, plays, and announcements may be written by individual learners. These written products may be assessed in terms of clarity and organisation of creative ideas. The mechanics of writing may

also be evaluated such as spelling, punctuation, capitalization, handwriting, and usage.

In Summary

There are many techniques available in assessing pupil achievement in the curriculum. The following, among others, represent diverse ways of assessing pupil achievement:

1. Teacher-made tests including the use of essay, true-false, multiple-choice, completion, and matching test items.
2. Standardized achievement tests.
3. Checklists.
4. Behavioural journal entries.
5. Sociometric devices.
6. Discussions.
7. Diary and log entries.
8. Other approaches such as construction, dramatization, and written products of learners may also be evaluated.

REFERENCES

Anderson, Scarvia B., and John S. Helmick (Editors). *On Educational Testing*. San Francisco: Jossey-Bass Publishers, 1983.

Ediger, Marlow. *Developing the Relevant Elementary Curriculum*, Kirksville: Northeast Missouri State University Stenographic Office, 1974.

Kubiszyn, Tom, and Gary Borich. *Educational Testing and Measurement*. Glenview, Illinois: Scott, Foresman and Company, 1984.

Marshall, Jon Clark, and Loyde Wesley Hales. *Classroom Test Construction*. Reading, Massachusetts: Addison-Wesley Publishing Company, 1971.

Martuza, Victor R. *Applying Norm-Referenced and Criterion-Referenced Measurement in Education*. Boston, Massachusetts: Allyn and Bacon, Incorporated, 1977.

Nitko, Anthony. *Educational Tests and Measurement*. New York: Harcourt Brace Jovanovich, Inc., 1983.

Payne, David A. (ed.). *Curriculum Evaluation*. Lexington, Massachusetts: D.C. Heath and Company, 1974.

Remmers, H.H., N.L. Gage, and J, Francis Rummel. *A Practical Introduction to Measurement and Evaluation*. New York: Harper and Row, 1960.

Ten Brink, Terry D. *Evaluation, a Practical Guide for Teachers*. New York: McGraw-Hill Book Company, 1974.

Victor, Edward. *Science for the Elementary School, Fourth edition*. New York: Macmillan Company, 1980. Chapter Eight.

9

Inservice Education

Faculty members of an elementary school should be held accountable for having an updated curriculum in terms of objectives, learning experiences, and assessment procedures in the social studies. Thus, it is necessary to have a variety of approaches in inservice education.

Workshops to Improve the Curriculum

Each elementary school or several elementary schools may join efforts in improving the curriculum through the workshop approach. Processes that need to be followed in conducting relevant workshops include the following desired criteria:

1. The theme of the workshop should be decided upon cooperatively by the participants. Thus, relevant themes may include *(a)* implementing recommended trends in teaching in the elementary school, *(b)* using inquiry approaches in teaching social studies, *(c)* developing teaching units and resource units, *(d)* using problem solving approaches in teaching-learning situations, *(e)* providing for individual differences in reading content, *(f)* implementing concepts pertaining to nongradedness and open space education, *(g)* using team teaching in the curriculum, *(h)* updating procedures to evaluate pupil achievement, and *(i)* utilizing appropriate sequential learning experiences for pupils.
2. The general session should be utilized to help participants identify relevant problems in teaching. Thus, teachers may identify such relevant problems as *(a)* stimulating pupil interest in learning, *(b)* guiding the slow learner in achieving to his or her optimum, *(c)* developing meaningful tasks for pupils in open space education, *(d)* planning objectives,

learning experiences, and evaluation procedures cooperatively in a true team teaching situation, *(e)* coping with discipline problems in the class setting, *(f)* helping the disadvantaged child, and *(g)* making teaching aids to provide for individual differences in the curriculum.

3. Committees should be formed to work on problems identified in the general session. Committee membership should *(a)* be voluntary, *(b)* meet the needs of participants, and *(c)* help individuals to solve problems in teaching students.
4. Individual study is necessary in providing for personal differences among participants in the workshop. Individuals may work in the direction of solving problems pertaining to *(a)* selecting relevant units of study, *(b)* choosing textbooks and other reading materials appropriate for a given set of learners, *(c)* evaluating the current curriculum in terms of criteria, and *(d)* maintaining an updated curriculum.
5. Consultant services must be available at the workshop. The consultants may help workshop participants to clarify issues and problems, suggest resources for participants, and present possible solutions to problems.
6. An adequate library must be available for participants. College and university level textbooks dealing with the teaching of elementary school subjects should be available to participants for study. Elementary school textbooks with accompanying teacher's manuals should also be available for study to participating members in the workshop. Recent professional journals pertaining to teaching elementary students should be a part of the professional library for workshop participants. Films, filmstrips, slides and tapes on the elementary curriculum may also be beneficial for faculty members in the workshop to use in the solving of problems.
7. The number of sessions in the workshop as well as the duration of each session should be decided upon cooperatively by workshop participants. Each faculty member should donate an adequate amount of time for professional improvement, as well as have enough time available to take care of personal needs and responsibilities.
8. The physical facilities necessary in having a good workshop and the arrangement of furniture conducive to generating ideas in the solving of problems should be such that they facilitate increased achievement on the part of individuals in the workshop. The serving of refreshments and meals should be given careful consideration when workshops are being conducted. Individuals in a workshop setting should get to

know each other well so that mutual trust and confidence may become an important outcome or objective of the workshop.

Faculty Meetings and the Social Studies

Faculty meetings in an elementary school can be used wisely in improving the curriculum. Properly developed criteria need to be utilized in implementing concepts pertaining to improving the elementary school program through the use of faculty meetings.

1. Each faculty member of an elementary school should have ample opportunities to provide input in terms of the agenda to be used at a faculty meeting.
2. All faculty members should have numerous opportunities to serve on a committee to arrange problem areas for consideration on an agenda.
3. The agenda should be ready for faculty member study, approximately, two days before meeting.
4. Faculty members should identify relevant problems to discuss at a faculty meeting. These problem areas may include changing from the use of basal texts to a more individualized approach in reading content, using management systems in teaching students, and integrating science, social studies, mathematics, as well as language arts, into the elementary curriculum.
5. Participants in a faculty meeting may volunteer to serve on a committee of their own choosing to solve relevant problems. Individual study in attempting to resolve an identified problem may also become an inherent part of the faculty meeting concept to improve the curriculum.
6. Adequate resource materials should be available to help individuals in the area of problem solving. These resources may include college and university level textbooks in teacher education, professional periodical articles in this area, as well as related films, filmstrips, tapes, slides, and resource personnel.
7. Direct teaching of pupils using innovative ideas may also become an inherent part of these faculty meetings. Tape recording and video taping of lessons may provide participants needed data to improve teaching-learning situations in the elementary school.

Visiting Innovative Schools

Ample opportunities should be given to faculty members to visit innovative schools. Thus, teachers, supervisors, and principals may see firsthand what is being done in other schools to improve the curriculum. The following criteria should be inherent in selecting innovative schools to visit:

1. Faculty members should identify specific kinds of innovations they wish to observe, such as the nongraded school, inquiry methods of teaching, and team teaching. Ample background information pertaining to the innovation to the observed should become a part of faculty members.
2. The specific of visiting the innovative school or schools should be determined well ahead of time such as the time of arrival at the school to be visited and how the visitation will proceed during the day.
3. Ample time should be given to discuss observations made with faculty members of the innovative school.
4. It is important to evaluate innovations observed in terms of strengths and weaknesses.
5. In the local school setting with faculty participation, a discussion may be held pertaining to what factor facets, if any, of the observed should be adopted.

Using Video Tape

Video taping teaching performance has become increasingly popular. Portable video tape machines can now be purchased which are within the budget norms of most public schools. Thus, the classroom teacher may video tape his or her own teaching and analyze the results. Advantages of utilizing video tape to improve teaching performance include the following:

1. The teacher can actually see his or her physical appearance in teaching in a replay.
2. The teacher may notice if all pupils had ample opportunities to participate actively in the class setting.
3. Evidence can be obtained as to which learners dominate discussion sessions or which refrain from participating.
4. Pupils who appeared to lack interest in learning may be identified; learning activities can then be selected to obtain the interests of these pupils.
5. The teacher can notice if critical thinking, creative thinking, and problem solving methods were utilized adequately in teaching-learning situations.

Naylor and Diem wrote:

> Social Studies involves more than merely imparting facts to students; it includes teaching students how to learn. Skills are not an appendage to social studies instruction; they are an integral and important part of it. Skills need to be taught functionally, within the context of a larger unit of study. And they need to be taught

systematically. The steps involved in learning skills must be made explicit. Students need sufficient time to develop skills and frequent opportunities to use them. Learning skills is a cumulative process requiring continuous attention, reinforcement, and refinement.

6. More evidence can be obtained in terms of pupils attempting to disturb other learners.
7. Proper sequence in learning experiences may be evaluated more thoroughly.
8. Portable video taping may be utilized by the teacher to evaluate his or her own teaching in a nonthreatening way. Thus, the principal or supervisor does not need to observe the actual teaching situation as it occurred in the class setting or on video tape. The teacher is then utilizing self-evaluation in assessing teaching performance.

The use of video tape machines certainly can be an excellent way to assess teaching performance by those involved directly in instructing learners. The following guidelines are recommended to be used when assessing teaching effectiveness through the use of video tapes:

1. The teacher shouid attempt to obtain a random sampling of teaching behaviour. Attempts should be made in identifying weaknesses and working in the direction of remedying these deficiencies.
2. Periodically, a principal or supervisor should assist the teacher in evaluating the quality of teaching.
3 The teacher should guide pupils in utilizing inquiry approaches in learning. Thus, many responses would come from pupils pertaining to higher levels of thinking such as analyzing content, presenting hypotheses, and assessing, and assessing content in terms of stated guidelines.

Using Tape Recordings to Evaluate Teaching

The use of tape and cassette recording may be an effective way to aid in improving teaching performance. The classroom teacher may tape record his or her own teaching and analyze the results. The teacher may notice the following when listening to a replay of teaching and learning as recorded by the tape or cassette recorder:

1. Pupils are adequately praised for improved performance.
2. Learners have adequate opportunities to ask questions and make ample contributions in discussion sessions.
3. Each pupil is treated with respect in the class setting.
4. The teacher does not lecture or engage in lengthy explanations which may be meaningless to pupils.

5. Pupils are encouraged to participate in ongoing learning experiences.
6. Concise and clear directions are given by the teacher.
7. The amount of time given to pupils to reflect on information and knowledge obtained as well as to engage in obtaining information to solve problems is adequate.

Disadvantages which may be listed in using tape recorders to record teaching performance are the following:

1. The visual facet of teaching is completely omitted.
2. There needs to be a broader dimension of evaluation of teaching other than listening to recorded voices.

Observational Visits by the Supervisor

It is important that the elementary principal or supervisor make an adequate number of observational visits to the class setting. Criteria to follow in making these observational visits include the following:

1. It is best if teachers invite the principal or supervisor to the class setting to observe specific facets of teaching and learning such as the culmination of a unit. Following the observational visit, the teacher and supervisor may wish to evaluate the quality of teaching in the class setting.
2. The supervisor may also wish to schedule observational visits with teachers. Perhaps ultimately, the supervisor may visit classrooms unannounced in an informal manner. Prior to visiting a classroom, the supervisor should become thoroughly familiar with the possible achievement levels of pupils in the class to be observed. It is always good for teachers and supervisors to have much information about each pupil in school to be used in improving the quality of instruction and supervision.

Following the observational visit, the teacher and supervisor cooperatively should discuss observations made during the observational visit. Thus, the quality of educational objectives, learning experiences, and assessment procedures could be evaluated. Specifically, the teacher and supervisor could assess *(a)* grouping procedures utilized, *(b)* balance among objectives such as understandings, skills, and attitudes, *(c)* sequence of learning activities, *(d)* providing for individual learners, *(e)* ways of assessing learner achievement, *(f)* methods of monitoring pupil growth, *(g)* additional needed commercially prepared teaching materials, *(h)* the need to make and prepare teaching aids, *(i)* appropriate means to assess pupil achievement, *(j)* needed innovations in the public schools, and *(k)* new psychologies of teaching and learning such as humanistic versus S—R theory.

Team Teaching and Inservice Education

Team teaching has much to offer in terms of inservice growth for teachers. If two or more teachers cooperatively plan the objectives, learning experiences, and assessment procedures in teaching a given set of pupils, team teaching is in evidence. In team teaching the following opportunities in inservice education are available:

1. Teachers may learn from each other in planning sessions devoted to teaching a given set of learners.
2. Team members may also assess the quality of teaching done by each individual teacher in ongoing units of study.
3. A team cooperatively can assess pupil achievement and thus learn from each other as to diverse perceptions held about pupils as well as means of evaluating learner progress.
4. Members in a teaching team may share ideas pertaining to *(a)* arranging bulletin board displays, *(b)* various learning experiences available for pupils, *(c)* learning centers and open space education, *(d)* programmed materials available for teaching, *(e)* learning packets available for pupils, *(f)* pupils working on committees, *(g)* processes of values clarification, *(h)* management systems in education, and *(i)* behaviour modification techniques.

The Professional Library

All elementary schools should have space available and subscribe to educational periodicals pertaining to updating curriculum areas in the elementary school. Criteria to be utilized in selecting professional periodicals for elementary teachers may be the following:

1. The journals contain articles which would guide teachers in doing a better job of teaching in the elementary school.
2. Manuscripts in reputable professional educational journals should contain content pertaining to philosophies of education as well as to theories of learning.
3. Teachers, principals, and supervisors should cooperatively decide which educational journals a given school should subscribe to.
4. Educational journals selected should have content which is clear to read and contain relevant content as perceived by faculty members of a given school.

The professional library for faculty members of an elementary school must contain the following facilities:

1. The professional journals are kept and clearly marked on open shelves.

2. Faculty members have easy access to these journals in the school setting or for home use.
3. Facilities for reading journal articles are comfortable and attractive for faculty members of an elementary school.
4. Participants in the professional library area have ample opportunities to discuss and evaluate innovative ideas in education.

The principal or supervisor of an elementary school should *(a)* introduce selected journal articles to teachers, *(b)* discuss innovative content with teachers, *(c)* encourage the use of recommended procedures in teaching and learning, *(d)* attempt to increase holdings in the professional library to include not only reputable journals but also textbooks and audio-visual media which may become sources of content to improve the curriculum, *(e)* provide ample opportunities for teachers to engage in reading professional literature, and *(f)* be a democratic leader in inspiring teachers to improve all curriculum areas in the elementary school.

Involving Lay Citizens

The aid of lay citizens can be widely used to improve the curriculum. The following, among others, are ways to utilize lay citizens in improving the curriculum:

1. Conducting a survey to determine what parents and others would feel should go into developing an effective curriculum. Results from the survey should be evaluated in moving toward a more effective curriculum for all learners.
2. Conducting meetings involving selected lay people to determine purposes of the elementary school. Faculty members and lay citizens should be active participants at these meetings.

Micro-Teaching

Micro-teaching can give teachers valuable insight into the art and skill of teaching. Micro-teaching emphasizes standards such as the following to improve the curriculum:

1. The lessons are short that teachers would teach, approximately five to ten minutes.
2. Small numbers of pupils are utilized in teaching the short lessons.
3. The teacher tries out a new teaching skill such as initiating a lesson properly or ending a lesson in an effective manner. It is important to video tape teaching performance in these mini-lessons.
4. A nonthreatening environment is necessary to try out a new teaching skill.

5. After practicing the teaching of a specific skill, the teacher alone may assess the completed teaching-learning situation. Through the use of video tape, the involved teacher and other evaluators may give suggestions to improve the performance of a specific teaching skill. Following the evaluation, the teacher may again practice the use of that particular teaching skill, such as initiating a lesson properly.
6. Skills that teachers could practice in micro-teaching situations include *(a)* beginning a lesson appropriately to obtain the interest of pupils, *(b)* using inquiry methods of teaching, *(c)* explaining content in the meaningful manner, *(d)* developing the art of asking stimulating questions, *(e)* diagnosing needs of individual pupils, *(f)* helping pupils inductively and deductively perceive purpose in learning, *(g)* guiding individual pupils to achieve continuous progress, *(h)* helping pupils to identify problems, *(i)* ending a lesson in a manner which maintains pupil interest, *(j)* stimulating pupils to develop appropriate hypotheses, *(k)* helping learners gather data from a variety of reference sources, *(l)* guiding pupils in testing and assessing hypotheses, *(m)* assisting pupils in achieving a desirable sequence in learning, *(n)* evaluating pupils progress, and *(o)* utilizing nonverbal communication effectively in teaching-learning situations.

Thus, micro-teaching emphasizes the practicing of specific teaching skills in a nonthreatening manner. The duration of these lessons is short, lasting perhaps, five to ten minutes. The number of pupils involved in these lessons should be small, perhaps five or six involved learners. The use of video tape provides a teacher with needed feedback to improve the performance of a specific teaching skill.

In Summary

There are numerous ways available to improve the curriculum. Among these approaches are the following:

1. Utilizing the workshop concept.
2. Implementing the faculty meeting concept.
3. Visiting innovative schools.
4. Using video tape in evaluating the quality of teaching.
5. Utilizing tape and cassette recorders in ongoing learning experiences.
6. Conducting observational visits to the class setting.
7. Having a good professional library for faculty members.
8. Involving lay citizens in working toward curriculum improvement.

9. Using micro-teaching to improve the social studies curriculum. Orlich, *et. al*. wrote:

   Not all of the decisions are made as the result of systematic and organised planning. Sometimes the choices are made intuitively. The use of intuition in teaching is quite prevelant. Many choices must be made intuitively because the rapid pace of the classroom learning demands instant decision-making. In these instances, teachers depend on experience and quick thinking to provide the most appropriate instructional technique. We may assume that the intuition of the experienced teacher is likely to be superior to that of the novice. Intuition is like an option in that its usefulness is dependent on the experiential background of which it is based. Yet, in many cases, teachers depend on intuition when systematic and organised planning would be more appropriate. For example, a teacher may believe that a new activity ought to be offered in this school setting, so a particular course of action is taken. Sometimes these "hunches" prove to be right and the results are beneficial to the students. But sometimes they are not effective or are inappropriate for the needs of the learners.

REFERENCES

Association for Supervision and Curriculum Development. *Role of the Supervisor and Curriculum Director in a Climate of Change*. Washington, D.C., ASCD, 1965.

Feyereisen, Kathryn, et. al. *Supervision and Curriculum Renewal: A Systems Approach*. Englewood Cliffs: Prentice-Hall, Inc., 1970.

Hass, Glen, et al. (Eds.), *Readings in Curriculum*. Second Edition. Boston: Allyn and Bacon, Inc., 1970.

Naylor, David T. and Diem, Richard. *Elementary and Middle School Social Studies*. New York: Random House, Inc., 1987.

Orlich, Donald C. et al. *Teaching Strategies*. Second Edition. Lexington, Massachusetts: D.C. Heath and Company, 1985.

Rodgers, Frederick, *Curriculum and Instruction in the Elementary School*. New York: Macmillan Publishing Company, Inc., 1975.

Roe, William H. and Drake, Thelbert L. *The Partnership*. Second Edition. New York: The Macmillan Company, 1980.

Wiles, Kimball, and John T. Lovell. *Supervision for Better Schools*. Fourth Edition. Englewood Cliffs: Prentice-Hall, Inc., 1975.

10

Objectives in the Language Arts

It is important for teachers, principals, and supervisors to study and evaluate relevant objectives for pupils to achieve. The following sources may be utilized in gaining information pertaining to relevant educational objectives:

1. Reading content from recent textbooks written for undergraduate and graduate students in teaching education programs on the college and university level.
2. Studying ideas written in recent periodical articles in professional education journals.
3. Attending professional meetings relating to teacher education and improving the curriculum.
4. Visiting progressive schools and talking with professionals pertaining to ways of improving the curriculum.
5. Reading research studies relating to determining and selecting educational objectives.

Educational objectives should be categorized so that rational balance may exist among the diverse kinds which pupils may achieve. One category scheme that can be used pertains to understandings, skills, and attitudinal general objectives. Understandings objectives comprise important facts, concepts, and generalizations which learners are to achieve as a result of teaching. Understandings objectives to achieve in the language arts could be the following:

1. Various techniques to utilize in reading to identify new words.
2. Diverse purposes involved in comprehending written content such as skimming and scanning, reading for factual information, and gaining a sequence of ideas.

3. Appropriate methods to use in the spelling of words.
4. Guidelines to follow in giving an effective oral presentation within a group setting.
5. The importance to communicate ideas effectively to others.
6. Different purposes involved in communicating ideas orally such as in conversing, discussing, interviewing, introducing, and solving of problems.
7. The need to reveal legibile handwriting exhibited through proper letter formation, spacing of letters and words, alignment of words, proportion of letters within words, and slant of individual letters.
8. The need for unity of content within a paragraph and the necessity of having appropriate sequence of paragraphs.
9. The need to listen for a variety of purposes, such as listening for facts, main ideas, generalizations, sequence of ideas, as well as engage in listening critically and creatively.
10. Differences in meaning between the concepts of standard and nonstandard English.
11. Generalizations pertaining to how the English language operates.

Relevant skills objectives for pupils to achieve could be the following:

1. Reading for a variety of purposes such as reading to acquire facts, generalizations, main ideas, sequence of ideas, evaluate content, engage in divergent thinking, and solve problems.
2. Identifying new words through the use of phonetic analysis, syllabication, context clues, picture clues, structural analysis, and configuration clues.
3. Developing increased proficiency in the correct spelling of words.
4. Writing for a variety of purposes such as in business letters, friendly letters, poems, stories, announcements, thank you notes, and congratulatory messages.
5. Developing increased skill in utilizing oral communication for a variety of purposes, such as in conversation, discussions, dialogs, panel presentations, creative dramatics, buzz groups, and oral reports.
6. Working cooperatively with the teacher and other learners in developing recommended guidelines to be used in evaluating learning experiences in oral communication.
7. Developing increased skills in writing legibly to communicate written content effectively.
8. Developing skills pertaining to the mechanics of writing such as in proper capitalization and punctuation.

9. Using the concepts of stress, pitch, and juncture when communicating oral content to others.
10. Utilizing diverse sentence patterns in writing such as the subject-predicate pattern; subject-predicate-direct pattern; subject-linking verb-predicate adjective pattern; subject-linking verb-predicate noun pattern; and the subject-predicate-indirect object-direct object pattern.
11. Developing proficiency in using various types of sentences such as interrogative, imperative, declarative, and exclamatory sentences.
12. Developing increased skill in expanding sentences through compounding, modifying, subordinating, and using appositives.
13. Being able to write diverse kinds of poetry such as couplets, triplets, free verse, quatrains, limericks, tankas, and others.
14. Putting more of the child's own thoughts and feelings into creative writing.
15. Developing adequate reading, writing, speaking, and listening vocabularies.

Attitudinal Objectives in the Language Arts

It is of utmost importance for pupils to achieve relevant attitudinal objectives. Achieving attitudinal objectives will also aid pupils in attaining important understandings and skills objectives. Positive attitudes toward learning aid in achieving understandings and skills objectives. The following may be vital attitudinal objectives for learners to achieve:

1. An attitude of appreciation in desiring to know how the English language can be described.
2. An appreciation for contributions of linguists in improving the language arts curriculum.
3. An attitude of interest in the history and development of the English language.
4. A desire to develop increased proficiency in listening, speaking, reading, and writing.
5. An attitude of respect toward the contributions of classmates in listening, speaking, reading, and writing.
6. Wanting to read as an appropriate leisure time activity.
7. Desiring to be more creative in speaking and in writing.
8. Wanting to evaluate one's own achievement in the language arts in terms of appropriate standards.
9. Desiring to participate in teacher-pupil planning pertaining to selecting objectives, learning activities, and evaluation procedures.

10. Wanting to improve in the mechanics of writing when communicating content to others.

Specific Objectives in the Language Arts

Selected educators are recommending that precise, specific objectives be utilized in teaching-learning situations. This has many advantages providing that creative thinking, critical thinking, and problem solving are emphasized adequately in teaching-learning situations. Specific objectives should emphasize the following criteria:

1. The objective should state what learners are to achieve as a result of teaching.
2. Learning activities selected by the teacher should guide students in achieving desired objectives.
3. It can be measured if the stated objective(s) have been achieved.

The writer recommends the following additional criteria when writing specific objectives:

1. An adequate number of objectives comes from pupils in ongoing learning experiences.
2. Teacher-pupil planning is utilized to determine educational objectives, learning activities to achieve objectives, and assessment procedures in evaluating learner achievement.

The following are examples of specific objectives in the language arts:

1. The pupil will write a haiku poem.
2. The learner will identify a problem area and write a related solution.
3. The pupil will write a story of at least three hundred words using a title of his/her own choosing.

Advocates of specific objectives recommend that goals be stated prior to teaching so that the direction of learning may be determined before pupils engage in ongoing learning activities.

Outcomes Within Learning Experiences

There are selected educators who state that objectives for learners to achieve cannot be determined prior to teaching. These educators would say that from selected learning experiences, pupils achieve ends of their own choosing. Activities for pupils then should achieve the following outcomes:

1. Obtain pupil's interests.
2. Help pupil's perceive purpose in learning.
3. Provide for diverse achievement and capacity levels.
4. Aid pupils in identifying problems and questions.
5. Increase teacher-pupil planning.

6. Involve learners in evaluating their own achievement.
7. Learners being involved more in the decision-making process.
8. Pupils respecting other individuals.
9. Improved sequence in learning.
10. Intrinsic motivation being present on the part of the learner rather than extrinsic motivation.

Learning Centers and Open Space Education

Advocates of open space education have made many important contributions in improving the curriculum. The teacher in open space education plays a different role in teaching-learning situations as compared to more traditional practices in education. The following guidelines should be followed by teachers who are actively involved in open space education:

1. Pupils are involved in determining what to learn and the media to be used in learning.
2. Pupils engage in decision-making practices pertaining to which learning center to participate in.
3. The teacher guides and stimulates pupils in learning; lecturing, assigning, reprimanding, forcing, and dictating are concepts not associated with open space education.
4. Pupils with teacher guidance are involved in determining content of diverse learning centers.
5. Learners have ample opportunities to work in small groups at different learning centers in the class setting.
6. Good human relations are emphasized very strongly in open space education.
7. Sharing of ideas gained at a specific learning center and also with the class as a whole is significant in open space education.
8. Pupils sequence their own learnings when making selections as to which goals to achieve as well as learning activities selected.
9. Self-evaluation by learners is vital.
10. The integrated curriculum is advocated rather than the separate subjects approach.

To implement the above listed statements involving open space education, the following are given as examples pertaining to possible learning centers in the language arts curriculum:

1. ***Reading center.*** At this center each pupil would have ample opportunities to select a library book written on his/her achievement level. The library books at this center should pertain to various topics and titles, thus providing for the interests of each child in the class setting. After having

completed the reading of a library book, the child may have a conference with the teacher to reveal comprehension of what has been read. The child may also indicate comprehension in reading library books through the following ways:

(*a*) Sharing ideas with other learners.

(*b*) Developing a related diorama.

(*c*) Completing a mural with other learners who have read the same library book.

(*d*) Dramatizing what has been read (this would involve creative dramatics and pantomiming).

(*e*) Presenting an oral report to the class using related pictures and other audio-visual materials.

2. ***Listening center.*** Here, pupils individually or in committees may select tape recordings to listen to. The teacher may wish to prepare task cards for this learning center. From the task card, the child may select which task to work on. The tasks will vary in levels of complexity in order to provide for individual differences in the class setting. The child may reveal comprehension as a result of answering questions from a task card. Or, he/she may select a task which pertains to a problem solving activity whereby needed information is obtained from recorded voices.
3. ***Speaking center.*** Pupils working at this center may practice using the concepts of stress, pitch, and juncture when communicating content orally to others. Cassette recorders may be used by learners to record the spoken voice and notice changes in meanings of selected sentences when emphasizing the concepts of stress, pitch, and juncture. For example, pupils can notice changes in meanings of a sentence when commas are left out in writing or when pauses are not clear between words when communicating content orally:

Jim Allen Ralph Henry Bob Martin and Linn went to the picnic. (There, of course, is a lack of clarity as to the number of people who attended the picnic.)

4. **Spelling center.** Spelling textbooks may provide learning experiences for pupils at this center. It is good to pretest pupils to determine present individual achievement levels. Thus, each learner can be working at a different achievement level as compared to other children in the class setting. Once a child has acquired the correct spelling of a given set of words, the teacher, aide, or another child can test the individual child's mastery of these spelling words. Each child can work at his/her own optimum rate of speed in mastering the spelling of selected sets of words within the adopted spelling textbook.

Each pupil with teacher guidance may also select a specific set of words to master in spelling. The individualized set of spelling words could come from units of study in social studies, science, mathematics, and the general area of language arts, including reading. Once a child feels he has learned to spell a selected set of agreed upon words, he may be tested to insure mastery.

The teacher should guide pupils in using these spelling words in a variety of functional writing situations such as in writing business letters, friendly letters, announcements, plays, poems, and stories.

5. ***Writing center.*** Ample opportunities need to be given learners to put ideas in writing. Pupil's individually may select a picture, from among several, to write about. Pupils should be encouraged and rewarded to write creatively. Originality and uniqueness of content are to be encouraged.

Pictures as well as objects should be present in the classroom setting to encourage pupils in writing diverse kinds of poetry such as free verse, triplets, couplets, quatrains, tankas, and limericks. These pictures and objects may also stimulate learners in writing creative stories. Within these stories, at the proper stage of development, pupils may be guided in thinking and writing about the setting, characterization, and the plot of the story.

6. ***Vocabulary center.*** At the vocabulary center, pupils may be guided in attaching new meanings to words as well as learning to use in a meaningful way new concepts and content. Thus, pupils may view and discuss selected pictures and objects with the ultimate goal of developing a richer listening, speaking, reading, or writing vocabulary.

Pupils in the class setting may also discuss new terms read about in library books. They may also discuss vocabulary terms heard from viewing television programs or listening to radio broadcasts.

Learners may also be guided in attaching meaning to new words encountered in reading through the use of context clues. For example, a child reading a sentence such as the following may not know and understand the meaning of the italicized word:

The boy rode his *bicycle* to town.

Numerous words would make sense to take the place of the unknown new word which in this case happens to be "bicycle." Other words that would be meaningful within that sentence would include "horse," "donkey," and "tricycle." With the use of phonetic analysis, the child would associate the beginning letter "b" which has a consistent sound with words that begin like "bed," "boy," "bay," and "bail." A bicycle, of course, is something to ride on and is used much more frequently in riding to town as compared to the use of a horse, donkey, or tricycle. Pupils then need many experiences in reading to use context clues in determining the meaning of new words.

7. ***Audio-visual centers.*** Pupils should have ample opportunities to view filmstrips, slides, and films of their own choosing. These presentations could provide background information in setting the stage for creative writing. Audio-visual presentations may provide background information for pupils in a quality reading readiness program. Later on, in a more formal program of reading, pupils generally have an easier time in learning to read, since familiarity of content is in evidence due to having developed adequate background information within a reading readiness program.

The audio-visual center may also provide background information for pupils to use in diverse kinds of speaking activities, such as conversing, discussing, and interviewing.

8. ***Puzzle center.*** The teacher and/or pupils at the appropriate stage of development may make crossword puzzles. By filling in the blank spaces on the crossword puzzles, learners may be guided in developing to an optimum level in vocabulary development. Pupils individually or in committees may work on these crosswords puzzles. The puzzle center could be increased in scope to include the playing of games pertaining to the language arts curriculum. Games may be made or purchased commercially pertaining to helping pupils in spelling, word recognition, and vocabulary development. These games should be on the understanding level of pupils. New learnings would be developed by pupils and at the same time success can be in evidence for pupils.

9. ***Dramatization center.*** After selected pupils have completed reading a library book, they may wish to dramatize its contents to others. Formal dramatization may be used whereby play parts are written by a committee of learners. Cooperatively, these learners decide upon and designate who is to play the role of each person in the play. Scenery may be developed by committee members to go along with the formal dramatization.

The final presentation may be given to other learners in the class setting or to other classrooms of pupils.

Creative dramatics may also be used to present content to listeners in the class setting. The content may come from having listened to a story or library book read by the teacher. Content for the creative dramatization may also have come from the telling of a story by the teacher. Pupils in creative dramatics spontaneously develop speaking parts as the need arises. Pantomiming may also be used to convey the contents of a story or library book to viewers. The spoken voice is not used in pantomiming.

Summary Statements on Open Space Education

Within a structured environment determined by the teacher, pupils have much leeway in determining what to learn in open space education. Thus, pupils are involved in decision making. It is important for pupils to learn to work together harmoniously in open space education. Humaneness is an important concept to emphasize in this method of providing learning activities for pupils.

In Summary

Objectives should be selected carefully which pupils are to achieve. There should be rational balance among understandings, skills, and attitudinal objectives in teaching-learning situations involving the language arts. Attempts should be made by teachers, supervisors, and administrators to state objectives precisely (specific objectives) when writing goals for learners to achieve. These objectives, however, must contain relevant learnings for pupils to achieve such as critical thinking, creative thinking, and problem solving. Ample opportunities must be given learners in determining objectives, learning experiences, and evaluation procedures.

REFERENCES

Corcoran, Gertrude B. *Language Arts in the Elementary School. A Modern Linguistic Approach*. New York: Ronald Press Company, 1970. Chapters One, Two and Fifteen.

Dallmann, Martha. *Teaching Language Arts in the Elementary School*. Second Edition. Dubuque, Iowa: William C. Brown Company Publishers, 1971. Chapters One, Two and Three.

Funk, Hal D., and DeWayne Triplett (Eds.). *Language Arts in the Elementary School: Readings*. Philadelphia: J.B. Lippincott Company, 1972.

Hatchett, Ethel L., and Donald H. Hughes. *Teaching Language Arts in Elementary Schools*. New York: Ronald Press Company, 1956. Chapters Five-Thirteen.

Keith, Lowell, et. al. *Contemporary Curriculum in the Elementary School*. New York: Harper and Row, Publishers, 1968. Chapters Three and Four.

Reisman, Fredricka and Payne, Beverly. *Elementary Education*. Columbus, Ohio: Marrill Publishing Company, 1987.

Saylor, J. Galen, and William M. Alexander. *Curriculum Planning for Better Schools*, 1974. Chapters One, Two and Three.

Stewig, John Warren. *Exploring Language Arts in the Classroom*. New York: Holt, Rinehart and Winston, 1983.

Tiedt, Iris M. *The Language Arts Handbook*. Englewood Cliffs, New Jersey: Prentice-Hall, 1983. Chapters One and Two.

11

Theories of Learning and the Language Arts

It is important for teachers of language arts to develop recommended guiding principles when selecting objectives, learning activities, and evaluation procedures in the language arts curriculum. All teachers possess something that guides them in teaching-learning situations if this can be verbalized or not. Thus, a teacher may believe strongly that textbook writer in the language arts have relevant learnings that all pupils need to develop sequentially. A different teacher believes that much rote learning and memorization are methods to use in acquiring complex knowledge, skills, and attitudes. This same teacher then has a selected theory of learning which is a guide in implementing the curriculum. It may well be that a teacher of this description cannot describe orally or in writing which theory of learning is adhered to. The theory of mental discipline, emphasized in the United States prior to the 1900's, may then be in evidence. Basic principles back of the theory of mental discipline would be the following:

1. Difficult content must be learned by pupils to exercise the muscles in the mind.
2. Memorization of content is important to exercise the muscles in the mind.
3. A formal classroom setting is needed so that pupils may learn much content.
4. Content objectives become important to the exclusion of skills and attitudinal objectives.

Stimulus-Response Theory of Learning

Stimulus-response school of thought in terms of how pupils learn is very important for all educators to be knowledgeable about. This theory emphasizes the following criteria:

1. Programmers may determine what pupils are to learn, using microcomputers or textbooks.
2. Pupils progress forward very slowly at each sequential step of learning.
3. Learners know immediately if their response to an item is correct or incorrect.
4. Reinforcement is inherent in programmed learning. Thus, pupils basically are correct in each sequential step in learning.

The use of behaviourally stated objectives also stresses stimulus-response psychology in teaching-learning situations. Behaviourally stated objectives generally follow the following criteria:

1. Specificity is important in the writing of stated objectives.
2. It must be possible to measure pupil achievement after instruction, to determine if the desired ends have been achieved.
3. Learning activities are selected in terms of having pupils achieve the desired objectives.
4. The objectives are stated in terms of what pupils will be learning.

The following are examples of behaviourally stated objectives in the language arts:

1. Each pupil will spell correctly nine out of ten words.
2. The pupil will write a haiku poem.
3. The pupil will write a two hundred word paper on a topic of his own choosing.
4. Pupils will write a sentence following each of these sentence patterns:
   (a) Noun-verb or subject-predicate.
   (b) Noun-verb-noun or subject-predicate-direct object.
   (c) Noun-verb-noun-noun or subject-predicate-indirect object-direct object.
   (d) Noun-linking verb-predicate adjective or subject-predicate-predicate adjective.
   (e) Noun-linking verb-predicate noun or subject-predicate-predicate nominative.
5. The pupil will write a paragraph of forty words using a topic sentence.
6. Given a paragraph of fifty words, the pupil will find five errors in spelling.

In each of these objectives, the teacher can determine if pupils have or have not achieved the desired end or ends.

Behaviourally stated objectives written by the teacher for teaching-learning situations differ from programmed learning in the following ways:

1. Behaviourally stated objectives may be achieved by pupils in more than one class session. Pupils need to follow learnings sequentially determined by the programmer in programmed learning.
2. Sequential steps in learning using behaviourally stated objectives are not as specific as compared to programmed learning. In programmed learning, the pupil moves forward very gradually from one sequential step to the next.
3. The teacher will need to do much of the evaluating when assessing pupil achievement in terms of behaviourally stated objectives, whereas in programmed learning, the pupil generally knows immediately if he is right or wrong after making a response by noting the answer given by the programmer.
4. The classroom teacher writes behaviourally stated objectives for teaching-learning situations whereas the programmer determines what pupils are to learn in programmed learning.

The following would be an example of programmed learning in the language arts:

1. Which word has a different beginning letter as compared to the other two words? (bat)
   bat cake cat
2. Which two words of the following have the same beginning letter?
   (bat, ban)
   apple bat ban
3. Which words in the following set have the same beginning letter?
   (bat, ban, banana)
   bat ban cat banana dad
4. Which of the following words have two beginning letters which are alike?
   (bin, bit)
   bin cat bit saw

Sequential steps for pupils to achieve are smaller in programmed learning as compared to the use of behaviourally stated objectives written by the teacher. In programmed learning as well as in using behaviourally stated objectives, the following criteria must be followed:

1. It definitely can be measured if pupils have been successful in achieving desired objectives.
2. Pupils are to be successful in each sequential step of learning.
3. The child does not sequence his or her own learning; the teacher or programer determines correct order of experiences in learning for pupils.

Criticisms given of stimulus-response school of thought in terms of how pupils learn include the following:

1. It is mechanistic and emphasizes lower level of cognition on the part of learners.
2. Attitudinal objectives may be slighted in teaching-learning situations.
3. Sequence and content in learning should be determined more by children as compared to programmers and/or teachers.
4. Selected pupils may find that this approach in teaching does not harmonize with their own individual learning styles.
5. A single method used extensively in teaching may not aid in developing and maintaining pupil interest in learning.

Gestalt Theory of Learning

Gestaltists emphasize the importance of wholistic learning. Thus, individuals have as tendency to perceive content in terms of the wholeness of the situation. After perceiving the wholeness of an object, scene, or situation, specific facets or parts of the whole are then noticed. In reading and spelling, a pupil will view a complete word and then notice the parts that make up this word. In the teaching of reading then, the teacher may utilize the following teaching procedures in the gestalt approach:

1. The teacher would guide learners in getting an overview of an entire story before discussing relevant parts. Thus, in developing background information within learners prior to reading, related ideas would be stressed emphasizing content covering the wholeness of the situation.
2. In introducing new words which pupils would encounter in reading, learners see these words in sentences on the chalkboard prior to engaging in the act of reading. The words may then be analyzed phonetically to aid learners in gaining important learnings pertaining to word recognition and identification.
3. Pupils attach necessary meanings pertaining to the new words within context. Thus, meanings to words are not learned in isolation but within a wholistic situation such as in a sentence.
4. From these experiences above (numbers 1, 2, and 3), pupils are encouraged to ask questions for which related content can be obtained through reading.

Following the reading of content on an individual basis, content may be discussed answering previously identified questions or purposes. Further learning experiences emphasizing wholistic approaches in teaching and learning emphasize the following:

1. Pupils in a committee developing a mural pertaining to ideas gained from reading.
2. Selected learners cooperatively dramatizing content taken from the completed reading activity.
3. Individual pupils summarizing major generalizations achieved.

The gestalt school of thought in terms of stressing how pupils learn emphasizes wholistic learnings initially. These initial wholistic learnings then may be followed by analyzing facets or parts of the whole.

Structure of the Disciplines

Selected leading educators in the United States emphasize that pupils inductively develop key main ideas of a discipline. Thus, for example, college and university professors cooperatively would identify structural ideas pertaining to the academic discipline in which they specialize. Linguistics then may identify structural ideas such as the following which pupils would achieve inductively:

1. Diverse sentence patterns such as the subject-predicate pattern; the subject-predicate-direct object pattern; the subject-linking verb-predicate adjective pattern; the subject-linking verb-predicate noun pattern; and the subject-predicate-indirect object-direct object pattern.
2. Ways of expanding sentences through the use of modifiers, appositives, subordinate clauses, and compounding parts within a sentence.
3. Word patterns such as those which represent consistency between symbol and sound, *e.g.*, cat, hat, mat, fat, and bat, as well as understand word families where consistency is not in evidence between symbol and sound, *e.g.*., box and fox, or weight and neigh.
4. Difference in meaning of grammar as compared to usage in developing major concepts pertaining to the study of the English language.
5. The changing English language in terms of new vocabulary terms being added as well as meanings changing of selected words. Other changes are also identifiable such as spelling of words and word order in sentences.

In Summary

It is important for teachers, principles, and supervisors to study and develop a theory or theories of learning pertaining to the selection of objective, learning experiences, and assessment procedures. Faculty members in schools must be guided by relevant and agreed upon principles and theories of learning.

REFERENCES

Ausubel, D.P. *Educational Psychology, a Cognitive View*. New York: Holt, Rinehart, and Winston, 1968.

Becker, Wesley C. (Ed.). *An Empirical Basis for Change in Education*. Chicago: Science Research Associates, Inc., 1971.

Eliot, John (Ed.) *Human Development and Cognitive Processes*. New York: Holt, Rinehart and Winston, Inc., 1971.

Finn, Patrick. *Helping Children Learn to Read*. New York: Kandom House, 1985.

Gagne, Robert M. *The Conditions of Learning*. Second Edition. New York: Holt, Rinehart and Winston, 1985.

Hilgard, Ernest R. *Theories of Learning*. New York: Appleton-Century-Crofts, Inc., 1948.

Hyman, Ronald T. *Ways of Teaching*. Second Edition. Philadelphia: J.B. Lippincott.

Kim, Eugene C., and Richard D. Kellough, *A Resource Guide for Secondary School Teaching*. Fourth Edition. New York: Macmillan Publishing Company, 1987.

Kourilsky, Marilyn, and Lory Quaranta. *Effective Teaching*. Glenview, Illinois: Scott, Foresman and Company, 1987.

Looft, William R. (Ed.) *Development Psychology: A Book of Readings*. Hinsdale, Illinois: The Dryden Press, Inc., 1987.

Schell, Robert E. and Elizabeth Hall. *Developmental Psychology*. Fourth Edition. New York: Random House, 1983.

Torrance, E Paul, and R.E. Myers. *Creative Learning and Teaching*. New York: Dodd, Mead and Company, 1970.

Walcutt, Charles, child, et. al. *Teaching Reading, A Phonic/Linguistic Approach to Developmental Reading*. New York: Macmillan Publishing Company, Inc., 1964.

12

Organising the Language Arts Curriculum

Teachers, principals, and supervisors must think of relevant ways of organising the language arts curriculum. One can perceive of different patterns of curriculum organisation being represented on a continuum. Thus, the separate subjects curriculum would be represented by a point on a line toward one end of the continuum. Toward the other end of the continuum, a point on this same line would be represented by the integrated curriculum. Somewhat in between these two points on a line the correlated and fused approaches in developing the language arts curriculum would be inherent.

The Separate Subjects Language Arts Curriculum

In the separate subjects language arts curriculum, the following basic principles would be emphasized in teaching-learning situations:

1. Reading, writing, listening, and speaking should be emphasized in teaching-learning situations as being separate facets of vocabulary development. Each of these vocabularies would be developed in isolation in the class setting.
2. In learning activities involving writing, each of the language arts areas of grammar, handwriting, spelling, capitalization, punctuation, and content might be stressed in isolation in teaching-learning situations.
3. Reading instruction may be divided into the following categories: phonics instruction and other word recognition techniques, comprehension of content, and oral reading. Diverse purposes in reading may also be stressed in isolation from other curriculum areas in the elementary school. These purposes would include

(*a*) Reading to acquire facts.
(*b*) Gaining a sequence of ideas.
(*c*) Reading to follow directions.
(*d*) Reading critically and creatively.
(*e*) Acquiring main ideas and generalizations.

There are selected advantages in emphasizing the separate subjects language arts curriculum.

1. Pupils who experience difficulty at a particular time in a specific facet of the language arts, such as punctuation may receive needed help and guidance.
2. There is a tendency to emphasize each specific facet of the language arts in teaching-learning situations, such as capitalization, punctuation, usage, grammar, spelling and handwriting.

Disadvantages in relying too heavily upon the separate subjects language arts curriculum may be the following:

1. Each facet of the language arts becomes too fragmented such as separating phonics instruction from the actual act of reading, or discussing criteria for effective oral communication of content without emphasizing these standards in ongoing learning experiences involving speaking.
2. There may be very little transfer of learning from one situation to another if, for example, pupils are taught skills pertaining to oral communication of content and yet do not use these skills in various kinds of speaking activities within different curriculum areas in the elementary school. Thus, the separate subjects approach in organising the language arts curriculum would not be a relevant trend unless the teacher diagnoses a specific difficulty pupils may have, such as formation of letters in handwriting, for example, and works in the direction of remediation.

The Correlated Curriculum

In the correlated curriculum, the teacher could stress the relationship of two or more areas of the language arts curriculum. Examples of the correlated curriculum in the language arts are the following:

1. The teacher stressing quality handwriting in the area of spelling.
2. Improved proficiency in speaking emphasized in time devoted to oral reading.
3. Minimal learning in punctuation stressed at the time that experience charts are developed by pupils with teacher guidance.

4. Proper capitalization emphasized as being important while learners are writing business or friendly letters.

Advantages given for the correlated language arts curriculum are the following:

1. Pupils perceive that content is related such as standards pertaining to speaking and to oral reading.
2. Learners have opportunities to transfer learning from one facet of the language arts to a different facet.
3. Fewer separate learnings are needed in the correlated language arts curriculum as compared to the separate subjects approach.

Disadvantages of the correlated language arts curriculum may be the following:

1. It does not relate enough of the different language arts areas.
2. There are times when a specific area of the language curriculum needs emphasizing such as the correct spelling of a word within a selected context.

The Fused Curriculum

The fused language arts curriculum relates its component parts into a broader whole as compared to the correlated approach. Thus, in developing and experience chart by pupils with teacher leadership in a reading readiness program, the following language arts skills will be emphasized:

1. Speaking by involved learners.
2. Perceiving content being written on the chalkboard by the teacher.
3. Seeing the teacher write punctuation marks in sentences containing experiences given by the pupils.
4. Listening to the content presented by learners in the class setting.
5. Reading the completed content by involved learners.

Thus, the listening, speaking, reading, and writing vocabularies are brought in and developed in the above language arts learning activities involving the fused curriculum.

Advantages in utilizing the fused curriculum in the language arts involve the following.

1. Pupils perceive diverse facets of the language arts to be interrelated.
2. Learning becomes more meaningful to pupils as facets of the language arts are brought in as the need arises.
3. Artificial barriers pertaining to separating diverse facets of the language arts are no longer in evidence.
4. Less drill is in evidence when the fused language arts curriculum is used as compared to the separate subjects approach.

5. Learnings appear to become more realistic when content is taught as being related as compared to isolating diverse facets of the language arts.

Disadvantages of the fused approach in developing the language arts curriculum may pertain to the following:

1. A specific facet of the language arts curriculum such as capitalization may be overlooked when content is perceived as being related in terms of usage.
2. It may be more difficult to determine sequence in diverse facets of the language arts, such as sequence or order in the teaching of spelling.

The Integrated Curriculum

The integrated curriculum in the language arts would go a step further as compared to the fused approach in having pupils perceive content as being related. Thus, the integrated language arts curriculum would stress the following:

1. Subject matter loses its boundaries and borders.
2. Understandings, skills, and attitudes in the language arts are developed as needed.
3. Diverse curriculum areas such as mathematics, social studies, science, health, physical education, art, and music are brought into the language arts as needed.
4. The integrated curriculum may be called the functional curriculum since content may be utilized in problem-solving situation.

Grouping Pupils for Instruction

There certainly is a close relationship between the methods used in grouping pupils for instruction and approaches utilized in organising the curriculum, *e.g.*, separate subjects, correlated, fused, or integrated language arts learnings. Teachers, principals, and supervisors must think of the best approaches in grouping and guiding learners to achieve optimum development. Professional educators need to be highly knowledgeable pertaining to the philosophy behind each method utilized in grouping pupils for instruction. A specific plan or plans adopted in grouping pupils for instruction in selected schools should be based on sound criteria with which educators agree.

Open Space Education

Open space education has become rather popular in the United States. Basic generalizations pertaining to open space education would be the following:

1. Pupils in small groups work at learning centers in the class setting.

2. Learners may select which center to work at as well as select the task to pursue from a selected learning center.
3. Pupils are to learn to respect each other at the different centers of learning.
4. Humaneness in the learning environment is stressed as being very important.
5. Pupils order their own achievement in selecting activities.
6. The teacher structures the learning environment from which learners may choose ongoing experiences.

The following are selected examples of learning centers in the language arts:

1. A reading center in which pupils individually may select a book to read of their own choosing.
2. A writing center wherein pupils may select a picture about which to write.
3. A speaking center containing suggested topics to speak on. A cassette recorder may give a learner feedback pertaining to his own achievement.
4. A listening center in which learners listen to selected tapes of their own choosing. A task card at this center may help learners assess their own achievement in listening.
5. A spelling center in which pupils may select a list of words to master in spelling and use in functional writing situations.
6. A dramatization center wherein pupils look at possibilities listed on a task card for dramatizing and proceed with their choice.
7. Other possible learning centers may include a phonics center, a poetry center, and a construction or art center relating to ongoing experiences in the language arts.

Nongraded Schools

All public schools in the United States should deemphasize grade levels in teaching-learning situations. For example, selected third graders read better than certain sixth graders. Or, a specific group of fourth grade pupils achieve at a higher level in spelling as compared to a selected set of sixth graders. Thus, grade levels in many cases may mean very little in terms of learner achievement. What is important is that new learnings are being achieved by each learner and success in inherent in learning. Also, each individual pupils needs to achieve to his or her own unique optimal rate of achievement.

All public schools need to work in the direction of being ungraded. Each learner then would achieve relevant objectives in different facets of the language arts regardless of age level. Continuous progress should be in evidence for each learner.

Advantages of the nongraded school may be the following:

1. Grade levels are not considered when determining a child's present level of achievement. If, for example, a pupil is eleven years of age and achieves to his/her optimum by reading content written on what is normally the third or fourth grade level, these materials must then be used in ongoing learning experiences.
2. Ideally, pupils individually should experience continuous progress in teaching-learning situations. Feelings of success on the part of individual learners are then an inherent part of ongoing learning activities.

Disadvantages in utilizing the nongraded concept in grouping pupils for instruction may be the following:

1. Parents and the lay public tend to think of grade levels and graded textbooks in the school setting. (There are implications here for educating they lay public in terms of changing concepts pertaining to education.)
2. Teachers must keep relevant records pertaining to each child's achievement. Thus, new learning experiences should not duplicate nor be too far removed from previous learnings obtained by individual learners. Keeping adequate records for each learner at each step along the way in achievement can add to the heavy work load of professional teachers.
3. Learners tend to think they need, for example, to study from sixth grade commercially prepared textbooks if they are in the sixth grade. Many learners feel this way if these textbooks do or do not meet their personal needs. (Thus, learner attitudes also need to be changed in terms of interacting with learning activities on diverse achievement levels.)

Team Teaching and the Pupil

Team teaching has been a valuable asset in improving the public school curriculum. To be called a teaching team, the following criteria must be adhered to:

1. Two or more teachers must plan together the objectives, learning experiences, and assessment procedures for a given set of pupils.
2. Pupils are taught, generally, in large group sessions, committee work, and individual study.

Advantages given for team teaching include the following:

1. More than one mind is involved in determining what to teach (goals of instruction), as well as the means used to have pupils achieve desired ends (learning experiences) and how learners are to be assessed (evaluation).

2. Teachers may learn from each other in a democratic planning session (inservice education is then in evidence).
3. Selected teachers may do better in teaching when other professionals on the team assist in planning for instruction as well as help in evaluating teaching performance in the class setting.

Disadvantages of team teaching include the following:

1. There are teachers who would prefer not being members of a teaching team.
2. Selected teachers may feel uncomfortable teaching in the presence of other adults.
3. Planning sessions may be undemocratic and the thinking of one team member alone is then implemented in teaching-learning situations.

The Self-Contained Classroom

The self-contained classroom has much to offer in teaching-learning situations. Thus, a given teacher may teach a set of pupils in most of the curriculum areas, except perhaps music and art. The teacher in the self-contained classroom can

1. Get to know each pupil well and use this data to do a better job of providing for individual differences.
2. Help pupils perceive that diverse curriculum areas in the elementary school are related.
3. Keep the amount of time devoted to teaching each curriculum area flexible, thus using time flexibility for each curriculum area in providing for individual differences.

Disadvantages given for the self-contained classroom concept in teaching may be the following:

1. A specific teacher cannot teach all curriculum areas in the elementary school well. Thus, a teacher may not be interested in or have the skills to teach a specific curriculum area as compared to other areas.
2. Teachers need to specialize more in the teaching of a specific curriculum area. Adequate course work in content and methods should be taken by a teacher on the college or university level to qualify for a teaching position in a specific curriculum area such as the language arts.

Departmentalized Teaching

On the intermediate grade levels, there are educators who emphasize more of departmentalization in terms of grouping pupils for instruction. Thus, in a departmentalized set up the teacher may:

1. Become proficient in teaching one curriculum area only, such as the language areas.
2. Obtain preservice training on the undergraduate level qualifying the future teacher to specialize in teaching a specific curriculum area only. This individual would take the necessary professional education sequence as well as have adequate background training in such areas as semantics, linguistics, literature, speech correction, language development, public speaking, and diagnosing and remediation of problem areas in the language arts.
3. Make fewer preparations for each day of teaching since the language arts only or a different curriculum area will be taught.

Disadvantages of the departmentalized plan in grouping pupils for instruction may be the following:

1. The teacher does not get to know each pupil well enough to do a good job of teaching. There are, for example, too many learners that are taught in a given school day.
2. Content pertaining to the language arts may become too isolated from other curriculum areas such as social studies, mathematics, health, and science. Pupils should have ample opportunities to notice that diverse curriculum areas may be perceived as being interrelated.
3. Time devoted to each curriculum area is rigid. Pupils, for example, may spend forty to fifty minutes on the intermediate grade level where language arts is taught. After this amount of time has elasped, pupils must move to a different classroom for learning activities pertaining to another curriculum area.

Homogeneous Grouping and the Language Arts

Selected teachers of language arts prefer homogeneous grouping of pupils as compared to heterogeneous grouping. Thus, learners in a classroom will be more uniform in language arts achievement in homogeneous as compared to grouping pupils heterogeneously. The following, among others, may be advantages of homogeneous grouping:

1. It may be easier to teach a given set of learners where the range of achievement is not as great as compared to other plans for grouping learners for instructional purposes.
2. Learners individually may not look down upon others as much whose capability and/or achievement is not extremely different.
3. Pupils may be challenged more in learning where achievement is more uniform in the class setting as compared to heterogeneous grouping.

4. The class as a whole may be taught more frequently as compared to heterogeneous grouping.

Disadvantages pertaining to homogeneous grouping may be the following:

1. The class setting may be more democratic if mixed achievement levels are in evidence.
2. There still are marked differences in achievement of a given set of learners even if homogeneous grouping is being tried.
3. Pupils must become accustomed to being with others regardless of capacity and/or achievement levels. In society individuals tend to interact with others regardless of factors pertaining to language arts achievement.
4. The teacher may teach learners as if they are uniform in achievement.

Heterogeneous Grouping and the Language Arts

Selected educators recommend that pupils be grouped heterogeneously. Thus, a greater range of achievement in the class setting will be true in the language arts as compared to using homogeneous grouping. Advantages given for heterogeneous grouping may be the following:

1. Pupils can learn from each other regardless of capacity and/ or achievement levels. These learnings may include getting along with others in a atmosphere of respect involving individuals who may be greatly different from others in many ways.
2. Teachers need to provide for individual differences regardless of the method used to group pupils for instruction.
3. Provision can be made for individual differences by using open space education, individualized reading, programmed learnings, and other innovations in individualized instruction regardless of the plan used in grouping pupils for instruction.

Disadvantages which may be listed for heterogeneous grouping include the following:

1. It may be difficult to teach the class as a whole at selected intervals due to an extreme range of pupil achievement in the class setting.
2. Gifted and talented pupils may not achieve to their optimum when slow learners take up much of the teacher's time in teaching-learning situations.
3. Fast learners may not appropriate the contributions of slow learners in the class setting.

Schools Without Walls

The alternative school movement was rather popular in the United States. One type or kind of alternative school is the school without walls. Basically, all public schools have used the "schools without walls" concept in teaching-learning situations. Thus, purposeful excursions or field trips have become an important part of the curriculum. The use of field trips or excursions in teaching-learning situations may be represented on a continuum using a line. On this continuum, selected schools may strongly believe in and implement the use of many excursions in the curriculum. Toward the other end of this continuum, a public school may not implement any field trips related to units of study during a given school year. Most of the learnings gained by pupils in a school without walls take place in the community. These would be purposeful learnings that are planned in a class setting. Learnings obtained in the community may be assessed in the class setting. Listening, speaking, reading, and writing vocabularies can be emphasized thoroughly in the school without walls. Advantages given for schools without walls may be the following:

1. Realistic learnings are definitely in evidence with the use of excursions and field trips into the community.
2. Purpose is inherent in learning if pupils with teacher guidance have planned excursions.
3. Schools is not separated from society in that realistic learnings in the community can be obtained by pupils.
4. Students sequence their own learnings through teacher-pupil planning involving objectives, learning experiences, and evaluation procedures.
5. Interest in learning should be high on the part of students since they are involved in planning the curriculum.
6. Students must be responsible individuals since their concerns are important in terms of what is to be studied.

Disadvantages inherent in the school without walls concept in teaching learners may be the following:

1. This method of teaching may not harmonize with the learning styles of selected pupils. This would be true of any approach in grouping pupils for instruction as well as methods used in teaching.
2. Selected learners may not be responsible enough to participate in planning the curriculum.
3. Pupils may lose out on the basics in each of the curriculum areas.

The Dual Progress Plan

The dual progress plan in grouping pupils for instruction has much to recommended itself. On the intermediate grade levels social studies and the language arts may be taught as being related by one teacher. These two curriculum areas, as well as health, and physical education are taught on a graded or grade level basis. Science, mathematics, music, art, and foreign languages are taught using a departmentalized system in grouping pupils for instruction and are taught on a non-graded level of instruction. Intermediate grade pupils may experience both the self-contained concept as well as departmentalization in groping practices.

Advantages for the dual progress plan in groping pupils for instruction may be the following:

1. It is a more gradual way to introduce pupils to departmentalized teaching which is typical on the junior high school level. The change from the elementary to the junior high years may be abrupt if the self-contained room is emphasized from kindergarten through grade six and departmentalization is stressed in grades seven through twelve.
2. Teachers who like to teach a specific curriculum area such as science or mathematics may do so.
3. Pupils may experience teaching-learning situations from more teachers as compared to the self-contained classroom.

In Summary

Teachers, principals, and supervisors must become very knowledgeable and conversant about different approaches utilized in organising the curriculum. Thus, the separate subjects, the correlated, the fused, and the integrated curriculum represent diverse ways of organising each of the curriculum areas in the elementary school. There are advantages as well as disadvantages in using any one of these approaches in organising the language arts as well as other curriculum areas in the elementary school.

Related to the problem of how each curriculum area should be organised in the elementary school is the question pertaining to ways of grouping pupils for instructional purposes. Thus, teachers, principles, and supervisors must assess each of the following approaches in grouping pupils for instruction before any single plan is adopted:

1. Open space education and learning centers.
2. The nongraded school.
3. Team teaching.
4. The self-contained classroom.
5. Departmentalized grouping of learners.
6. Homogeneous grouping.
7. Heterogeneous grouping.
8. Schools without walls.
9. The dual progress plan.

REFERENCES

Anderson, Paul S. *Linguistics in the Elementary School Classroom*. New York: The Macmillan Company, 1971.

Anderson, Paul S. *Language Skills in Elementary Education*. Third Edition. New York: The Macmillan Company, 1979.

Beane, James A., Conrad F. Toepfer, Jr., and Samuel J. Alessi, Jr. *Curriculum Planning and Development*. Boston: Allyn and Bacon, Inc., 1986.

Berman, Louise M. *New Priorities in the Curriculum*. Columbus, Ohio: Charles E. Merrill Publishing Company, 1968. Chapter Eleven.

Ediger, Marlow and Digumarti Bhaskara Rao. *Language Arts Curriculum*. New Delhi, India: Discovery Publishing House, 2002.

Frost, Joe L., and G. Thomas Rowlan. (Eds.). *The Elementary School, Principles or Problems*. Boston: Houghton Mifflin Company, 1969. Chapter Thirteen.

Oliva, Peter F. *Developing the Curriculum*. Boston: Little Brown and Company, 1982.

Saylor, J. Galen, and William M. Alexander. *Planning Curriculum for Schools*. New York: Holt, Rinehart, and Winston, Inc., 1974. Chapters Five, Six, and Seven.

Taba, Hilda. *Curriculum Development, Theory and Practice*. New York: Harcourt, Brace, and World, Inc., 1962. Chapters One and Twenty-one.

Walter, Dick and Lou Carey. *The Systematic Design of Instruction*. Second Edition. Glenview, Illinois: Scott, Foresman, and Company, 1985.

Wilson, L. Craig. *The Open Access Curriculum*. Boston: Allyn and Bacon, Inc., 1971, Part II.

13

Learning Activities in the Language Arts

Learning activities must be carefully selected which guide pupils in achieving relevant objectives. Criteria should be utilized by those involved in the selection of learning experiences. These criteria should include the following:

1. The interests of learners are important to consider when selecting learning activities.
2. Learning activities must relate to the diverse learning styles that individual pupils have.
3. Learnings should be perceived as being sequential from the pupils's point of view.
4. Pupils must be guided in perceiving reasons for learning.
5. Diverse kinds of thinking should be emphasized in ongoing learning activities, particularly higher levels of thinking in the cognitive domain.
6. Pupils should attach meaning to what is being learned.
7. Learners must have ample opportunities to engage in problem-solving activities.
8. Decision making by pupils should be stressed in teaching-learning situations.
9. Pupils should be actively involved in learning and not behave as passive individuals.
10. Each pupil must be respected for present levels of achievement in understandings, skills, and attitudinal objectives and be guided in achieving continuous progress.

Teachers, supervisors, and principals must continually seek learning activities which guided learners in creative writing. Developing pupil proficiency in creative thinking and creative writing is a major goal in the language arts curriculum. Learning activities pertaining to creative writing will now be discussed.

1. From a library book or story that has been read, the pupil could write additional happenings. The pupil may also write a different ending to the completed library book or story.
2. The teacher could read a new story to pupils and stop at a given point. Pupils individually write an ending to the story. Voluntarily, pupils compare content that has been written. Ultimately, the teacher could read the rest of the story to pupils.
3. Pupils at a learning center select a picture to write about. Learners may write what happened prior to or after the scene in the picture. Pupils individually may write how the person or persons, animal or animals feel in the picture. They could also write how an inanimate object in the selected picture feels.
4. The teacher could give a brief beginning to a continued story. A committee of three or four pupils add one or two paragraphs to this story. Other committees in sequence may also add to the continued story.
5. From the object center in the class setting a pupil may write about three of these objects in developing a creative story. Unique, novel content is desired from pupils in final products pertaining to creative writing.
6. One child may write a beginning sentence for a creative story. A second pupil can add a sentence in sequence relating to the first sentence. Each learner in sequence adds additional sentences to the creative writing activity.
7. Pupils select an event from an ongoing social studies unit involving history and write weekly diary entries pertaining to that event. For example in the adventures of Marquette and Joliet sailing down the Mississippi River, what experiences did these explorers have specifically on a day-to-day basis?
8. A committee of pupils could write about what the United States would be like today if a selected event, such as World War I, had not occurred.
9. A child may be stimulated to draw an interesting set of lines using a variety of crayons on a sheet of paper. Learners exchange papers and write a paragraph or several paragraphs pertaining to these designs containing lines of diverse colors.

Writing Poetry

Pupils should have ample opportunities to listen to and write poetry. The teacher must think of ways to stimulate learners to write poems. The following methods should be considered by teachers as means to stimulate pupils to write poems:

1. The teacher reads carefully selected poems to pupils on their appropriate developmental level. The poems must be read with enthusiasm and interest on the part of the teacher. Hopefully, pupils will wish to write the same kinds of poems. For example, a teacher may read limericks to pupils whereby the latter may wish to write limericks.
2. Commercially prepared to teacher tapes can be played to learners in stimulating interest to write poetry. In the tape a stimulating voice could read and tell about haiku, thus developing interest within learners in writing haiku poetry.
3. The teacher may present orally two rhyming words to pupils; pupils in groups of two can develop a couplet whereby these rhyming words are used at the end of each of these two lines.
4. Pupils in small groups may think of three words which rhyme and cooperatively develop a poem of three lines (a triplet). The rhyming words come at the end of each of the three lines.
5. Pupils in a committee may suggest four words which rhyme to another committee of learners with the intent of writing a quatrain. As an end result, each committee of pupils would ultimately develop a poem containing four lines of rhymed verse.
6. Using objects in learning center, each pupil in the class setting may be stimulated in writing free verse. In writing free verse, rhyming of words is not necessary, and there is no requirement as to the length of each line. Thus, from the object center, a pupil may write about a model farm tractor in the following manner:

   A farm tractor can be big and powerful.
   Is used to pull implements.
   Looks beautiful when new.
   Is as powerful as a giant.
   Winds its way through the fields.
   Pulls a plow and tears the earth apart.

Spelling in the Language Arts

It is important for pupils to develop increased proficiency in spelling to communicate content more effectively to others. There are selected guidelines which teachers should utilize in the teaching of spelling.

1. Pupils should understand the meaning of and be able to correctly identify words prior to mastering these words in the area of spelling.
2. Learners should be able to use these new spelling words in sentences.

3. A variety of interesting learning experiences should be provided for pupils in learning to spell selected words.
4. A specific methodology should be used by individual pupils which will aid them to develop increased power in the correct spelling of words. This methodology includes *(a)* careful perception of the new word; *(b)* correct pronunciation of the new word and listening to sounds that each letter or letters make; *(c)* the pupil writing the word once and then checking with the correct spelling of that word; and *(d)* once the word has been spelled correctly, the pupil practices the spelling of that word in functional writing situations.
5. It is important for pupils to perceive purpose in learning to spell words.
6. Pupils should practice spelling words correctly within diverse writing activities such as writing business letters, friendly letters, stories, poems, announcements, and thank you notes.
7. The number of words that a pupil is to learn to spell correctly per week depends upon his/her present achievement level.
8. An individualized spelling program is recommendable. Each child's list of spelling words may be planned with teacher guidance utilizing words that come from units of study in social studies, science, mathematics, and other curriculum areas. A recommended series of spelling textbooks may also be used in individualizing spelling programs for learners. Each pupil in the class setting will be achieving at a different rate of speed as compared to others in mastering the spelling of a set of words.
9. Creative teaching methods should be used in helping learners to spell words. From a list of spelling words, learners may write a creative story, poem, or engage in other kinds of creative writing activities.
10. Pupils should be rewarded for volunteering to learn to spell additional new words. Praising pupils for improved performance in spelling can spur learners on to greater efforts.

Handwriting in the Language Arts

Legible handwriting on the part of pupils is important in effectively communicating content to others. Legibility in handwriting is the major objective for pupils to achieve in this facet of the language arts.

General guidelines that teachers may follow in the teaching of handwriting include the following:

1. The handwriting curriculum must make provision for individual differences among pupils in the class setting.

2. Specific and general objectives in handwriting should be attainable by pupils.
3. The teacher may group pupils for instruction in handwriting. Desks can be moved quickly by learners in order that pupils who need the most assistance in handwriting instruction are sitting within a group as compared to learners who may need very little guidance.
4. Each pupil may evaluate his/her own achievement in handwriting by *(a)* comparing his own individual product with a model contained in a handwriting textbook, *(b)* comparing his own product with that of a reputable commercially prepared handwriting scale, and *(c)* comparing his present achievement in handwriting with earlier accomplishments in this area.
5. The teacher must give specific guidance to learners after diagnosing weaknesses such as the following in the area of handwriting:
   (a) Formation of specific letters.
   (b) Space between words and letters.
   (c) Alignment of letters and words.
   (d) Proper proportion of letters.
   (e) Neatness in the final product.
   (f) Proper slant of letters and words.
6. Pupils should be able to see models of good handwriting in the classroom. These models may be provided by the teacher and other learners.
7. A model of upper and lower case letters of the alphabet may be purchased from a reputable publisher in the area of handwriting and placed where it can be referred to by pupils as the need arises.
8. Reputable handwriting textbooks may provide excellent learning activities for pupils if the sequence of learning activities followed is based on student need.
9. Pupils should have ample opportunities to practice quality handwriting in functional writing situations such as in writing business and friendly letters, poems, stories, plays, announcements, and notes of sympathy.
10. Each pupil should be evaluated in terms of improvement over past performance and not compared unfairly against others.
11. Pupils should be encouraged to voluntarily display finished products in handwriting on the classroom bulletin board.

The teacher must follow recommended procedures in teaching so that each pupil may achieve to the highest development possible in legible handwriting.

Speaking Activities and the Pupil

Each child must develop optimal achievement in the area of oral communication. This is necessary so that effective communication of content is possible. There are many kinds or types of speaking activities. The following, among others, are important kinds of speaking activities for pupils:

1. Telling of stories.
2. Making of announcements.
3. Taking part in discussions.
4. Interviewing others.
5. Introducing visitors and guests.
6. Conversing with others.
7. Participating in panel discussions and debates.
8. Reading content orally.
9. Conveying ideas in creative dramatics.
10. Being a member of a buzz group.
11. Presenting oral reports.
12. Leading a small or large group discussion.
13. Responding to questions raised by other individuals.

It is important for teachers to provide an adequate number of learning activities to help pupils develop proficiency in each of the above named types of speaking activities. Guidelines that a classroom teacher must follow to assist each pupil to achieve well in the area of speaking are the following:

1. A relaxed classroom environment should be in evidence. Difficulties in oral communication of content may come about due to a tense, anxious learning environment.
2. Pupils individually should be treated with respect by other learners and by the teacher.
3. Each child should be guided in feeling that he/she is an important human being and has status.
4. The teacher should guide pupils to become active participants in the class setting. Thus, the child feels that he belongs to the group in the class setting.
5. Models for good speaking can come from the teacher, pupils, tapes, records, resources persons, and content contained in library books.
6. Pupils are not forced to make changes in speaking; an inward desire to improve in oral communication should be an ultimate goal.
7. The teacher may give guidance in helping pupils overcome deficiencies in speaking; however, the teacher must realize his/her area of responsibility here and be aware of difficulties in speaking which involve the help of specialists.

8. Definite goals in oral communication must be in evidence for each pupil. These objectives must be attainable.
9. Pupils should have ample opportunities to evaluate their own achievement in speaking in terms of stated realistic objectives. The learner may assess his own achievement in speaking in terms of stated realistic objectives. The learner may assess personal achievement in speaking by listening to his/her recorded voice pertaining to a specific learning activity involving oral communication.
10. Learners must perceive purpose in ongoing learning activities involving speaking.
11. Realistic situations in speaking should be inherent as learning experiences. Thus, for example, the pupil may engage in discussing solutions to problems which are realistic and life-like.

Listening and the Pupil

Pupils should become good listeners so that ideas, knowledge, and skills may be obtained. Courtesy is also involved when individuals listen carefully to the thinking of others. The teachers guides pupils in developing skills pertaining to improved listening. Selected criteria must be followed when helping each learner achieve optimum development in listening.

1. Standards for listening should be developed cooperatively between pupils and the teacher as guidelines for the former to achieve in listening. Periodically, pupil achievement in listening should be assessed in terms of these standards. This could involve self-evaluation by learners, or pupils with teacher guidance may evaluate learner progress in achieving the objectives.
2. Interesting learning activities should be inherent in the classroom setting involving listening. This will aid learners in becoming better listeners. Tape and cassette recordings, discussions, reports, films, filmstrips, and slides should contain content which is interesting to pupils.
3. Pupils should perceive reasons for listening to ongoing learning activities. Prior to the time that pupils are to become involved in a learning activity involving listening, purposes or reasons should be established for listening. Learners may then sense a necessity to listen to content carefully so that information may be obtained pertaining to the stated purposes or reasons for listening. It is important to stimulate pupils in raising questions prior to the learning activity involving listening so that an inward desire to listen carefully will be in evidence.

4. Special time must be set aside in the class schedule to provide specific learning activities pertaining to listening. For example, pupils could rest their heads on their desks, and with eyes closed, identify sounds the teacher is making. Individual pupils may also take turns presenting specific sounds to other learners under the same conditions. Sounds that could be made may include the crushing of paper, tapping of a pencil, snapping of fingers, and pouring of water.
5. During story hour, the teacher may ask interesting questions of pupils pertaining to content read. These questions should stimulate pupil interest in wishing to listen to content being read orally. Pupil listening may then be evaluated during story hour.
6. Task cards at listening centers can aid in evaluating pupil comprehension pertaining to listening to tape and cassette recordings. These tasks guide pupils in developing an inward desire to learn. Intrinsic motivation is important on the part of learners.
7. Reputable elementary school language arts textbooks have selected learning experiences which aid learner achievement in listening. The teacher can select experiences from these textbooks which assist learners to achieve to an optimal level.
8. The teacher must evaluate his/her own teaching to determine if explanations are repetitious. If content presented by the teacher is repetitious, pupils may come to depend upon statements being repeated. Poor listening may be encouraged through excessive repeating of ideas.
9. Learning activities need to be varied in the classroom setting in order to prevent boredom on the part of learners when listening to ideas being expressed. Boring routine, dull learning activities hinder in developing optimal achievement.
10. The teacher must present a model to pupils in the area of listening. When conversing and discussing content with children, the teacher must be a good listener.
11. Unnecessary noises can hinder pupils in the area of listening. It is important to have a learning environment which is conducive to good listening.
12. The teacher must accept each pupil as a human being having worth. Each child's progress in listening must be evaluated in terms of present levels of achievement. There are, of course, pupils who have grave personal and social problems. Situations such as these do not aid pupils in listening to content to the fullest of their ability. Each child must be treated

with respect regardless of race, creed, and socio-economic level.

13. The teacher must emphasize good listening in all curriculum areas. In special class sessions devoted to the teaching of listening, hopefully learners will transfer these attained skills to different curriculum areas in the elementary school.

Reading and the Child

Developing proficiency in reading is a very important objective for pupils to achieve. A person who reads poorly is greatly hindered in most cases in getting a good position, job, or vocation in life. It is difficult to experience an enriched life unless one has developed proficiency in reading.

It is important for early primary grade pupils to have and experience a good reading readiness program. Learning activities such as the following in a reading readiness program should guide pupils to do better in a more formal reading program later:

1. Developing an experience chart with the teacher

Pupils, first of all, would have a learning activity such as viewing a filmstrip or film, set of slides, scenes during an excursion, or a set of pictures. Following this experience, pupils with teacher guidance would present related content for the latter to record on the chalkboard or on a chart in neat manuscript letters. After the ideas have been recorded, pupils read the abstract words with the teacher pointing to the content as it is being read.

2. Having an object center. Here pupils discuss content pertaining to these objects. This learning activity guides learners in getting needed background information necessary for understanding related content in a formal reading program. The objects on the learning center may pertain to units on the farm, city, neighbourhood, and transportation. Later on, in a formal reading program, pupils read content related to these objects.
3. Labeling selected objects in the classroom. Pupils with teacher leadership select important items in the classroom and attach related labels written in neat manuscript style. Objects such as "chair," "table," "door," and "window" may have labels attached.
4. Discriminating between words and letters. The teacher prepares exercises for pupils to work in helping the latter notice likeness and differences between and among letters and words. In beginning lessons pertaining to visual discrimination, the child may, for example, tell which picture

is different from two other pictures. Two pictures, of course, would need to be identical in content. Later, in sequence, pupils could identify gross differences in printed words such as which word is different from two other words within a set: man boy man; girl girl machine; dog owl dog. Pupils may also cross out a letter that is different from two other letters in a set; l m l; b b a; y d y. In sequence, pupils should pick out a word or letter which is different from two other words or letters in a set; however, the discriminations are becoming more complex such as the following: l b l; o o a; c m m.

5. Using audio-visual aids. The use of video tapes, slides, filmstrips, films, pictures, and tapes can give pupils much background information pertaining to what pupils will be reading later in a more formalized reading program. In utilizing these audio-visual materials, pupils gain much needed content relating to pets, the zoo, the circus, children at play, the home, and the school. Major concepts and generalizations are acquired by learners when interacting with these learning activities.
6. Developing skills in hearing likenesses and differences in sounds. Pupils must develop proficiency in the area of phonetic analysis. Learners should make continuous progress in associating sounds with abstract symbols represented by letters and words. In a reading readiness program, pupils may listen to poetry containing rhyme read by the teacher. Pupils at the appropriate stage of development give words which rhyme with each of the following: cat; ball; tin; and cold. In proper sequence in learning, pupils give words which begin with the same beginning sound as the following words; call; baby; same; and game. It is good to use pictures and objects pertaining to the abstract words whenever possible. Leanings acquired by pupils should become meaningful. Pupils need to understand what is being taught. Pictures are good to use in teaching. The pictures aid pupils in getting needed background information. They also assist pupils in using picture clues in the act of reading. If a pupil, for example, cannot identify the word "cat" in a sentence, the picture on the printed page may show a cat, thus helping pupils to select appropriate unknown words in reading. Context clues are also important to use in reading whereby a new unknown word makes sense within a sentence. In a sentence, "I see a ....," there are many words that make sense in context. The following words, as examples, would make sense; boy, girl, dog, man, tiger, woman, map, cat, and cow. There may be, as was stated previously, a picture of a cat on the printed page. However,

other animals or people may also be in the same picture such as a dog, a man, and a woman. The learner needs another approach to use in recognizing new words such as phonetic analysis. The first grapheme of the unknown word "cat" is the letter "c". The words "cat" and "cow" would now fit in as appropriate words within the sentence, since they have the same beginning sounds. However, the word "cat" has a different ending sound as compared to the word "cow". "I see a cat" would pertain to reading the intended sentence correctly as written by the author.

7. There are patterns of sentences with which pupils should become familiar. These include the subject-predicate pattern (Jack runs); the subject-predicate-direct object pattern (Michael threw the ball); The subject-linking verb-predicate adjective pattern (The dog was tall); the subject-predicate-indirect object-direct object-pattern (Jim gave Ivan some candy); subject-linking verb-predicate noun pattern (Miss Smith is a singer). Pupils should also become familiar with approaches used in expanding sentences such as in using modifiers and appositives within each of the above listed patterns of sentences. Equally important ways of expanding sentences pertain to compounding verbs, nouns, adjectives, independent clauses, and adverbs in sentences as well as in using dependent clauses.
8. Pupils should understand word patterns such as ban, can, dan, fan, man, pan, ran, tan, and van. By changing the initial consonant in each of these words, a new word is in evidence. These words follow a pattern or structure. Linguists strongly emphasize patterns as far as recognizing words and sentences is concerned.
9. In beginning reading experiences, young pupils encounter words where there in consistency between symbol and sound such as in the following words: hat, cat, mat, fat, rat, and bat. In later reading experiences pupils read words where irregularity in spelling is in evidence.

Advantages which may be given for linguistic approaches in the teaching of reading are the following:

1. Young readers obtain security in reading when words are consistent in terms of sound-symbol relationship.
2. Pupils may perceive order or structure of sentences and words in the English language.

Disadvantages inherent in a linguistic approach to the teaching of reading are the following:

1. Meaningful content cannot be written where a family or a pattern of words is used only, in written content for beginning

readers. Written sentences for all age levels of pupils in the elementary school contain words where there is consistency as well as a lack of consistency between symbols and sounds.
2. Meaningful words in reading are those which are perceived to be relevant in the lives of the learners.

The language experience approach in teaching reading may be valuable to many learners in realizing optimal achievement.
1. Content for reading comes from the learner. Pupils present ideas based on personal experiences to the teacher. The teacher records these ideas for learners on the chalkboard.
2. The ideas expressed and the abstract words used in the experience chart are meaningful to pupils when reading the recorded content.
3. Pupils experience security in reading since they presented content for the experience chart.

Disadvantages of the language experience approach in reading are the following:
1. Pupil's achievement in reading may indicate the need to use more complex words than those given on an experience chart.
2. When content for a single experience chart comes from several or many learners, the needs of a single individual may not be met. Experiences are unique to an individual pupil.

The Initial Teaching Alphabet (ITA) has been used in selected elementary schools in the United States. There are basal reading series using. ITA symbols. There are forty-four symbols representing forty-four sounds. Pupils are to experience consistency when relating a sound to a symbol. Irregular spelling of words is not a problem when using ITA symbols in reading and writing activities. Silent letters are omitted in reading and writing words using ITA. No differentiation is made between upper and lower case letters using ITA except that a capital letter is taller than a lower case letter.

Advantages given when using ITA symbols in reading instruction are the following:
1. There is consistency basically between each symbol and its related sound in ITA.
2. Pupils experience security in reading and writing when this consistency is in evidence.

Disadvantages which may be given in using ITA are the following:
1. There is not set of letters or symbols whereby perfect consistency is in evidence between each symbol and its related sound.

2. Pupils must always make the transfer after having used ITA symbols to traditional ways of spelling and reading words. Selected ITA symbols vary greatly in appearance from those used in traditional writing.

In Summary

It is important to help each pupil develop optimal proficiency in understandings, skills, and attitudes in listening, speaking, reading, and writing vocabularies. Content may be presented meaningfully to others when speaking and writing. Relevant ideas may be obtained through the language arts skills of reading and listening. Recommended criteria must be followed in teaching-learning situations pertaining to guiding each pupil in achieving to the optimum in different facets of the language arts curriculum.

REFERENCES

Arnstein, Flora J. *Poetry in the Elementary Classroom*. New York: Appleton-Century-Crofts, 1962.

Burns, Paul C., and Leo M. Schell. (Eds.) *Elementary School Language Arts, Selected Readings*. Chicago: Rand McNally and Company, 1973.

Burrows, Alvina T., et. al. *New Horizons in the Language Arts*. New York: Harper and Row, Publisher, 1972.

Chenfield, Mimi Brodsky. *Teaching Language Arts Creatively*. Second Edition. New York: Harcourt Brace Jovanovich, Publishers, 1987.

De Stefano, Johanna S., and Sharon Fox. (Eds.) *Language and the Language Arts*. Minneapolis: Burgess Publishing Company, 1966.

Donoghue, Mildred R. *The Child and the English Language Arts*. William C. Brown Publishers, 1971.

Norton, Donna E. *The Effective Teaching of Language Arts*. Second Edition. Columbus, Ohio: Charles E. Merrill Publishing Company, 1985.

Smith, James A. *Setting Conditions for Creative Teaching in the Elementary School*. Boston: Allyn and Bacon, Inc., 1966.

Sutherland, Zena, and May Hill Arbuthnot. *Children and Books*. Seventh Edition. Glenview, Illinois: Scott, Foresman Co., 1986,

14

Issues in The Language Arts Curriculum

There are selected issues in the language arts which have not been resolved. Students of education must be avid readers of trends and issues in the language arts with the intent of adopting new ideas in the public schools using rational criteria as evaluation techniques to assess these innovative ideas.

Handwriting as an Issue

Pupils do need to develop legible handwriting so that content may be effectively communicated to others. The methods or approaches used in teaching handwriting certainly are an issue.

1. Should handwriting textbooks be used to develop pupil proficiency for all learners? Or, can teachers guide learners in handwriting achievement without the use of textbooks in this language arts area?
2. If a handwriting textbook is used in teaching-learning situations, should each child be guided in developing sequential learnings pertaining to every page in order as it exits within the book? Or, should each learner complete those exercises in a handwriting book where a need exists pertaining to achieving selected objectives?
3. Does the use of handwriting textbooks guide learners in experiencing continuous progress in the area of handwriting? Could pupils achieve continuous progress in this facet of the language arts without the use of handwriting textbooks?

Thus, as an important issue in the language arts curriculum, one can ask relevant questions pertaining to the use of handwriting textbooks in guiding learners to achieve to their optimal level when communicating written content to others.

Phonics Instruction as an Issue

A frequent question raised pertaining to the teaching of reading relates to phonics instruction in the elementary school.

1. How much phonics should be taught in order to be able to identify new words in the reading curriculum?
2. Should phonics be taught to each learner? Are there better ways to help selected learners become proficient in using word recognition techniques other than through phonics instruction?
3. How can balance be maintained in teaching-learning situations among diverse techniques to identify and recognize new words, *e.g.*, phonetic analysis, configuration clues, picture clues, context clues, syllabication, and structural analysis?

   Rubins wrote:

   Teachers should not present initial consonants in isolation from words. Since letters do not have sounds, but are merely representations of them, it is not correct to refer to the sound of b or g. Teachers may state a number of words beginning with the initial consonant. They may ask the children to listen to the words ball, book, and bee. They should write the words on the board. Then they should ask how ball, book, and bee are similar. They all have the same beginning letter b. They all start with the same sound. Teachers can then give a list of words that begin with b and ask students to state some others like big, book, and balloon.

Use of Spelling Textbooks as an Issue

Many elementary schools in the United States use spelling textbooks to develop pupil proficiency in the correct spelling of words. Questions that might be raised about this approach in teaching-learning situations may be in the following:

1. Are the words contained in weekly lists of words in spelling functional in the lives of pupils?
2. Are learners able to spell these words correctly in functional writing situation after they have been mastered as revealed in a test?
3. Can pupils perceive purpose in learning to spell a list of words which they have not identified as being relevant?
4. Are teachers able to provide for individual differences in terms of the number of words mastered per week when spelling textbooks provide major learnings for pupils in this facet of the language arts curriculum?
5. Do spelling textbooks contain learning experiences which pupils find meaningful and interesting?

Direct Instruction in Listening as an Issue

It is important for pupils to become proficient listeners as a method of obtaining new information as well as in showing respect toward others in situations, involving oral communication of content. There are selected issues which may be discussed pertaining to teaching listening in the elementary school.

1. Can skills in listening be taught directly to pupils, or does good listening occur only within a stimulating environment in which interesting content is being presented?
2. Does direct teaching of skills in listening have transfer value in that there is a carry-over of these skills to different curriculum areas in the school setting?

Using Textbooks and Workbooks as an Issue

Certainly, language arts textbooks and workbooks can provide valuable learning experiences for pupils. No teacher, basically, would be able to creatively develop objectives, learning experiences, and evaluation procedures for each curriculum area taught in a self-contained classroom without the use of the selected basal textbooks providing a framework for pupils learning. The issue centers itself more around the methods used when language arts textbooks and workbooks provide major learnings for pupils.

1. If textbooks an workbooks are followed sequentially, as written by the authors in providing learning activities, does this aid pupils perceiving proper sequence in learning?
2. Could teachers creatively develop a better language arts curriculum than that presented in textbooks and workbooks?
3. Which criteria would writers of elementary school language arts materials need to follow when developing content for learners which is interesting, meaningful, purposeful, and makes provision for individual differences.

Specific Plans of Reading Instruction as an Issue

There certainly are many methods available in teaching reading in the elementary school. Each plan of instruction has its strengths and weaknesses.

1. Do pupils actually select library books on their own individual unique reading levels in individualized reading, or are books selected for reading based on those which can be completed with little or no effort?
2. Do all pupils actually read a library book during time set aside for individualized reading?
3. Is it good teaching procedure for pupils in beginning reading instruction to use Initial Teaching Alphabet symbols when

traditional symbols need to be understood and used at a later time?

4. Do schools have an ample supply of library books which have ITA symbols when supplementing basal readers which utilize these symbols in teaching-learning situations?
5. Is it realistic to have pupils in beginning reading instruction learn to read words which follow a specific pattern? Attempt to build meaningful sentences using the following pattern or structure of words: bat, cat, fat, hat, mat, nat, rat, sat, and vat.
6. Does the use of basal readers provide for unique interests and rates of learning that individual pupils have?
7. What kind of reading program would be in evidence if experience charts alone would be used in teaching-learning situations involving reading instruction?

Grammar in the Language Arts Curriculum

Pupils in the elementary school, especially in the intermediate grades, have spent a considerable amount of time in the study of grammar. Thus, pupils have attempted to learn to classify words within sentences in terms of specific parts of speech such as nouns, verbs, adverbs, adjectives, pronouns, prepositions, conjunctions, and interjections. They have also learn to tell how words are used within a sentence such as a word or words being used as

(a) The subject of the sentence.
(b) The direct object.
(c) The object of the preposition.
(d) An indirect object.
(e) A predicate adjective or predicate noun.
(f) An adverb or adverb phrase.
(g) An adjective or adjective phrase.
(h) Gerunds, infinitives, and participles.
(i) Independent or dependent clauses.

Pupils in the study of grammar also learn to classify sentences in terms of the following types:

(a) Declarative (states a fact or opinion and ends with a period).
(b) Interrogative (asks a question and ends with a question mark).
(c) Exclamatory (reveals strong feeling and ends with an exclamation mark).
(d) Imperative (issues a command or request and ends with a period).

Thus, pupils spend much time in the study of grammar in the elementary school. There are selected issues which may be identified pertaining to the study of grammar.

1. Does a study of grammar aid pupils in achievement in the areas of speaking and writing?
2. Can learner interest be developed in the study of grammar?
3. Do teachers use a variety of learning activities in the teaching of grammar so that memorization of content and rote learning are minimized?
4. Is there a transfer of learning from content learned in grammar to other curriculum areas in the elementary school.

Standard and Nonstandard English

Much has been written about the issue of changing pupil's speaking behaviour from nonstandard to standard English. In American society a premium is placed upon individuals being able to speak and write using standard English. One can, no doubt, express content equally clearly using nonstandard English. The following are examples of standard and nonstandard English:

1. He is going to walk to school. (standard English)
   He goin to walk to school. (nonstandard English)
2. He is not ready yet. (standard English)
   He ain't ready yet. (nonstandard English)
3. The dog and the cat are scrapping. (standard English)
   Da dog and da cat are scrappin. (nonstandard English)

Thus, in speaking either standard or nonstandard English, content may be clearly presented. Middle and upper class individuals socio-economically prefer and stress the importance of standard English in functional speaking and writing situations.

Issues that arise in these two value systems are the following:

1. Should pupils be guided in switching from nonstandard to standard English?
2. What approaches should be utilized in helping pupils change from nonstandard to standard English?
3. How can pupils who speak nonstandard English continually respect themselves and their heritage when learning to speak standard English?
4. Can pupils learn to speak and write standard English in the school setting and still communicate content with feelings of respect using nonstandard English in the home setting?
5. Should teachers "correct" learners in the school setting who use nonstandard English?

Norton wrote:

Traditional grammar is considered prescriptive, because it provides a series of rules for constructing sentences and classifying parts of speech. In contrast, structural grammar is referred to as descriptive grammar, because it describes words according to form classes, and describes sentence patterns or positions of words in sentences. Transformational grammar is built on the work of the structuralists, but extends grammar into the meaning of language. Whereas structural grammar is concerned primarily with syntax, transformational grammar is concerned more with semantics and the generating of sentences. The term transformation refers to the division of sentences into kernal sentences and the transforms or variations that can be developed from these basic sentences.

Evaluating Pupil Progress in the Language Arts

There are numerous ways to assess pupils achievement in the language arts. Frequently, much emphasis has been placed upon the use of standardized tests in the evaluation process. These tests have the following advantages:

1. An individual pupil's achievement in school may be measured against the norms of the test.
2. These tests are generally highly reliable in that consistency of results is in evidence on the part of learners.

Disadvantages given in using standardized tests are the following:

1. Selected items are not valid in measuring learner achievement.
2. Not all facets of pupil development can be measured using standardized tests, *e.g.*, skills in speaking, creative writing, and achievement in listening.

Thus, numerous approaches must be utilized in assessing learner progress in the language arts.

Manuscripts versus Cursive Writing

There is a relevant issue pertaining to the teaching of manuscript versus cursive writing. In most elementary schools, pupils on the early primary grade levels begin with manuscript writing. This is due to the following reasons:

1. The content in textbooks and library books is printed in manuscript writing. Thus, there is a relationship between writing in manuscript letters and printed content that pupils read.
2. Manuscript letters are easier to form as compared to cursive letters.
3. Pupils have better control over their finer muscles when engaging in manuscript writing as compared to cursive writing.

Pupils, however, ultimately need to switch from manuscript to cursive writing. Cursive writing, generally, is expected of adults, although manuscript writing is being accepted more and more in terms of adult usage. There are selected elementary schools in which pupils begin their own writing experiences using cursive letters. The following problems arise pertaining to the teaching of handwriting using manuscript or cursive letters:

1. When should pupils begin using either manuscript or cursive symbols in handwriting experiences?
2. If pupils begin with manuscript symbols, when should the change-over be made to cursive writing.
3. Which methods are best to use in the teaching of handwriting when either manuscript or cursive letters are to be in the evidence?

In Summary

There are numerous issues which have not been resolved in the language arts curriculum. Teachers, supervisors, and principals should certainly become highly knowledgeable about these issues and take a position based on understanding and thought. Issues which need to be resolved in teaching the language arts include the following:

1. The use of handwriting textbooks for pupils.
2. The teaching of phonics in the reading curriculum.
3. The utilization of spelling textbooks for learners in teaching-learning situations.
4. Direct instruction in developing pupil proficiency in listening.
5. Diverse plans and programs of instruction in the curriculum area of reading.
6. The teaching of grammar in guiding pupils to communicate ideas more effectively in speaking and writing.
7. The use of standard versus nonstandard English in oral communication.
8. How pupil achievement should be assessed in the language arts.
9. Manuscript versus cursive writing in the language arts curriculum.

REFERENCES

Burns, Paul C., et al. *The Language Arts in Childhood Education*. Second Edition. Chicago: Rand McNally and Company, 1971.

Knight, Lester N. *Language Arts for the Exceptional: The Gifted and Linguistically Different*. Itasca, Illinois: F.E. Peacock Publishers, Inc., 1974.

Lamb, Pose. *Guiding Children's Language Learning*. Second Edition. Dubuque, Iowa: William C. Brown Company Publishers, 1971.

Norton, Donna E., *The Effective Teaching of Language Arts*. Columbus, Ohio: Charles E. Merrill Publishing Company, 1985.
Rubin, Dorothy, *Diagnosis and Correction in Reading Instruction*. New York: Holt, Rinehart, and Winston. 1982.
Petty, Walter T. (Ed.). *Issues and Problems in the Elementary Language Arts*. Boston: Allyn and Bacon, Inc., 1968.
Schell, Robert E. and Elizabeth Hall. *Developmental Psychology Today*. New York: Random House, 1983.
Silberman, Melvin L., et. al. *The Psychology of Open Teaching and Learning*. Boston: Little, Brown, and Company, 1972.
Smith, James A. *Creative Teaching of the Language Arts in the Elementary School*. Second Edition. Boston: Allyn and Bacon Inc., 1973.
Stewing, John Warren. *Exploring Language Arts in the Elementary Classroom*. New York: Holt, Rinehart, and Winston, 1983.

15

Poetry in the Language Arts

An important type of reading for elementary age pupils is to read poetry. There are pupils who love to read poetry and unfortunately others either are neutral or react negatively to its reading. My hope in this writing is that all pupils will read and react more positively to diverse forms of verse and their contents. Pupils in classrooms where I have supervised student teachers and cooperating teachers are somethat eager to express their opinions about the study and writing of poetry. Some of the recorded comments we have written down of these opinions include:

1. I do not understand what is written.
2. I would rather read stories from library books.
3. The language used is confusing.
4. I like to read poems that rhyme.
5. I would rather do something else than read.
6. I like poetry that has animal content.
7. I like to read poetry and other literature.
8. I do not like to memorize poetry.
9. I feel that the words used in poems are difficult to understand.
10. I wish more time would be given to the study and reading of poetry.

From the above comments, it is quite obvious that there are mixed feelings toward the reading of poetry. Certainly, the teacher will need to establish objectives in which each pupil learns to love the studying and reading of poetry. This can be a difficult task and yet the teacher needs to try to get pupils actively engaged in units of study pertaining to poetry in the elementary school. We would suggest that a major goal of instruction should be to assist pupils to love and appreciate poetry. Additional objectives include obtaining meaning and understanding of poems read, desiring to write different forms and types of poems, working harmoniously with others in reading and writing of poems, increasing vocabulary development through poetry writing, improving reading skills in word recognition and comprehension (Ediger, 1997), relating poems read to different curriculum areas in the elementary school, building and developing background information to use in diverse subject matter areas in the curriculum, as well as increasing in the desire to learn, grow and achieve. To write quality poetry, the pupil needs background information. The teacher needs to have a rich learning environment in the classroom. We believe in having many learning centers in the classroom so that learners may look at what is at each center. Objects, items, audio-visual aids, realia and library books with other print materials need to be located at each of these centers. The teacher needs to introduce each center briefly as well as motivate and assist pupils to move forward with achievement in poetry writing. Pupils need to browse through books containing poetry. First, lets take a look at how the poetry curriculum may be organised.

Organising the Poetry Curriculum

Teachers need to think of how to organise the poetry curriculum so that more optimal pupil achievement is in evidence. We have observed teachers teach entire units on poetry as a separate subject. The unit involved here may be entitled "Reading and Writing Poetry". Why do selected teachers teach separate units on poetry? Depth teaching might then be involved in that the focus is upon poetry only in its many forms. Here, the teacher may have pupils concentrate on rhymed, unrhymed but with a certain number of syllables per line and no rhyme and no specific number of syllables per line. When readiness is in evidence, pupils may compare and contrast diverse forms of poetry studied and written. Ingredients in poetry writing may also be emphasized here with imagery, alliteration and onomatopoeia. In the separate subjects approach of units on poetry in the elementary school, pupils may focus in depth upon what goes into the different forms of verse to emphasize poetry in its diverse manifestations.

For example, in studying, imagery, pupils may learn in depth what is involved here with metaphors and similes. Thus, pupils need to understand that metaphors do not require words including *like* and *as*. Creative comparisons may then be made: The moon, a yellow flame of gold, moves rapidly in space. Here, the moon is compared creatively with, "a yellow flame of gold". This is a metaphorical comparison.

A second form of imagery is to use similes whereby the words "like" and "as" are used to make creative comparisons: The clouds in the sky look like sheep walking on the blue grass. The simile her is "like sheep walking on blue grass". Thus, a creative comparison is made between "The clouds in the sky", and "sheep walking on blue grass".

In addition to the separate subjects poetry curriculum, the teacher may also wish to correlate reading and writing poems with different curriculum areas. Here, the teacher attempts the best possible to have pupils directly relate each poem studied to social studies, science, mathematics and the language art areas. Thus, if a social studies unit on the Civil War is being taught, the teacher may assist pupils to read and study literature written during this war. Social Studies and literature are being correlated. Perceiving relationship of knowledge by pupils is a major goal of the correlated curriculum. There are fewer separate subjects to be taught in a given day. The elementary school curriculum tends to be crowded as it is and teachers do welcome certain curriculum areas to be correlated.

In correlating social studies and poetry, one pupil in the fifth grade wrote the following quatrain containing patterns of rhyme:

The Holy Land
Moslems, Christians and Jews
Each have their own unique views
Mosque, Church or Temple
Religion is taught as an example.

When pupils perceive that knowledge is related, it becomes easier to remember what had been learned. Why? One idea obtained triggers off others that are related. In a separate subjects poetry curriculum, the pupil may perceive content in isolation and thereby not sense that facts, concepts and generalizations can be learned as a unity or as ideas related to each other. There are fewer separate subjects to teach if correlation of content is in evidence.

A third way of organising the poetry curriculum is to stress an integrated curriculum. Here, the teacher leans upon social studies, science, mathematics and literature, among other academic disciplines, to provide content for poems written by pupils. Each academic discipline tends to become blurred with the integrated curriculum. Pupils then have even greater chances of understanding how knowledge can be related. Many educators would argue that pupils here should retain subject matter in memory longer due to using it and in this case not being a separate subject.

How the teacher wishes to organise the poetry curriculum depends upon many factors. These include the number of curriculum areas taught which can be emphasized satisfactorily as related by the teacher. Sometimes the integrated curriculum is also called the interdisciplinary approach for organising instruction.

One pupil wrote the following triplet with all ending words rhyming and indicating an inter-disciplinary curriculum:

The Dome of the Rock in the Holy Land
The Dome of the Rock has an octagonal design
(mathematics)
It is used for worship by the Moslems as a sign
(social studies)
With all of its beauty viewed by yours and mine
(art).

The poetry curriculum needs to be carefully developed with quality objectives, learning opportunities and evaluation procedures. In making these three decisions, the teacher also needs to think of organisations such as the separate subjects, the correlated and the integrated and the integrated approach in teaching and learning.

Alliteration and Onomatopoeia in Poetry Writing

Pupils with teacher guidance should learn to use alliteration in poetry writing. Poets use this device frequently in writing. Alliteration tends to stress two or more sequential words that begin with the same sound. Learners find it fascinating to create verse whereby the two or more initial sounds are the same in an ordered way. A committee of three children collaborated on writing the following containing alliteration:

The Dead Sea in the Holy Land
With salty sea water at sight
And low level elevation of land
I find the dear Dead Sea to lack life.

We feel that writing poetry with alliteration assists pupils in recognizing the role of phonics in reading. Creatively determining words that start with the same sound stresses sounds, not spelling. For example, the words *cent* and *sent* have identical sounds but these words are spelled differently with the initial consonant sound.

Another device that poets use in writing poetry is onomatopoeia. Here, words used must make the sounds that one hears in the natural environment. If one throws a rock into the water, the sound made is similar to splash! Thus, the word splash makes that sound, in degrees, when a rock is thrown into the water. A pupil I observed while supervising student teachers in the public schools wrote the following containing onomatopoeia in a science unit of study:

The Sound of Wind

Why does the wind sound like *swish, swoosh, slosh, slash* and *spash*? The unequal heating of the earth's atmosphere makes for movement of air.

The movement of molecules through the air say travel move and go!

The underlined words in the above poem seem to indicate in degrees the sound of wind. The pupil has included onomatopoeia in the first line only of this poem.

Poems That Rhyme

One important kind poetry does rhyme. Others do not. The following are examples of rhymed verse which pupils may write when readiness is in evidence (Ediger, 1988). Couplets contain two lines with ending words rhyming, such as in the following poem:

The Forty Niners
The Forty niners went to the West
To look for gold with great zest.

One teacher mentioned to one of us while supervising student teachers that the whole word method only or largely was used when she attended public schools. Major learnings came from studying rhymed verse. In her school, the teacher would have pupils brain storm ideas on how many words would rhyme with a particular word printed on the chalkboard. These listed words were then to be used in poetry writing.

Triplets have three lines with all ending words rhyming. From a brain storming session on ideas about the zoo, a committee of three wrote the following triplet:

The Zoo
I like to visit the zoo to see large lions
We have studied these animals in science
They live in a few nations with different biomes.

The quatrain was discussed above and needs a little review. Quatrains have four lines with lines one and two rhyming as well as lines three and four rhyming. Sometimes, all ending words rhyme of the four line poem. A dyad of two pupils wrote the following within a unit of study:

An Inventor
Thomas Edison invented the light bulb with much work
His efforts helped all to see better at night with little quirk
The light bulb was here to stay
And make life better with more pay.

Selected pupils like to work together with others in the classroom in writing a poem. The number here needs to be kept small so all may participate such as a dyad of two members of a maximum of four pupils writing collaboratively.

Limericks are a very popular kind of poem for pupils to write. Generally, this poem starts with the words "There once was a— The limerick has five lines comprised of a couplet and a triplet. Lines 1, 2, and 5 form a triplet whereas lines 3 and 4 form a couplet.

Kindness
There once was a man in a large city
Who felt sorry for poor people in a pity
He raised much money for the poor
And felt he needed much more
That wonderful man worked on a committee.

It is excellent if pupils volunteer to write poetry; however, there are learners who do not participate with intrinsic motivation and may need to be assigned to a committee which is highly accepting and provides for all pupils to succeed.

Unrhymed Verse

Many pupils are surprised that there can be unrhymed poetry which provides for interest and purpose on the part of the learner. They find free verse to be challenging and relatively easy to write. After all, pupils should enjoy reading and writing poems. Intrinsic motivation is important in all learning as an ideal. Many pupils are motivated from within and do not need inexpensive prizes as rewards for learning. For those lacking intrinsic motivation, the teacher may need to use an award system and, hopefully, pupils will wean themselves from extrinsic motivation as time goes on. We do not count verbal praise as extrinsic motivation. Honest praise is good for pupils and should be used judiciously. We believe that quality learning takes place best with intrinsic motivation, but a few pupils will need rewards and prizes as motivators. Two pupils wrote the following haiku containing five-seven-five syllables for each of three lines:

The Goat

The goal is a joy (five syllables)
In the grass among the trees (seven syllables)
A lovely sight seen!

A tanka has two more lines, each having seven syllables:

The Tall Camel
I like to see far (five syllables)
Where camels roam in deserts (seven syllables)
And chew scarce rare feed (five syllables)
Up, away go the camels (seven syllables)
Where grass and water abound. (seven syllables)

Writing Free Verse

Free verse is a very open-ended kind of poetry. There does not have to be any rhyme nor syllabication. Many pupils enjoy brain storming lines for free verse. The following free verse was composed by four pupils collaboratively:

The Shepherd
Alone with the sheep in the field
plays on the flute to maintain entertainment
watches and cares for each and every sheep
is careful with the little lambs
herds the animals to good grass
throws stones at cement fences
does not mind being alone
relishes time with the sheep
ever faithful and kind

In Conclusion

Pupils need to experience reading and writing different kinds and forms of poetry. There are rich meanings and messages in poetry. The novel use of words adds to the learning repertoire of pupils. There should be poems for pupils to read that deal with diverse topics and genres. The poems should be on appropriate reading levels of individual pupils for maximum achievement to take place. The teacher needs to read poetry frequently to pupils in an enthusiastic way. Each pupil may wish to collect his/her favourite poems for enjoyment and future reference. Pupils need to become motivated through the use of different stimuli in order to read and write more poetry. For selected pupils, reading much poetry has been a way of increasing skills in learning to read more proficiently.

REFERENCES

Ediger, Marlow (1997), *The Modern Elementary School*, Kirksville, Missouri: Simpson Publishing Company, 206.

Ediger, Marlow (1988), *Language Arts Curriculum in the Elementary School*. Kirksville, Missouri: Simpson Publishing Company, 29-36.

Rao, Digumarti Bhaskara and Pushpa Latha, Digumarti (1993). *Achievement in English*. New Delhi: Discovery Publishing House.

16

Reading in the Language Arts

Primary grades teachers need to be certain that pupils are off to a good start in reading. These early years of instruction are crucial in guiding pupils to have a positive altitude toward reading. Pupils should learn to enjoy reading and realize that many benefits accrue from the act of reading. The teacher needs to communicate to pupils that he/she loves to read and communicates these feelings to learners. An attitude of reading is a good endeavour which needs to be communicated to pupils. Not only should reading be enjoyable to pupils but also useful in its many manifestations. There are numerous things that a teacher can do to stimulate young children in becoming lovers of library books.

Strommen, and Mates (1997) conducted research into young children's ideas about the nature of reading and wrote the following:

> Our observations confirm that learning to read is a developmental process but show that a young child's age, word and later-level decoding skills, are not necessarily reliable indicators of what he/she understands reading to be, and, therefore, of what intervention may be useful.
>
> It is important for teachers to realize that a child's growth in ideas about what readers do an his/her growth in reading itself are interdependent. A fundamental goal of beginning reading instruction should be to move each child toward the understanding that readers reconstruct texts by using multiple strategies to interpret the language encoded by print and at the same time, to make it possible for the child to do this by providing information that will enable construction of appropriate strategies. With this is mind we make the following recommendations regarding children early literacy instruction.

1. Teachers of young children should initially stress a child's ideas about the nature of reading, written language and the written code, as well as his/her reading strategies and tailor reading experiences to the child's ideas about what readers do.
2. Teachers should ask themselves what new information could cause a child to rethink or interpret what he or she believes and challenge each child's non-conventional ideas through demonstrations that contradict his/her current thinking. For example, frequent re-readings of a particular text help to build a child's knowledge of written language, but may also promote the idea that reading is memorizing texts. If a child believes this is what readers do, then demonstrating that readers can and do read a variety of unfamiliar texts may contribute to a shift in the child's thinking.
3. Teachers should set expectations for a child's reading performance that always take into account the child's ideas about how readers read.

Developing a Love for Reading

The act of reading means that pupils are reading enjoyable and useful materials. Reading does not mean a study of phonics, nor lessons on syllabication. Rather, reading involves securing ideas, content and subject matter. Thus, reading stresses a form of holism in that concepts and generalizations are obtained from print materials. An immersed reader find few distractions and is actively engaged in what is being read. The interest factor in reading propels pupils to reach toward higher levels in reading subject matter. Thus, the pupil and the content to be read become one, not separate entities.

With active involvement in reading, the pupil should attach meaning to ongoing concepts and generalisations. Meaning is attached to what is being read. The abstract print then makes sense to the reader. Understanding of print materials assists pupils to like reading in its diverse purposes. Pupils learn to predict what comes sequentially in ongoing reading tasks. This helps the pupil to overcome difficulties in recognizing individual words when predicting in a contextual situation. Further reading will provide the pupil with clues as to the predictions being correct or incorrect. Holism is involved in reading ideas, not fragmented sounds or syllables. Learners need to feel they have control over what is being read. In other words, they are able to understand in a meaningful way that which is being read. Pupils have control over their own reading when they can break the code involving abstract symbols.

Does this mean that phonics needs to be taught in beginning reading? Good teachers have always brought in phonics instruction when stressing a holistic reading curriculum. The phonics is brought in contextually, not within isolated word analysis lessons.

Pupils need to develop a basic sight vocabulary of relevant words as they progress through the early primary grades. The sight vocabulary for reading needs to be developed within a viable context, not within isolated words presented by the teacher. A more meaningful procedure is then in evidence when contextually pupils achieve a vocabulary for reading whereby words are recognized at sight. In addition to a basic sight vocabulary, pupils need to attain basic learnings in phonics. Phonics has its many values when a pupil cannot determine an unknown word, but can identify this word through analysis such as in phonics. Thus, the pupil associates individual sounds with their related symbols. It does not take long before pupils can apply relevant phonics principles when unlocking unknown words in a contextual situation. Interest in reading should never be destroyed through the development of a basic sight vocabulary of words whereby these are known by immediate observation. Nor should phonics instruction in which pupils truly enjoy learning phonics within a contextual situation as the need arises. In have supervised many student teachers and cooperating teachers who have devised games to assist pupils to enjoy mastering new words which then are recognized at once through observation.

As the young child progresses in reading, he/she develops concepts pertaining to what a word is when seeing it in print. Usually, pupils individually also learn the letters within a word and the related sounds inherent in the word. There are words which contain letters that have a one to one correspondence with the related sounds. Other sounds need two letters such as the "th" sound in words such as "the", "this" and "that". Pupils need to do much reading with teacher guidance as well as by themselves so that increased skills in word recognition occur. The teacher also needs to read aloud to pupils so that the latter obtains concepts pertaining to content, sequence of ideas presented, punctuation, stress, pitch and structure of sentence patterns. Selections read aloud by the teacher should be interesting, understandable and purposeful. These reading selections might well serve as a basis for pupils liking or disliking reading instruction.

The Experience Chart

Experience charts are an excellent way for pupils to enjoy reading as well as extend their skills in this area. Here, the classroom of pupils or a smaller group has had an interesting experience such as looking outside the classroom window to notice the rain falling. After an ample period of time for observing the rain fall, pupils may dictate ideas to the teacher in developing an experience chart. These learners should understand the content presented to the teacher since a concrete situation was provided to children to think about. The teacher records subject matter on the chalkboard, when presented by pupils. As the ideas are given, pupils can see talk written down. A word processor may also be used to record pupil's ideas for the experience chart.

Once the ideas have been presented, the teacher guides pupils in reading the recorded ideas from the experience chart. Pupils read the content orally with the teacher as he/she points to each word or phrase. Here, pupils have opportunities to develop a basic sight vocabulary of words for reading. The content of the experience chart may be read over again as pupils desire. With re-reading, pupils are aided in identifying more and more words by sight. Also, pupils notice that talk is written down. These can be considered as written experiences for young peoples when they see talk written down. Thus, there are individual letters, words, phrases and sentences. Whatever is said by pupils can be recorded on the chalk-board or by using the word processor. Learners usually begin to make statement such as the following pertaining to the recorded contents in the experience chart:

1. Here are two words that begin or end with the same letter.
2. These two words rhyme.
3. These are long words or these are short in length.
4. These are the same letters in the two words but they make different sounds.
5. This word has taller letters as compared to that word.

It is quite obvious that pupils are making discoveries within the experience chart and appear to be interested in this activity at the same time. We have personally observed much enthusiasm when pupils engage in making discoveries by examining words and sentences.

When making comparisons among different experience charts with content provided by young children and recorded by the teacher, it is quite obvious that more sophistication is involved on the learner's part when sequentially experiences of this nature are provided. Ediger (1988) lists the following assumptions involving experience charts:

1. Pupils are actively involved in experiences which provide content for an experience chart.
2. Learners present ideas for the experience chart.

3. Pupils with teacher help read content pertaining to their very own experiences.
4. Learners may notice how ideas are written down using abstract letters and words.
5. The content in the experience chart is familiar to learners since it relates to their own personal lives.
6. The experience chart method may assist pupils to develop interest in reading.
7. Individualization is inherent in using experience charts since each child has unique experiences. Each child may then present content for a group or individual experience chart.

Pupils soon select library books to read and practice reading those same words that were experienced on the experience chart. Pupils should experience many reading activities so that learning to read is pleasurable and progress is made sequentially. Fountas and Pinnell (1996) wrote the following objectives for guided reading which serve well in all reading programs:

- It gives children the opportunity to develop as individual readers while participating in a socially supported activity.
- It gives teachers the opportunity to observe individuals as they process new texts.
- It gives individual readers the opportunity to develop strategies so that they can read increasingly difficult texts independently.
- It gives children enjoyable, successful experiences in reading for meaning.
- It develops the abilities needed for independent reading.
- It helps children learn how to introduce texts to themselves.

Young children need to achieve these broad objectives in reading sequentially. Success in each sequential step is important. Interesting and purposeful reading materials need to be in the offing. The reading teacher needs to know each pupil well so that a quality reading curriculum may be continuous and ongoing.

Guided Listening Thinking Activity

The Guided Listening Thinking Activity (GLTA) emphasizes the teacher choosing a library book which children would love to participate in. A large picture book for young children would suffice. The teacher asks the children to predict what the book would be about as the title and illustrations therein are viewed. The teacher then reads aloud to pupils a short section in which the height of action in the story is involved. Pupils then need to evaluate their original prediction or hypothesis. Each hypothesis must be respected and further hypothesizing encouraged for the rest of the story. Then the teacher may read to find out what did happen in the picture book. Higher levels of cognition need to be emphasized already on the early primary grade levels. Pupils should be encouraged to do critical and creative thinking as well as problem solving as early as possible in life. Higher levels of cognition are necessary in every day life with its many perplexities and difficulties.

After the reading of the picture book has been completed, the teacher may raise additional questions about the contents. It is salient to obtain pupil reaction to the contents. Pupils should be able to provide reasons for their answers given. Learners should also ask questions covering what was read from the picture book.

The GLTA is teacher directed. The teacher chooses the book to be read. He/she determines questions to be answered by pupils. The teacher stimulates pupils to make predictions, develop hypotheses, think at higher levels of cognition, set the classroom climate for the activity and provide support for each pupil. This does not mean that pupils are left out of the reading curriculum when the GLTA is being stressed. Rather, the teacher encourages pupils responses and is the leader in setting the stage and implementing the reading lesson. It is also child centered in that pupils are encouraged to make predictions and hypothesize. Pupils have opportunities to raise questions, especially at the end of reading the selection from the picture book. We believe with a teacher directed reading lesson, the pupil needs to be as actively involved as possible in responding to the questions of the teacher as well as the child raise questions of his/her own. Listening carefully and well is an important goal to stress in GLTA.

The Shared Book Experience

The shared book experience emphasizes more pupil participation in the actual reading of content as compared to the Guided Listening Thinking Activity in which the teacher does the oral reading and pupils follow along in their own books to achieve in word recognition and other elements in reading. The shared books experiences stresses the use of a Big Book. With the Big Book, all pupils in the group can clearly see the illustrations and print from where they are seated. Examples of two Big Book are *When the King Rides By* (Mahy, 1986) and *The Greedy Goat* (Bolton, 1986).

Contents in Big Books should have predictable subject matter for pupils so that they can rather readily determine what will come next in the story in sequence. The teacher introduces the Big Book to pupils by looking together at the illustrations therein. These illustrations are discussed and provide pupils with background information in order to understand Big Book contents more effectively. The pupils with the background information will be better able to read along with the classroom teacher from the Big Book. Predictions may be made by pupils in terms of outcomes of the story. These predictions may be checked at an appropriate point when reading the Big Book cooperatively. Higher levels of cognition is definitely a goal here, including critical and creative thinking as well as problem solving. These higher cognitive goals are to be encouraged and based upon the present developmental level of each pupil. Respect for the learner and his/her abilities is always important. Good citizenship and democracy need to be practiced continuously in the classroom.

When pupil read along together with the teacher from the Big Book, they learn to identify words which present problems in the teaching of reading. The experience chart approach made is so that pupils presented ideas for the chart with the teacher then reading together with the pupils the contents therein. The Big Book philosophy of reading instruction also emphasizes pupils learning to recognize words contextually while reading together with the teacher. At the end of the reading experience, the teacher may ask questions such as the following to provide interest in phonics:

1. Which words did you notice that started with the same letter or sound?
2. Which words end with the same letter and sound?
3. Which vowel letters in words make the same sound?
4. Which vowel letters makes a different sound when comparing two or more words?
5. Do you see words whereby two letters make a single sound?

Each of the above learning activities needs to be emphasized or adjusted to the present achievement level of pupils. Pupils should enjoy phonics activities. These experiences need to be positive for pupils and assist in developing word recognition skills. Phonics should not be taught for its own sake, but rather to assist learners to unlock unknown words. Phonics then has practical and utilitarian values and is not taught for its own sake.

When pupils and the teacher orally read together the contents from a Big Book, a type of choral reading is being emphasized. Learners may perceive sentence patterns which provide structure for the English language. Re-reading of a Big Book, especially if desired by pupils, is to be encouraged. We think most of us had our favourite books a children which we re-read many times, in my case. *The Little Red Hen* was read over and over again as a child! A major objective here is to guide pupils to want to read more literature and at a more complex level as optimal progress is being made by individual pupils. With re-reading, comprehension appears to increase, meaning that more complex questions may be discussed with pupils. Familiarity with words is important when assisting pupils in developing a basic sight vocabulary. Choral reading and re-reading assists pupils in achieving a core of functional words, necessary in becoming a good reader.

Word Banks and the Young Reader

One way to assist pupils to master words in reading is to stress the word bank concept. With the word bank, each pupil prints on a three by five inch card a word that has been mastered in reading. With the addition of new cards, each card having a word printed thereon, the pupil must alphabetize the set of words and rehearse the correct identification of each word. The reward to the pupil is to see the stack of cards get larger due to having mastered more words as sight words. The teacher could place an interesting sticker on each card as reinforcement.

There are pupils who enjoy making sentences from words in the word bank. Pupils could work in teams doing this. The point is to have pupils read words within context frequently and thus become better readers.

Peers may also work together by providing drill and practice experiences from the use of these work bank cards.

Word bank cards could also be grouped in terms of

1. Those having the same beginning sounds.
2. Those having the same ending sounds.
3. Those having the same vowel sounds.
4. Those having grave irregularities in spelling between symbol and sound.

As many uses as possible should be made of word bank cards. Games may be devised, sentences expanded and stories written with the use of these cards.

Story Book Time with Children

The teacher needs to read orally to pupils each day. Why? Here, pupils learn about a story, about vocabulary terms, about sequential ideas in a story, about sentence patterns, about characterization, about the setting of a story, about the plot, about the theme and messages presented by the author. Pupils also may learn to enjoy good literature for their developmental level. Perhaps, an individual child desires to read the same book during spare time or at home. Background information for the child's time to read has then come from the teacher's oral reading. There should be familiarity when the pupil reads the same book as compared to not having heard the contents read by the teacher. The teacher needs to become very familiar with children's literature so that pupils perceive a model to emulate. A few years ago while supervising a student teacher and cooperating teacher, we noticed how knowledgeable the latter was about library books for pupils. This teacher related library books with the books being read to children. We believe young children here were fascinated with the knowledge the teacher had about library books when integrating different sources. Thus, a good characteristic of a teacher who reads orally to pupils is that he/she likes children's literature. The horizons of the primary grade teacher need to be expanded in knowing about recent books that have come out in children's literature as well as remaining informed about older books of high quality, the later being important to Perennialists. Perennialism, as a philosophy of education, believes that the enduring ideas in time and space are important and not recently published books.

The primary grade teacher should also read enthusiastically to pupils. Learners are very attentive to these read aloud sessions if the teacher shows love and enjoyment of oral reading of library books. As the oral reading progresses, the teacher needs to show related illustrations in the book to pupils. There should be adequate time for pupil to comment about the illustrations and content. If the comments from pupils seem endless, the teacher may politely say that we have time for one more pupil. Otherwise, it is wholesome and good for children to react to what is contained in a library book.

The teacher needs to observe pupils when reading aloud to notice the pace at which learners can understand the content. I have observed teachers read too rapidly whereby pupils seemingly cannot understand the contents. The opposite has been true also in which the content was read too slowly by the teacher. Remember, pupils can listen to and comprehend content more rapidly as compared to the reading that they do. Thus, pupils read more slowly as compared to comprehending content listened to. With practice and feedback from pupils being read to, the teacher can adjust the speed of reading aloud to what pupils can process in terms of subject matter listened to.

Voice inflection which includes stress, pitch and juncture is very important in oral reading to pupils. Certain words need to be stressed more than others so that proper interpretation is an end result. A monotone says all words with the same stress, but a dynamic speaker places more stress on specific words as compared to others so that meaning in interpretation is in evidence. Proper pitch is important also when reading aloud. Thus, selected words are pitched higher or lower than others. Why? Whatever is said involves interpretation by the speaker as well as by the listener. If all words are pitched on the same level, a monotone results. By pitching words properly, there are better chances for appropriate communication. It is much easier to secure the attention of others with proper pitch of words as compared to a monotone voice. And by pitching words appropriately, the reader of library books to pupils emphasizes what he/she wishes to communicate. Proper pauses or juncture needs to be in evidence in oral reading of children's literature. Juncture then indicates that the reader pause where commas, periods and other punctuation marks are located. By omitting or slighting punctuation marks, distortion in meaning of content read certainly can be an end result.

In our teacher education classes, we do emphasize university students reading well orally to peers, according to quality criteria and also that they received practice in the schools in reading orally pupils at different age and achievement levels. This is vital for a good teacher.

The teacher should have good eye contact with each pupil as the read aloud continues. This indicates that a teacher is communicating with all pupils and watches the attention span of pupils. Pupils do need to be attentive and engaged when the teacher reads aloud content from sequential library books. Literature read to children needs to be carefully chosen by the teacher. Hopefully, the contents will be interesting and enjoyable to pupils whereby these learners will have an inward desire to achieve in reading skills and attitudes. The teacher needs to choose a variety of genres in literature so that the diverse interests of pupils is met. Teachers usually tend to become knowledgeable about which library books would fascinate learners when being read aloud to pupils.

It is good teaching practice for a teacher to read privately the library book which will be read aloud to pupils later. A definite strategy should then be developed by the teacher as to how the library book should be introduced to pupils. Here, readiness factors enter in as to what to do to assist pupils to like the new book to be read aloud. Certainly, the teacher should discuss the illustrations at the beginning of the books with children, prior to reading, so that there is more familiarity of learners with the content to be read aloud sequentially. By thinking of procedures to use when reading each library book, the teacher soon develops a repertoire of skills which assist in gaining the attention of pupils in desiring to read children's literature. I think it is good procedure too for a teacher to read aloud these library books he/she enjoys. After all, the positive attitudes should have their affects within listeners. A special time needs to be set aside each day for oral reading of children's literature so that pupils realize the importance of this activity. Primary teachers always set aside time after the one hour noon recess for oral reading of children's literature to pupils. The read aloud had a tendency to make for a relaxed feelings and we believe, provided readiness for studying in the next curriculum area.

We should the teacher be when reading aloud to pupils? We have noticed teachers for read aloud at different places when supervising student teachers in the public school, such as

1. Being seated in front of the classroom.
2. Being seated in a chair while pupils are nearby seated on the carpet.
3. Being seated on the floor on an even level with the pupils.
4. Being seated in the middle of the classroom.
5. Being in a standing position and moving around the classroom while reading aloud to pupils.

Individualized Reading

Once children have developed an adequate number of basic sight words for reading, they may become involved in individualized reading. Here, there needs to be an appropriate number of library books for pupils to select from in choosing a book to read. The titles need to indicate different genres to provide for the interest needs of individual pupils. Also, the library books must be written on diverse achievement levels so that each pupil may choose a book which harmonizes with his/her present achievement level in reading. Content which is too complex to read frustrates the reader. Subject matter that is too easy might well become boring to the reader. Thus, there are library books which are on the reading level, not frustration nor boring level, for pupils to select from for individualized reading.

These library books should be displayed at a learning center in an interesting manner to capture pupil attention. A bulletin board with neatly displayed book jackets of new library books should also assist pupils to develop interest in individualized reading. The teacher should tell a few interesting things about a library books as it is held up for learner viewing. Hopefully, this will also assist in whetting the appetites of pupils for individualized reading. The primary grade teacher needs to think of different strategies in developing within pupils a desire to select and read sequential library books. The pupil is the chooser, not the teacher, as to which library book a pupil is to read. The teacher offers assistance if pupils are hesitant in choosing or if they do not find an appropriate library book to read.

The individual pupil then chooses a library book to read at the learning center. Usually, a learner will select a book that refers to a preferable genre and is on his/her reading level. Sometimes, a pupil needs to select a different library book to read due to the complexity of the original book selected. Once a pupil has settled down to read silently, the library book chosen, a good reader or teacher aide may assist pupils with word identification. Each pupil should be given adequate chances to determine an unknown word before assistance is given in word recognition. Primary age pupils need to become as independent in identifying words as possible. Sometimes, a few pupils become too dependent upon the teacher for word identification. Through the use of content clues and phonics, a pupils can identify many words which generally would be unknown to the reader (Ediger, 1997).

Following the completion of silent reading of a library book, the pupil should have a brief conference with the teacher. Here, the involved pupil reads a short selection to the teacher from the library book. The teacher may also choose the selection to be read orally by the pupil in the conference. The primary grade teacher may then observe errors made by the pupil in oral reading and assist in remedying the problems areas. Which problems do pupils reveal on oral reading on the primary grade levels? Student teachers and cooperating teachers whom we supervised have enumerated the following:

1. Omitting words. This can be a major problem if meaning is distorted when reading the selection. Sometimes when "a", "an," and "the" are omitted by learners in reading in the conference setting, the meaning may not change any.
2. Adding words. When the young child adds words that are not in the reading selection, the resulting meaning may or may not change. Pupils do add the article "the" with no change in meaning of the sentence. Other words added may really distort the meaning of what is read.
3. Disregarding punctuation marks. If commas are omitted when words are in a series, the meaning will be greatly distorted. The same is true if a period is omitted and a run on sentence is an end result. Errors made by pupils provide a basis for determining objectives to stress in the reading curriculum.
4. Hesitating too long before pronouncing words. Frequent hesitations, lasting each five seconds or longer, do hinder pupils in reading with understanding. Generally, a library book is too complex for reading if hesitating before word pronunciation hinders pupils in attaching meaning to what is being read.
5. Repeating what has been read correctly.

Teachers of individualized reading need to record the types of errors made by pupils in reading aloud in a conference setting after the letter has completed the reading of a library book. These reading errors should be examined and then noticed if remediation instruction is necessary. As was indicated, some types of errors may not be important enough to stress in remediation work. Thus inserting or omitting articles, among other kinds of errors, might be quite minimal in a holistic approach of reading instruction where by learners may become skillful in predicting what will follow in sequence in reading.

In the conference within the individualized reading program, pupils and the teacher need to appraise comprehension of the learner. We would suggest that the teacher stress higher levels of cognition in individualized reading. Thus critical and creative thinking, the problem solving need adequate emphasis in the conference involving pupil and teacher. The teacher needs to have a good working knowledge of children's literature when an individualized reading program is in evidence.

We would suggest that the teacher read children's literature, keeping a file on each book read as to its contents, as well as reading reviews of new library books for pupils to read. There are excellent reviews of children's literature in *The Language Arts* (See bibliography entry of the National Council Teachers of English) as well as in *The Reading Teacher* (See bibliography entry of the International Reading Association). The teacher should become very familiar with Caldecott and Newbery Award winning library books. The Caldecott Award is given to the author of the best illustrated library book written for children whereas the Newbery Award is given to the author, also annually, who wrote the best judged content. There are other awards given annually to the best writer of the year in children's literature such as in Missouri the Mark Twain Award is given for writing the best judged children's library book.

Every year, a Children's Literature Festival is held on the Truman State University Campus. I (Ediger) have served as member of the Children's Literature Festival Committee for several year. Live authors speak to children and show the written works. As this Festival, children are divided into small groups of ten so that there are ample opportunities for pupils to ask questions of the authors. Children make some very positive informal comments about the festival during its sessions. Some of these comments which I heard in passing were the following:

1. I didn't know good authors were living individuals. I thought they had to have died sometime ago to be called an author.
2. I am thrilled to see an listen to an author.
3. One author even signed his signature to a library book I now have!
4. I like to ask questions of live authors that I could never have asked before.
5. I have written letters to authors but never listen to one talk to us.

In a questionnaire provide pupils directly after the Children's Literature Festival, the following were rated high with a 4 to 5 average rating, as marked by pupils in the questionnaire:

1. The festival was truly worth attending.
2. The pupils listened carefully to authors as they talked about writing their books.
3. I learned much about the children's books discussed.

The lowest rating was given to one author speaking in too quiet a manner when presenting his library book to children.

A Children's Literature Festival seemingly does much to interest pupils in the reading of library books. This observation was confirmed by teachers of pupils attending the Festival. Seemingly, pupils did more reading that previously. Motivation to read had increased. Many pupils read library books written by the authors who appeared at the Festival. Apparently, the authors had provided readiness or an introduction to reading the library books. It does help pupils in wanting to read a book if they have become familiar with it in one way or another. Modelling by authors at the Festival is a powerful factor in encouraging pupil reading of books.

We have observed to how Sustained Silent Reading (SSR) can offer to children a positive model for reading. In one school I visited, everyone in the elementary school building read during a certain time of the day, usually twenty minutes in length. When the word "everyone" is mentioned, this included the custodian and cafeteria workers. Pupils can then notice that people do read and there must be something enjoyable and valuable in doing so. One very important model for pupils in reading is the primary grade teacher. This teacher needs to be enthusiastic about reading and what has been read. One of us noticed a second grade teacher tell about Plato's *The Republic* she had read the previous summer in a university graduate class. She told pupils of how Plato had divided people into three class—the rulers of the nation, the military personnel and the artisans or workers. This teacher showed pictures of present day adults and asked pupils which of the three categories of Plato's Republic they would come under. Pupils were fascinated with the discussion and were actively engaged in the activity. We do believe pupils will remember sessions such as these and consume more literature now as well as when they progress through the different levels of schooling.

In Conclusion

Primary grade reading teachers need to provide a variety of concrete, semi-concrete and abstract experiences for pupils so that a solid foundation is laid for successful reading. The instruction should be as holistic as possible so that pupils read content, not work on isolated sound/symbol relationships. The act of reading is holistic whereby learners need to perceive the whole of the selection read. This leaves room for the teaching of phonics as needed. Some children will need much less phonics as compared to others. How much phonics is to be taught depends upon the needs of individual pupils.

To identify unknown words, contexts clues are important for pupils to use. Further help for pupils in unlocking unknown words is to use phonics. Teachers and pupils need to realize the upper limits of phonics use. There are letters which are rather consistent between symbol and sound. However, there are many weaknesses or limits in phonics use, such as in the following words: phone, through, rough, flight, among others. Here, the relationships between individual sounds and symbols do not harmonize in most cases.

The primary grade reading teacher needs to have all pupils experience initial successes with continual optimal progress emphasized for each child. No child should be permitted to fall through the cracks to be a failure (Ediger, 1998).

REFERENCES

Bolton, F. (1986), *The Greedy Goat*. New York: Scholastic Book Services.

Ediger, Marlow (1988), *Language Arts Curriculum in the Elementary School*. Kirksville, Missouri: Simpson Publishing Company, 19.

Ediger, Marlow (1998), "Goals of Reading Instruction", *Experiments in Education*. 26(1), 11-18.

Ediger, Marlow (1997), "Reading and the Psychology of Teaching", *The Educational Review*. 103(3), 41-45.

Ediger Marlow and D. Bhaskara Rao (2003). *Teaching Language Arts Successfully*. New Delhi, India: Discovery Publishing House.

Fountas, Irene C. and Gay Su Pinnell (1996), *Guided Reading Good First Choice for all Children*. Portsmouth, New Hampshire: Heinemann, 1 and 2.

International Reading Association. *The Reading Teacher*. 800 Barksdale Road, Newark, Delaware 19714.

Mahy, M. (1986), *When the King Rides By*. Bothel, Washington: The Wright Group.

National Council Teachers of English, *The Language Arts*, 1111 Kenyon Road, Urbana, Illinois 61801.

Strommen, Linda Teran, and Barbara Fowles Mates (1997), "What readers do: Young Children's Ideas about the nature of reading", *The Reading Teacher*. 51(2), 106.

17

Writing and the Language Arts

The reading and writing curriculum correlate well with each other. Why? Very often, reading experiences provide the springboard for writing. Thus, a variety of kinds of poetry may be written based on content acquired from reading. Diverse kinds of rhymed and unrhymed poems may then be written. Literary elements such as characterization, setting, plot, irony, theme and point of view may be rewritten or elaborated upon by pupils from having read a given story or selection. Creativity should be a major objective of pupil writing. Novelty, uniqueness and originality of content from pupil writing, should be wanted. Written work should emphasize cutting across all academic disciplines. Written work then has no single academic discipline to stress but writing across the curriculum should be the objective of instruction (Ediger, 1997).

There are definite assumptions pertaining to writing. These assumptions are the following:

1. Pupils learn to write by writing.
2. Proficiency in oral language assists the learner to do a better job of writing.
3. Success in writing helps pupils to extent major goals to improve continuously in written work.
4. Writing seemingly is the most difficult of the four areas of vocabulary development—listening, speaking, reading and writing, but each needs to be emphasized to assist pupils to achieve as optimally as possible.
5. Pupils individually learn to write, but each pupil may learn much through collaborative endeavours in writing. Pupils learn from each other in writing.

6. Writing needs to be taught as being interrelated with grammar, punctuation, spelling, vocabulary, syntax, semantics, structure in the English language, handwriting, whole language and phonics.
7. Written work cuts across all academic disciplines whenever print discourse is used.
8. Pupils need to write for a variety of audiences such as the teacher, parents, friends, brothers and sisters among others.
9. Sequence in writing improvement begins with the pre-school years, including scribbling and occurs throughout adulthood.
10. Written work should be useful whereby application is made of print discourse, as well as be creative for leisure type and utilitarian activities.

The teacher needs to focus upon the above named objectives in teaching writing and their inter-relationship with the other areas of the language arts. Writing must be related to all academic disciplines when written work is being stressed. These ideas are expressed further in basic goals that pupils need to acquire in on-going lessons and units of study. Pupils are to:

1. Write frequently to record ideas in print discourse.
2. Experience the relationships among listening, speaking, reading and writing.
3. Expand literary experiences in incorporate written expressions.
4. Use a variety of purposes to convey meanings in writing.
5. Experiment with diverse genres and subject matter when engaged in writing.
6. Attend to conventions in writing such as quality punctuation, capitalization and grammar.
7. Edit personal work and the work of others in writing by using collaborative endeavours.
8. Appreciate writing skills possessed and enjoy what has been written.
9. Utilize reading and children's library books as spring-boards in writing in their diverse manifestations.
10. Indicate pride in being successful in listening, speaking, reading and writing.

Leadership from the principal is vital. The principal and the teacher need to work together for the good of the child in attaining more optimally in the school setting (Ediger, 1998).

Creative Writing and Poetry

An important source for writing is to use content from basal texts and library books, among other print discourse sources, to engage pupils in written work. Through reading, viewing objects, items, illustrations and audio-visual materials directly related to what is/has been read, might well encourage creative poetry writing by learners. Discussions pertaining to what has been read might also impress pupils to apply what has been learner in poetry writing.

First of all, let's take a look at writing poems which rhyme. Many pupils like to write poetry which contains rhyme. There are numerous patterns in rhyming poetry. Early primary grade pupils who can hear rhyme may wish to write couplets, individually or in a small committee. A couplet contains two lines with ending words rhyming. These young learners may wish to dictate the couplet for the teacher to print in neat manuscript letters. Dictated poems may be saved for re-reading by pupils in class. Later on, and for all pupils, learners may wish to write triplets containing three lines. With a triplet, all ending words rhyme. A slightly more difficult poem to write in the quatrain. Here, with four lines of verse, all ending words need to rhyme or lines one and two as well a lines three and four should rhyme.

The limerick has five lines with lines one, two and five rhyming as well as lines three and four rhyming. Limericks generally begin with "There once was ... The limerick may be written as follows:

There once was a man of great height
He always seemed to be up tight.
He swatted a bee
and landed in the sea
That wonderful man of great light.

There are pupils who cannot hear rhyme or may wish to write unrhymed poetry. The haiku is a favourite of many people to write. The hakiu contains three lines with the following sequence: five syllables for the first line, seven for the second line, and five syllables for the third line. The following hakiu is an example:

Birds
Birds fly without rest
Where do they get the power?
I do not know why.

A tanka is a slight variation of the haiku and has a total of five lines with the following number of syllables for each line: five, seven, five, seven, and seven. The following tanka presents a model:

The Arctic in Winter
The blasts of cold air
Keep the polar bear on ice
Whither the young cubs?
Walking on the tall iceberg
Never mind the cold weather.

The haiku and the tanka above were written by elementary age pupils whom we observed when supervising student teachers and one of us cooperating teachers in the public schools. We find that pupils like to write poetry when background information has been experienced and motivation to write is there.

Free verse has no rhyme and no syllabication involved for writing. One pupils whom one of us observed in the classroom wrote the following free verse:

The horse
gives us rides when wanted.
is fed well in the barn.
exercises much during the day time.
loves to be petted.
wants to be noticed.
desires to be comfortable all year long.
hates files and gnats in summer.
eats grass in summer and grain/hay in winter.
wants to please others.
may ever be grateful for good care.

In the writing of poetry, pupils need to use elements that poets apply in writing verse creativity. One element is onomatopoeia which stresses words written to make echoic sounds. The following emphasize words making their very own sounds: splish, splash, swoosh and slash. The relationship will not always be sound made in the environment. These words also bring in a second element poets use in writing and that is alliteration. With alliteration, two or more sequential words start with the same sound. In this case, the "s" sound is made. A third element is imagery. Imagery has two dimensions and these are similes and metaphors. Similes connect two phrases, in general, such as in the following example of a poem written by a pupil: The cloud of smoke looked like a billowing lion. Thus, the 'cloud of smoke' is compared with "a billowing lion". The word *like* connects the two phrases. Another word used in smiles to make these creative connections is the word as *e.g.* "The crow caws as a coughing giant. Metaphors as a second element of imagery, do not have the words "like" or "as" to make these novel connections. For example, the following imagery pertains to a metaphoric approach: "The egg in the pan bubbles tiger like in the water." There is no connector, such as *like* or as between. "The egg in the pan" with "bubbles tiger like in the water."

Writing in Journals

Journal writing is quite popular as an activity for children in the elementary school. There are numerous items that might be written in a journal. Here, many peoples record what they have experienced in a reading lesson such as summaries of content read and discussed in the classroom, vocabulary terms learned in a lesson or unit of study, results discussed from a test taken, and/or impressions acquired from a study of characterization, setting, plot, theme, point of view and/or messages of the writer of stories and literature in general.

Some pupils write journal items each day. Others write once a week or biweekly. We suggest encouraging pupils to write each day, but at least once a week. Pupils need to do much writing in order to become proficient in written work. Practice makes for proficiency in writing. We do much writing of manuscripts for publication and at the beginning, our written work left much to be desired. With effort put forth, we have been quite successful in having our manuscripts published in educational journals. We are convinced that most pupils can communicate effectively in writing if there is adequate practice, assistance from the teacher and from parents in the home setting, encouragement from many, a stimulating environment to provide ideas for writing and a designated place for writing with the necessary materials.

Journal writing should have important purposes such as the following for the writer: to be more observant of happenings in every day life, to keep record of ideas and events, to use models that stress quality writing and to establish meaning in life's endeavours. It is important for the pupil to carry his/her journal and a pencil along, in order to record important things in life. What might go into journal writing?

1. Happening in class that were of interest.
2. Content read from library books as well as the basal textbook.
3. A sketch of something that is difficult to write about.
4. Poems that were of personal interest.
5. Letters written and received.
6. Frustrations felt in writing.
7. Descriptions on items and objects that fascinate the writer.
8. A creative description of a modified setting, characterization, plot, theme, point of view and other elements of a story read.
9. Statements on what you would like to be or become in the future.
10. Play parts of a story in literature or unit in the social studies.

Writing A Personal Experience

Pupils tend to like telling incidence about their own life and times. The personal experience involves a part of the person's life time. The learner needs to choose what is personally relevant and what might be important to the reader of the essay. Sometimes, pupils have so much to write about that the reader feels overwhelmed in its reading. At the opposite end of the continuum, selected pupils just cannot get started in writing a personal experience. Readers like to know which events truly shaped the history of the writer. The pupil also needs to write how he/she fits into wider social roles in life.

A narrative account of events then needs to be shared with peers. The account actually involves a part of the history of the individual doing the writing. Some important pointers for the writer of the essay are the following:

1. Think of what is truly relevant to write about in your life and times.
2. Select an event that is clear and distinct. The event(s) should be written about in detail.
3. Describe each incidence carefully so that readers may role play selected characters in the story of life. There needs to a character, setting and plot in the historical account.
4. Sequence the order of events in the writing so that it makes sense to the reader.
5. Write details which assist the reader to be an inherent part of the story.
6. Use depth coverage in writing about the major events or characters in the writing.
7. Emphasize dialogue in the writing to breath life into the personnel experience.
8. Build the major events or incidence of a story up to a climax.
9. Write for a target audience and identify this audience.
10. Give each person in the essay should have a name.

Writing An Outline

Outlining salient subject matter may be a good way to learn about main ideas, subordinate ideas and details. When a person reads, he/she needs to sort out what is of major importance as compared to that which is less salient. To view each sentence as having the worth of others, robs the reader of securing important ideas. With the explosion of knowledge, in behooves the reader all the more to arrange content read in terms of major versus minor ideas. Otherwise, the reader is bombarded with ideas which do not lend themselves to remembering effectively what has been read. The teacher needs to model good outlining habits to pupils. Peers may also assist each other in outlining subject matter read.

When pupils outline content read or the spoken voice listened to, careful attention needs to be paid to major as compared to more minor ideas. Let us suppose we are reading/listening to an essay on Bears. The first major division of the presentation is, "Looking for food". The first major division of the presentation is, "Looking for food", is a phrase. A subdivision may indicate the kinds of food being looked for. The pupil doing the outline may write the following kinds of foods—fish, rodents, seals and birds. The latter animals emphasize details. A second major division under the heading *Bears* might be, "Finding shelter". A subdivision here might be the kinds of shelter which are acceptable, such as caves, an old deserted building, the side of a mound of dirt and among intertwined branches.

Questions that might the raised pertaining to outlining include the following:

1. How long should the outline be? This depends upon the length of the reading selection being outlined. Or a teacher might assign the length of the outline.
2. How many main major division are there in an outline? This depends upon how many broad ideas there are in a selection that is being read and outlined. We would say that a reading selection of 250 words will generally have two major divisions. Rules in outlining say that there need to be two major divisions at least under one title or topic. There also need to be two subdivision, at least, under a major division. There also should be a least two details under a subdivision. What if *two of each* (such as main divisions, subdivisions and details) cannot be found? Then put the data within the statement preceding the two items of lesser value.
3. Should there be a sentence outline or a phrase outline? This depends upon the teacher and the pupils involved in writing the outline. We prefer the sentence outline since each sentence says something that is complete in meaning. In my thinking, phrases lack the clarity that sentences possess. The above examples emphasized a phrase rather than a sentence outline. We will now write a model sentence outline:

The Holy Land

A. A region that is sacred to Muslims, Jews and Christians.

1. There are Five Pillars of the Muslim religion.
    - *(a)* The Hajj at Mecca, Saudi Arabia is made at least once during the life time of a devout Muslim.
    - *(b)* The Holy Book of the Muslims is *The Koran*.
2. The Pentateuch, the first five books of the Old Testament, is holy to devout Jews.
3. The Church of the Holy Sepulcher is a holy place to devout Christians inside the walled city of Jerusalem.

B. A region made up of the Mediterranean climate has rainy weather from October to April.

The above outline contains two major divisions, such as in A and B. It has three subdivisions such as the numerals 1, 2 and 3. Two details are in evidence such as a and b under the first subdivision. As more content is read, additions may be made to this outline.

Writing An Opinion

A personal perspective of a writer contains a point of view or an opinion. Generally, the writer wants to be understood in terms of what is believed in the opinion. The writer may challenge his/her own point(s) of view in the writing. Sometimes, through writing, the writer wants to understand the premises better of his/her own ideas. By writing about personal beliefs, the writer may also clarify and critically evaluate thoughts brought forth. The following are selected pointers for the pupils in writing about his/her opinions:

1. Choose something that has been on your mind for a long time.
2. Assist readers to comprehend and understand your beliefs.
3. Be yourself in the written content. ... Do not write about someone else's opinion.
4. Use your own distinct style in writing.
5. Write in the first person.
6. Use examples and details in your writing to make meaningful the opinions expressed.
7. Write on what "bugs" you.
8. Take a point of view which represents your thinking on an issue.
9. Give your thinking on capital punishment, the creation story or the evolution of the universe or the pros and cons of governmental spending on social projects.
10. Write about your favourite pet peeve.

Proofing your writings provides numerous opportunities for reading ideas and content. The final copy should be one that you are very proud of.

Writing on How Something Should be Done

There are numerous occasions when we are asked to provide information on how something is to be done. Directions need to be given frequently on assembling a mower, repairing a kitchen appliance, installing a door bell and building a deck, among other items. People tend to be curious on how something works as well as why something does not work. We believe children find it interesting and challenging to write about something within their area of readiness involving how to do something. The "how to" essay may also involve providing explanations about an event or reasons for an occurrence or happening. There are a plethora of writings that stress how to do something. We would want pupils individually to be involved in determining content for developing the how to essay. Pupils do need to be ready in terms of subject matter acquired so that writing on how to do something is possible.

We have the following suggestions when pupils write the "How To" paper. The pupil needs to choose a topic that he/she understands well and can explain it to pupils. It is truly frustrating when one is asked to do something that is not conceivable. Second, the content should relate to what others do not understand and need assistance in its doing. Third, the writer should have an audience that needs to have this information conveyed. This means that content needs to be written on the understanding level of the target audience. The writer needs to determine what it is that the reader might lack in understanding. There might be something in the how-to-essays that clarifies that which makes for confusion on the part of the reader. Proper sequence needs to be in offing when writing clearly and distinctly the order of steps involved in how to do something. The ordered steps should not be isolated from each other, but rather follow a related set of ideas. Thus, the sequential steps follow a relationship, not an isolation from each other. Step one is related to step two while step two is related to step three and so on.

The following additional pointers are salient in an How To Do It paper, as well as in all written work:

1. Eliminate redundant ideas.
2. Modify vague statements that are relevant otherwise, so that the reader may follow directions carefully and implement successfully what was given in the essay.
3. Try the steps written in the "How To" paper to see if they work.
4. Proofread very carefully that which was written.
5. Have a peer try out what is written in the essay.

Writing and Problem Solving

Developing problem solving skills is important for elementary age pupils presently as well as in the future at the work place. Seemingly, problems are with us continually. Selected problems may be solved rather quickly. Others are much more time consuming in solving. What is important is that pupils learn to identify and solve problems. The first flexible step is to identify the problem. Clarity is involved when identifying problem areas. Data is then gathered in order to offer solutions to the problem area. Information then is available for an hypothesis. The hypothesis is a tentative answer to the problem. The hypothesis is tentative and subject to testing. A real live situation needs to be used for testing the hypothesis. If evidence warrants, the hypothesis is rejected. New data or information then need to be gathered. This results in a new hypothesis which is again subject to testing in a life-like situation. If results indicate, the hypothesis may then be accepted.

There are numerous reasons pupils need to learn to write information essays. New information has come out on a topic and the learner believes others need to be informed of the new content. Perhaps, there is a need to inform individuals about the necessity of selected current events items that have just come off the news network. The major purpose here being to inform learners and others about the newness of the situation. Information then is being shared. There is so much new information coming out that it is difficult to stay abreast of what is new. We certainly do live in an information age and individuals feel so limited when they can only learn to know a small amount what is new content. If we think to internet and all the information that is therein, if baffles the individual who thinks of possible ways to learn as much as possible. Newspapers and news magazines attempt to keep individuals informed as to what is going on. But the amount of information coming therefrom is overwhelming. There are selected pointers that may be provided pupils when writing the information essay. These are the following:

1. Try to be as objective as possible when reporting information. The information does not represent opinions, feelings and subjective thoughts.
2. Remember that the writer is writing for human beings and not automations.
3. Write facts, not opinions, to be presented in an appealing way.
4. Delimit the topic to what can be accurately covered and in detail. Overly broad topics may be too complex to cover as compared to a more delimited approach.
5. Cover your delimited topic in a comprehensive way be discussing the five w's—who, what, where, when and why. Shallow and survey methods of reporting information may not stand up under scrutiny. Depth coverage of information will influence the reader much more so as compared to survey procedures.
6. Be as accurate as possible in reporting information. Sources of information need to be checked for reliability and accuracy.
7. Make certain that the information being reported is new and not something that is a rehash of previously presented ideas.

8. Have pupils perceive the new information being reported as related to what was known previously.
9. Sequence ideas presented effectively so that readers perceive the relationship of new knowledge to what was presented previously.
10. Use drawings, diagrams, figures and illustrations to report information clearly and accurately.

In an information age, pupils need to be able to present content accurately and in depth. The information needs to be as factual as possible and yet it needs to be presented in an appealing manner. It is always important to secure learner attention in reading written work.

Writing to Describe

Descriptive writing is very important to a pupil. Why? Each pupil needs to learn to describe something as accurately as possible. In conversing with others, individuals are asked to describe something such as a car, bicycle, house, and/or a place, among others. When pupils are ready, they should have sample opportunities to describe something that is purposeful in their lives. When going to the doctor's office, we are asked to describe how we feel, what the pain is like and the kinds of foods we like to eat frequently. When engaged in descriptive writing, the writer needs to be as accurate as possible when describing an object a musical performance and/or a delicious meal at a banquet, among other things.

Generally, a good conversationalist can converse well and in conversing, decisions enter in. There are selected excellent pointers that may be given in order that pupils write well in descriptive writing:

1. Have something worthwhile to describe. Worthwhileness is an important concept to stress in writing since pupils do better in writing when a purpose or reasons are involved in written work.
2. Have a peer evaluate the descriptive writing product to notice accuracy, in particular, in the written product.
3. Appraise the sequence of ideas in the descriptive writing. Good sequence or order of sentences can assist to clarify the descriptive writing product.
4. Have major ideas be supported with details, whose ideas are of lesser value but do add emphasis upon the major ideas.
5. Use adjectives wisely in your writing since these words describe nouns used as subjects and objects.
6. Develop pupil interest as much as possible when writing to describe. Due to interest factors, the reader might continue to pay attention to the entire written product.

7. Use adverbs effectively to describe. The descriptive adverbs modify verbs, adjectives and other adverbs within the framework of descriptive writing.
8. Check for meaning within the written product. Meaningful statements assist in improving any descriptive writing product.
9. Pay careful attention to the mechanics of writing such as correct punctuation, capital letters, spelling of words and indentation of paragraphs among other items.
10. Proofread and modify weaknesses in the descriptive writing paper.

Narrative Writing

Narrative writing tells a story. Pupils need to do much reading of narrative stories so that they will understand the elements that go into this type of writing. Thus, there needs to be good models of narrative writing for pupils to emulate. Much interest then might be developed in the writing of narration. Interest is powerful factor in learning. Interest in writing might well propel children to pupil forth effort in narrative writing. Pupils, too, need to perceive reasons for writing narrative content. These reasons should be stated deductively by teachers as well as inductively. There are times when prizes and awards in extrinsic motivation allow a pupil to really buckle down to write narrative forms of stories.

When readiness factors permit, the pupil with teacher guidance may begin using the elements of writing narrative accounts.

There are definite pointers for the teacher to point out to pupils when narrative writing is in the offing:

1. Have pupils understand the important ingredients of narrative writing by reading stories that clearly point out what narrative writing is.
2. Permit pupils to use a familiar story for revision and thus stress, heavily, sequence of happenings in the story.
3. Provide quality continuity when pupils are heavily involved in writing sequential happenings in narration.
4. Read aloud narrative accounts so that pupils understand sequence in narration.
5. Guide pupils to choose a character that will be fully described in the narrative account.
6. Assist learners to write a setting for the character that will interest the reader.
7. Help pupils write a theme for the story. The theme will be the underlying message in narrative writing.
8. Let pupils develop a point of view in terms of someone telling the sequential events in the writing.

9. Have pupils write a plot which tells what actually happened in the story. The plot must keep the reader reading to find out what really happened in the story.
10. Use conversation in the story whereby quotation marks indicate what a character said at a specific time.

As is true of all writing done by pupils, the teacher needs to have conferences with pupils individually and collectively so that optimal progress for each pupil is possible. A writer's workshop might assist individuals to improve in the area of writing.

Writing to Assert

Information written by the learner, at times, will need to be backed up with logic and evidence based upon research. Assertions go beyond opinions, feelings and subjective knowledge. The assertion attempts to prove selected ideas, concepts and generalizations. Quality reasons given by the writer to make these assertions include strong and consistent logic, as well as good research which is accurate and reliable.

Sometimes, a writer believes that too many people have inconsistent ideas that are based on partial truths and poor research. The record then needs to be straightened out. There are selected pointers for pupils to become more proficient in developing written content which does hold water:

1. The central idea of the essay must be assertion, not opinions, feelings, attitudes and subjective thoughts.
2. Vocabulary terms in the essay should be clear and meaningful. Peers and the teacher who proof-read may need to point out the fallacy in logic used as well as terms that are vague and fail to communicate.
3. With critical thinking, the essay may need to be analyzed into important parts which then make it possible to take out and weaknesses in the assertion.
4. Ample evidence must be given to substantiate the assertion.
5. The evidence presented at diverse places in the essay needs to be sequential and related, not in terms of isolated fragments.
6. Evidence presented needs to be written in a manner readable to the audience or target group.
7. Research information may be presented in terms of graphs, charts, illustrations, tables and figures.
8. The summary of the essay needs to present a generalization which draws conclusions, supporting the assertion.
9. The assertion made will need to be written in a serious manner, but in a way which facilitates the reading thereof.
10. Clarity in writing and direct communication is necessary.

Oral discussions whereby pupils need to defend statements made, could be a pre-requisite in writing assertion essays. These learning opportunities provide background experiences for pupils in being able to defend statements made. Assertions should be backed up with supportive information which is logical and research based.

Evaluation Within an Essay

Individuals seemingly are always evaluating ideas, objects and statements made. Their worth and accuracy is then being evaluated. Quality criteria need to be used in the evaluation process. Otherwise, the evaluative statements may have little worth. There are definite pointers that may be given to assist the writer in writing an evaluation essay:

1. There needs to be clarity on what is being evaluated.
2. Comparisons need to be made between and among comparable items. Apples and oranges should not be compared since they are different fruits and the comparisons a writer makes depend upon the feelings and subjective ideas of the evaluator.
3. Evaluative statements should be valid in terms of the topic presented in the essay.
4. Clarity in the criteria used to judge the worth of something is a must.
5. There seems to be an opposite and equal reaction to many statements made in society. The writer must allow for other points of view, presented by listeners, that may have much merit.
6. Statistical devices should be used to support evidence in the evaluation process, such as tables, charts, graphs, figures and research data.
7. Sequential statements should be made to support the evaluation process.
8. Evidence to support an evaluation should be significant, not minor ideas nor trivial content.
9. Bias and prejudice need to be avoided in the evaluative statements.
10. Defend what has been written, based on logic, reason and objective data.

Writing Business and Friendly Letters

Business and friendly letter writing are two kinds of written work which have high utilitarian values. Most people write both kinds of letters to serve personal needs.

The business letter needs to have a heading to show where it came from such as the street and its number, the city and state as to its origin and the present date. Convention indicates these items should be on upper right hand side of the business letter. The inside address should be located on the left hand side of the letter. The inside address indicates to whom the letter is written, street address, city and state with zip code number. The greeting is directly below the inside address. The body is the major part of the business letter and pertains to what is being ordered in terms of merchandise or other requests; followed by the closing and the signature. Thus, a model business letter might look like the following:

Heading
D-43, S.V.N. Colony
Guntur 522006
Andhra Pradesh
India
August 15, 2002

Inside Address
Bowen Book Company
1849 Skyview Hall Drive
Kansas City, Missouri 69981
Greeting
Dear Sir:
Body

I would like to request a price list of current books you have on education. Your prompt attention to this would be greatly appreciated since our class is studying the educational systems of different countries.

Thank you
Closing
Sincerely Yours
Signature
D.B. Rao

The friendly letter has the same format as the business letter above, except the inside address is not necessary. The reason for this is that in friendly letter needs to contain personal experiences of the writer which would be of interest to the receiver of the letter. I would suggest here that the writer of the friendly letter include such items as the following:

1. Hobbies and interests being pursued.
2. Vacations that were taken.
3. Weekend trips experienced.
4. A new addition to the family.
5. Gifts given and received during holidays, birthdays, and other special events during the year.
6. An unusual event or happening.

Before a letter is sent, careful proof-reading needs to be in the offing. Politeness is involved when business and friendly letters are carefully and accurately written. Receivers of letters need to be clear as to the meaning of content written. Writing in long hand needs to be proofed in terms of clarity in handwriting. It is difficult to write legibly in long hand. Pupils should have ample experiences in using the word processor when conveying information in business and friendly letters.

Writing to Persuade

There are occasions when individuals need to persuade others in writing as well as orally. Selected educators have stated that persuasion is the most important kind of essay writing. Frequently, there are no right or wrong positions on an issue. Therefore, the individual, having strong feelings about one side of the issue, may use persuasive powers to have others, who initially disagreed, change their minds. When voting for officers at any level of government, the candidates running for office take different positions on an issue. Each candidate attempts to persuade voters to accept his/her position when voting. Liberals versus conversations, agriculture versus business, pro-choice versus pro-life, as well as pro-labour versus pro-business provide opportunities to hear and determine how each person stands on an issue. The position taken may represent how the candidate will vote in an election.

Some pointers that may assist pupils in being able to persuade others include the following:

1. Select a position on an issue which you agree with wholeheartedly. Write a persuasive essay to support your contention. Attempt to influence others to accept you point of view.
2. Write the essay for a selected audience. The audience should tend to believe the other side of the issue.
3. Do possess clarity in terms of where you stand. Your position should be very clear in the essay.
4. Argue, using logic, to substantiate your thinking on the issue.
5. Focus on the one issue so that your argument will be stronger and more influential.
6. Provide evidence which strengthens your point of view.
7. Appeal to the feelings and emotions of the reader when presenting your argument(s).
8. Establish credibility in your writing so that readers will wish to share your position on the issue.
9. Sequentially, order your statements to support your point of

view on the issue. The best supportive statement comes toward the end of the essay. The attention of the reader must be kept so that the most powerful influence comes toward the end of the essay.

10. Clarity in the writing of ideas is important with a variety of vocabulary terms used to convince others. Redundancy in writing makes for less influence over the unconverted reader. Arguments given must be direct, logical and used to obtain converts from the uncommitted.

Being able to influence others is very important in a democracy. There are many ideas and points of view on the many issues in society. Peaceful means of resolving these issues is important. Too frequently, violence is resorted to in society to influence others toward a certain position or point of view. The pro-life versus pro-choice issue is a good example. There needs to be rational means with debate and persuasion used to convince others to join a particular group having a specific point of view. Democracy in society emphasizes the freedom to express and listen to diverse sides of an issue. The atmosphere here must be such that listeners and readers might make up their own minds, after hearing the different points of view on an issue.

Finding Time to Write

If pupils are to become proficient writers, when will there be time to do much teaching of writing? I have noticed student teachers and cooperating teachers use different time schedules to permit increased time for writing. Numerous elementary school teachers indicate that there needs to be a scheduled period of time to have pupils be actively involved in writing for different purposes. Perhaps, two to three thirty minute periods are then given to teaching writing each week. Here, pupils are provided guidance and direction in writing. A definite type of writing might then be emphasized such as narrative or expository writing.

A second approach in finding time to teach writing is to relate writing with all curriculum areas in the elementary school. For example, there are many writing activities then that can be stressed in the social studies. Poetry writing might then be correlated with a thematic unit in the social studies (Ediger, 1997).

Third, before the school day begins, there could be writing instruction as well as writing projects for pupils. Pupils may write collaboratively or individually. It is good to provide choices for pupils as frequently as possible.

Fourth, pupils need to be encouraged to write in the home setting. Through parent/teacher conferences, a way may be worked out whereby the home setting becomes conducive to pupil writing.

Definite goals in writing for pupils to achieve might be discussed with parents.

Fifth, writing clubs have been successful in many schools. These clubs meet after school. The Writing Club has specific goals for learners to attain in writing. Sharing of written products might be an end goal to stress. Pupils may learn from each other and challenge learners to achieve at a more optimal level in writing.

Sixth, pupils should definitely be encouraged to write when assignments and tasks have been completed. Some of the finest writing comes from pupils when they write in their spare time during the school day!

In Conclusion

There are many kinds of writing activities for pupils. Pupils need to develop proficiency for a variety of types of writing. Hopefully, pupils individually will achieve more optimally in writing. With writing experiences, pupils engage in reading also. Writing and reading cannot be separated. What is written will be read. Sometimes the re-reading is done many times since the end product needs to be proofed and become a quality written product.

We would like to end the writing and reading connection by indicating ways to motivate writers to increase proficiency in print discourse. How might pupils then be motivated to increase writing skills and products?

1. Developing a classroom that is very rich with materials which encourage writing by pupils.
2. Encouraging pupils to write content pertaining to their very own interests and purposes. The content then for writing comes from the learner.
3. Providing rich experiences from which pupils enjoy writing in their diverse manifestations.
4. Showing interest and respect for pupil's writings.
5. Building on the interests of pupils to encourage participation in many purposes in writing.
6. Building a classroom environment for writing that is free from ridicule, embarrassment and fear.
7. Giving adequate time before, during and after the school day for pupils to truly become proficient in writing.
8. Assisting pupils to use the mechanics of writing well without losing out on quality ideas for written expression.
9. Helping pupils to feel confident when sharing ideas from writing.
10. Evaluating pupils progress in writing which encourages, but does not destroy interest in written work (Tiedt, 1983).

A quality program of evaluation needs to be in evidence to appraise pupil progress in the language arts and reading. This is true also in appraising pupil achievement in motivation. The teacher needs to evaluate, continuously, pupil progress in motivation. Motivation needs to be there to have pupils attain worthwhile objectives in the language arts/reading curriculum (Ediger, 1996).

REFERENCES

Ediger, Marlow (1997), *Teaching Reading and the Language Arts in the Elementary School*. Kirksville, Missouri: Simpson Publishing Company, 135-44.

Ediger, Marlow (1997), *Social Studies Curriculum in the Elementary School, Fourth edition*. Kirksville, Missouri: Simpson Publishing Company, 168-83.

Ediger, Marlow (1996), *Elementary Education*. Kirksville, Missouri: Simpson Publishing Company, 107-17.

Ediger, Marlow and Bhaskara Rao, Digumarti (1996). *Science Curriculum*. New Delhi: Discovery Publishing House.

Ediger, Marlow (1998), "The Principal of the School", *Reading Improvement*, 35: 45-48.

Tiedt, Iris M. (1983), *The Language Art Handbook*, Englewood Cliffs, New Jersey: Prentice-Hall, 184.

18

Spelling and the Language Arts

Pupils need to become good spellers to communicate effectively with others. Spelling is a tool to use to make known personal needs as well as to communicate feelings and appreciations. Correct spelling of words will always be necessary, even with the mass amount of technology available to many in society. Why? a person does not always have a computer at a specific place to process words. If the word processor is available, individuals still need to spell words reasonable close in accuracy for the spell checkers program to work and be effective. Thus, if a word is misspelled greatly, spell checkers will not list the needed correct spelling of the word on the monitor. Then too, sometimes it is more convenient to use long hand in writing rather than starting a computer up and using the attached printer. A personal message written in long hand may convey information to the reader better as compared to a printed document. How then might pupils be assisted to become proficient spellers?

Guidelines for Teaching Spelling

We would like to state selected guidelines which good teachers have used successfully in the teaching of spelling. First, pupils should understand the meaning of words to be mastered before studying their spelling. Meaning theory suggest that if pupils understand context, they will learn more effectively and depth learning may then be in evidence. Teachers need to take time for pupils to give definitions and/or be able to use a word contextually within a sentence. Some words are difficult to define and should then be used by the learner in a meaningful sentence. If a word can be defined and a pupil is ready to explain the meaning, he/she should do so. We believe that being able to use a word in a sentence and with a clear meaning, the learner is then ready to study the correct spelling of that word. We hope that words mastered in spelling will also be retained in memory for reading content as well as for writing in different academic areas. It is good if a pupil makes use of spelling words in many ways such as in reading those same words in literature, social studies, science and mathematics content. If pupils do not identify words correctly or a halting procedure is used in reading, the chances are comprehension will suffer in the process.

Second, the teacher needs to provide a variety of learning opportunities to assist pupils in learning to spell words correctly. Do I approve of the use of spelling textbooks in guiding pupils in learning to spell? It is not the textbook that is good or bad, but it depends upon how they are used by pupils and the teacher. There can be selected fascinating activities for learners within the confines of a spelling textbook that has been carefully chosen. Thus, here are activities that truly benefit and make spelling enjoyable. For example, in one lesson in a spelling textbook, there are the usual list of words for pupils to master. How are they to achieve this task? One approach in the text is to have pupils fill in blank spaces in sentences given, whereby the words for the fill in, come from that list. Pupils can be very attentive in doing this when application is made of the new words to be mastered in spelling. Seemingly, many pupils are interested in this activity even though it does occur generally in each weekly lesson. We think that the activity has variation each week due to changing words that are used to fill in the blank spaces within sentences. The teacher should always observe pupils to notice if boredom sets in and, if it does, to switch to a different experience. The teacher cannot do a prefect job of varying activities when boredom sets in, but he/she can do the best possible to keep pupils on task. With twenty to thirty pupils in a classroom, it is difficult to provide for individual needs of all pupils. Additional tasks in a textbook to be used to help pupils learn to spell words correctly are cross word puzzles that use words from the weekly list in the spelling text. Friendly and business letters are to be written using selected words from the spelling list. The teacher needs to be creative in text use in teaching spelling by thinking of and implementing other learning opportunities than those indicated in the weekly lesson.

Third, we believe that pupils should develop a definite methodology in learning to spell words. A good speller, no doubt, has a workable method of learning to spell words correctly. Those who do not spell words correctly, in many cases, may need a new methodology in mastering the correct spelling of words. We like the method that many pupils have used correctly in learning to spell. Thus, the pupil needs to look at the new word carefully. It is doubtful that a teaching strategy will work if the pupil here does not look at the word carefully if pupils are truly focusing upon a word to acquire in correct spelling. Next, the pupil should pronounce the word correctly. Spelling errors are made due to inaccurate pronunciation of words. Hopefully, the pupil will listen to all the sounds with that word being studied for mastery in spelling. Involved sounds need to be associated with the correct graphemes or symbols. The learner than should practice writing the word once. The written word may then be checked with the correct spelling. Too frequently, pupils are asked to write a word five or ten times immediately; the word written might be misspelled then ten times. Better it is, to write the word once and check accuracy of spelling. Once the word is spelled correctly, the pupil may wish to write it several times in a contextual situation.

Fourth, pupils need to perceive reasons for learning to spell a given set of words, be if from the textbook or from other sources. Purpose is vital for success in learning to spell words correctly. The teacher may say why it is important to learn to spell words correctly in a specific lesson. A deductive approach is then in evidence. Inductive procedures may also be used such as a teacher asking questions of learners so that the latter understands the merit of learning to spell a given number of words correctly. Extrinsic rewards are used by some teachers to motivate pupils to study and master the new set of words in spelling. Thus, a teacher may say how many words need to be spelled correctly by Friday to receive a prize. These prizes are generally visible to pupils. Learners then know what to do to receive the award. We recommend that if extrinsic awards are given for learning, pupils should, as soon as possible, feel a desire from within to learn to spell words correctly as an intrinsic motivational device. The extrinsic rewards should be removed as soon as possible and not become a crutch or lever used to spell words correctly.

Fifth, pupils should learn to spell words correctly in a contextual situation. The new words are then used in functional situations. Words and their correct spelling are meaningful within a practical endeavour. We recommend that pupils determine useful ways to spell words correctly within contextual situations. The learner may then use the new words when writing an invitation for his/her birthday party. Further uses include writing business and friendly letters, content in greeting cards, prose and poetry, poetry, narrative and expository accounts, short stories, announcements and thank you notices, among other functional writing activities.

How many words should a pupil learn to spell correctly per week? This depends upon the present achievement level of the involved learner? To be sure, too many words may be required for a pupil to master in spelling. The opposite extreme would be too few words are learned to spell words correctly in a given time interval. The teacher needs to observe each pupil and notice what a reasonable number of words might be. There is nothing sacred about mastering twenty spelling words per week in the third grade, for example. It is important always to challenge pupils to do their very best in all curriculum areas.

Sixth, the spelling curriculum should be as individualized as possible. To some educators this means that each pupil should have a unique set of words to master in spelling. These words may come from those the learner misspelled from diverse writing activities the preceding week. The number of words in this list must be adjusted to fit the abilities of the individual learner so that too many or too few words are not required for mastery within a designated time. This seems to work fairly well in the spelling curriculum provided that learners do not refuse to use words in writing unless they are spelled correctly. The reason for doing this pertains to keeping the number reasonable of those words misspelled and needing to be studied for mastery. Another approach that might be used pertains to adjusting the number of words from the spelling textbook that need to be spelled correctly per week. Pupil A then may find it easy to learn to spell all words correctly plus a bonus list of words per week. Pupil B might be able to spell ten of the twenty words correctly per week. Once Pupil B has experienced success, he/she might become motivated to increase the number of words spelled correctly per week. We have noticed that pupils who are successful do volunteer to do more work then formerly and go beyond minimal levels. It takes time and effort for the teacher to make these adjustments for individual pupils. But with good teaching, teachers attempt to provide for individual differences among learners in the classroom. Even though the spelling curriculum is individualized, there may be pupils who wish to work collaboratively. Learning styles differ from one pupil to another such as wanting to work interpersonally or by the self as contrasted with interpersonal or committee work. Here, pupils should have a voice in how they wish to study and learn, individually or in a group, to achieve more optimally in spelling.

Seventh, we recommend that creatively be stressed in pupils learning to spell words. So often, spelling is taught as role learning and memorization. Rather, the pupil should have ample opportunities, to spell words correctly within creative poetry and prose written or within plays and stories written. Here, we recommend that pupils evaluate correct spelling of words after the creative product has been completed, not during the writing endeavour. Pupils may wish to assist each other when correct spelling of words is emphasized at the end of the creative writing experience.

Eighth, we recommend strongly to provide incentives for pupils to volunteer to learn to spell more words correctly, than those assigned or even going beyond the bonus words. It is surprising what pupils will do to put forth effort when the sky becomes the limit. Intrinsic motivation certainly can come into being when pupils feel rewarded and successful in learning. The teaching of spelling is not known to be the most stimulating curriculum area, but the teacher can work in the direction of it becoming motivating and challenging.

Which Words Should Pupils Master in Spelling?

This question has been debated for a long time. There are teachers who assume that the spelling text alone contains salient words for pupils to master in spelling. The text has had a long history of use in teaching and learning situations. We have looked at spelling texts that came out in the early 1930s. These books had lists of words only for pupils to memorize in spelling per week. There were no suggested learning activities. The teacher each week needed to work out all learning activities that would assist pupils in learning to spell each word correctly. Presently, there are teachers who believe that no spelling texts be used and believe better teaching is an end result. A well chosen textbook should definitely not hinder good teaching. Ingenious teachers can stimulate pupils to learn with interesting activities that capture pupil attention. No textbook needs to be followed religiously in terms of the recommendations in the manual. The good teacher chooses from among the different activities stresses in the manual section. Additional learning opportunities are brought into the teaching and learning situation that provide for individual differences among pupils. No writer of quality materials would suggest following the manual 100 per cent. Writer realize that the teacher is the one to implement the teaching suggestions and must vary the kinds of learning opportunities provided for pupils so that securing the attention of pupils is there and pupils are actively engaged in learning. No using a basal textbook, in and of itself, does not make for good teaching. The teacher is there to study and implement teaching strategies that assist pupils to attain relevant objectives in the spelling curriculum.

If the teacher uses words for each pupil that the latter missed in everyday functional writing, the teacher still needs to have quality approaches in teaching so that individual pupils learn and achieve. Pupils need to be motivated when attempting to master the spelling words missed in daily writing. The number per week to be mastered needs to be adjusted to what a child can achieve in a reasonable manner. Certainly, a pupil may experience failure if too many words need mastering or become bored if too little is expected in a given time interval.

There have been successful teachers whom we have observed that emphasize spelling words that have been chosen for pupils to master which are based on research study of pupils' writings were selected by the teacher within a list for mastery learning by local pupils. The Dolch List (1954) has been used in teaching spelling by many teachers, even though it is not a recently developed list. This list has 220 words that Dolch's research found should be learned by pupils as sight words. This might then cut down on the number of errors that pupils make in spelling as well as in word identification in reading. These are the most frequently occurring words in spelling errors in pupils' writing, according to Dolch. We feel the Dolch List still has much merit because these words are commonly used by pupils in everyday writing and reading today. The word list is not divided by grade levels but is contained in one listing. We recommend that teachers study pupils' writings to notice which words are used most frequently. Teachers should be involved in doing research and may come up with a revision of the Dolch List. With personal computers in the school and in the home, the statistical procedures, we believe, have been greatly simplified and become user friendly. With personal computers and assistance from educational researchers, teachers now have more opportunities to engage in research and attempt to solve classroom problems than ever before.

There are numerous statements of objectives in spelling that educators have developed over the years. We believe the following are worthy for teachers to emphasize in the curriculum:

1. Assist pupils to master those words which are needed in order to express oneself clearly and accurately in writing.
2. Guide pupils to achieve good study habits which assist the learner to pursue diverse kinds and types of writing experiences. Preservance is a key concept here. Pupils need to establish plans in writing, work toward their achievement and personally monitor progress. We have noticed pupils who attempt to give up too soon on assigned or voluntary written work. Encouragement by peers and the teacher will go a long

way in motivating learner achievement. Pupils pride in achievement aids in setting higher goals in spelling within the writing activity.

3. Develop within pupils a set of standards in learning that will help pupils to spell words correctly. These standards involve using phonics to make associations between symbol and sound where this consistency is in evidence. Pupils also need to learn to spell selected words by sight when the consistency between symbol and sound and sound just is not there. Correct pronunciation of words is important so that spelling errors are not made due to that factor.
4. Help pupils to realize that correct spelling is a social courtesy and incorrect spelling may reflect negatively upon the pupil.
5. Direct quality teaching to have pupils, when ready, learn keyboard skills to use the personal computer to engage in writing. This is necessary for all pupils. Spell checkers can do much to minimize spelling errors when word processing is used. Computers are increasing becoming user friendly.
6. Provide friendly assistance to pupils who need help in spelling so that success can be stressed as much as possible in the writing curriculum. A good speller in the classroom may also provide this help. If the latter approach is used, change or rotate who gives the assistance. Each pupil also needs to pursue his/her own interests in purposeful learning.
7. Emphasize the interest factor by letting pupils choose the topic to write on, regardless of the purpose involved. Thus, if pupils are to write limericks, the learner may select within that framework the contents of the limerick. Interest goes a long way in providing effort for learning.
8. Let pupils work together in the writing activity involving spelling. Observe theat each is participating actively in the spelling/writing experience.
9. Involve pupils in self-evaluation as well as the teacher participating actively in appraising learner progress. Collaboratively, a learning community may be developed that stresses quality writing in the curriculum.
10. Establish quality sequence in pupils learning to spell words correctly. If pupils are involved in determining which words need to be learned in spelling, a psychological spelling curriculum is in evidence. Sequence then resides within the learner, not in other sources. Should the teacher determine sequence in pupil learning to spell words, a logical approach is in evidence since the teacher determines the order of learning activities for pupils (Ediger, 1988).

Pupils should definitely realize that spelling and reading are related, not isolated entities. Being able to spell more words correctly as time goes on should reflect learners' increasing abilities to become better readers. The goals of spelling and reading instruction should develop confidence in the learner to achieve at a higher level commensurate with inherent abilities of the involved pupil (Ediger, 1998).

Cautions in Learning to Spell Words

There are selected cautions that teachers need to be aware of when teaching spelling. Pupils and the teacher should not go overboard on phonics when correct spelling of words is being emphasized. Thus, there are numerous words that lack consistency between symbol and sound such as my, pie, buy, sigh, kite, white and bye. Each of these words contains the long in sound and yet that sound is spelled differently from word to word.

Second, pupils need to learn to spell vital words that are truly useful. Too frequently, words listed in a spelling textbook may not be important enough for pupils to learn to spell. We believe the teacher needs to study word lists in spelling texts, if used and ascertain the worth of learning to spell each word. There is so much to learn that it behooves the teacher to choose carefully what pupils are to learn.

Third, if pupils are to learn to spell a given set of words, they should make application of what has been learned. Much forgetting occurs of mastered words in spelling if there are no related practical endeavours, meaning that applying what has been learned is important. We believe much time is wasted in learning if pupils are tested only, on the number of words spelled correctly on Friday and yet the involved pupil perceives no practical application of these kinds of learning activities.

Fourth, too frequently, memorization of correct spelling of words is emphasized and yet meaningful experiences are lacking. Generally memorization is done for the sake of passing a test and in this case to receive a good grade from the teacher. We would like to see the evaluation process change to where more emphasis is placed upon pupils' making application of words being studied for correct spelling in ongoing lessons and units of study.

Fifth, pupils in many cases lack readiness factors for learning to spell words correctly. What are these readiness factors? Certainly, a pupil should also be able to use the new words being studied contextually in a sentence that makes sense. Pupils individually need to use the proper tools at hand to analyze parts within a word such as grapheme/phoneme relationships. For those irregularly spelled words, a basic sight vocabulary needs to be developed by learners.

Sixth, too often, pupils in a class are taught as if all possess readiness for the same number of words to be mastered in spelling. Pupils are individuals, not a mass of objects. Learners come with feelings, dreams and hopes. The need to be treated as human beings with much worth. Thus, the teacher needs to help each pupil to learn as much as possible. The opportunity for pupil learning is now and we need to take advantage of these opportunities.

Seventh, there is a lack of emphasis upon diagnosis and remediation when teaching spelling. We need to determine why pupils individually are making errors in the incorrect spelling of words. Do pupils go by phonics too much when learning to spell words and yet one or more of these words are not that phonetic in sound/symbol relationships? Is legible handwriting a cause for improper; spelling of words? Pupils need to experience as much success as possible so that motivation is there to learn, grow and achieve.

Technology and Spelling

There definitely is room for technology use in the spelling curriculum. Its use is one way to strengthen teaching and learning in ongoing lessons and units of study. Computer use should be made available to teachers and learners. The software content of the computer should not duplicate with other materials of instruction, but should provide learning activities which also assist pupils to improve in the area of spelling. There are drill and practice exercises which truly help pupils to achieve more optimally. Words here need to be highly useful with strategies of learning that provide for each pupil's ability level. The drill and practice experiences give learners an opportunity to rehearse the correct spelling of words. There are needs for drill and practice so that pupils may practice and retain the correct spelling of words at a more optimal level of achievement. Much of what we remember has been presented to us in different ways using a variety of learning activities. Here software and computer use can provide this variety with innovating ways and procedures displays on the monitor. Also, there are numerous games that pupils may engage in individually or collaboratively that stress the correct spelling of words, as shown on the monitor. These games may provide wholesome competitive activities between two or three sides. Thus, in rotation, one side may score points for the correct spelling of one or more words whereas the two other sides or single side, in sequence, may come back with spelling other words correctly to score points. The winner has the most words spelled correctly. Games in spelling are good for pupils to play competitively, if appropriate attitudes are in evidence.

Tutorial software programs provide new words for pupil mastery, as shown sequentially on the monitor. Diverse learning opportunities are provided so that pupils may master these new words in spelling. Also, there are simulations that attempt to represent life-like situations whereby pupils are to engage in problem solving in virtual reality. The encounters here are quite realistic and provide for situations involving higher levels of cognition such as critical and creative thinking as well as problem solving. At the same time, pupils are engaged in attempting to spell words correctly. Since a more utilitarian situation is involved in simulations, pupils tend to find these activities to be challenging and real.

We find that pupils engaging in using the word processor to write creatively or functionally is one of the better ways to stress correct spelling of words. Here, pupils need to be proficient in spelling during the actual composing situation when using the words processor. It is true that spell checkers does provide much assistance in helping pupils make corrections in spelling. However, the commands provided by the learner in writing content into the computer need to be very close in correct spelling or spell checkers cannot provide the correct spelling on the monitor of the word processor. All pupils, when ready, should master use of the word processor to write prose, poetry, or utilitarian content. Mehlinger (1997) asks the following provocative questions when using computers in the curriculum:

1. How would teachers teach if textbooks were replaced by small multi-media devices that serve as both computer and communications tool?
2. What would school libraries be like when students have access to the libraries of the word?
3. How would teaching change when students can contact experts who know more about a single topic than the teacher?

These are three excellent questions that need pondering for all educators. We recommend both technology and textbooks, carefully chosen, be used to provide for individual differences among learners. Diverse kinds of materials need to be used in teaching and learning. Individuals posses diverse learning styles and the professional teacher attempts to harmonize instruction with pupil learning styles. Bermman and Tinker (1997) discuss a seminar method of instruction with the use of technology:

Many teachers who experiment with on-line courses report being overwhelmed with enrolments of 10 or 12 students because they set up e-mail conversations with each student. The better model is more than a seminar, in which the teacher determines the topic and activities, encourages substantive interactions among students, monitors and shapes the conversation and promotes and atmosphere in which students respond to one another's work. This model results in more conversation, is far more likely to be constructivist and builds on the rich learning that takes place in groups.

Collaborative endeavours that stress the learning of correct spelling of words within purposeful writing activities certainly do emphasize positive ways in the use of technology. Interactions among learners do tend to make for higher levels of cognitive endeavours within the framework of critical and creative thought as well as problem solving.

Handwriting, Spelling and Print Discourse

Illegible handwriting may be major cause for incorrect spelling of words. Handwriting as a separate subject is receiving much less emphasis than formerly. When attending the elementary school years from 1934 to 1942, handwriting received considerable time for instruction; approximately, fifteen minutes per day was spent in handwriting instruction. We learned to write in the air to form individual letters correctly. The making of ovals so that no line was crossed with another received much emphasis as did push and pull exercises, again with no strokes crossing each other. May be these activities had something to do with a transfer value in becoming better handwriters. We truly doubt if this was the case, however. Probably, more time should have been given to the actual writing of prose and poetry, as well as other forms of print discourse. Thus, use needs to be made of what has been learned in handwriting experiences.

What might the teacher do to assist pupils to improve in handwriting? Here, the teacher needs to give much attention to child growth and development characteristics. A lengthy period of time given to handwriting instruction may not harmonize with psychomotor skills and readiness of the learner. Much tension may be built up by the leaner if he/she is required to write extensively. Activities may be changed so this does not occur, such as changing to a reading experience. It is always good procedure in teaching to observe the attention span of pupils to notice when sequential activities need to be changed. We strongly recommend handwriting be taught within an ongoing activity involving purposeful writing. Application might then be made of what is being emphasized in terms of objectives in instruction. Handwriting and content written become one, not separate entities.

The objectives of handwriting need to be chosen carefully so that relevance is in evidence. The making of ovals and push/pull exercises were eliminated from the elementary school curriculum some time ago due to a lack of significance involved. To spend hours and hours on drill pertaining to a set of letters certainly is misusing teaching time. We believe legibility is a key concept to emphasize in the handwriting arena. A pupil does not need to conform specifically to models of upper and lower case letters of the alphabet presented in a handwriting text. The model letters, however, may be used as a guide for pupils to develop legibility in handwriting. If we can read a pupil's written products readily, then we are satisfied with the quality of his/her handwriting. If illegible handwriting is in evidence, then objectives of instruction need to be developed and implemented so that the child becomes a writer of legible content.

Pupils should feel successful in ongoing experiences. Thus, a pupil is making progress over his previous work in handwriting. Learners should not be compared with each other in legible handwriting. Why? Pupils individually are at different achievement levels in using neuromuscular skills. Teachers need to develop interest within pupils in achieving at a higher level in handwriting. Three kinds of objectives need to be stressed in handwriting. These are knowledge objectives whereby pupils have the needed content about legible letters, words, phrases, sentences and paragraphs to write in a illegible way; skills objectives whereby learners use what has been learned; and attitudinal objectives in which learners develop positive feelings in wanting to improve over previous levels in handwriting.

More specifically, objectives of instruction in handwriting should achieve the following:

1. How to form letters legibly.
2. How to align letters appropriately.
3. How to space letters and words properly.
4. How to stress proper proportion of letters within words.
5. How to achieve overall legibility in written discourse.
6. How to appraise the self in the quality of handwriting exhibited.
7. How to emphasize neatness in all written products as final copies.

Skills objectives should emphasize the following:

1. Form letters and words illegibly.
2. Align letters and words properly.
3. Appropriate proportion of letters and words.
4. Proper spacing of letters and words.
5. Self-evaluation in achievement in general as well as specific skills in handwriting.

6. Neatness in the handwriting arenas.

Attitudinal objectives for pupils to achieve should place importance on the following:

1. Desiring to improve in the area of handwriting.
2. Wanting to improve in the area of letter information.
3. Developing positive attitudes toward having proper proportion.
4. Feeling a need to space words and letters properly.
5. Voluntarily assessing personal achievement in handwriting.
6. Emphasizing neatness in activities involving handwriting.
7. Respecting the progress of others in handwriting.

There needs to be proper balance among understandings, skills and attitudinal objectives in handwriting. Pupils do need knowledge pertaining to what makes for quality handwriting, but the knowledge needs to be implemented as skills. Hopefully, positive feelings as attitudes within learners will develop as a result.

Quality Handwriting Across the Curriculum

Good handwriting that is legible needs to be stressed throughout the different curriculum areas in the school setting.

Thus in mathematics, written work of pupils becomes difficult to evaluate unless good handwriting is there. Good handwriting needs to infiltrate numerals written as well as story or words problems composed by learners. Reports written such as biographies of famous mathematicians provide more opportunities to have pupils practice proper handwriting skills.

In science, pupils individually or in committees may write up the results of a science experiment, a method of procedure in doing an experiment, a report written on a self selected topic in science, bar or line graphs developed on temperature readings on a daily basis, notes written on content read in science from a well known encyclopaedia, an outline written from a variety of reference sources in science, criteria written on being an effective member of a discussion group in science, as well as summaries on main ideas obtained from a video tape.

In social studies, pupils may write business letters to order free and inexpensive materials pertaining to an ongoing unit of study, friendly letters to pen pals, generalizations involving content read from diverse reference sources, relevant facts in reaction to a question raised by pupils in the classroom, as well as announcements to other classes to come to visit the pupil's classroom to observe completed projects related to an ongoing unit of study in social studies. Additional learning opportunities involving handwriting in the social studies include the following:

1. Speaking parts for pupils involving early days of Puritans in the New World.
2. Directions written for making a relief of the continent being studied in the social studies.
3. Standards may be written for evaluating an oral report.
4. An outline might be written to cover content pertaining to conclusions reached on an important selection read from social studies materials.
5. Hypothesis written involving one or more hypotheses written in a problem solving activity.
6. Notes taken on a selection in reading in the social studies.

In the literature curriculum, there are many opportunities for pupils to practice handwriting, including the following:

1. Labeling objects in the classroom in a reading readiness program.
2. Using handwriting texts as the need arises, such as for a model in the writing curriculum.
3. Developing experience charts written by pupils with teacher guidance in a reading readiness class.
4. Writing ideas involving reading for a variety of purposes, such as from critical reading, reading to follow directions, factual reading, reading for a sequence of ideas, creative reading, reading for main ideas and reading to develop generalizations.
5. Pupils need ample time to do practice forming letters correctly, writing letters and words with proper alignment, slanting letters correctly, spacing words and letters properly and using proper proportion of letters.
6. Pupils with teacher guidance need adequate time to write news articles. The resulting newsletter could be sent home weekly, bi-weekly, or monthly on important happenings in class.

In the health curriculum, the following writing experiences involve handwriting:

1. Learners may take notes on a talk given by a physician pertaining to improved health practices in everyday living.
2. Main ideas might be written on a set of slides or illustrations presented by a registered nurse on improving healthful living in the community.
3. Each pupil might write a personal experience chart pertaining to content from a filmstrip related to a facet of healthful living.
4. Letters may be written to the city council making recommendations on improving a polluted area.

5. Menus may be written for a week on implementing balanced diets in the school lunch program.
6. Business letters may be written to order free and inexpensive materials relating to an ongoing health unit of instruction.

In Conclusion

Handwriting errors certainly may cause spelling errors. The teacher needs to do much diagnosing to ascertain why pupils misspell words in writing. Writing needs to be emphasized in all curriculum areas. Improved communication results when quality spelling and handwriting are involved. Courtesy is also inherent when the learner exhibits the best spelling and handwriting in ongoing contextual writing activities. Purposeful writing experiences propel pupils to put forth effort to attain worthwhile objectives. Quality knowledge, skills and attitudes as three categories of objectives should be achieved by pupils. Pupils need to practice much writing so that increased proficiency is in evidence. The writer has treated spelling and handwriting within the broader perspective of writing. Spelling and handwriting skills can best be developed in context within the writing activity. Successfully learners in writing will increase their abilities in spelling and handwriting. Careful selection of objectives, learning opportunities and evaluation procedures need to be in the offing.

REFERENCES

Ediger, Marlow (1998), "Goals of Reading Instruction", *Experiments in Education*, published by the SITU Council of Educational Research (in India), 11-19.

Ediger, Marlow (1988), *Language Arts Curriculum in the Elementary School*, Kirksville, Missouri: Simpson Publishing Company, 73-81.

Dolch, Edward W. (1955), *Methods in Reading*. Champaign, Illinois: Garrard Publishing Company.

Mehlinger, Howard D., "The Next Step", *Electronic School*, A22-A24.

19

Phonics and the Language Arts

Word recognition skills help readers identify words while reading. One skill is sight word recognition, the development of a store of words a person an recognise immediately on sight. Use of context clues to help in word identification involves using the surrounding words to decode an unfamiliar word. Both semantic and syntactic clues can be helpful. Phonics, the association of speech sounds (phonemes) with printed symbols (graphemes), is very helpful in identifying unfamiliar words, even thought the sound-symbol associations in English are not completely consistent. Structural analysis skills enable readers to decode unfamiliar words using units larger than single graphemes. The process of structural analysis involves recognition of prefixes, suffixes inflectional endings, contradictions and compound words, as well as syllabication and accent. Dictionaries can also be used for word identification. The dictionary re-spelling that appears in parentheses after the word supplies the word's pronunciation, but the reader has to know how to use the dictionary's pronunciation key to interpret the re-spelling appropriately.

Children need to learn to use all of the word recognition skills. Because they will need different skills for different situations, they must also learn to use the skills appropriately.

An overall strategy for decoding unfamiliar words is useful. The following five step strategy is a good one to teach:

1. use context clues;
2. try the sound of the initial consonant, vowel, or blend in addition to context clues;
3. check for structural clues;

4. use phonics generalizations to sound out as much of the word as necessary; and
5. consult the dictionary (Burns, Roe and Ross, 1996, 152-53).

There is considerable debate pertaining to how much phonics should be taught in the reading curriculum. Whole language approaches tend to minimize the teaching of phonics. Advocates of whole language believe that pupils will learn to read well when holism in content read is emphasized. For example, pupils together with the teacher here look at a Big Book that all can see clearly to discuss the illustrations. This activity assists pupils to obtain background information so that the resulting print will be understood better. Pupils also speculate on what the print material in the Big Book will be about. The pulls and the teacher then read aloud the contents in the Big Book. Pupils may see the printed words as the oral reading activity progresses. If they do know them or they don't pulls can determine what each word is through reading aloud together and follow along in the print material. Re-reading is recommended since all pupils have their favourite stories and like to hear them again. Before I was able to read to myself, I liked to hear the Katzenjammer Kids comic strip read over and over again. The contents therein were quite predictable since the Katzenjammer Kids always did something mischievous; the father and the captain never liked to work while mama did all the work.

Big Books read with children should contain predictable content in that pupils have security in knowing something about what will happen in the story. With re-reading and predicable content, pupils learn to identify many words. These identified words become sight words. With a core of sight words in the repertoire, pupils may then read content at a more sophisticated level. With the Big Book approach, pupils are not hindered in sequential thinking when attempting to recognize an unknown word. Enjoyment of the story being read should then be in the offing. If pupils are stumbling along with word recognition, they may learn to dislike the act of reading. Rather, pupils need to focus upon interesting content contained in the Big Book. There are teachers who teach some phonics along with Big Book use. Thus, there may be games that pupils play in phonics related directly to the content read. Pupils then study words which have the same beginning letter and sound. They may compare short and long vowel sounds in words following a pattern such as: cap—cape, hat—hate, fat—, nap—nape and can, cane, among others. Teachers in whole language also stress words that end alike and words that rhyme. By having pupils find which word, for example, starts like 'bat', pupils may enjoy the phonics learning activity. It is not drill in a complete scope and sequence program of phonics, but rather learners locate words with a pattern and these words came from print materials read.

Phonics Integrated with Content from Reading

The view that reading consists of its simultaneous application of many different skills has important implications for our understanding of the successes and failures that readers experience as well as the kinds of educational programs that we should implement. The reason for this is that in reading, as in all cognitive activities, there are many roads that lead to Rome. There are many paths to successful reading and hence many paths to successful reading instruction. On the other hand, failure to read may result from deficiencies in any of the sub-skills of literacy. On the other hand, readers with strong skills in one facet of reading are bound to be able to compensate for possible weaknesses in other skills. We already have seen, for example, how second language readers use their comprehension and inferential skills to compensate for a lack of vocabulary and word identification skills. Thus, it is true that readers not only can fail to accomplish literacy for many different reasons, but also can succeed for different reasons (Van Den Broek, 1996).

We do not agree with a phonics program that has a scope and sequence of its own whereby lesson after lesson emphasizes phonics. Why? 1. The lessons become much too abstract for young pulls on the primary grade levels. 2. Phonics is separated from the act of reading whereby reading for ideas should be the key component of a quality reading program. 3. Pupils experience much drill when phonics becomes a separate subject area. 4. Teachers find it difficult to obtain pupil interests in sequential lessons in phonics. 5. Learners have a difficult time to determine reasons for all the emphasis upon "How" to read.

An approach in the teaching of phonics needs to stress reading for content and ideas as well as mastering key concepts pertaining to word recognition. There needs to be rational balance between whole language and phonics. Now we are left with the problem of what makes for balance between whole language and phonics. Now, we are left with the problem of what makes for balance between the two—phonics and whole language. We would give much more importance to reading for ideas as compared to phonics. Why? We read to secure ideas, not to associate sounds with symbols. Relating sounds to symbols emphasizes keys to unlocking unknown words. It is not an end in and of itself. Phonics should never be taught as an end, but it is a means to an end. If phonics knowledge and use is more important than being a tool to unlock unknown words, then we are stuck with a strong scope and sequence program in phonics. Phonics then may be taught for its own sake. Here, we believe a mistake is made when phonics is conceive to be good for its own sake whether it assists pupils in reading well or not. Compare that line of thought with phonics being a tool to use when needed to determine the word that is not being identified.

Sometimes, even with strong context clues, a pupil cannot identify an unknown word. Perhaps, in these cases, a pupil may unlock an unknown word through identifying the initial consonant and then using context clues. A strong case can be made for emphasizing phonics as needed. If a pupil then cannot identify a word after being given adequate opportunity to do so, the teacher may need to stress selective facets of phonics which are useful here, such as the initial consonant "m" when the word "modify" is encountered and not identified. There is that teachable moment when the teacher needs to emphasize what is salient and in this case, a phonetic element. Phonics also may be taught in the context of basal reader use. Thus, when pupils are to read a story or selection from the basal, the teacher may print on the chalkboard in neat manuscript style the new words pupils will encounter when they are to read silently or orally. Generally, these new words will come from the manual section of the basal. The teacher points to each new word as he/she and the pupils pronounce them. This procedure may be used more than once per lesson if the need exists. The point is that pupils should be able to recognize these same words when reading. It still will be necessary as the act of reading is in evidence for the teacher or a good reader to pronounce words not known to the teacher. The pupil needs to be helped after allowing not known to the reader. The pupil needs to be helped after allowing five seconds, in general, before the unknown word is pronounced. Pupils not knowing a word should attempt to the best possible to determine it during these approximate five seconds. When pupils have ample opportunities to see the new words in near manuscript print, prior to oral or silent reading, the chances are they will identify many of these in the ongoing reading experience.

What about a phonics program that has a scope and sequence of its very own? Pupils should realize that a consonant sound is made with an obstruction by the speaker between the throat and the lips. This is true of all consonant sounds. When thinking about the teaching of single consonants, the teacher or committee of teachers need to decide when these should be taught. There are individual consonant letters that are very consistent with their individual sounds. The following consonants are very consistent between grapheme/phoneme—b, d, f, h, j, i, m, n, p, r, s, t, v, w, and y. With high frequency of use, I would stress the importance of pupils learning the following consonants: b, d, m, n, p, r, s, t, and w. These consonants have very few exceptions to being consistent between symbol and sound. The following are some exceptions.

1. The letter "b" is silent in the word "debt".
2. The letter "p" is silent in the word "pneumonia".
3. The letter "s" sounds like a "z" in the word "resides".
4. The letter "w" has a "wh" sound in words such as "why". "what", and "when". When I was an undergraduate student in a teaching of reading class, the instructor mentioned strongly that the "wh" sound is made with pronouncing the "w" and then at the same time blowing the light out an a candle. We think in most cases we cannot distinguish between the two initial consonant of "w" with the words "where" and "when".

In context, then, single consistent consonants, between symbol and sound, need to be taught. These are very helpful for learners to use in addition to context clues to unlock unknown words. Functional use should be made of these consonants. They are not to be learned for their own sake, but rather for application and use.

Short vowel sounds are next in importance for pupils to study. The consonant/vowel/consonant pattern are relatively easy for many pupils. These sounds are common in such words as the following: run, sun and bun. These words pattern with a short "u" sound. Ran, ban and man pattern with the short "a" sound. Hen, men and pen pattern with the short "e" sound. Sit, pit and hit pattern for the short "i" sound. Cot, lot and tot pattern with the short "o" sound.

Long vowel sounds can have a pattern when taught to pupils. For example, there are numerous words that follow the consonant/vowel/consonant/silent "e" (CVC silent e) pattern, such as bake, cake, make, fake, sake and lake. Vowel digraphs include sail, pail, mail and rail. Here, there are two vowel letters that come together with the first being long and second silent in sound.

Initial consonant digraphs taught by the teacher may assist many pupils to become proficient in word recognition. Generally, two consonant letters make for one sound. These individual letters cannot be taken apart and make sense, such as the following: "th" as in thought; "sh" as in shine; "ch" as in chair; and "ph" as in phone. The words listed here for the consonant digraphs are commonly used words. The consonant digraphs listed are used very frequently. Within context, there are pupils who need assistance here since the separate letters do not make for consistency between symbol and sound.

Ending consonant digraphs are more difficult for pupils to master as compared to those coming in the beginning. Many pupils have been guided to improve reading through identification of ending consonant digraphs such as: ch as in bench, sh as in push and th as in width. Games may always be played with pupils to see if they can provide additional words that have a beginning or ending consonant digraph. One of us observed a student teacher and her cooperating teacher have pupils brainstorm consonant blends and pupils wanted the lesson to continue beyond closing time. There was excitement and interest in continually naming more consonant blends.

Consonant blends or clusters are made up of two or three letters, each making its separate sound. The sounds come rather close together. There are pupils who have difficulty making these blends of two consecutive letters with their individual sounds. Her are some common blends: bl as in blow and blue; cr as in cry, crystal and crow; fr such as in fruit, frail and fry; sn such as in snow, snail and snake and str such as in street, stray and strike.

Phonograms are interesting of many pupils to experiment with. Phonograms are short words found within a larger word. Examples of pupils discovering phonograms are the following: at as in hat, eat as in seat and ate as in skate. Sometimes a new "unknown" word is not impossible to identify. Thus, the word may appear unknown, but the learner knows enough about phonograms that he/she can identify the word correctly.

There are pupils who face an "unknown" word until they notice familiarities therein, such as a prefix. There are very common prefixes that hold true quite consistently. These include un meaning not such as unpopular and im meaning not such as in impolite. The unfamiliar becomes familiar when pupils notice suffixes such as less as in childless and ful such as in cupful. By noticing the familiar such as the root word and adding either the prefix and/or suffix, many pupils can determine what the new word is.

Diphthongs may cause selected pupils problems in word recognition. Why? Here are two vowel letters that are together and yet their sound is different then any short or long vowel sound as well as being different in pronunciation. The following are examples: oil (the oi letters make a unique sound) and oy as in oyster (the oy make a unique sound also). These sounds are not like the individual letters or like a short or long vowel sound would make.

Another problem in sound/symbol relationships are words governed by a final "r". Notice the following words: fir, fur, fer, a syllable as in transfer. The first word "fir" refers to a fir tree. The second "fur" refers to the hair on an animal, such as "The dog had shaggy fur". The third "fer" is common as a suffix to many words. Sometimes, there are no governing principles in analyzing an unknown word. With the sight method in oral cooperative reading by pupils and the teacher, an unknown word becomes a known word. The following words, for example, follow a spelling pattern, but their individual pronunciations certainly do not: though, through, tough, bough, cough and dough. These words are spelled in an irregular manner and must be learned as sight words, even though a spelling pattern is there.

We generally oppose in teaching phonics prior to the time it is needed. To be functional, phonics should be taught when the need arises. Thus, when a pupil is reading silently or orally, he/she may need assistance on word identification. There is that teachable moment in time when a pupil might well benefit from selected phonics learnings. Thus, if a pupil is reading. "The Henry family liked to take—during holidays", the pupil may not know the word in the blank space. When using context clues, there are many words that would fit in according to meaning theory. The words that do not begin with the correct initial consonant can then be eliminated. If the pupil does not know the sound that goes along with the initial consonant letter, he/she may now be taught the grapheme/phoneme correspondence.

There is another suitable time to teach phonics and that is when learners may see patterns pertaining to the word not identified in oral or silent reading. Not always, of course, are there patterns in evidence. But, when a pupil does not identify the word "soil" in reading, he/she may be assisted to notice words which pattern such as boil, toil and spoil. The patterns approach has helped many pupils to identify unknown words when reading. Then too, a pupil who does not identify the word "soil" when reading may be asked to give other words that begin like "s" or end like "I". Why is this important? The teacher may then appraise if the pupil can see and hear these phonemes/graphemes.

The question always arises as to the teaching of phonics to pupils who truly cannot hear sounds. A colleague of one of us as a sophomore in college in teacher education could not hear sounds. He was an avid reader and comprehended well. At the time he was doing student teaching during his sophomore year for a sixty hour certificate, he was called down during a lesson taught. The calling down occurred in front of pupils being taught.

The student teacher had stated in the elementary school class that a vowel sound in reading was long when actually it was a short vowel sound. A colleague felt very badly for this happening and was ready to quit student teaching. At the last moment he decided to continue and be certified with a sixty hour certificate for teaching. This colleague had taught for forty-two years at the same time he was dying of cancer. His teaching was done on the fifth and sixth grade levels where phonics instruction in reading was minimal. He seemed to have done well as a classroom teacher. This teacher should no doubt rely very heavily upon whole language approaches when teaching pupils. This might not always be possible when the pendulum swings to a heavy dose of phonics for all pupils. One thing my colleague did during his teaching years was to mark vowel sounds carefully before each day of teaching. He checked with a dictionary as to the accuracy of the making.

Basic Principles in Teaching Phonics

There are basic principles that teachers should adhere to when teaching phonics to primary and intermediate grade pupils.

1. Pupils should be ready for the new lessons to be taught. This would include learners having an attention span adequate in duration. They should be able to hear likenesses and differences in sound.
2. Pupils should experience lessons in phonics that are taught in an interesting manner. This would mean that drill would be greatly minimized and stimulating games would receive primary emphasis in the teaching of phonics.
3. Pupils need to experience sequence in ongoing lessons and units of study. One of the most important factors in teaching is that pupils perceive learning activities as being sequentially more difficult and yet readiness is there for attaining goals in phonics instruction.
4. Pupils need to be attentive during the time phonics is taught. If pupils are not attentive, they will not benefit from ongoing instruction. A teaching strategy needs to be in evidence whereby pupils develop and maintain their attentiveness.
5. Pupils should experience success in learning. If pupils experience failure, the chances are they will not benefit much from phonics instruction.
6. Pupils should receive feedback on how well they are achieving in phonics instruction. In this way, pupils know what they need to concentrate on in phonics lessons.

7. The teacher needs to monitor pupil progress in phonics. Thus, there are indications that pupils are achieving and learning if careful monitoring is done.
8. Pupils need to use what has been learned in phonics; otherwise phonics may be learned for its own sake. The only reason for teaching phonics is for pupils to become capable readers and spellers. Knowledge needs to be used and application made to new situations encountered.
9. Pupils need to assist each other in learning about and using phonics in reading instruction.
10. Pupils should appraise themselves personally to notice progress in phonics knowledge acquired and application made.
11. Teachers need to evaluate themselves to notice what pupils have achieved and work for improved instruction.
12. Objectives chosen for phonics instruction need to be relevant and achievable by learners.
13. Learning opportunities in phonics should provide for individual differences regardless of ability levels and socio-economic status.
14. Evaluation techniques should be aligned with the stated objectives so that the objectives provide direction for instruction.
15. The phonics program needs to be assessed frequently and modified to provide the best instruction possible for each pupil.

We need to emphasize again that phonics should be taught as a means to an end, not an end in and of itself. The end being to produce readers who enjoy reading and like to solve problems through the act of reading.

Philosophies of Phonics Instruction

There are diverse philosophies of education stating how phonics should be taught. One philosophy stresses the basics idea whereby there is essential information that needs to be taught to all pupils. Phonics is conceived to be the basics by selected authors in education as well as teachers. These individuals believe that phonics is rather consistent between symbol and sound. Thus, the grapheme/phoneme correspondence makes it so that teachers can be certain that consistencies do exist between symbol and sound as pupils learn to read.

Advocates of the basics believe that there is a core of phonics principles and generalizations that pupils should learn and use. More people then would learn to read then ever before, according to advocates. A strong scope in phonics needs to be identified. The scope or breadth of phonics content to be taught needs to be identified. Specialists in phonics instruction should be on committees to choose what is silent to teach pertaining to phonics. These phonics learnings might be graded so that pupils and parents would know what the minimal level of achievement should be for pupils to achieve on a grade level or at the end of a semester. The determining of when phonics objectives should be emphasized in teaching stresses the concept of sequence. Thus, there are phonics objectives that would be taught on the kindergarten, first and/or second grade level. There are teachers who emphasize a very strong program of phonics with a well developed scope and sequence.

Reasons given for a strong program in scope and sequence in phonics are the following:

1. The English alphabet is rather consistent in stressing each grapheme (symbol) equals a phoneme (sound).
2. The key to success in reading is becoming an independent reader and that is through the study and use of phonics.
3. Once the graphemes/phonemes have been mastered, pupils can do more and more independent reading.
4. Pupils can enjoy ideas in reading when studying and using phonics. It is not an either/or situation such as either studying and using phonics versus obtaining ideas and enjoying reading.
5. Phonics instruction can be made enjoyable with games and stimulating exercises. The teacher may use a phonics text or workbook in teaching and still promote pupils interest in learning to read.

There seems to be general agreement that good auditory and visual discrimination are pre-requisites for learning sound-symbol relationships. We know that children must be able to distinguish one letter from another and one sound from another before they can associate a given letter with a specific sound. Visual discrimination refers to the ability to distinguish likenesses from differences among letters and auditory discrimination refers to the ability to distinguish likenesses and differences among sounds. To achieve these skills, children must first understand the concepts of like and different among forms. Also to achieve auditory discrimination, children must first have phonemic awareness or the awareness that speech is composed of separate sounds (phonemes). They must be able to hear sounds with words or they will be unable to form mental connections between sounds and letters (as quoted in Burns, Ross and Roe, 1996).

Somewhat toward the opposite end of the continuum, there are teachers who believe in holism, only, in the teaching of reading. They stress pupils reading the entire story or reading selection without having lessons on phonics. These teachers believe that phonics instruction destroys interest in reading. Thus, pupils with teacher assistance should read the selection together. In this way, all pupils can orally read the content and identify all words. Re-reading is also stressed so that pupils and the teacher read over again the same selection. Generally stories chosen are quite predictable in that pupils have some idea of what will occur in sequence. Predictability of content assists pupils to ascertain what the unknown words are in pronunciation and in meaning.

Individualized reading is a holistic approach in reading instruction. The teacher here needs to have a rather large supply of library books from which each pupil will select sequential content to read. Learners generally select sequential books to read that are interesting and on their own unique reading level. Positive attitudes should be an important and on their individual reading level. After the completion of reading a library book, a conference is held with the teacher to determine comprehension and reading skills of the pupil. Attention is paid to phonics individually or in a committee when pupils reveal a need for help. It is important to notice that pupils reveal help needed as they read orally to the teacher a chosen selection. Assistance is provided pupils then as the need arises in reading and not before any selection is to be read.

Reasons given for using whole language approaches in teaching phonics within a quality reading program are the following:

1. Pupils learn phonetic elements within context as library books are read and holistic procedures in reading are emphasized.
2. Ideas acquired are the major ingredients of a good reading program for pupils. With interest and purpose in reading, the pupil hurdles many difficulties in reading, including associating sounds with symbols.
3. Pupils need to read to become better readers, not study phonics for its own sake.
4. The whole is greater (content in reading) than the sum of the parts (phonics).
5. Phonics is a tool to be used to obtain ideas from reading, not an end in and of itself.

In a psychological reading curriculum which is child cantered, the pupil is strongly involved in a selecting objectives, learning opportunities, and evaluation procedures. This is the heart of a pupils centered curriculum in reading. Humanism as a psychology of learning is then being emphasized. A humane reading curriculum, according to its advocates, stresses the individual learner being involved in decision making in the reading curriculum. The pupil is at the center of developing the reading curriculum (Ediger, 1997).

Behaviourism and the Reading Curriculum

Behaviourism a psychology has had much influence in education. With behaviourism, objectives for pupil achievement are stated prior to instruction and in measurable terms. Teachers can even announce prior to teaching what pupils are to learn from the lesson. It is very precisely written in the objective as to what each pupil is to learn. The learning activities are aligned with the objectives. The teacher then ultimately measures, after instruction, what pupils have achieved that was stated in the objectives. A pupil either achieves or does not achieve an objective since each is stated very precisely. Reasons given for using behaviourally stated objectives in teaching are the following:

1. Learning standards are written with precision so there is certainly in knowing what pupils are to learn or have learned.
2. Careful selection is given to objectives when each is very important and carefully defined in measurable terms.
3. Clarity is involved when communicating pupil results to parents. The results can be given in numerical terms.
4. Much attention can be paid to sequencing of objectives so that pupils experience as much success in learning as possible.
5. Pupils may receive continuous feedback on how well they are achieving.

Phonics objectives for pupil attainment may be stated precisely or behaviourally. Careful selection of phonetic elements to be taught needs to be inherent in the stated objectives. A good teaching strategy needs to be in the offing so that pupils may achieve the sequential objectives. The teacher ultimately appraises pupil achievement to notice if objectives have been achieved.

In Conclusion

There are numerous decisions to make in the teaching of reading. First, which objectives should pupils achieve? There are implications here for stressing holistic approaches in teaching of reading versus analytical procedures. The objectives chosen will reflect one's beliefs pertaining to the teaching of reading. Under which conditions do pupils learn to read best? Second, which learning opportunities should be selected so that pupils will achieve the stated objectives. This includes the role of the basal textbook in the teaching of reading. In addition to basals, there are many other materials in reading instruction as learning opportunities such as the use of CD ROMS, computer packages (drill and practice, tutorial, games, simulations and diagnostic approaches), Big Books, picture books, library books, encyclopaedias, filmstrips and slides with accompanying print materials, among others.

Third, how should the reading curriculum be organized? There are numerous procedures available such as a separate subjects approach involving reading and literature only; correlation such as reading/language arts and social studies taught as being related; fused curriculum such as reading/language arts, social studies, science and mathematics, taught as being related. The inter-disciplinary reading curriculum integrates subject matter from all disciplines of knowledge. Problem solving procedures are best to use in inter-disciplinary approaches in instruction. Regardless of the academic disciplines, the subject matter is used which assists in solving a problem.

The role of the reading teacher is to stimulate pupils to identify problems within the framework of a stimulating environment. After a problem has been clearly identified, related information is gathered to solve the identified problem. ... Based on the data, a hypothesis is developed in answer to the problem. The hypothesis needs to be specific so that it can be tested. The hypothesis is tentative, not an absolute. With further reading experiences, as well as use of audio-visual activities, the pupil with teacher guidance tests the hypothesis. The hypothesis, as a result of testing, may be accepted as is, refuted, or modified. ... Problem solving skills are usable in all curriculum areas, as well as in the societal arena.

Curiosity of the learner is salient when he/she selects a library book to read. With curiosity, interest accrues. Interest in a particular topic may well spur pupils on to a greater desire to read (Ediger, 1997).

Fourth, how should pupil achievement be evaluated? There are many techniques to use in evaluating pupil progress in reading. These include standardized and norm referenced tests, teacher written tests, teacher observation, anecdotal records, checklists and rating scales, pupil self-evaluation, as well as peer appraisal. The purpose of evaluation is to determine how well the pupil achieving in reading. A philosophy of constructivism in evaluation may also be emphasized in that pupils reveal in context what has been achieved in word recognition techniques and in comprehension. This can provide feedback to the teacher and the pupil in deciding upon what he/she needs to emphasize as objectives.

A quality reading program then stress the following:

1. Each pupil begins at a point where he/she is ready to achieve as optimally as possible.
2. The learner experiences continual progress successfully in reading.
3. The four vocabularies—listening, speaking, reading and writing—are integrated in a quality reading program.
4. Word recognition skills, such as phonics, syllabication, context clues and structural analysis, are taught within a framework of interesting content to be read.
5. Major emphasis is placed upon reading literature, not analyzing words into component parts.
6. Multimedia approaches are used to motivate pupils so that an inward desire in learning to read inherent.
7. Problem solving, critical and creative thinking, as well as application are salient concepts stressed in teaching reading.
8. The best sequence is used to guide each pupil toward optimum achievement in reading.
9. Learning to read as a life time endeavour is stressed.
10. The use of relevant research results is important in the teaching of reading (Ediger, 1997).

REFERENCES

Burns, Paul C., Betty D. Roe and Elinor Ross (1996), *Teaching Reading in Today's Elementary Schools*. Boston: Houghton Mifflin Company, 114.

Ediger, Marlow (1997), *Teaching Reading and the Language Arts in the Elementary School*. Kirksville, Missouri: Simpson Publishing Company, 32.

Ediger, Marlow (1997), *Teaching Reading and the Language Arts*. Kirksville, Missouri: Simpson Publishing Company, 37.

Ediger, Marlow (1997), "Perspectives in Teaching Reading", *Reading Improvement*. 34 (2), 52-53.

Van Den Broek, Paul (1996), "On Becoming Literate: The Many Sources of Success and Failure in Reading", *the first R. every child's right to read*, Graves, Van Den Broek and Taylor, (Editors), 193.

20

Vocabulary Development and the Language Arts

Developing a rich listening, speaking, reading and writing vocabulary is important in all curriculum areas. In the reading curriculum, in particular, a quality vocabulary needs to be achieved by each pupil. One reason that pupils do not read well is that they do not possess a functional vocabulary for reading. Enriching and developing pupil vocabularies should be a major goal in each academic disciplines. The following are reasons for teachers guiding learners to possess a rich vocabulary:

1. Subject matter and ideas are expressed with more clarity and accuracy.
2. Proficiency in the work place might well depend upon individuals having a quality vocabulary.
3. Individuals seemingly have more prestige if their listening, speaking, reading and writing vocabularies and adequately developed.
4. Greater enjoyment of reading is in the offing if a person has a rich functional vocabularies.
5. Vocabulary development is salient in problem solving. A person with a rich vocabulary should have a better opportunity to develop his/her vocabularies.
6. Conversations carried on with other persons require a rich vocabulary. There needs to be an appropriate number of words used that carry intended meanings.
7. Variety in selecting words to convey accurate meanings is necessary in speaking and writing, the outgoes of the language arts.
8. Use of diverse terms and concepts in speaking and writing adds variety to quality communication. Vocabulary

development becomes a tool to take in, such as listening and reading, as well as provide communication to others within the framework of speaking and writing.

Very closely related to the background knowledge required for reading a text is vocabulary knowledge. ... By about the third grade and certainly by the fourth grade, most of the selections of the newer reading programs are drawn from independently published materials, as compared to selections created by a publisher for inclusion in their series. The newer basals are virtually anthologies. Authors of the selections are professional writers using the best words available from the general vocabulary to communicate their ideas. Thus, the kind of vocabulary control found in the older basals is not in evidence in current programs. The sophisticated vocabulary in the selections from the newer basals has both positive and negative potential for students. The negative potential is obvious—too many unfamiliar words will cause comprehension problems. The positive potential is also obvious—children can add words to their store of vocabulary.

Vocabulary development strategies for each story lesson begin with the identification of a subset of words that developers believe may cause meaning or decoding difficulty. These words are listed in the teacher's manuals. By the third or fourth grade the programs assume competent decoding: most of the words noted in the teacher's manuals are of the meaning variety difficulty. These words become "target words" for vocabulary development activities. Traditionally, the development of word meaning is attended to by instructional events that occur prior to reading, during reading and after reading. ... (Beck, 1984).

Developing the Vocabulary of Learners

The reading teacher needs to select quality objectives for pupils to achieve in the areas of vocabulary development. These objectives need to emphasize that is relevant and functional in vocabulary development. Certainly, pupils should be able to use what has been learned. Learning should not be for its own sake but rather be for personal use and application in society. Important vocabulary terms should be acquired by pupils. Adequate time must be given in choosing what pupils need to learn in vocabulary development. This cannot be hurried, because vocabulary development emphasizes that which must be learned in depth, not survey approaches.

Objectives pertaining to vocabulary development need to stress securing the interests of pupils in ongoing lessons and units of study. Ways of developing and maintaining pupil interest in learning must be emphasized in vocabulary studies. If pupils do not reveal interest in learning, they will not achieve as optimally as possible.

There needs to be objectives reflecting pupils working collaboratively. Within the cooperative endeavour, pupils listen to others and use oral communication with opportunities to achieve in vocabulary development. There are definite social goals here in that pupils need to learn to work harmoniously with others. And yet pupils also should be able to work by the self and achieve on an individual basis.

Vocabulary development emphasizes that pupils seek purpose in learning. Purposeful learning in vocabulary development means that pupils perceive reasons for learning. I think that one cannot stress too strongly that vocabulary development for pupils should have as a goal that purpose is involved in learning. Purposeful learnings have as a goal that pupils perceive the values inherent in vocabulary activities. If these values are lacking, the teacher should stress other vocabulary development lessons for learners.

Objectives in vocabulary development need to emphasize the importance of meaningful learnings. If meaning is lacking, the chances are pupils will memorize terms and concepts for testing purposes only or largely. Meaning stresses the importance of pupils understanding that which has been learned. Use cannot be made of a new vocabulary term unless understanding of prerequisites in vocabulary terms is prevalent. With prerequisites, background information is needed to attach meaning to vocabulary terms being studied.

Objectives in vocabulary development for pupils should emphasize pupils experiencing the concept of providing for individual differences. There are pupils who learn more rapidly that others while some pupils take more time to learn the same content/skills as written in the statement of objectives. Each pupil regardless of socio-economic level must be accepted as a human being and taught in a manner which provides for all pupils.

Learning Opportunities to Achieve Objectives

To achieve vital objectives in vocabulary development, the teacher needs to select worthwhile activities for pupils. These activities need to be selected carefully so that each pupil's achievement is as optimal as possible. Pupils should not be labeled as being fast, average, or slow learners. Rather all should be accepted and develop feelings of belonging to the group.

To achieve objectives in vocabulary development. We recommend selected learning opportunities that student teachers and cooperating teachers whom we supervise have used successfullv.

Each day the teacher should read aloud to pupils during story time. The book chosen should interest pupils and keep their attention. Voice inflection using proper stress, pitch and juncture should be in the offing when the teacher reads during story time. Word, should be pronounced clearly and accurately. The teacher should have good audience contact with listeners. For young children, it is especially good to show the book's illustrations to pupils as the library book is being read. Throughout the story time activity, pupils should understand an increased number of facts, concepts and generalizations. Knowledge received provides background information for more complex ideas that should be forthcoming. Knowledge is sequential and cumulative for learners. A love for learning by pupils might be a further end result when the teacher reads orally to pupils during story time.

A second activity stressed pupils discussing ideas obtained from listening to the library book read or from personal reading pursued. Through discussion participation, pupils should learn effective ways of working within a small or large group setting. Pupils should learn to be polite, accepting and cooperative in the discussion learning activity. Being a good listener, valuing the thinking of others and actively participating in a polite manner should help a discussion to move forward in quality. Thus, the processes of being a member of a discussion group need to be emphasized continuously.

Then too, during the discussion, pupils should achieve quality ideas, facts, concepts and generalizations. Learners need to stay on the topic to achieve subject matter learnings during a discussion. Straying from the topic at hand merely wastes time. Ideas need to circulate within the group so that all have opportunities to participate. Active participation by each pupils should be an objective. Use of language during a discussion helps pupils to achieve more optimally in speaking. This translates content acquired to be used to comprehend subject matter in reading. The content and vocabulary gained by the learner might then provide background information for reading. Generally, what pupils are able to discuss represents meaningful subject matter. The subject matter might then provide the necessary knowledge, prior to reading, which helps pupils to understand increasingly complex vocabulary read.

Third, it is good to have once or more listening centers in the classroom. There are excellent cassette tapes related to an ongoing lesson on unit of study. Information gleaned from listening to a tape may guide pupils to answer related questions contained at the center. The information might well assist pupils to use this as background content to understand better what will be read from a basal or library book.

At the listening center, pupils may choose sequential tapes to listen to, for a variety of purpose. These purposes might well be the following in listening for:

1. Facts, concepts and generalizations.
2. Information to use in problem solving.
3. Critical thinking purposes such as separating facts from opinions, accurate from inaccurate information and fantasy from reality.
4. Opportunities to do creative thinking in the reading curriculum such as coming up with novel, unique ideas and originality in thought.
5. Obtaining directions in reaching a certain place.
6. Securing a main idea when relating facts, concepts and generalizations.
7. Obtaining the setting of a story.
8. Securing ideas pertaining to characterization within a writing.
9. Determining the plot of a selection in reading.
10. Understanding the theme of the speaker.

Fifth, the reading teacher needs to have one or more speaking centers in the classroom. Listening (discussed above) and speaking are interrelated. We will mention some activities here that emphasize speaking more than listening.

1. Giving oral reports on library books read, related directly to the ongoing lesson and unit of study being taught. The oral report should follow good sequence in content presented. The ideas need to be presented clearly and at an appropriate rate of speed so that listening comprehension is optimal. The pupil presenting the oral book report needs to have the content well in mind. An outline, in proper form, should be used to convey the contents therein. The presenter of the book report should have good eye contact with the audience. Reading for enjoyment and for solving problems are two purposes in having pupils become proficient in reading.
2. Having pupils video-tape their individual oral book reports given to the class. Here, pupils individually or with a peer may appraise the quality of the oral report given. Standards used to appraise may be the same as under number two above. The contents of the videotape may also evaluate distracting mannerisms of the speaker such as rubbing the nose excessively. It is good to have the presenter appraise the quality of his/her own oral report in terms of quality standards. Vocabulary terms are developed from the reading of library books as well as from the oral presentations given of library book content.

3. Interacting with audio-visual materials to locate information for problem solving. The AV materials may include videotapes, CD ROMS, films, filmstrips, large illustrations, snapshots enlarged for class viewing with an opaque projector, internet and worldwide web, as well as computer packages. Among others. With pupil interaction with AV materials of instruction, there are many opportunities to gather information for a committee project such as developing a mural. The mural must be planned cooperatively with all participating and no one dominating collaborative endeavours. After the planning, the implementation of the plan comes in sequence. With implementation, each pupil on the committee does his/her fair share of the work. The project represents the best work each pupil can do. Thus, neatness, accuracy and attractiveness becomes key ingredients when appraising the mural. Art work correlates well with reading. Through art, pupils may reveal what has been learned. Vocabulary development is definitely inherent in planning, implementing and appraising the project.

Sixth, ample emphasis should be placed upon pupils doing much writing. With writing, pupils read their own written products as well as read those of other learners whose works are posted on the bulletin board. Reading and writing cannot be separated from each other but are complimentary. There are numerous forms of written work that pupils may engage in. Journal entries should be written freely to indicate what had been learned in a given lesson. Diary entries may be written each day and should be dated. These diary entries portray what pupils learned for a day. As pupils write these diary entries, they read written content. In this way pupils also review that which was learned previously from reading and re-reading diary entries covering subject matter learned. Additional written work may include in following:

1. Logs—logs summarize what was contained in diary entries for one week. Clarity of ideas and proper sequence is important in writing logs.
2. Book reports—these relate to an ongoing lesson or unit of study. Meaningfully content in an appropriate order must be inherent in the written work.
3. Outlines—here proper style needs to be used such as Roman numerals to indicate main ideas, capital letters in sequence to indicate subordinate ideas and Hindu-Arabic numerals to reveal details. The subordinate ideas relate directly to the main ideas whereas the details tell more about the subordinate

content. Outlines are very helpful to use in giving a report on a certain topic to classmates. Thus, the oral report will have improved sequence to ideas presented as well as if the pupil forgets certain ideas, the outline is there to aid memory in oral communication.

3. Poems—poetry written in any lesson should relate to an ongoing lesson or unit of study. There are opportunities for pupils to write poetry in each curriculum area. There can be unrhymed verse written such as free verse. Or poetry written may contain rhyme such as couplets, triplets, quatrains and limericks. Poetry written may also include a selected number of syllables per line such as Haiku (5-7-5 syllables for each of three sequential lines). Tanka contains 5-7-5-7-7 syllables per line for each of five lines.

It is quite obvious that there are many writing opportunities for pupil pertaining to each curriculum area and within each lesson taught. Pupils engage in much reading, re-reading and proofreading when engaging in writing experiences. Vocabulary development opportunities are numerous.

Seventh, pupils may engage in developing a dictionary. Even though there are pictured dictionaries, grade level dictionaries, unabridged dictionaries, as well as glossaries in basal textbooks, it can be highly profitable for pupils individually or in committees to develop their very own dictionaries. Why? Perhaps, there are many new words brought into the lesson or unit of study by the teacher. It is good to alphabetize these new words and write meaningful definitions for each. Dictionary entries need to be functional so that they may be used as needed to obtain contextual information. It is good for pupils to be able to alphabetize and re-read the necessary entries.

Eighth, pupils and the teacher should engage in story telling activities. Content for the story needs to follow a certain order to be meaningful to the listener. Thus, sequence of ideas in story telling is important! A clear speaking voice with proper enunciation helps the oral presentation to be more effective. Having a pleasant speaking voice with quality eye contact with listeners assists in the communication of the story. When pupils hear stories told, especially pertaining to a specific library book at an interest center, interest in reading that book tends to be generated. Background experiences are also developed within pupils for reading additional books in ongoing lessons and units of study.

When engaging in story telling, pupils should be developing poise and gracefulness in the process. Pupils need ample opportunities to appear before others in informal and formal experiences. No doubt, skills and attitudes are being developed here that will have life-long values and worth. Shy pupils, in particular, need to appear before others in a variety of roles so that feelings of poise and worth are inherent. The confidence that can come from these experiences might well have carry over values to other endeavours.

Tenth, reading co-operatively in small groups can provide much enjoyment and interest in literature. Being with others is a favourite leaning style of selected individuals. They prefer to work together rather than working on an individual basis. Pupils too receive practice in reading. Cumulative practice should make for increased knowledge, skills and attitudes toward reading. With co-operative reading, three or four pupils may take turns reading a library book. If one copy only of a library book is available, sequential pupils may read aloud as the others in the group listen carefully to the contents. The contents may also be tape recorded so that individual pupils may re-read the library book. Then, if a word is not known in identification, the recorded voice provides the needed information.

If multiple copies of a library book are available, the small group of three or four pupils may follow along in their own library book as the sequential oral reading takes places. Thus, one person reads aloud as the others in the committee follow along in their own library book. Shared reading experiences has many intrinsic rewards for pupils. There should also be ample opportunities for those who like individual endeavours to read a book by themselves.

Eleventh, there should be many objects and items at an interest center whereby pupils may discuss each. I have observed many aquariums and terrariums in classrooms which provide stimulating situations for pupils to provide content for an experience chart. Sometimes a teacher has numerous potten plants in the classroom which may provide pupils an opportunity for informal conversation and also ideas for an experience chart. A rich learning environment helps pupils to think about the contents. The resulting ideas assist pupils to use oral language, engage in written work, read about similar situations or subject matter and/or listen to the thinking of others. A stimulating environment needs to be in the offing so that pupils have purposes for engaging in reading and language arts activities. For example, on the early primary grade level, pupils may observe and experience objects on an interest center. They may then provide content to the teacher who is return prints in neat manuscript letters what pupils have said and discussed. After the write-up of the contents, the pupils with the teacher pointing to words and phrases being read may comprehend the ideas presented into his experience chart. This approach is sound in that:

1. Pupils have the background information to begin with by looking at and discussing objects at the center.
2. Pupils presented ideas for the experience chart. Learners then have chances to speak and to listen to others. What is said should be meaningful since it is based upon personal experiences of pupils. When the teacher points to words and phrases, he/she together with pupils read orally content from the experience chart. Here, young learners should be developing an enriched vocabulary with a larger basic sight vocabulary. These sight words become the building blocks for future reading activities. The contents of the experience chart may be re-read as pupils desire. Many pupils like to read over again what has been read previously. Practice here assists pupils to retain basic sight words better than would otherwise be the base.

Twelfth, a quality spelling program should help pupils to become better readers. There are numerous places where spelling words in vocabulary development may come from for pupils to master. Individualized spelling stresses learners mastering a reasonable number of words that come from what was missed in spelling words correctly from every day writing occurrences. The teacher needs to decide here how many of these misspelled words can be spelled correctly within a week or whatever the designated time would be. Words may also come from a quality basal spelling text, new words in a lesson for pupils to master as listed in the basal reader, words that research states are important for pupils to master in spelling such as the Dolch list (1955). As pupils practice the correct spelling of words, they are becoming involved in vocabulary development and reading. Learners need to see print as often as feasible in order to become good readers. Spelling need not be dull and dry with memorization of words. Rather pupils should experience interesting activities by;

1. Using these words in writing letters to parents and friends, developing a related cross world puzzle and playing games with peers.
2. Working with peers in learning to spell words correctly. Co-operative learning may be a preferred style of learning for selected pupils.
3. Pantomiming the meaning of selected words. This could involve the playing of charades whereby a pupil chooses a word for spelling at random from a box, pantomimes it and

then asks others in the classroom to identify which word is involved.

4. Dramatizing the spelling word. A pupils may select a spelling word at random and use puppets or marionettes to dramatize its meaning. Classmates may guess what the spelling word is. Creative dramatics may also be used. Here, the pupil chooses a word at random from a box and uses words and actions to indicate which word is being focused upon. The word wanted is not mentioned orally in the creative dramatics presentation. Several pupils could also be involved in this activity.

How much of the spelling curriculum should stress inductive and how much deductive thinking? We would suggest a balance between the two approaches. Thus, when using a spelling textbook in teaching, the teacher assigns words for pupils to master. This is a deductive approach. Furthermore, the teacher has pupils learn a strategy for learning to spell these words such as:

1. Looking at the spelling word carefully.
2. Saying the word accurately.
3. Saying clearly the parts of the word, such as pronouncing each syllable carefully and accurately.
4. Writing the new word without looking at it.
5. Comparing the written word with that contained in the basal spelling textbook.

The teacher here is emphasizing a deductive method of spelling words correctly. Why is this a deductive approach? The teacher has determined what and how pupils are to learn.

An inductive approach stresses pupils being involved in curriculum development such as, pupils seeing how many homonyms or synonyms to find in a homonym/synonym hunt. Pupils might have suggested this activity when studying a unit containing a few of these words. Also, the teacher may have suggested the activity and pupils individually or on teams volunteered to see how many could be found. The sky is the limit in the number to be located. Perhaps, the teacher needs to have a balance between deductive versus inductive approaches in having pupils learn in the area of spelling. If a basal spelling text is used and there are a few rhyming words in a weekly list, pupils could locate additional ones to go along with those given in an inductive approach in learning. With a deductive procedure, the teacher may challenge gifted learners with additional words to master in spelling in addition to those listed in the text. By studying the correct spelling of words, pupils should increase their skills in vocabulary development and reading.

Thirteenth, we recommend pupils learn to spell relevant words contained in computer packages. There are drill and practice activities, tutorial, gaming and games, simulation and diagnostic/ remedial packages. Reading teachers need to evaluate each package carefully to determine which relevant words in spelling pupils should master. Use should be made of spelling words for retention to take place. Spelling words may be used to write:

1. Friendly and business letters.
2. Notices, announcements, plays, reports, poems and stories.
3. Names and addresses.
4. Birthday greetings and holiday messages.
5. Notes of sympathy and condolence.

As pupils participate in these writing activities, they need to proof-read content. The skills of reading are very much in evidence then. The spelling curriculum should be based upon words that pupils need to learn to spell. The needs of pupils are very important when developing any curriculum area. Beyond the goals of learning to spell words correctly are skills in reading for a variety of purposes that should be upper most in the minds of learners. Narrative, expository and creative writing should all be emphasized in ongoing lessons and units of study. Vocabulary development is an essential part in any listening, speaking, achieve as optimally as possible in vocabulary development and its related component—reading.

What then should be guidelines to use in assisting pupils in vocabulary development?

1. Word study should be integrated with prior knowledge and with learning in the content areas.
2. Word study should involve intensive "deep" study of some words, involving many exposures to the words in meaningful contexts, both in and out of texts.
3. Teachers should engage in direct teaching or modelling, talking explicitly about word meaning and structure.
4. Students should be actively involved in instruction; an important side effect of this involvement is the development of favourable attitudes toward words and word learning.
5. Students should be taught strategies for learning new words independently.
6. Teachers should introduce words in meaning "families" so that semantic and structural relationships among the words are made explicit.

These principles are more applicable at the intermediate grade levels and beyond, when student's cognitive development has advanced to the point where they can explicitly deal with increasing conceptual abstraction. Nonetheless, you will see aspects of these principles at work; in work study at the primary grade level as well .... (Templeton, 1997).

In Conclusion

There are numerous opportunities for pupils to engage in vocabulary development. Each curriculum area provides these learning activities to increase proficiency in the use of vocabulary terms. The teacher needs to establish objectives, learning opportunities and evaluation procedures within individual academic areas to guide pupils in acquiring a rich listening, speaking, reading and writing vocabulary. The objectives of instruction need to stress relevant, functional words for pupils to master. Learning opportunities in vocabulary development should assist pupils to achieve the stated objectives. These activities need to be interesting, purposeful and meaningful. Evaluation procedures to appraise learner performance in achieving objectives need to be valid, reliable, varied and encourage further learning.

Ayyappan (1997) listed the following sequence in vocabulary development:

The confrontation phase emphasize the teacher presenting relevant data pertaining to the concepts as well as important related definitions. Students then generate questions pertaining to the concept or vocabulary term. Phase two is the concept information phase. Here, students compare the attributes given and relate them to form the concept of vocabulary terms taught. Learners discuss with other pupils the distinguishing features to identify the concept.

In phase three, the teacher obtains responses from pupils in a stimulating discussion. Pupils then identify similarities and differences from the information presented. Pupils hypotheses are then appraised involving the tentative concept. In phase four stressing the concept development phase, the teacher presents related tasks for pupils to complete pertaining to the concept stressed. Probing of pupils knowledge pertaining to a concept is important. References are also made to the textbook while discussing the concept. The major classroom interactions are:

1. Teacher interaction/introduction/information.
2. Activities for pupils include media interaction, consulting text, and peer interaction whereas feedback includes evaluation and teacher interaction (Ayyappan 1997).

One of the finest procedures in vocabulary development, one of us have observed in supervising student teachers and cooperating teachers, was the Hilda Taba inductive method used with a class of sixth grades. Here, the two teachers had pupils view a filmstrip on *Life on a Manor*. The teachers, after having pupils view the contents in the filmstrip, asked:

1. Tell us in a single word or phrase what you learned from watching the filmstrip. The following responses were given by pupils; castles, moats, draw bridge, the mill for grinding grain, oxen pilling a plow, peasants cutting wheat by hand, peasant cottages, the three field approach in farming, fallow, boblemen, tournaments, page, knight, guilds, apprentice, master and wars.
2. How would you combine or join together the concepts you mentioned for number one above? Here, a variety of answers were given in and for an open-ended question. One grouping of vocabulary terms given by pupils was the following:
   Oxen pulling a plow, peasants curring wheat by hand, the three field approach in farming and fallow were joined together.
3. What name would you give to the joined together vocabulary terms? The answer provided was "cultivating the soil".

REFERENCES

Ayyappan, R. (1997), *Concept Development in Electronics at Higher Secondary Level*. Coimbatore, India: Bharathiar University, Ph.D. thesis.

Templeton, Shane (1997), *Teaching the integrated Language Arts*, Second Edition, Boston: Houghton Mifflin Company, 287-88.

21

Patterns and Structure of the English Language

Students need to learn the involved patterns of sentences in the English language as well as the inherent structure. Learning subject matter through the perception of order and modified change makes it more interesting and easier to learn. Students then first of all should sequentially learn sentence patterns as they progress through the public school years. These sentence patterns may be made quite lifelike and meaningful to students.

Sentence Patterns

There are approximately five sentence patterns in English although there is not universal agreement on this. A first sentence pattern to consider is the subject predicate pattern. This pattern may be shown with two words such as, "Dogs bark." Seeing an actual dog doing this is certainly within reality. Or, a student playing the role of a dog and then doing a bark can provide a model for the subject predicate pattern. Illustrated scenes may be drawn or cut out from magazines to show, "Dogs bark." The dramatizations, the drawings, and/or cutting out illustrations may be viewed first and then students describe and write what is happening in each situation.

After seeing the sentence on the chalkboard, students may give a different subject such as cats, owls, and turkeys. They will usually respond with cats, owls, and turkeys do not bark. This provides opportunities for vocabulary growth. Students may say that cats meow, owls hoot, turkeys gobble. And this is correct. The subject predicate pattern of sentence still stands.

Other words may be given for "bark" in the sentence "Dogs bark," like "howl," "grumble," and "pant." However, the sentence pattern still stays the same with the subject predicate pattern. By playing with words in forming sentence patterns, the student creatively is learning about new words, terms, vocabulary, and arrangements.

A second sentence pattern emphasizes the subject—predicate—direct object pattern, as in "The boy ate candy." The question may be raised by students as to which word is the predicate. At this point, the predicate is the action word in the sentence. The only word which deals with an action here is "ate". The subject part of the sentence is relatively easy to determine; thus, the student may ask the question, "*Who* art?" The answer is "boy." "Boy ate" then forms the skeleton of the sentence. Additional words may be given in place of "boy," such as girl, man, woman, and Dan, among others. Words which students may provide in place of "ate" are swallowed, chewed, loved, and disliked. Next, students may give words which take the place of "candy." The sentence pattern still stays the same, being the subject—predicate—direct object pattern. The question learners may now raise pertains to how does one determine the direct object. The answer is, "The boy ate *what*? The word needed here would be *candy*. There is one word left in the sentence—The boy ate candy. This word is "The." The article "the" would not need to be discussed here unless students desire to do so and are ready for the concept of "the being an article. An article here answers the question of *which* boy. It could be "This," "That," or "A" boy. Articles, at this point, need not be discussed when thinking of sentence patterns; however student questions cannot and must not be ignored. Words supplied to change the subject, predicate, and/or direct object should come from the student. An inductive approach in learning should be stressed. Responses to questions then come form learners. Questions from students should also be invited freely and continuously. A stimulating and challenging learning environment needs to be in he offing. Whatever is taught must be sequential and learners need to be *ready* for each new concept and generalization taught (Ediger, 1999, Chapter Eight).

Third, the subject—predicate—predicate adjective sentence pattern may be taught such as, The girl is tall." Here, a linking verb "is" is used. There are few linking verbs so that students can master these in a short time. The following are commonly used linking verbs—is, are, am, was, were. Lining verbs in a predicate adjective sentence pattern join together the subject of the sentence with an adjective, such as "The men were joyful." The word "joyful" is an adjective in that it describes the subject "men." Thus, what kind of men were they? They were *joyful* men, not sad nor unhappy. Students tend to enjoy providing different words for the subject, the linking verb, and the predicate adjective. Scenes here may be drawn and illustrated pertaining to the subject, linking verb, and the predicate adjective sentence pattern.

A fourth sentence emphasizes the subject, linking verb, and predicate noun pattern, such as "The man is a golfer." The linking verb joins the subject and the noun which means and refers to the same person. Thus, man = golfer and the latter follows the linking verb. As homework, students and their parents could think together about reality situations whereby one = the other, such as man = truckdriver, woman = secretary, and boy = player. These words may then be joined together in a subject—linking verb—predicate noun sentence pattern.

A fifth sentence pattern stresses the subject—predicate—indirect object—direct object pattern. This sentence pattern is very similar to the subject—predicate—direct object pattern such as "Ray sent a letter," An indirect object may be added to this sentence such as "Ray sent Bill a letter." Indirect objects answer the question "to whom?" Thus, Ray sent *what*? The answer is "letter," To whom was the letter sent? The answer is "Bill." Very often on gift giving occasions, students will use sentences such as following, containing an indirect object:

1. Arthur gave John a toy *car* for his birthday present.
2. Marie presented Anne a *doll* for a Christmas gift.
3. Ben gave Jody a candy *heart* for Valentine's Day (Ediger and Rao, 2000, Chapter Seven).

The above named five sentences patterns are the most common of all in the English language, although there is not perfect agreement on this.

Highly practical uses may be made of different sentence patterns. Students need to have ample opportunities to write using the different sentence patterns. There are a plethora of writing activities which may be emphasized to incorporate sentence pattern use. These include the following:

1. Prose and poetry.
2. Birthdays and announcements.
3. Plays and dramas.
4. Diaries and logs.
5. Outlines, summaries, and precis' writing.
6. Evaluations, opinions, and letters to the editor.
7. Business and friendly letters.
8. Note taking in class, writing on hobbies, and informing others on plans for specific holidays.
9. Assessment of ideas in an ongoing classroom experience.

10. Minutes taken of a club meeting or organisation (Ediger, 1997, 114-117).

Modifiers to Extend Sentences

Sentences are bare indeed if the skeleton only, is written as in the following:

1. The boy ran (subject predicate pattern).
2. Larry caught the ball (subject—predicate—direct object pattern).
3. The roses are beautiful (subject—predicate/linking verb—predicate adjective pattern).
4. Judy is a singer (subject—predicate/linking verb—predicate noun pattern).
5. Alice taught Mary a song (subject—predicate—indirect object—direct object pattern).

There is need then to add modifiers to make sentences more meaningful and inclusive. One form of modification which may be used is adjectives, other than predicate adjectives which are a part of the skeleton of a sentence. Thus, adjectives modify or change meanings within a sentence. In sentence pattern number one, immediately above, there are words which can provide a more accurate and thorough meaning of the word boy, such as what kind of boy is he? The following adjectives modify "boy:" tall, kind, active, short, and slender. Phrases, as a group of sequential words, may, also be used as adjectives, as in the following underlined part: The boy *with the blue trousers* ran. "With the blue trousers" modifies the word boy and tells more about him.

In addition to adjectives, adverbs may modify verbs, adjectives, and other adverbs, such as in sentence pattern number two above "Larry caught the ball," Larry caught *How*? slowly, gently, rapidly, and eagerly. Here, an adverb modifies a verb. Phrases may also be used as adverbs as in the following telling *how* Larry caught the ball:

1. By leaping in the air.
2. By making a shoe string catch.
3. Without effort (Ediger, 1977, 49-51).

Appositives may be used to expand sentences in the following way using sentence pattern number three above: The roses, plants around the yard, and beautiful. Here, roses equals plants. *Plants* is then in apposition with roses. In sentence pattern number four above, Judy is a singer, several added appositives expand the sentence and information pertaining to Judy:

1. Judy, a teacher, is a singer. Judy equals teacher and the word teacher is an appositive with no verb in between.

2. Judy, a local artist, is a singer. Judy equals artist which is an appositive.
3. Judy, an entertainer of long standing, is a singer. Judy equals entertainer.

Clauses, might also expand a sentence and provide additional information about a topic, person, or event. From sentence pattern number five with a subject, predicate, indirect object, and direct object (Alice taught Mary a song), a compound sentence can be in evidence by adding another independent clause: Jane played the piano. The two independent clauses then become a compound sentence: Alice taught Mary a song, and Jane played the piano. The conjunction "and" joins two equal value clauses, both being independent, and each will stand meaningful by itself (Ediger, 2000, 6-13).

Dependent clauses do not stand with meaning by themselves such as "After Alice taught Mary a song." The dependent clause does make sense when joined in a related manner with the independent clause as in "After Alice taught Mary a song, Jane played the piano. This sentence then becomes a complex sentence, when differentiating it from a compound sentence. "After Alice taught Mary a song." Is *dependent* upon "Jane played the piano" to make sense. It is an adverb dependent clause since it modifies the verb "played" and tells "*when*" "Jane played the piano." Dependent clauses may also be adjective and noun.

The subject, predicate, indirect object, and direct object pattern of sentence may also be extended through the use of modifiers. To extend any sentence pattern, one may use adjectives and adverbs, as well as appositives, and dependent clauses. Modifiers add information about subjects, predicates, and direct/indirect objectives. Students with teacher guidance may have exciting, motivating class sessions in classifying sentence patterns as well as in extending sentences. One of the most exhilarating observational visits made by the author as supervisor of student teachers in the public schools was to observe a sixth grade class using and experimenting with different words, phrases, and clauses to expand sentences being discussed by the class as a whole, followed by small group discussion, and individual work. Students used what had been learned when writing different forms of poetry, rhymed and unrhymed. The class as a whole, small groups, and individual endeavours were in evidence to meet learning style needs of students (Searson and Dunn, 2001).

Types of Sentences

Learning sentence patterns and ways of extending sentences helps students to become better readers and writers when understanding the structure of the English language. Understanding and using different sentence patterns and expanding each sentence pattern, as needed, helps learners to understand the English language, in a functional way. Attaching meaning to four basic types of sentences assists students to further understand how the English language operates.

1. Declarative sentences make a statement of fact or opinion as in the following:
   (a) Nita rode a bicycle.
   (b) She appears to enjoy reading.

   Declarative sentences end with a period and the spoken voice drops in a lowered pitch at the end of the sentence.
2. Interrogative sentences ask questions and have a question mark at the end of the sentence as in the following:
   (a) Is Albert coming to the picnic?
   (b) How old is he?
3. Imperative sentences issue or give a command or request as in the following:
   (a) Open the window.
   (b) Please close the door.
4. Exclamatory sentences show *strong feeling* and end with an exclamation mark, as in the following:
   (a) Bob hit a home run!
   (b) Alice just now made a three pointer to win the basketball game! (Ediger, 1999, 3-11).

Once students perceive the differences in the above named four sentence types, they may use these in functional writing as well as in oral communication. Each sentence may also be classified in terms of sentence patterns. Students may experiment in how to expand each sentence pattern. Learning the structure of the English language can be fun as well as being highly informative in improving reading, writing, speaking, and listening skills. What has been learned may be revealed in numerous ways (Gardner, 1993).

REFERENCES

Ediger, Marlow (1995), "Shared Leadership in the Curriculum, *Reading Improvement*, 32 (4), 114-117).

Ediger, Marlow (1997), *Teaching Reading and the Language Arts*. Kirksville, Missouri: Simpson Publishing Company, Chapter Eight.

Ediger, Marlow, and D. Bhaskara Rao (2000), *Teaching Reading Successfully*. New Delhi, India: Discovery Publishing House, Chapter Seven.

Ediger, Marlow and D. Bhaskara Rao (2002), *Language Arts Curriculum*, New Delhi, India: Discovery Publishing House.

Ediger, Marlow (1977), "Guidelines for Selecting Experiences in Teacher Preparation," *College Student Journal*, 11 (1), 49-51.

Ediger, Marlow (2000), "Why Aren't Needed Changes in Education Implemented?" *College Student Journal*, 34 (1), 6-13.

Ediger, Marlow (1999), "Reading in the Social Studies Curriculum, *Experiments in Education*, 27 (1), 3-11.

Gardner, Howard (1993), *Multiple Intelligences: Theory into Practice*. New York: Basic Books.

Searson, Robert, And Rita Dunn (2001), "The Learning Styles Teaching Model," *Science and Children*, 32 (5), 22-26.

22

Evaluation of Achievement in Language Arts

The teacher must think of and use a variety of approaches in assessing pupil achievement in the language arts. Evaluation of pupil progress in the language arts should be comprehensive. Thus, many facets of a child's development are evaluated including:

(a) Social development.
(b) Emotional achievement.
(c) Academic learning.
(d) Physical development.

The teacher must assess pupil achievement continuously. Thus, as regularly as possible, each facet of a child's development must be assessed. Evaluation must also stress the importance not only of the teacher assessing pupil achievement but also the learner and involved parents being actively involved in quality programs of assessment. Thus, cooperative appraisal of achievement and development is important.

Evaluation of learner progress must be emphasized in terms of stated objectives. Certainly, one cannot assess learner achievement unless it is in terms of criteria, standards, or objectives.

Teacher Observation in Assessing Achievement

There are many facets of pupil learning that the instructor may evaluate through the use of teacher observation.

1. The teacher may observe which pupils have difficulties in identifying new words in reading and work in the direction of remedying these problems areas. Specific problems in word recognition should be pin-pointed such as using context clues,

phonetic analysis, syllabication, picture clues, structural analysis, and configuration clues.

2. Learner comprehension in reading may be assessed by noticing which pupils do or do not respond to identified purposes such as acquiring facts, main ideas, generalizations, and sequence of content. Critical and creative reading skills also should be assessed.
3. At a discussion center, the teacher may observe the quality of interaction among participants. Thus, pupils may be evaluated in terms of desirable agreed upon criteria in the discussion.
4. At a writing center, the teacher may observe the quality of creative ideas expressed in the written product. Pupil achievement in properly using the mechanics of writing can also be appraised.
5. When pupils present a purposeful oral report to the class, the teacher may assess the quality of the presentation using desirable standards in the evaluation procedure.

Teacher-made Tests and Pupil Evaluation

At selected intervals the teacher may wish to write appropriate test items to evaluate learner achievement. The following sample test items have been written to indicate how this procedure may be utilized in assessing pupil achievement in the language arts.

1. Which of the following words is spelled correctly? (Multiple-choice item)
   (a) Apple *(b)* Aple *(c)* Appl *(d)* Aplle
2. A noun is a word which may be changed from singular to plural in number.
   (True-false item)
3. Matching test

(a)	Nouns	———	connecting or joining words
(b)	Verbs	———	may refer to a person, place, or thing
(c)	Adjectives	———	words revealing strong feeling
(d)	Adverbs	———	may be changed from past to present tense
(e)	Conjunctions	———	modify verbs
(f)	Interjections	———	modify nouns

4. Discuss important standards which need to be followed in writing a good paragraph. (Essay item)
5. ______________________ contains two lines of rhymed verse. (Completion item)

There are selected standards which teachers must follow in writing test items to assess pupil achievement.

1. The items must be written on the understanding level of pupils.
2. Pupils must have an adequately developed writing vocabulary to respond to selected teacher-written item such as essay and completion items.
3. Items on a matching test must be homogeneous; thus, the items pertain to one topic or facet of the language arts such as parts of speech only, paragraph writing only, or usage items.
4. Adequate information must be written for completion items so that learners may determine needed content relating to blank spaces. The following completion item lacks adequate content; ____________________, ____________________, and ____________________ are ____________________.
5. Test times written to assess pupil achievement should attempt to measure relevant learnings only. Too frequently, pupils respond to the irrelevant and the unimportant.
6. All responses to the stem of a multiple choice item should be plausible. There should be no clues in the stem of the multiple choice item as to which response would be correct.
7. Tricky, vaguely written test items do not measure pupil achievement. These kinds of items definitely should be omitted in teacher developed test.
8. In evaluating responses to essay items, ideas written by pupils are more important then the mechanics of writing, such as spelling, handwriting, capitalization, and punctuation. The mechanics of writing then may be separated from written content in assessing learner achievement.

   Hopkins and Stanley wrote:

   Tests provide objective measurements on which educational decisions are based. From the standpoint of instruction, tests provide for feedback, motivation, and overlearning. From that of administration, they facilitate "quality control", program evaluation and research, classification and placement, selection, accreditation, mastery, and certification. From that of guidance, they serve to diagnose special aptitudes or abilities.

Rating Scales and Checklists

Rating scales and checklists may also be used to evaluate pupil achievement. In using the rating scale, the teacher must determine relevant behaviours of pupils to assess. The following is a model rating scale:

Name of pupil ____________________ Date__________

	good	average	needs improving
Can write topic sentence well	___	___	___
Has unity of content within a paragraph	___	___	___
Displays appropriate sequence in paragraphs	___	___	___

In using a rating scale device to assess achievement, the teacher must evaluate each student in terms of what can be expressed considering capacity and past achievement of the involved pupil. The teacher may forget individual pupil achievement unless selected observations are recorded.

The teacher must write relevant behaviours on a checklist when using this device to assess learner achievement. The following is an example of a checklist:

Name of pupil ____________________ Date __________

(Check the area or areas pupils need guidance in.)

1. The pupil speaks clearly when participating in discussions.
2. The learner respects ideas presented by others.
3. The pupil interacts with the thinking of others in a discussion.

The following criteria and considerations should be followed by teachers when developing and using scales and checklists to assess pupil achievement:

1. Only relevant behaviours should be written.
2. Behaviours should be specific and clearly stated.
3. Pupils should be involved in assessing their own achievement.
4. Feelings of the teacher will vary in making judgements when pupils are assessed at selected intervals.
5. Results from the assessment need to be used to improve the curriculum for each pupil.

Conferences and Assessing Achievement of Learners

Teacher-pupil conferences may be an excellent approach to use in assessing learner achievement. The following criteria should be emphasized in the conferences:

1. Mutual respect should be exhibited toward participants in the conference setting.
2. The thinking of the teacher and pupil must be respected.
3. Problem areas and possible solutions should be discussed in the conference.
4. Positive attitudes toward these conferences need to be developed and maintained.

Possible problem areas that can be identified through conferences could be the following:

1. The child's feeling toward reading content from library books.
2. Specific difficulties that the pupil experiences in writing, such as agreement of subject and predicate, recognizing sentence patterns, reading content orally with voice inflection, and writing paragraphs using appropriate sequence.
3. The learner using appropriate stress, pitch, and juncture when presenting content orally.
4. Specific problems that a child may have in speaking such as difficulties in articulation, voice control, or rate of speaking.
5. Difficulties a learner may experience in handwriting such as writing legibly, using correct letter formation, and aligning letters and words properly.

Parent-teacher Conferences

Parents certainly must be involved in ongoing programs of assessing pupil achievement. The child spends much time with parents or guardians. Thus, parents can have tremendous influence over their offspring. Relevant criteria must be adhered to in parent-teacher conferences.

1. There must be relaxed environment in assessing pupil achievement.
2. Respect for contributions made in a conference is a necessity.
3. Anger and hostility toward others definitely must not be a part of any conference.
4. Problem identification and possible solutions to these problems are key concepts to emphasize in parent-teacher conferences.
5. Results of any conference should not be used as a negative lever against pupils.
6. The teacher needs to be well prepared for the conference in having possible relevant items to discuss.
7. The major purpose of conducting parent-teacher conferences is to identify important problem areas and work in the direction of having an improved curriculum for each learner.
8. Notes should be written by the teacher for future reference when additional conferences are held.

Topics for consideration in a parent-teacher conference should be carefully selected. The support of parents must be enlisted in attempting to provide for each child in the class setting. The following are examples of areas to discuss in parent-teacher conferences:

1. Guiding pupils in developing a desire to engage in creative writing in the home.
2. Listening to the child read orally to parents in the home.

3. Having an adequate number of library books for pupils in the home setting.
4. Taking pupils on trips to nearby museums, libraries, and places of interest.
5. Reading library books orally to preschool pupils containing interesting and meaningful content.
6. Discussing ideas with children in the home setting to encourage listening and speaking skills.

Much information pertaining to a child can be obtained from parent-teacher conferences.

1. How parents feel toward their offspring.
2. What aspirations or goals parents have for their children.
3. How parents help their children in school work.
4. Concern shown by parents toward the child's achievement in school.
5. Willingness on the part of parents to cooperate with the teacher in developing an improved curriculum for pupils.

The teacher must be a good listener in a parent-teacher conference. This would be important for the following reasons:

1. To identify relevant problems with parents which need solving in order than an improved curriculum may be implemented for each learner.
2. To gather data pertaining to parental acceptance of each child.

The above obtained data must only be used to improve the curriculum for each individual learner.

Diaries, Logs, and Pupil Evaluation

Diaries and logs may be utilized effectively in appraising achievement. Learners reveal previous learnings obtained by writing diary entries and logs. Diary entries are written on a day to day basis by one child or by a committee on a rotation schedule. Logs are summaries written by a committee of pupils at selected intervals. All pupils in a class should have ample opportunities to experience the writing of diary or log entries.

The following is written as an example pertaining to diary entries in a unit of study pertaining to the Middle East:

September 1 (Monday). We studied about the Dead Sea which is about 1300 feet below sea level. There is no outlet from the Dead Sea; thus, the water has about 28 per cent mineral content. This makes it easy for anyone to float in the Dead Sea with no knowledge of swimming.

September 2 (Tuesday). Jericho is one of the oldest continuously inhabited cities on the face of the earth. It is a beautiful garden spot surrounded by desert land. Dates, oranges, bananas, grapefruit, figs, and pomegranates are grown here. Irrigation provides an adequate supply of water to grow crops.

September 3 (Wednesday). The Judean Hills located between Jerusalem and Jericho look like mounds of sand dumped at different points. Jericho is about 700 feet below sea level while Jerusalem is about 2500 feet above sea level. The Judean Hills start to green in January and look very dry by September—the reason being that rain falls in Palestine only from November to April. There is no rain from April to November.

September 4 (Thursday). Old Jerusalem has a wall which surrounds it. The present wall around old Jerusalem was completed in 1542 by the Turks. There are very few cars driven inside the walls of Old Jerusalem; this is due to very narrow streets.

September 5 (Friday). The church of the Holy Sepulchre was built by the Crusaders in 1099 A.D. This church was built over the place where Crusaders believed Christ had been crucified and entombed.

Logs may be written at selected intervals by pupils to summarize previous learnings. Thus, in a unit on magnetism and electricity, the following summary statements may be written by pupils:

There are many different kinds of magnets such as bar, horseshoe, and electromagnets. Magnets have a north pole and a south pole. Poles of magnets can be determined in that opposite poles of magnets attract whereas like poles repel.

There are many advantages in having pupils individually or in committees write diary entries and log items:

1. Pupils reveal what has been learned previously.
2. Learners determine what is relevant to record.
3. Pupils can be creative in expressing ideas obtained.
4. Learners may select which committee they wish to participate in.
5. The mechanics of writing may also be assessed.

Standardized Tests

At selected intervals, it can be good procedure to use standardized tests to assess pupil achievement in areas such as *(a)* reading comprehension, *(b)* vocabulary growth, *(c)* purposes in reading, *(d)* capitalization, *(e)* spelling, *(f)* punctuation, *(g)* usage, and *(h)* grammar.

Results from standardized tests may be used to guide pupils in the following ways:

1. To diagnose pupil difficulties in different facets of the language arts.

2. To utilize data in developing a relevant language arts curriculum.
3. To select learning activities which aid pupils in achieving important objectives.

Results of standardized tests should not be utilized in the following negative ways:

1. As a "lever" against a child to work up to grade level achievement pertaining to the present grade level the child is in.
2. A uniform curriculum in terms of scope and sequence for all learners.
3. Teachers teach learnings contained in the test to pupils.

Sociometric Devices

Very frequently committee work is used in ongoing units of study in the language arts. All educators would agree that social development of pupils is of utmost importance. Thus, there are many reasons for emphasizing committee work:

1. To help pupils develop increased proficiency in getting along well with others.
2. To guide learners to gain relevant information as a result of having worked in committees.
3. To aid pupils in emotional adjustment through satisfying experiences in committee work.

In Summary

There are many techniques available to evaluate each pupil's achievement. Many approaches need to be used to assess learner achievement. Results obtained must be used to improve the curriculum.

Mehrens and Lehmann wrote the following summary statements, among others, on evaluation in education:

1. Measurement and evaluation are essential to sound educational decision making.
2. The term test often suggests presenting a standard set of questions to be answered.
3. The concept of measurement is broader than that of testing. We can measure characteristics in ways other than by giving tests.
4. Evaluation is the process of delineating, obtaining, and providing useful information for judging decision alternative.
5. Every person must at some time make educational decisions.
6. A good decision is one that is based on relevant and accurate information. The responsibility of gathering and imparting that information belongs to the educator.

REFERENCES

Calder, Clarence R., Jr. and Eleanor M. Antan. *Techniques and Activities to Stimulate Verbal Learning*. New York: The Macmillan Company, 1970.

Hopkins, Kenneth D., and Julian C. Stanley. *Educational and Psychological Measurement and Evaluation*. Sixth Edition. Englewood Cliffs, New Jersey: Prentice Hall, Inc., 1981.

Langacker, Ronald W. *Language and Structure*. New York: Harcourt, Brace, and World, Inc., 1968. Manning, Duane. *Toward A Humanistic Curriculum*. New York: Harper and Row, Publishers, 1971. Mehrens, William A., and Irvin J. Lehmann. *Measurement and Evaluation in Education and Psychology*. Third edition. New York: Holt, Rinehart and Winston, 1984.

Newman, Harold (Ed.) *Effective Language Arts Practices in the Elementary School*. New York: John Wiley and Sons, Inc., 1972.

Ober, Richard, et. al. *Systematic Observation of Teaching*. Englewood Cliffs: Prentice-Hall, Inc., 1971.

Ragan, William B., and Gene D. Shepherd. *Modern Elementary Curriculum*. Sixth Edition. New York: Holt, Rinehart, and Winston, Inc., 1982. Chapter three.

Raths, James, et. al. (Eds.). *Studying Teaching*. Second edition. Englewood Cliffs: Prentice-Hall, Inc., 1971.

Remmers, H.H., et. al. *A Practical Introduction to Measurement and Evaluation*. New York: Harper and Row, Publishers, 1960.

Taylor, Ronald L. *Assessment of Exceptional Students*. Englewood Cliffs, New Jersey: Prentice-Hall, Inc., 1984.

Walsh, Bruce W., and Nancy E. Betz. *Tests and Assessments*. Englewood Cliffs, New Jersey: Prentice-Hall, Inc., 1985.

23

The Social Sciences and the Social Studies

The social sciences provide content for the social studies. History may be treated by selected academicians as an area of the humanities, and will be stressed as a discipline providing subject matter for the social studies. Rational balance among the diverse disciplines needs to be emphasized in the social studies. Social studies stresses a study of people from diverse perspectives and thus adequate emphasis needs to be placed upon the following academic disciplines largely:

1. History with its study of relevant past events and how this has affected human beings within the social studies unit being developed and implemented.
2. Geography in which human beings are studied within a given carefully defined region.
3. Political science and its stress placed upon how people are governed. The laws, rules, and regulations in a region, state, and/or nation affect people live there.
4. Economics and its role placed upon people buying goods and services needed to survive as well as to enrich the lives of human beings.
5. Anthropology and its emphasis placed upon culture and culture's influence upon human beings.
6. Sociology with its stress placed upon how institutions in society affect human behaviour. These institutions include religion, government, economic, education, and organisations joined by people (Ediger, 1996, 17-20).

History in the Social Studies Curriculum

To examine and study the influence of history upon the human being, students need to achieve carefully chosen objectives within carefully designed social studies units emphasizing how the past has influenced the present. In a unit pertaining events following World War One, the student may learn about decisions made by the victorious powers affecting happenings presently in the Middle East such as

1. The Hussein/MacMahon correspondence whereby the land of Palestine was promised to the local Arabs who later became known as the Palestinians.
2. The Balfour Declaration in which the land of Palestine was promised as a homeland to Jews.

These conflicting promises made for problems between Arabs and Jews. With mass immigration of Jews to Palestine, conflict between the settled Arabs and newly arrived Jews was bound to arise, resulting as one of the reasons for fighting and wars between opposing sides of Palestinian Arabs versus Israel. The land of Palestine was then wanted by both Jews and Arabs. Cause and effect thinking is very important in history. Historians always look for causes of events (Ediger, 1998, 53-59).

Geography in the Social Studies

With the increased amount of information pertaining to news items and happenings reported in different media, it behooves he learner to become proficient in identifying places where the events took place. The listener to news happenings needs to have a world map and a globe available to pinpoint where these happenings transpired.

There are five identified themes by the National Council for Geographic Education (NCGE), which teachers should use to incorporate and implement in the geography curriculum. These five themes are the following:

1. ***Location***: Position on the Earth's Surface. Absolute location stresses location of a place by using degrees of latitude, north or south of the equator and longitude, east or west of the prime meridian. Any place on the earth's surface may by located when being given the number of degrees north or south of the equator as well as the number of degrees east or west of the prime meridian. Likewise, any city location may also be given in degrees north/south of the equator and east/west of the prime meridian.

Relative location, for example, may be given of a place when speaking of the nation of Jordan being west and adjacent to Iraq, or Lebanon being east of the Mediterranean Sea.

2. ***Place:*** Physical and Human Characteristics. The physical, characteristics, for example, may then be described for Amman, the capital city of Jordan. Amman is located on seven hills and has approximately one million people located here. One of the seven hills is called Jebel Amman which has the large, well known Bishop's School, surrounded by many small shops and streets, filled with automobiles.
3. ***Regions:*** How They Form and Change. A Region emphasizes unity of characteristics which distinguishes it from other regions. For example, the Mediterranean climate in the Middle East generally has rain from November to April and basically no rainfall from April to November. Much of the land is desert in nature but does have a fertile triangle. Within the desert, there are oases which make a desert spot bloom.

   Jericho, the oldest continually inhabited city of the planet earth, would be a desert, except for a flourishing spring which provides water to make for a garden spot. The Mediterranean climate is relatively homogeneous when compared to other climates on the planet earth. The Middle East region, for example, can be clearly differentiated from the Polar areas in terms of annual rainfall amounts, temperature readings, as well as how the land can be used.
4. ***Human—Environment Interaction.*** Advantages and disadvantages exist in the natural environment in selecting places for habitation. Fertile soil, adequate supplies of clean water, and chances to use water transportation as in port city locations provide opportunities for large scale settlements whereas desert, polar, and equatorial climates are much less likely to support human habitation.
5. ***Movement:*** Humans Interacting on Earth. People living and moving in an uneven manner on the planet. Some live in rural areas, small cities, villages, towns, or metropolitan areas. As they travel and move around, goods and services are purchased and used as well as communication taking place among people and places/regions. In the nation of Jordan, people have flocked to the large city of Amman, the capital, to seek employment in factories, industries, and in small shops. It is a bustling, busy city but has high rates of unemployment due, in part, to the influx of many Palestinian refugees. Movement of population has been from the rural areas to the

large urban city of Amman. In rural areas where much of the land is desert, villagers farm in the fertile valleys, adjacent to the hills. East of Amman, the areas are completely desert with no inhabitants, basically. Learnings such as these may be similar/different from other regions stressing human—environment interaction.

Each of the key, themes may be integrated into the social studies curriculum. Thus, any area chosen for social studies units may incorporate the five themes of place, location, region, human-environment, and movement pattern characteristics as identified by the National Council for Geographic Education (1994).

Map and Globe Skills

There are a plethora of map and globe knowledge/skills which students need to develop sequentially in emphasizing geography in the social studies. The concepts of meridians, parallels, latitude, and longitude have important meanings for students. The following are important generalizations for students to achieve as objectives in the social studies (Ediger, 2001, 209-210):

1. Meridians are imaginary lines running north and south on a map or globe.
2. There are many meridians and they all intersect at the north pole and at the south pole. Mercator projections on maps do not show this intersection since intersection of parallels does not occur at the north/south poles. Rather the meridians on a Mercator projection are at a ninety degree angle to each parallel, making for distortions, especially at the north and south regions.
3. To measure distances north and south of the equator, one measures along a meridian.
4. The farthest number in degrees one can measure north of the equator is ninety. This is the north pole region. The Tropic of Cancer is located twenty-three and one half degrees north of the equator.
5. The farthest number in degrees one can measure south of the equator is ninety degrees. This is the south pole region. The Tropic of Capricorn is located twenty-three and one half degrees south of the equator.
6. To measure distances east or west of the prime meridian, one measures along a parallel.
7. There is a distance of fifteen degrees between regions for each hour of time difference. This is discussing time zones, in moving from each to west or west to east on a parallel, a difference of one hour of time is in evidence for every fifteen

degrees in longitude. Longitudinal lines fifteen degrees apart measure one hour of time on the planet earth.

8. The low latitudes are located between the tropic of Cancer and the Tropic of Capricorn.
9. The high latitudes are located in the Arctic and Antarctic circle. From the North Pole and going twenty three and one-half degrees south is the Arctic circle. From the South Pole and going twenty-three and one-half degrees north latitude is the Antarctic circle.
10. In between the low latitudes (Torrid Zone) and the high latitudes (Frigid Zone) are the middle latitudes (Temperate Zone).

Objectives for teaching a specific unit of study emphasizing geography/map and globe skills might well stress the above named goals. Generally, teachers may wish to modify selected ends and add others. Adaptation to the local social studies unit being taught as well as to the involved learners needs adequate emphasis in the curriculum. Social studies curriculum development is a creative process needing much thought and problem solving. A variety of learning opportunities need to be implemented so that each student may achieve vital ends of instruction.

Political Science and the Social Studies

People then have a past which then brings in history into the social studies. They live in a place and region; thus geography is also emphasized in the social studies. A further problem is that there needs to be rules, regulations, and laws which govern human behaviour. Governing requires laws which are fair to each person.

In the classroom setting, rules can be established which can be considered fair to most students. Rules such as the following may then need to be developed by students with teacher guidance:

1. Each student needs to respect others in the group setting.
2. Each learner needs to develop a caring attitude when assisting others as is necessary.
3. Each regulation to govern behaviour may need to be revised periodically when purpose indicates modifications are necessary.
4. Each person should feel he/she is a definite member of the group or committee.
5. Each individual should feel that personal contributions are welcomed.

When groups/committees are working together, the following criteria need to be followed:

1. All should participate and no one dominate.
2. Encouragement of ideas to further committee work should be in the offing.
3. Ideas discussed should flow between and among individuals and not among the few.
4. The talents of each person need to be utilized fully in committee work.
5. Students individually have responsibilities to make the collaborative endeavour successful with active participation.
6. The teacher also has an important goal in assisting, encouraging, and helping students to be successful in ongoing committee work.
7. Adequate materials of instruction must be accessible to students including reading, nonreading, and technology kinds of learning opportunities.
8. The committee members with teacher guidance need to assess their total and individual achievement.
9. Each student should engage in journal writing to indicate what has been learned in terms of vocabulary terms, concepts, main ideas, and subject matter in general.
10. Diary entries may be kept by the committee to indicate what has been learned collaboratively on daily basis Parker, 2001.

Units of study emphasizing political science need to stress those dealing with local government, among other levels of governing. On the local level, students need to study issues by reading news accounts of happenings in city and county government. They need to participate in local government by writing and sending letters showing concern over items being considered at council meetings. Social studies units stressing the importance of the city manager, mayor council, and commission forms of local government then become salient to implement. Students need to learn about and understand the role(s) of each member of local government. Carefully designed units of study need to be in the offing which contain quality well thought through aims of instruction. In these political science units, balance among cognitive, affective, and psychomotor objectives for student achievement must be emphasized and implemented.

Units on state government also provides much information and news as to proceedings, happenings, and issues being considered. A well informed constituency is needed to become actively involved in state government in capacities which are challenging for students in the social studies.

Units of study on the federal level of government may become a part of content dealing with local and state government. A good working understanding of the constitution together with the Bill of Rights are musts for students in a democracy. Goals for students to achieve in political science are the following:

1. Acquire knowledge of the three levels of government—local, state, and federal—which is useful presently in decision making as well as for voting in elections in the future.
2. Integrate school and society by taking an active role in societal institutions. Here, learners with teacher guidance may, for example, visit and present a program for senior citizens. Community service projects are important for social studies student participation.
3. Reveal patterns of behaviour indicating democracy as away of life such as accepting and valuing others (Curriculum Advice: Center for Civics Education, 1994).

Economics and the Social Studies

Within social studies units, students should acquire a good understanding of economic concepts. Each person lives in an economic world and buys goods and services. After providing concrete and semi-concrete examples of *goods* many individuals purchase, the social studies teacher may have students tell about goods which they have purchased. Pictures of purchased items by the student or his/her parents may be brought to school by learners. These need to be discussed in depth. No doubt, the related concept of *services* will also accrue as an economics vocabulary term. Brain storming services which are purchased by parents can make for a fascinating learning opportunity. No value judgments are made on each contribution made here by students. Ideas are to be generated and not criticized. Additional economic learnings for students to achieve are the following:

1. ***Production.*** Goods and services are produced. The means of production of selected goods and services need to be studied/ understood by students with teacher guidance. Thus, for example, there are certain steps which farmers follow in producing wheat such as plowing and disking the land to rid the fields of weeds in summer, harrowing the land in getting it ready for seeding in fall, and the actual seeding of the land. Hopefully, the result will be a good crop of wheat next summer. The actual wheat is considered as *goods* whereas the process of grinding the grain for making flour for baking is a *service* provided by commercial milling companies. The loaves of bread which will eventually accrue at bakeries is again labeled as goods.

2. ***Consumption.*** Human beings are consumers of needed/desired goods and services. Bread, for example, purchased at a supermarket is eaten together with other food items in the home and school lunchroom setting.
   Interesting discussions need to be conducted in the classroom of the many items of food, clothing, and shelter which are consumed by students/parents. Some items are purchased consumed based on need whereas others are based on *wants*. Sometimes, the wants exceed the *resources* or money available for making purchases. Choices then need to be made as to what to buy and what to give up.
3. ***Distribution.*** Goods and services need to be distributed from processors to selected places, such as super markets, in order that they may be conveniently purchased by consumers for consumption. Decisions are made in terms of what to buy. In classical economics, the law of supply and demand operates. Competition among products is there to determine which goods/services will survive based on consumer needs and wants.
4. Opportunities costs are experienced by individuals preparing for a job, occupation, or profession. There are trade offs as to the rewards which will be experienced or lack thereof for workers at the work place. A trade off may occur, for example, when considering the amount of time spent working versus the amount of income to be received in one of the professions. Thus, among other considerations, a person in the professions may be willing to sacrifice much time in order to increase income levels.
5. ***Scarcity.*** Scarcity of items to be purchased may be in very short supply thus driving up the costs. Or, products may be very plentiful and lower prices are then in evidence. Costs of petroleum have come in this category of being in short supply and then at other times being more plentiful. The price of gasoline at the pump as well as the price of home heating fuel is dependent upon how much petroleum is available and ready for consumption (National Council on Economic Education, 1999).

Each of the above concepts may be taught in the separate unit of study of economics or be integrated into a social studies unit. They are vital to understand since each person has a different lifestyle/culture in an economic world in which goods and services are purchased and consumed.

Issues also need to be identified carefully in terms of student understanding and meaning pertaining to the world of economics.

What transpires in one area of the world does affect other regions on the planet earth. These learnings, among other information sources, may be accessed on the World Wide Web and might well include

1. Economic interests versus protecting the natural environment.
2. Understanding the proposed privatization of Social Security.
3. Attaching meaning to the North America Free Trade Act (Risinger, 2001).

Anthropology and Sociology in the Social Studies

As a last social science discipline to be discussed, students do need to understand human behaviour from the point of view of culture. Culture, studied by both anthropologists and sociologists, is a powerful factor in helping to modify and determine, in part, how individuals behave react, and think. The author has since 1971 studied. The Old Order Amish in rural Bloomfield, Iowa. How the prevailing culture there influences human beings can be noticed in the following ways, among others:

1. The kinds of dress worn such as women with prayer caps, long dresses reaching to the ankles basically and long sleeves coming down to the wrists. The material for the dresses is always a plain color, no stripes nor checks.
2. The means of transportation such as a carriage pulled by a horse. Automobiles are not owned by he Old Order Amish. Automobile transportation, however, is rented for long distance travel.
3. Farming methods with horse drawn equipment used for plowing, disking, and seeding of the farm land. Cutting of grain raised is done with a binder pulled by draft horses. A threshing machine is used to separate the chaff and straw from the grain. Self propelled combines are not owned by the Amish but may be hired to cut/thresh grain stalks in the field.
4. Few Old Older Amish actually farm since the family size is large, six to ten children per family approximately, and there is not enough land available for all to farm. Also, prices for farm products are extremely low making it difficult to make a living by doing farming. Amish men then work for others doing farm related kinds of work such as carpentering, bricklaying, and lumbering. In Old Order Amish communities close to larger cities, Amish work in small food stores, factories, butcher shops, wood working shops, and bakeries.
5. Amish worship every other Sunday in each other's homes, as well as in barns in summer and late spring/early fall. Men and boy sit on one side of the building whereas women with

small children and girls on the other for worship services (Ediger, 1997, 339-342).

In each social studies unit where applicable, students may then study indepth the music, art, architecture, games played, foods eaten, attire, religious beliefs, marriage, ceremonies, and other customs of a given subculture or society. Learners are then studying the culture and how it influences beliefs and values of a specific group of people, identified for study.

REFERENCES

Curriculum Advice; Center for Civic Education (1994), Calabasas, California: National Standards for Civics and Government.

Ediger, Marlow (2001), "Maps, Globes and the Social Studies," *Teaching Social Studies Successfully*. New Delhi, India: Discovery Publishing House, pp 209-210.

Ediger, Marlow (1996), "Activity Centered and Subject Centered Curricula," *The Educational Review*, 102 (1), 17-20.

Ediger, Marlow (1998), *The Holy Land*. Kirksville, Missouri: Simpson Publishing Company, 52-59.

Ediger, Marlow (1997). "Examining the Merits of Old Order" Amish Education, Education, 117 (3), 339-343.

Ediger, Marlow and Digumarti Bhaskara Rao (2001), *Teaching Social Studies Successfully*. New Delhi: Discovery Publishing House.

National Council on Economic Education (1999), *The Standards in Economics Survey*. Washington, DC: NCEE.

National Council Geographic Education (1994), *Geography for Life;* National Geography Standards. Washington DC: NCGE.

Risinger, C. Frederick (2001), "Teaching Economics and the Globalization Debate on the World Wide Web," *Social Education*, 65 (6), 363-365.

Parker, Walter (2001), *Social Studies in Elementary Education*. Upper Saddle River, New Jersey: Prentice Hall, Inc, Chapter Four.

24

Philosophy of Education and the Social Studies

The social studies teacher must be well grounded in the philosophy of education. A philosophy of education gives guidance and direction in the selection of objectives, learning activities, and assessment procedures. Teachers of social studies need to study different schools of thought to develop a philosophy of their own.

Experimentalism in the Curriculum

Experimentalism as a philosophy of education stresses the following in teaching-learning situations:

1. Problem solving activities are important for learners. Pupils with teacher guidance identify problems and work in the direction of obtaining needed solutions.
2. Realistic situations in teaching and learning are important. Thus, pupils engage in problem solving activities which are life-like and relevant.
3. Problem-solving activities pertain to what is useful in society.
4. All disciplines of knowledge may be utilized in the solving of problems.
5. Dualisms in teaching-learning situations are eliminated. Thus, a child's efforts in learning would come about from inherent interests in ongoing opportunities to learn. Effort and interest are not separated.
6. As a result of experience, the pupil modifies his perceptions and efforts.
7. The whole child is involved in learning. The intellectual, emotional, social and physical achievement of pupils must then be stressed in the school, class, and larger environment.

8. The school environment is perceived as being as directly related to society as possible.
9. Pupils are actively involved in learning. Passive individuals in ongoing learning experiences does not reflect the thinking advocated by experimentalists.
10. Integration of experiences would be important in the thinking of experimentalists. Subject matter areas would lost their borders and boundaries in problem-solving activities.
11. Democracy is a form of government and also a way of life in the school and community setting.

There are important implications for teaching-learning situations involving the thinking of experimentalists:

1. Each unit of study in the social studies emphasizes that pupils engage in problem-solving activities.
2. Pupils and the teacher must develop a stimulating learning environment using a variety of activities so that learners may truly feel a need to identify relevant problems.
3. Pupils should experience as much reality as possible when perceiving and identifying needed problems for solution in society.
4. The teacher of social studies must guide pupils to perceive purpose in ongoing learning experiences. Thus, the whole pupil may become involved in ongoing learning experiences. This would be true if active involvement in committee work, in particular, is in evidence. Learners are wholeheartedly involved in learning—intellectually, emotionally, socially, and physically.
5. The teacher guides pupils in utilizing a variety of resources in attempting to solve relevant problems. Subject matter boundaries and borders lose their identity in problem-solving activities.
6. Pupils with teacher guidance develop criteria in terms of standards of conduct for the class setting. Thus, pupils have ample opportunities to be involved in decision-making practices as to the kind of classroom climate desired.

Idealism and the Curriculum

Idealists generally emphasize that ultimate reality goes beyond the use of the senses. An individual has ideas pertaining to what reality is really like. Many idealists would also adhere to the following conclusions:

1. What is observable is not what is of most importance. Thus, what is really important in life must be sought after and is not easily found.

2. There are universal laws which are important for every human being to seek and abide by. These are standards of morality, such as the golden Rule equivalents.
3. The thinking of human beings changes in time in terms of what is important in the area of values, beliefs, standards, and ideals.
4. The liberal arts are important in the curriculum. What is vocational should be delayed until general education has been completed.
5. Ideas and abstractions are more important for pupils as compared to learnings gained from using the senses, or using concrete materials.

The teacher who adheres to the philosophy of idealism in teaching—learning situations stresses the following:

1. Social studies content provides pupils with selected ideals which give direction and guidance in life.
2. Pupils with teacher guidance should spend ample time in examining standards, criteria, and beliefs to live by. In any unit of study in the social studies, pupils will encounter value systems of selected individuals, cultures, and nations.
3. An idea or subject centered curriculum should be in evidence. Pupils need to attain worthwhile facts, concepts, and generalizations.

Realism and the Curriculum

The teacher who stresses realism as a philosophy of education in teaching-learning situations emphasizes the following:

1. Pupils can know ultimate reality as it really exists.
2. There is much permanency in the world; conditions are not in a state of continual transition as other philosophical schools in education seem to think.
3. Essential learnings can be identified which pupils need to achieve. These learnings may be identified in any curriculum area in the school setting. The use of behaviourally stated objectives is important.
4. Real and life-like learnings are salient for pupils to acquire and achieve desired ends. Concrete materials would be used heavily in teaching.

The teacher embracing the philosophy of realism in teaching learning situations would not emphasize the following:

1. Abstract ideas to the exclusion of realness and what reality is actually like.
2. Change and instability in the environment to the exclusion of that which is permanent. Seasons of the year and their causes,

the planets and their order of rotation and revolution, and explanations of natural phenomena such as earthquakes and hurricanes, for example, represent stability and permanency in the universe.

Existentialism and the Curriculum

The existentialist point of view is important for teachers to consider in the social studies curriculum. Existentialists adhere to the following standards of thought:

1. Each individual is responsible for making moral choices in society.
2. Choices that are made may result in feelings of anxiety, unhappiness, guilt, loneliness, stress, and even alienation.
3. Each person must be creative in interpreting knowledge, concepts, and facts. Knowledge is subjective, not objective.
4. Human beings individually must seek and find purpose in life. Purpose is not given to the person but must be sought.

The teacher of social studies emphasizing existentialist philosophy of education stresses the following in teaching-learning situations:

1. Values clarification in ongoing units of study. Learners in a variety of learning activities and in diverse unit titles may engage in making decisions pertaining to that which has most worth. Ample opportunities must be given to reflect upon values selected in a given situation.
2. Pupils should study the life history of selected individuals to determine what choices these individuals made in life. Careful consideration should be given to the effects these choices had on others.
3. Adequate emphasis must be placed upon learners being creative in art work, construction activities, dramatizations, creative writing of prose and poetry, and story telling.
4. Pupils must be guided in exploring diverse vocations, pursuits, hobbies, and interests. Pupils will then have numerous opportunities to seek that which has purpose and meaning.
5. The classroom environment should be supportive of creative thinking and work of learners.
6. Pupils should have ample opportunities to examine their own values and find freedom to modify these beliefs intrinsically.
7. Much pupil input into the curriculum is important.

The following generalizations definitely would not be consistent with existentialist thinking:

1. The teacher lecturing to pupils about desired values which the former feels should be adopted by learners.

2. Instructors determining objectives for pupils to achieve, learning activities to attain these objectives, and assessment procedures to evaluate achievement of learners. Pupils should be heavily involved in decision-making.
3. Pupils feeling they must experience much drill and practice so that satisfactory test results are an end result.
4. Each pupil being compared with other learners in the class setting to determine who is successful in ongoing learning activities.
5. A rigid, formal classroom environment where each pupil conforms to teacher-developed standards in the class setting.
6. Learning activities which require little or no pupil originality or uniqueness of thought.
7. Content presented as being strictly factual.
8. The feelings of pupils being ignored in the school and class setting.
9. No pupil-teacher planning of the curriculum.

In Summary

Teachers, supervisors, and principals must understand major tenets of different schools of thought in the philosophy of education. Educators must perceive how teaching and learning would be emphasized in the philosophical schools of thought such as experimentalism, idealism, realism and existentialism. Each teacher, principal, and supervisor must develop his or her own unique philosophy based on study and thought pertaining to teaching and learning in the class setting.

REFERENCES

Brubacher, John S. *A History of the Problems of Education*. Second Edition. New York: McGraw-Hill Book Company, 1966.

Kahane, Howard. *Logic and Philosophy A Modern Introduction*. Belmont, California: Wadsworth Publishing Company, 1982.

Morris, Van Cleve, and Young Pai. *Philosophy and the American School*. Second Edition. Boston: Houghton Mifflin Company, 1976.

National Society for the Study of Education. *Modern Philosophies and Education*. Chicago: University of Chicago Press, 1955.

Pai, Young, and Joseph T. Myers (Eds.). *Philosophic Problems and Education* New York: J.B. Lippincott Company, 1967.

Ryan, Kevin and James Cooper. *Those Who Can Teach*. Boston: Houghton Mifflin Company, 1984.

25

Designing the Social Studies Curriculum

The teacher needs to give careful consideration to the design of the curriculum for elementary children. Each pupil should be guided to achieve to his or her optimum in terms of understandings, skills, and attitudinal objectives. Thus, it is necessary to place adequate emphasis upon the design of the curriculum. The design of the curriculum should follow these criteria:

1. Each pupil should achieve continued success in learning.
2. Learners need to experience appropriate sequence in ongoing experiences.
3. Pupils should experience integrated learning experiences with adequate emphasis being placed upon content cutting across boundaries and borders of diverse academics disciplines.
4. Learning opportunities must take into consideration previous understandings, skills, and attitudes developed.
5. Pupils individually should have ample opportunities to develop will socially as well as to achieve to their optimum in working on an individual basis.
6. Adequate emphasis needs to be placed upon pupils developing well intellectually, emotionally, socially, and physically.
7. Pupils need to participate in learning activities which require a relatively quite environment such as in reading social studies content as well as participating in activities which require physical movement and manual dexterity.
8. The teacher needs to select objectives, tasks, and appraisal techniques in teaching-learning situations, as well as pupils with teacher guidance identifying relevant goals, learning experiences, and assessment procedures.

Social Development and Achievement on an Individual Basis

Pupils need to develop well socially. Thus, individuals are able to interact well with others in a group setting. Additional reasons inherent in guiding pupils to achieve well socially would be the following:

1. The school is a social setting comprised of pupils, teachers, custodians, cafeteria workers, the principal, the supervisor, and other workers such as remedial reading specialists and guidance counselors. Thus, it behooves the teacher in guiding pupils to be able to interact well with others.
2. Much content is learned from other human beings; thus it is important to be able to possess necessary skills in human relations to develop well intellectually, physically, socially, and emotionally.
3. Satisfying human relations aid pupils in feeling successful in the school setting. One facet of development that all human beings need to be successful in is the area of good human relations.
4. Teachers need to emphasize considerable committee work in a quality curriculum. Pupils need to interact well with others in order to accomplish relevant goals within a group setting.
5. Politeness, as a valued asset in society, demands that each human being develop optimally in the area of social development and group interaction.

It is important then for teachers to select an adequate number of learning experiences which guide pupils to achieve to their full potential in social development. Pupils may work in committees using open space education and learning centers. Centers such as the following may be developed which could guide pupils in interacting well with others in a committee setting:

1. A writing center. Pupils could cooperatively develop a poem, story, or engage in research.
2. An art corner. Here pupils may cooperatively plan and develop a mural.
3. A construction center. Pupils within a committee may decide upon the kind of industrial arts project to be developed relating to an ongoing unit of study. Following this decision, learners with teacher leadership may implement their decisions directly relating to the construction activity.
4. A reading station. Pupils may share content of library books and stories read in a group setting.
5. A dramatization corner. Selected learners cooperatively may plan and implement a dramatization related to ongoing

learning experiences. Thus, pupils again have opportunities to work harmoniously together with other learners.

6. A story telling center. Here pupils may take turns telling creative stories to others in a committee setting.
7. A listening center. Pupils may listen to selected tapes and share major ideas gained using agreed upon criteria for committee work.

Criteria need to be emphasized when learners work in a committee setting. Cooperatively, pupils with teacher guidance may develop guidelines such as the following:

1. Pupils should respect the thinking of others.
2. Each pupil needs to contribute to his or her optimum in committee work.
3. No one should dominate committee endeavours.
4. Evaluation of pupil achievement within the committee setting must be positive and facilitate rather than hinder learner progress.
5. Each pupil should have ample opportunities to choose which task to pursue within a committee setting.
6. Ideas in a discussion should flow within the committee rather than from chairperson to participant only.

Pupils also need to have numerous opportunities to work individually on selected learning activities. Situations in life demand that human beings individually engage in profitable experiences. Thus, the school setting may emphasize learning experiences such as the following:

1. Pupils selecting and reading library books and stories of their own choosing.
2. Each pupil may select approaches to reveal knowledge gained from units of study. Art work, written products, oral reporting, written reports, and construction projects may provide ways for pupils to reveal learnings obtained from ongoing units of study.
3. Learners individually may select a research problem and gather needed information in attempting to arrive at a solution.
4. Each child could select a club or organisation to joint in the school setting in which the student could select a project of his/her own choosing to work on.
5. After completing a given assignment, the child may choose the next learning activity such as engaging in art work, or in a construction project, or participating at a writing center.

The learner should find experiences satisfying, fulfilling, and rewarding when working on a learning activity involving individual efforts.

The Integrated Curriculum

Social studies lends itself well to placing emphasis upon the integrated curriculum. Too frequently in the past, social studies has been taught in terms of separate academic disciplines. Thus, separate units of study have been emphasized pertaining to geography only, history only, or political science only. It is important for pupils to develop learnings in depth pertaining to each of the disciplines emphasized in elementary school social studies such as history, geography, political science, economics, sociology, and anthropology. Learners must also perceive content from these social science disciplines as being interrelated. Using problem solving approaches in teaching-learning situations can aid pupils to perceive that facts, concepts, main ideas, and generalizations are related. Thus, the fused social studies curriculum may become a reality in teaching-learning situations. Pupils should also perceive the relationship of science, music, art, and physical education, as an inherent part of a good social studies program. In a common social studies unit on "Communication in the United States", pupils with teacher guidance may

1. Develop telegraph sets; thus, principles of science may be brought into the ongoing social studies unit with learners studying electromagnets and how they operate.
2. Write selected verse relating to content being studied; attempts may be made in setting the words to music.
3. Plan and develop individual illustrations, friezes, murals, and dioramas pertaining to a major generalizations being studied.
4. Engage in rhythmic activities relating to main ideas contained in the ongoing unit of study.

Selected problems need to be identified and attempts made at remedying these situations pertaining to the implementation of the fused or integrated curriculum:

1. Each social science discipline should receive adequate emphasis in the social studies curriculum.
2. Content should not be fused or integrated for the sake of doing this. Rather fused and integrated content should make learnings more meaningful to pupils.
3. Selected pupils may need to develop learnings in depth pertaining to a specific curriculum area or to a facet of this curriculum area. The concept of diagnosis should be implemented to determine when the separate subjects curriculum needs to be emphasized in ongoing learning activities as compared to fused and integrated approaches.

Developing the Total Child

In educational history, much emphasis has been placed upon the intellectual development of the learner. At the turn of the last century, more emphasis has been placed upon learners achieving well in other facets of development also, such as social, emotional, and physical. The curriculum must help pupils achieve to their optimum in all four facets of development-intellectual, social, emotional, and physical. The following learning experiences are mentioned to reveal learning opportunities pertaining to all areas of a child's development:

1. Participating in critical thinking, creative thinking, and problem solving activities (intellectual development).
2. Learning to play games of a specific country being studied in social studies (physical development).
3. Working together with other learners in a committee to develop a mural or frieze (social development).
4. Choosing a library book to read voluntarily or freely selecting a task to complete at a learning center (emotional development).

Why should the total development of pupils be emphasized in the school and class setting?

1. Each facet of development influences the achievement of a different area of growth such as positive attitudes or feelings (emotional growth) aid in achieving well in intellectual achievement if self-fulfillment of human beings is to be in evidence. A person who is not well developed socially, for example, will be greatly handicapped when attempting to achieve well in situations involving the world of work as well as in more informal interactions with other human beings.
3. With more leisure time available for many American citizens as compared to earlier times, it is imperative that positive recreational pursuits are in evidence. Thus, for example, the emotional development and physical achievement of individuals are of utmost importance.

Readiness for Learning

To achieve to the optimum in a given unit of study, pupils need to obtain adequate background experiences. The teacher needs to guide pupils to achieve in the following areas in terms of readiness for learning:

1. The pupil must have enough background information to benefit from a new unit of study.
2. If these prerequisites have not been met, then objectives need to be stated at an easier level. Pupils need to be successful in achieving new goals in the social studies.

3. A variety of learning activities may be provided to assist learners in securing necessary readiness experiences to benefit from ongoing tasks, such as the use of picture, films, slides, filmstrips, discussions, and field trips.
4. Problem solving approaches may be utilized to guide learners in achieving necessary prerequisite learnings. Within the framework of problem solving, critical thinking may be utilized to appraise necessary content in arriving at solutions. Creative thinking may be used to arrive at unique and novel solutions to problems.
5. Feedback from learners should be utilized in determining if pupils are ready for achieving new objectives.
6. Pupils should have ample opportunities to raise questions in a stimulating environment for learning. The individual learner will reveal where he/she is presently in achievement.
7. The teacher needs to guide pupils to engage in self evaluation. Thus, learners may be involved in assessing readiness for learning.
8. The teacher must attempt to select those learning experiences which will guide pupils to experience continuous progress and success in achieving new objectives.
9. Using appropriate pretesting techniques can aid in determining if pupils are ready to benefit from stated objectives in a new unit of study. Thus, discussions may be utilized in determining where pupils are presently in social studies achievement.

Teacher-Pupil Planning

To emphasize democracy as a way of life in the school setting, pupils must have ample opportunities to engage in helping to plan objectives, learning experiences, and assessment procedures. Teacher-pupil planning can become an important part of the elementary school curriculum. There are many opportunities during any school day for learners to engage in teacher-pupil planning.

1. The content of learning centers may be developed through teacher-pupil planning.
2. Bulletin board displays might be an end result of teacher-pupil planning.
3. Problem areas for an ongoing unit may be developed through teacher-pupil planning.
4. Reference sources utilized in problem-solving activities may be cooperatively identified.
5. Standards of conduct can be developed by pupils with teacher guidance.

6. Selected objectives for a unit of study can be identified cooperatively involving pupils and teachers.
7. Means of evaluating pupil achievement during and at the end of a unit may be planned by pupils with teacher leadership.

There are important standards to follow when teacher-pupil planning is utilized as a learning activity in the school setting:

1. All should participate with no one dominating the discussion.
2. Ideas should be presented to the total group and not a few individuals only.
3. Ideas should be discussed and evaluated in depth.
4. Content presented should flow among members within the committee and not between individuals only.

The Learning Environment

Teachers must give careful consideration to the quality of learning environment in the school and class setting. Thus, pupils must experience a quality environment for learning which would aid each to achieve optimal development. Educators, generally agree upon the following standards pertaining to an atmosphere which is conducive to pupil achievement and development:

1. A relaxed environment should be in evidence where pupils may get needed materials as well as share content with others.
2. A supportive climate needs to exist in which pupils feel that concern for their welfare is in evidence.
3. Pupils individually are rewarded for achieving at an optimal rate of growth.
4. Mutual respect is there for pupils and teachers in the school and class setting.
5. Pupils' rights and the rights of teachers are of mutual concern in ongoing learning experiences.

Child growth and development characteristics must be thoroughly considered when determining the quality of learning environment for pupils in the class and school setting. Primary grade pupils may exhibit the following characteristics:

1. They generally follow the teacher eagerly in terms of expectations.
2. Much physical movement is necessary since these pupils basically are continually on the move when freedom of choice is given in term of activities to participate in.
3. Gradually, these pupils tend to interact more with each other as they progress through the primary school years.
4. The finer muscles are not developed as well as the larger muscles. Thus, handwriting and writing activities in general may cause stress and strain if excessive time is given to these kinds of learning activities.

Intermediate grade pupils tend to reveal general behaviour such as the following:

1. Peer culture is becoming increasingly important where as adult influence may become less important.
2. With more background information, intermediate grade pupils may become more proficient in critical thinking and problem solving as compared to primary grade pupils.
3. Intermediate grade pupils are continually increasing their skills in using the finer muscles. Learning opportunities involving writing experiences can be stressed more frequently as compared to the primary grade levels.
4. Intermediate grade pupils are continually becoming more proficient in social interaction.
5. Intermediate grade pupils should and do become increasingly more independent from adult direction.

The following factors need to be emphasized in ongoing units of study:

1. Pupils must have ample opportunities to work within a committee framework. Skills in positive human relations are important for pupils to achieve. Everyday living stresses the importance of individuals getting along well with others.
2. The use of the larger muscles should be encouraged throughout the public school years. The use of the larger muscles involve experiences such as running, jumping, hopping, skipping, and throwing.
3. Skill in the use of the finer muscles must be continuously emphasized in teaching-learning situations. Refined movements of the human being such as in writing activities should be emphasized in terms of child growth and development characteristics.
4. Critical thinking, creative thinking, and problem solving need to be emphasized throughout the pupil's school years. Life in society demands proficiency in these highly important cognitive skills.
5. Good attitudes must be developed within all learners since optimal achievement in all facets of growth may take place only if affective objectives are achieved by learners.

In Summary

Teachers of social studies, supervisors, and principles must give careful consideration to the design of the curriculum. Factors such as the following must be taken into consideration when designing the curriculum:

1. Social and individual achievement on the part of pupils.
2. Integration or fusion of content in ongoing units of study.

3. The total child being perceived as important in teaching-learning situations.
4. Proper sequence in pupil learning being in evidence.
5. Adequate emphasis being placed on teacher-pupil planning in the social studies.
6. Quality learning environments being stressed.

REFERENCES

Frost, Joe L., and G. Thomas Rowland (Eds.). *The Elementary School, Principles and Problems*. Boston: Houghton Mifflin Company, 1969.

Hass, Glen. *Curriculum Planning*. Fourth Edition. Boston: Allyn and Bacon, Inc., 1983.

Hass, Glen, et. al., (Eds.). *Readings in Elementary Teaching*. Boston: Allyn and Bacon, Inc., 1971.

Joyce, Bruce R., et. al. *The Structure of School Improvement*. New York: Longmans, 1983.

Oliver, Albert I. *Curriculum Improvement*. New York: Dodd, Mead and Company, 1965.

Steeves, Frank L. (Ed.). *The Subjects in the Curriculum*. Indianapolis: The Odyssey Press, 1968.

Stratemeyer, Florence, et. al. *Developing a Curriculum for Modern Living*. New York: Bureau of Publications, Teachers College, Columbia University, 1957.

26

The Integrated Curriculum in the Social Studies

Social studies as one curriculum area in the elementary school may be taught in terms of utilizing the separate subjects approach pattern in organising the curriculum. Thus, units of study could pertain to each of the following separate social science disciplines:

1. History
2. Geography
3. Political science
4. Economics
5. Anthropology
6. Sociology

In examining the social science discipline of history, the following historical units of study could be taught using the separate subjects approach in curriculum organisation:

1. The Age of Discovering New Lands
2. Developing Colonies in the New World
3. The Beginnings of a New Nation
4. Struggling Against European Controls
5. A Dividend Country at War
6. Settling the Western Areas of the United States
7. The United States—A World Power
8. Events Leading to a Modern United States

Each of the above named units of study pertains to a study of selected events and issues of the past or a study of history. No doubts, a few of the other social science disciplines would be brought into each of these social studies units. For example, in units pertaining to "The Age of Discovering New Lands," considerable emphasis would need to be placed on where these new lands were located and where the explorers came from to discover new areas. Thus, the social science discipline of geography would be important in this unit of study.

It utilizing geography as a separate subject to determine the social studies curriculum, the following units of study may be emphasized:

1. Using Maps and Globes
2. Desert Areas of the World
3. How People Live in Rain Forest Regions
4. Major Farming Regions in the World
5. The Arctic and Antarctic Regions

Again, other social science disciplines will become a part of each of the above named units of study which have geography as the core. For example, in studying a unit on "Desert Areas of the World," pupils may study the history of people living in a selected desert region.

In units of study pertaining to political science, the following may be relevant for pupils:

1. Municipal Government—How It Works
2. Our State and Its Government
3. The United Nations
4. Our Federal Government
5. Voting in Elections
6. Laws and How They Affect Us

Units of study emphasizing economics as a separate subject in organising the social studies curriculum include the following titles:

1. Producing Goods and Services in the United States
2. Visiting the Neighborhood Shopping Center
3. The Assembly Line at Work
4. Inflation, Recession, and Depressions
5. Exports and Imports of the United States

Specific social studies units that would pertain to anthropology and sociology may emphasize the following:

1. Visiting the Old Order Amish and the Hutterites
2. Culture in American Society
3. The Bedouins of the Middle East
4. Minority Groups in the United States

It would be difficult to teach social studies units pertaining to anthropology and sociology without emphasizing the other curriculum areas in the elementary school. The integrated curriculum in elementary school social studies could be implemented rather fully in the disciplines of sociology and anthropology since music, art, architecture, sports, foods, customs, and religious beliefs of people would be emphasized in ongoing units of study.

Kim and Kellough provide the following reasons for planning a coherent curriculum:

1. To insure program continuation, your plans are available for a substitute teacher.
2. To evaluate your teaching, your plans may be a criterion recognized and observed by the administration.
3. To provide mechanism for vertical (K-12) articulation, *i.e.*, scope and sequence curriculum development.
4. To prepare for the individual differences of the students within your class.
5. To prevent classroom-control problems: the teacher who has planned carefully is less likely to have severe discipline problems.
6. To serve as a criterion for self-evaluation by the teacher.

Emphasizing the Integrated Social Studies Curriculum

The teacher of social studies must place heavy emphasis upon the integrate curriculum in teaching-learning situations if this is to be become reality. Integration of content in the social studies may come about through teaching-learning situations such as the following:

1. Emphasize problem solving as a way of life in school as well as outside the school setting.
2. Stimulate pupils to ask questions within the confines of a rich learning environment.
3. Use open space education and learning centers in guiding pupils to relate content.

Emphasizing Problem Solving

The teacher in each unit of study must ask stimulating questions of pupils. Thus, pupils may be guided in using a variety of reference sources in attempting to solve these problems. Ultimately, a hypothesis relating to the problem may be developed and evaluated. In gathering content to solve problems, no effort should be given to utilize a specific academic disciplines only. Emphasis rather should be placed upon obtaining information relative to solving specific problem areas.

Problem areas which social studies teachers may identify and guide pupils in solving may be the following pertaining to a unit of study on the Middle East:

1. Why is the Middle East crisis in evidence today?
2. How do customs of Jews and Arabs differ from each other?

How are they alike?

3. Compare Arab and Jewish culture in the following areas:
   (a) Music, art and architecture
   (b) Sports, dress, and foods
   (c) Religious beliefs.

Pupils intrinsically could be motivated to ask challenging questions. Through the use of appealing bulletin board display, pictures, objects, models, charts, graphs, and reading materials, the social studies teacher may guide pupils to identify questions and problems. With the use of these materials within the framework of learning activities, the pupil, for example, may ask questions such as the following related to a unit on Japan:

1. Why is Japan a leading manufacturing nation?
2. How do farming methods used in Japan differ from those used in the United States?
3. How does Japanese music differ from that of the United States? How is it alike?
4. In general, what is considered to be important in Japanese arts products?
5. What are selected representative food dishes in Japan? How does Japanese food differ from that eaten in the United States? How is it alike?

In problem-solving activities in the class and school setting, pupils gather data or content from a variety of reference sources in attempting to arrive at a solution or partial solution. Data sources to solve problems may come from any one, several, or all of the social science disciplines emphasized in elementary school social studies. Generally, content from social science disciplines will be related and integrated when serving as a basis for pupils engaging in problem-solving activities.

Critical Thinking and the Integrated Curriculum

Pupils in the social studies need to have ample experiences in the area of critical thinking. Critical thinking emphasize cognitive skills such as the following:

1. Analyzing content in order to develop depth learnings pertaining to facets of ideas being examined.
2. Examining pros and cons pertaining to content being evaluated.
3. Separating factual data from that which is fantasy in nature.
4. Categorizing content which is accurate as compared to inaccurate.
5. Being able to distinguish between fact and fiction when reading content.

6. Taking a position on an issue after adequately analyzing ideas in an ongoing learning experience.

In the area of critical thinking, students tend to relate content from diverse social science disciplines. Perhaps, a situation in life is being analyzed in terms of viewing human beings from the following points of view:

1. Selected events of the past (history).
2. The natural environment (geography)
3. Goods and services produced and consumed (economics)
4. Laws, rules, regulations, and authority (political science)
5. Customs, values, beliefs, and culture (anthropology)
6. Norms in society, sanctions to uphold these norms, and groups behaviour of individuals (sociology).

Ultimately, after thinking critically, pupils may put together or synthesize knowledge in coming up with a generalization.

Synthesizing Content in the Social Studies

After pupils have adequately analyzed content in an ongoing unit of study, it is necessary to guide learners in relating knowledge or in attempting to integrate ideas. For example, in a unit of study on Brazil, after having analyzed relationships that exist between the climate of that nation and the kinds of agricultural products produced there, pupils need to synthesize content. Thus, pupils may realize generalizations such as the following:

1. The kind of soil, amount of rainfall, and actual temperature aid the Sao Paulo area is being a leading producer of coffee beans (geography).
2. The large amount of coffee produced in Brazil allows this nation to export this product to other nations in the world (economics).
3. Many changes are occurring in Sao Paulo due to technology, inventions, ideas, and movement of people in this large city (history and sociology).

Pupils must have related ideas, facts, and concepts to develop each of the above named generalizations. The third generalization emphasizes more social science disciplines being related or integrated as compared to generalizations one and two. However, even in generalizations one and two, it is difficult to focus upon geography only or economics only. Other social science, disciplines will also be brought in as the need arises such as history, anthropology, sociology, and political science.

In Summary

Pupils must experience ample learning opportunities which guide in the direction of integrating content in the social studies.

The following kinds or types of experiences will help pupils inperceiving that content in ongoing units of social studies is correlated, fused, and related:

1. Engaging in the solving of real problems.
2. Using critical thinking processes in ongoing units of study.
3. Synthesizing facts, concepts, and generalizations.

Pertaining to inquiry methods, Savage and Armstrong wrote:

> Inquiry has some features that clearly differentiate it from the other instructional approaches. One of these features has to do with what the teacher does. In an inquiry lesson, for example, responsibility for gathering data shifts from the teacher to the students. Pupils must decide what information they need. They are encouraged to ask the teacher questions to get this information. This represents a reversal of the more typical pattern, in which the teacher interrogates the pupils.

REFERENCES

Blitz, Barbara. *The Open Classroom, Making It Work*. Boston: Allyn and Bacon, inc., 1973.

Doll, Ronald C. *Curriculum Improvement: Decision Making and Process*. Sixth Edition. Newton, Massachusetts: Allyn and Bacon, Inc., 1986.

Herman, Wayne L., Jr. *Current Research in Elementary School Social Studies*. London: The Macmillan Company, 1969.

Joyce, Bruce R. *New Strategies for Social Education*, Chicago: Science Research Associates, Inc., 1972.

Kim, Eugene C. and Kellough, Richard D, *A Resource Guide for Secondary Teaching*. Fourth Edition. New York: Macmillan Publishing Company, 1987.

Kourilsky, Marilyn and Guaranta, Lory. *Effective Teaching*. Glenview, Illinois: Scott, Foresman and Company, 1987.

Medley, Donald M. et. al. *Measurement-Based Evaluation of Teacher Performance*. New York: Longman, 1984.

Owen, Steven, et. al. *Educational Psychology*. Second Edition. Boston: Little, Brown and Company, 1981. Chapter Nine.

Savage, Tom V. and Armstrong, David G. *Effective Teaching in Elementary Social Studies*. New York: Macmillan Publishing Company, 1987.

Skeel, Dorothy J. *The Challenge of Teaching Social Studies in the Elementary School*. Second Edition. Pacific Palisades: Goodyear Publishing Company, Inc., 1974.

27

Providing for Individual Differences in the Social Studies Curriculum

There are selected differences among pupils which must be considered thoroughly in order to provide for all learners in the class setting. Thus, pupils differ from each other in interest, capacity, achievement, social development, socio-economic level, and psychomotor skills. These traits will now be considered in the order presented above.

Pupil Interest and the Social Studies

There are selected learners in the class setting who feel that social studies is the most interesting curriculum area in the elementary school. Others may feel neutral toward the values to be gained from studying units of study in the social studies, or that it is the least interesting curriculum area in the elementary school. Why do selected pupils feel that social studies is the most interesting curriculum area as compared to those who may dislike studying this curriculum area?

1. The teacher provides for a variety of learning experiences such as the use of excursions, reading activities, films, filmstrips, tapes, slides, pictures, study prints, discussions, resources personnel, and panel work.
2. Plans for grouping pupils are utilized which guide pupils to experience continuous progress such as in the nongraded school.
3. Each pupil is praised for progressing well in the social studies.
4. The teacher is interested in teaching the social studies and this enthusiasm is reflected within learners.
5. Learning activities are selected by the teacher on the basis of capturing pupils' interests.

6. Teacher-pupil planning is utilized in determining objectives, learning experiences, and assessment procedures.
7. The teacher uses feedback from pupils in evaluating when to change learning experiences to something which is more interesting to pupils.
8. The family in the home setting discusses news items and other content pertaining to the social studies.

There is much then that teacher can do in attempting to obtain the interests of pupils in the social studies.

Capacity of Pupils and the Social Studies

Native capacity of learners may be an important consideration to keep in mind when thinking of pupils who achieve well in the social studies as compared to those who may gain less rapidly in this curriculum area. No intelligence test, of course, accurately measures native capacity of pupils. Even the best intelligence tests have their weaknesses in attempting to appraise native capacity. This is true for the following reasons.

1. It is difficult to separate native capacity from opportunities to learn on the part of any student.
2. Test writers have a difficult time in the writing of items on any examination which might truly reflect the native capacity of any individual.
3. A pupil's score on an IQ test generally varies from the first time to the second time the same or an alternate form of the test is taken even when the intervening interval is short between the two times the test was taken.

High capacities on the part of pupils should aid in pupil achievement in the social studies due to the following reasons:

1. If the pupil has considerable native intelligence, chances to develop more complex concepts and generalizations should increase.
2. Schools tend to emphasize abstractions in ongoing learning experiences. Pupils with high IQ's can generally handle abstract content better then learners who have less to show in the area of mental maturity.

Pupils with high intelligence quotients may be guided in the following ways to realize optimal achievement:

1. Do additional tasks at selected learning centers; these tasks require more complex levels of thinking.
2. Engage in research activities requiring a variety of learning experiences.
3. Present research findings to classmates.
4. Interview resource personnel to gather data pertaining to selected problem areas.

5. Plan learning activities with the teacher which would be challenging and purposeful.
6. Work on art and construction projects which would clarify selected concepts and generalizations in depth.

Pupils with below average capacity may need to have the following experiences in ongoing units of study in the social studies.

1. Concrete and semi-concrete learning activities need to be utilized more so than those stressing the abstract.
2. Sequence in learning must be adjusted to where each pupil is presently.
3. Easier tasks must be provided for those pupils who do not have the native capacity that faster achievers possess.
4. Teacher-pupil planning may aid in adjusting learning activities to the present achievement level of slow learners.
5. A variety of learning activities must be in evidence so that all learners may be successful in the class setting.

It is important to provide for all learners regardless of capacity levels. Each pupil is important and has great worth. The teacher must perceive her overall goal in teaching to help and guide each pupil in realizing his/her highest potential. It is important then to continually study each pupil in order to determine where his or her present achievement level is. The teacher may then determine which learning opportunities would be most beneficial for each child in the class setting.

Pupil Achievement in the Social Studies

It is vital to guide each pupil to achieve optimal development in the social studies. Pupils, of course, differ much from each other in achievement in the social studies as well as in other curriculum areas in the elementary school. How can the teacher of social studies aid each pupil to progress well?

1. Use teacher-pupil planning in selecting relevant units of study.
2. Have pupils within a structured frameword select what they wish to learn.
3. Let learners individually pace their own achievement in terms of rate of speed.
4. Reward each pupil for improved performance.
5. Permit pupils to have ample opportunities in assessing their own achievement with instructor guidance.
6. Have adequate materials from which pupils may learn.
7. Carefully develop appropriate teaching strategy to initiate, develop, and culminate ongoing units of study.
8. Use inductive approaches adequately in the teaching of pupils.

9. Use stimulating teaching materials when expository methods of instruction are used in ongoing learning opportunities.
10. Give pupils assistance and guidance when necessary in teaching-learning situations.
11. Do not label pupils such as being "dull", "slow", and "disinterested".
12. Provide for different styles of learning in the class setting.
13. Respect all pupils regardless of race, creed, and socio-economic levels. Naylor and Diem wrote:

    Every child possesses certain physical, emotional and social characteristics that make him or her unique. For the most part these differences fall within a range of anticipated norms. Exceptional children, however, fall outside these normative standards. Some have mental or learning impairments that cause them to perform significantly below grade-level norms. And some children have visual, auditory, speech, or orthopedic impairments that may or may not affect their ability to meet grade-level standards.

    Not so many years ago, handicapped children were denied equal access to public schooling. With the passage of Public Law 94-142, that situation has changed dramatically. Many handicapped children are now being mainstreamed into regular classrooms for part or all of the school day. Not every handicapped child is well served by placement in a regular classroom, but many are. The goal of mainstreaming involves more than the mere presence of handicapped children in a regular classroom.

Social Development and the Pupil

Pupils differ much from each other in social development. Thus, learners individually may exhibit behaviour such as the following when interacting with others.

1. Being shy, withdrawn, and reserved.
2. Exhibiting aggressive behaviour in wanting to dominate others.
3. Revealing kind, friendly, and polite behaviour.
4. Being overly polite and wishing to impress others.
5. Talking "down" to other individuals.
6. Being aloof and impersonal.
7. Avoiding the discussion of controversial issues.
8. Showing feelings of mistrust to others.
9. Being a showoff and wishing to entertain others.
10. Revealing tremendous leadership capacity.
11. Being quiet and studious.
12. Wanting to be the "strong person" in a group.
13. Disagreeing constantly with others.
14. Being considerate of others.
15. Holding grudges for long periods of time.

The teacher must study individual pupils in terms of present levels of attainment in social growth and guide learners in living rich, full lives. Each child needs to experience that which is fulfilling. Thus, pupils must experience a learning environment filled with diverse kinds of experiences which are interesting, meaningful, and purposeful. Adequate emphasis must be placed upon learners engaging in committee work if social development is to be in evidence. Committee work, in and of itself, definitely will not guide pupils in achieving well socially. Each pupil must experience success and satisfaction within committee settings in order that positive social development may be in evidence. The teacher then must plan learning centers or arrange pupils in committee work which will foster skills in the area of social development.

1. Pupils with teacher aid plan and implement worthwhile standards of conduct in the class setting. These criteria must stress the importance of the total growth of each individual, including social development.
2. Pupils with the supervision of the teacher initiate, develop, and evaluate a mural pertaining to content in an ongoing unit of study.
3. Learners in a committee write and present a short play relating to a unit of study.
4. With teacher guidance, a committee of learners constructs models relating to content being studied in social studies units.
5. Within a committee setting, pupils plan and execute a dramatization such as creative dramatics or a pantomime.
6. Pupils engage in conversation in the class setting. Proper standards for conversing should be stressed in this learning activity involving oral communication.

Socio-Economic Levels and the Pupils

Pupils come from diverse socio-economic levels in the home and community setting. Thus, pupils may come from homes such as the following:

1. There is barely enough income to obtain the necessities of life.
2. The parent or parents are unemployed and depend upon welfare funds in order to obtain food, clothing, and shelter.
3. Selected pupils come from a very favorable home environment with adequate income and loving parents.
4. A child lives with a grandparent; the child was not wanted by the parents.
5. There are seven children living with one parent in a one bedroom house; the combination living and dining room is

very small. The parent finds it very difficult to obtain enough money to provide for the needs of these children.

Many other descriptions could be given of pupils who come from favourable as well as unfavourable home environments.

What can the teacher do to provide for individual differences among pupils who come from homes representing diverse socio-economic levels?

1. Accept all pupils as human beings having much worth.
2. Assess each pupil to determine present levels of achievement. The curriculum may then be adjusted to present achievement levels of learners.
3. Encourage each child to achieve to his/her own optimum rate of achievement. Do not force pupils in the class setting to achieve at the same rate at the same time in any given curriculum area.
4. Attempt to determine the learning style of each pupil and provide learning experiences beneficial to each learner in the school and class setting.
5. Have adequate knowledge pertaining to the home and community environment of each pupil. The teacher needs to use this information to improve the curriculum for each learner.
6. Have pupils with teacher guidance, sequence their own progress in learning.
7. Hold frequent conferences with individual pupils to obtain feedback to improve the curriculum.
8. Use unsigned questionnaires to obtain information for pupils on interests, hobbies, and talents.
9. Use a variety of evaluation techniques to obtain data from each learner to improve the curriculum.
10. Show genuine interest in each pupil.

Psychomotor Skills and the Pupil

Pupils need to achieve well in the psychomotor domain. Thus, pupils must develop skill in the use of the muscles or eye hand coordination. Learners will be at different levels of achievement here as is indicated by the following examples:

1. Jimmy is in the fifth grade and has little or no interest in baseball, basketball, or other athletic endeavours. He has difficulty catching a baseball thrown from a nearby area.
2. Carl is proud of being the fastest runner among classmates. He actively participates and excels in games involving physical movement.
3. Alice, a third grade child, prefers to watch others rather than participate in the playing of games.

4. John, a sixth grade student, wants to become a professional basketball player. He spends as much time as possible playing basketball, as well as engaging in other sports, in the home and school setting.
5. Mary, a fourth grade pupil, is almost always chosen first when teams are formed to play either baseball or basketball. Pupils admire her for performing as well as any boy in athletic events.

Pupils do admire others who are able to use their muscles well. Pupils who are proficient in the playing of games may enjoy considerable status. What can the teacher do to guide pupils in developing needed skills in the psychomotor domain.

1. Develop an environment whereby pupils respect each other regardless of present achievement in the psychomotor domain.
2. Stimulate pupils in wanting to participate in learning experiences involving the psychomotor domain.
3. Develop positive attitudes within pupils pertaining to the use of the muscles in teaching-learning situations.
4. Integrate an adequate number of psychomotor objectives into the social studies curriculum.
5. Have pupils engage in learning activities in which success may be experienced.

The following are selected learning experiences in the social studies for pupils in the psychomotor domain:

1. Pupils learn representative folk dances pertaining to the unit presently being studied.
2. Learners play games that children play in other countries of the world, as these units are being studied.
3. Pupils engage in construction activities as they relate to ongoing units of study.
4. Learners develop a mural, a frieze, or individual sketches directly related to the ongoing unit of study.
5. Puppets and marionettes are made by pupils individually or in a committee.
6. Pupils dip candles, make butter, or engage in similar process activities in the social studies.

In Summary

Definite provisions should be made for individual pupils in the class setting.

Differences that exist among pupils in the school and class setting include the following:

1. Differences in pupil interest in ongoing learning experiences.
2. Differences in capacity among learners.
3. Differences in achievement among learners.

4. Differences in social development.
5. Differences in socio-economic levels.
6. Differences in psychomotor development.

It behooves the teacher to study each pupil thoroughly in terms of the above named characteristics. The teacher of social studies needs to set realistic goals for each pupil to achieve in all facets of development. Relevant learning opportunities need to be provided for pupils in order to achieve these objectives. Evaluation of pupil achievement is then necessary to determine if desired objectives have been met.

Karel wrote the following pertaining to individual differences:

1. All children are special. They have different needs, and they learn at different rates and in different ways.
2. It is the responsibility of the school to meet any needs of children that are educational in nature.
3. The learner is to be trusted. Positive teacher perceptions can increase effective intellectual functioning.
4. Every child is entitled to an education suited to his or her learning style.
5. Instructing large groups, though outwardly efficient, has many liabilities. If is effective for some learners, ineffective for others.
6. All children do not have to be taught everything. Some children learn without school instructions; some children must be taught the same thing in many ways.

REFERENCES

Goodwin, William L., and Herbert J. Klausmeier. *Facilitating Student Learning*. New York: Harper and Row, Publishers, 1975.

Karel, Rose. *Teaching Language Arts to Children*. New York: Harcourt Brace Javanovich, Inc., 1982, page 105.

Smith, B. Othaniel. *Fundamentals of Curriculum Development*. Second Edition. New York: Harcourt, Brace and World, 1957.

Schell, Robert E., and Elizabeth Hall. *Fundamental Psychology Today*. Fourth Edition. New York: Random House, 1983, chapters ten and eleven.

Van Til, William. *Curriculum: Quest for Relevance*. Second Edition. Boston: Houghton Mifflin Company, 1974.

Wright, Betty Atwell, et. al. *Elementary School Curriculum, Better Teaching Now*. New York: The Macmillan Company, 1971.

28

Creative Experiences in the Social Studies

In society life demands that individuals be creative in solving personal and social problems. Personal problems which need to be solved in a creative way include the following:

1. Selecting a job, occupation, or vocation.
2. Buying a house or place of business.
3. Financing one's purchasing of a house or place of business.
4. Selecting a college or university to attend and financing the costs of education.
5. Making friends.
6. Joining selected clubs and organisation.

Social problems that need solving in society include the following:

1. Preventing war and racial discrimination.
2. Providing all individuals in society with quality opportunities in life, such as good jobs, education, and housing regardless of race or creed.
3. Avoiding inflation and unemployment.
4. Preventing hunger and a lack of nutrition.
5. Working in the direction of helping individuals to get along well with others.

Personal as well as social problems in society demand creative solutions. Learning activities for pupils involving creative thinking become very important. What are selected learning experiences for pupils to aid in developing creative thinkers?

Writing Poetry

Pupils may express their own thoughts and feelings in a creative way through the writing of poetry. Pupils may be stimulated in writing poems at a learning center or when the class is taught as a whole. Pictures, objects, discussions, transparencies, tapes, excursions, filmstrips, slides, and films may be utilized as learning experiences to stimulate pupils in desiring to write poetry in a creative manner pertaining to ongoing social studies units. Kinds of poems to write include couplets, triplets, quatrains, limericks, haiku, tanka, and free verse.

Making Models

Creative behaviour may be expressed by pupils individually or in committees in the making of models related to ongoing units of study.

1. In a unit on "Early Southern Colonies in the New World," pupils may develop relevant parts of a model on Jamestown Colony. Much research will go into the development of this model.
2. A model castle may be constructed pertaining to a unit on "The middle Ages." A cardboard box may be used in making the model. A knife is utilized to cut the configuration of the castle. Ultimately, tempera paint can be used to put in details on the castle. Much research will generally be done to complete this project successfully. Pupils will need to look at pictures and read content on castles. A learning activity such as this may branch out to understanding the kinds of rooms contained in a castle, how the land was farmed near the castle, the role of the church in the lives of people during the Middle Ages period, and the relationship of noblemen to kings.
3. Pupils may develop sack, stick, and sock puppets pertaining to a unit on "The Neighbourhood Supermarket." Pupils may play the role of workers in the supermarket with the use of these puppets. Related background scenery should be developed pertaining to the using of these puppets. No doubt, as the puppets are made and used, pupils will find additional content is needed to develop a presentation for the class. A good reference center is then needed to guide pupils in getting needed information.
4. In a unit on "Our School," first grade pupils with teacher guidance may take an excursion to carefully view the school building and its surroundings. Following the excursion, the teacher may guide learners in developing a flat map portraying features viewed during the excursion. A large sheet of paper, covering approximately one-sixth of a traditional classroom, should be placed on the floor. The directions on the flat projection harmonize with exact directions in the out-

of-doors. Pupils with teacher direction make models or draw pictures of buildings, sidewalks, and streets on the map. Other data may also be put on the map such as stop signs, signal lights, and speed limit signs. Children in the school setting realize that reality can be placed in a smaller area such as in a map.

Processing Items

Pupils should develop relevant understandings, skills, and attitudes pertaining to processing selected items related to ongoing units of study.

1. In a unit entitled "Visiting a Diary," pupils should experience how butter is made. This could bring in a study of the past or history with the use of butter churns in the class setting. If possible, pupils should have an opportunity to visit a dairy where butter is made to observe present day practices in this area. Pupils can participate in processing raw materials in the making of butter in the class setting.
2. If pupils are studying a unit on "Colonization in the New World," they could dip candles using approaches and procedures of Puritans and Pilgrims. Reference sources need to be utilized by learners to get necessary data on performing the process of making candles. Pupils should use the candles in the class setting to provide light. Learners can notice the differences between candle light and electric lights to provide illumination in the class setting.
3. Pupils should experience the making of cloth with the use of a loom. Pupils with teacher guidance may make a loom. The loom can also be purchased. If pupils, are studying a unit on the American Indian, learners may make and weave cloth. In units pertaining to the American Indian and other minority groups, it is only appropriate to deemphasize stereo-types. Accurate concepts and generalizations need to be developed by pupils pertaining to minority groups and their many contributions.

Music and the Social Studies

Pupils learn much about a country or culture by listening to musical recordings. If pupils are studying a unit on the Middle East, they learn much from listening to musical recordings pertaining to that area of the world. The following understandings, skills, and attitudes may be acquired from listening to these recordings:

1. How Arab and Israeli music differ from that of other nations.

2. Which instruments are a part of the recorded music of the Middle East.
3. What content is mentioned rather frequently in the recorded music.
4. Develop an appreciation for music of the Middle East area of the world.

In the unit on the Middle East, pupils could participate in the following music and creative expression activities:

1. Writing poetry (couplets, triplets, quatrains, as well as limericks and setting the words to music).
2. Drawing a picture pertaining to content heard in recorded music.
3. Writing stories pertaining to feelings obtained from listening to recorded music.
4. Singing songs written about the Middle East area in a creative manner.

Dramatic Activities

Pupils may exhibit creative behaviour, as well as have learnings become realistic, when participating in dramatizations. There are several kinds of dramatic activities that pupils may participate in.

Pantomiming as one kind of dramatization may help pupils breathe life into understandings gained from ongoing units of study. When pupils participate in pantomiming, no spoken words are utilized. The following, among others, could be appropriate learning experiences for pupils involving pantomiming:

1. In a unit on "Manufacturing in Our Community" pupils could play the role of assembly line workers after having taken an excursion to a factory. The pantomime can be evaluated by participators in terms of accuracy and completeness. Additional information may need to be obtained pertaining to working on an assembly line. Various kinds of reference materials give pupils needed information.
2. If first grade pupils are studying a unit on the farm, they may pantomime the role of workers involved in farming. For example, after pupils have viewed a modern poultry farm, they could pantomime the approaches used to feed and water laying hens in cages as well as the gathering of eggs from a conveyor belt.

Creative dramatics involves the use of spoken language as the need arises. Spontaneously, pupils use language as the situation calls for this in creative dramatics. The following are situations where creative dramatics may be utilized as learning experiences:

1. Pupils studying a unit on "Visiting Australia" may develop a dramatization in a visit to a cattle station.

2. In an ongoing unit on "Living in Brazil," pupils may dramatize selected events related to the growing of coffee. Background content is necessary in planning for the dramatization. Related films, filmstrips, slides, pictures, encyclopaedias, library and trade books, as well as information received from knowledgeable resource personnel can aid learners in getting background information. Following the presentation of the dramatization, learners find that additional information is necessary to clarify content. The dramatization can branch out to other learnings in the previously mentioned unit on Brazil. Thus, pupils may wish to learn about the geography, government economic system, culture and traditions, as well as the history of Brazil.

Formal dramatizations should not be used frequently in the elementary school social studies program for the following reasons:

1. They consume much time in preparing to the exclusion of other purposeful learning experiences.
2. Polished performances are not generally considered an important domain of the elementary school curriculum. These performances are reserved for the high school level. Participation in formal dramatizations does provide for individual interests on the secondary school level.

Formal dramatizations in the elementary school social studies program may involve learning activities such as the following:

1. In a unit on "The Age of Discovery," a committee of intermediate grade pupils could write a play on happenings to Columbus and his men as they sailed to the New World on the Pinta, Nina, and Santa Maria. Parts in the play could be ready by individuals. Costumes and scenery may also be developed for the play. Pupils with teacher guidance plan each facet of developing and presenting the play.
2. Pupils with teacher supervision may decide which facets of a unit on "Visiting Japan" lend themselves to play writing. Pupils volunteer to write the play. A second committee of pupils complete objects needed by the actors to perform their role. A third committee plans and designs scenery for the play. Parents should be invited to view the presentation in the class setting.

Criteria to follow when pupils engage in formal dramatizations include the following:

1. The development and presentation of the play guide learners to achieve desired objectives.
2. The time allotted to completing the formal dramatization must harmonize with priorities in the curriculum.

3. All pupils in the class setting experience worthwhile learning activities.
4. The formal dramatization must not be a polished performance to the extent that pupils lose out on other worthwhile learning activities.

Creative Writing in the Social Studies

There are numerous opportunities that pupils must have pertaining to creative writing in the social studies. The following may be worthwhile learning experiences for pupils in ongoing units of study:

1. In a unit on "Colonial America" pupils may creatively reconstruct, based on research, day by day experiences of a child in that period of time.
2. Pupils individually may select a picture from several at a writing center in a unit entitled "Living in Great Britain" and write about what might have happened prior to or after the chosen illustrated scene.
3. When studying a unit on the Middle East, pupils write diary entries relating to Bedouin life. Creative reconstruction of experiences is important.
4. Pupils on the first grade level when studying a unit on "Living in the City" dictate content to the teacher for recording on constructing a skyscraper, visiting a department store, or riding to work on the subway.
5. Pupils individually or in a committee write on feelings developed when listening to recorded music pertaining to a specific country.
6. After viewing a video tape on an area or country being studied, pupils may think of problem areas which they would like to have solved. The identified problems would relate to gaps in knowledge pupils perceived as they viewed the contents of the video tape.
7. After reading a library book related to an ongoing unit of study, pupils individually write a different ending, or a completely different story as compared to that contained in the library book.

Art Work in the Social Studies

There are many occasions when pupils exhibit creative behaviour in the area of art. Thus, pupils may participate in learning experiences such as the following:

1. In a unit on "Living on a Farm," pupils individually develop a farm scene using media of their own choosing.

2. Pupils in a committee develop a mural on "Visiting Japan" Cooperatively, these learners would need to decide upon the content to be placed in the moral.
3. A committee of learners decides upon the content to be put in a frieze. Each learner assumes ultimate responsibility for his or her illustration to be put in a frieze. Five separate scenes may become the end results of this frieze. A variety of art media should be utilized.
4. Dioramas could be developed by learners individually or in a committee. The contents of the diorama are represented in three dimensional form.

Problem Solving in the Social Studies

Pupils may reveal creative behaviour in problem solving activities. Generally, pupils will proceed through the following steps flexibly when engaging in the solving of problems:

1. From a stimulating learning environment, identify relevant questions which require research in obtaining possible solutions.
2. Use appropriate learning activities based on the present achievement level of pupils to get needed related information.
3. Develop hypotheses (possible solutions) related to the identified problems. View the consequences of each hypothesis.
4. Engage in more data gathering from a variety of reference sources to check hypotheses.
5. Revise or refute hypotheses, if necessary.

Learners need to be stimulated to identify problem areas. To provide a stimulating learning environment, the teacher may have the following learning centers for pupil involvement in a unit pertaining to the Middle East:

1. An interesting caption should appear on a bulletin board display with pictures on the Golan Heights area, the Sinai penisula, the West Bank of the Jordan, and the Dead Sea area.
2. A slide presentation can be shown on the Middle East including scenes on the Old City of Jerusalem, the Judean Hills, the Dome of the Rock (a Moslem mosque), and the Jewish Wailing Wall.
3. Pupils may listen to a newscast. Newscasts tend to contain items on the Middle East.

From the pervious learning experiences mentioned, pupils begin to identify problems which they perceive to be relevant.

Following the identification of problem areas, pupils should be introduced to related reference sources. The following data sources give pupils needed content when attempting to solve problems:

1. Maps, globes, charts, graphs, and tables.
2. Encyclopaedias, library and trade books, reputable almanacs, and pamphlets.
3. Daily newspapers, weekly news magazines, and classroom newspapers written specifically for children.
4. Filmstrips, films, tapes, pictures, objects, and video tapes.
5. Models, excursions, and presentations by resource personnel.
6. Experiments, dramatizations, and debates.
7. Panels, discussions, interviews, and committee work.
8. Software packages.

After obtaining adequate data to a problem area, pupils need to develop a hypothesis or hypotheses. Developing hypotheses involves understanding, skills, and attitudes such as the following:

1. Critical assessment of content obtained.
2. Creative approaches in reconstructing information.
3. Original conclusions being achieved from obtained data.

The final steps in problem solving include

1. Gathering more information from a variety of reference sources to evaluate the accuracy of the stated hypothesis.
2. Changing the hypothesis if evidence warrants.

In Summary

There are many approaches or ways in which pupils reveal creative behaviour.

1. Pupils write poetry related to ongoing units of study.
2. Models may be developed by learners revealing creative thinking.
3. Pupils with teacher guidance process relevant items in ongoing units of study.
4. Efforts in setting words to music can stress creative behaviour within selected pupils.
5. Dramatic activities provide for individual differences in the class setting.
6. An ample number of learning experiences involving creative writing should be emphasized in the school setting.
7. Content in the social studies may be expressed through art work.
8. Problem solving activities encourage creative behaviours.

REFERENCES

Bremer, Anne, and John Bremer. *Open Education, A Beginning*. New York: Holt, Rinehart and Winston, 1972.

Burns, Paul C. and Betty L. Broman. *The Language Arts in Childhood Education*. Fifth edition. Boston: Houghton Mifflin Company, 1983. "Writing Creative Poetry" Pages 205-212.

Chenfeld, Mimi Brodsky. *Teaching Language Arts Creatively*. Second edition. New York: Harcourt Brace Jovanovich, 1987. Chapter 9 "Write? Of course Write".

Dennis, J. Richard and Robert J. Kansky. *Instructional Computing*. Glenview, Illinois. Scott Foresman and Company, 1984.

Ediger, Marlow. *Language Arts Curriculum in the Elementary School*. Kirksville, Missouri: Stenographic Office of Northeast Missouri State University, 1983. Chapter 4, "Poetry in the Elementary School".

Howes, Virgil M. *Informal Teaching in the Open Classroom*. New York: The Macmillan Company, 1974.

Jarolimek, John, and Huber M. Walsh (Eds.). *Readings for Social Studies in Elementary Education*. Third Edition, New York: Macmillan Publishing Company, 1974.

Shive, R. Jerrald. *Social Studies As Controversy*. Pacific Palisades. Goodyear Publishing Company, Inc., 1973.

Smith, James A. *Creative Teaching of the Social Studies in the Elementary School*. Boston: Allyn and Bacon, Inc., 1967.

Thomas, R. Murray, and Dale L. Brubaker. *Curriculum Patterns in Elementary Social Studies*. Belmont, California: Wadsworth Publishing Company, Inc., 1971.

Tiegs, Ernest W., and Fay Adams. *Teaching the Social Studies*. Boston: Ginn and Company, 1959.

29

Current Affairs in the Social Studies

A relevant current affairs program is necessary in the elementary school. Current affairs instruction can keep the school curriculum updated. This would be true for the following reasons:

1. What is happening presently is being emphasized in a quality current affairs program.
2. Pupils may keep abreast of happenings in different fields of knowledge such as social studies and its separate contributing disciplines, namely history, geography, political science, economics, sociology, and anthropology; science and its contributing disciplines such as biology, chemistry, botany, zoology, physics, geology, astronomy, and space travel; and new findings and knowledge in mathematics, health, and literature.

Current affairs instruction in elementary school social studies is important for the following reasons:

1. Boundaries of countries and nations change.
2. New presidents, prime ministers, and kings become leaders in given countries.
3. Wars erupt between and among nations.
4. Friendships change between countries as well as among countries on the face of the earth.
5. Catastrophes happen in selected areas of the world such as earthquakes, volcanic eruptions, floods, famines, and other natural phenomena.
6. The concentration of wealth changes within selected countries on the face of the earth. For example, the oil-producing nations have accumulated large concentrations of wealth.

7. Economics conditions change from prosperity, for example, to recessions and depressions.
8. Concerns change within a country. A country, for example, may change its concerns about inflation to that of avoiding a recession or depression.
9. Countries and nations on the face of the earth face situations involving rapid change in culture, beliefs, and values.

Learning Activities and Current Affairs Instruction

Learning activities in the area of current affairs should be *(a)* interesting, *(b)* meaningful, *(c)* individualized, *(d)* purposeful, and *(e)* satisfying to the learner.

There are many kinds of learning experiences for pupils in current affairs instruction.

1. Pupils may be encouraged to report in class relevant happenings in the news. Contents of the report can then be discussed in class.
2. The teacher can have pupils listen to newscasts on radio during the regular school day. A discussion of the contents of the newscast is important to clarify learnings as well as to stimulate pupils to pursue selected topics, concepts, and generalizations further.
3. Pupils could bring selected news clippings to class for discussion purposes.

These clippings could be arranged around a world map. Colored yarn may be used to connect the event with the area or place where it happened on a world map.

4. For homework, pupils might listen to a radio or television newscast to gain relevant information pertaining to a problem or question identified in class.
5. Each pupil could develop a riddle pertaining to a news item. Others learners can guess the answer to this riddle.
6. A pupil may pantomime the contents of a selected news item. Others learners may guess what information is being pantomimed.
7. Pupils in a committee may plan and develop a frieze pertaining to selected items from a completed newscast.
8. Each pupil can develop an illustration pertaining to a selected news item.
9. Learners in a committee may complete a diorama based on content from a specific newscast.
10. A committee of pupils may wish to dramatize selected facets of content from a newscast.
11. Each pupil may write a summary of main ideas covered in a newscast listed to in the class setting.

12. Selected items on a newscast may lend themselves to pupils engaging in the writing of poetry, such as couplets, triplets, quatrains, haiku, and limericks.
13. Pupils may engage in predicting what will happen next after having listened to selected news items.
14. Learners may critically assess decisions that were made in government on the local, state, and national levels.
15. Pupils individually may write true-false, multiple choice, matching, completion, and essay items on current affairs happenings.
16. Pupils could present a newscast of their own after editing items from a radio newsreport.

Jarolimek wrote the following on the development of bulletin boards.

> The teacher should prepare a display of interesting news pictures and stories to which the child turn for information concerning current affairs. Because items on the news bulletin board should be changed frequently, it should be in a place in the room where children pass regularly. A point near the doorway is a good location.
>
> It is good procedure to discuss the significance of the news articles in class before they are posted on the bulletin board. The display should contain items of national and international import as well as items of local interest, sports stories, developments in science, people in the news, perhaps even oddities and jokes for variety and spice. It is helpful to have various sections of the bulletin board specifically designated for such groupings as local news, science in the news, news of our country, and global happenings. This serves as a means of organising the display in a meaningful way.

Objectives and the Current Affairs Program

Pupils should achieve relevant objectives as a result of interacting with interesting, meaningful, and purposeful learning experiences.

Understandings objectives which pupils may achieve in the current affairs program could include the following:

To develop within the pupil an understanding of

1. Economic changes that are occurring in selected countries on the face of the earth.
2. Strife and conflict that is apparent between and among opposing nations as well as within a country.
3. How geography influences the way people live in given countries.
4. Relevant historical events that lead to a selected country's current status.

5. Customs, values, beliefs, and ideals that people presently possess and strive toward.
6. Diverse socio-economic levels in specific cultures and societies.
7. Ways of governing individuals within selected countries.

Adequate emphasis needs to be placed upon skills objectives for pupils to achieve.

Thus, pupils may achieve skills such as the following:

1. Read current affairs content with understanding.
2. Locate content from various reference sources which provide background experiences.
3. Takes notes on current affairs items.
4. Develop an outline pertaining to information obtained.
5. Present an oral report on relevant current affairs items utilizing recommended criteria in reporting content to learners.
6. Listen to radio newscast using a variety of purposes in listening such as comprehending facts, directions, main ideas, sequence of ideas, generalizations, and critically assessing information presented.
7. Thinking creatively about content pertaining to events and issues that are current.

Attitudinal objectives that may be emphasized in the current affairs include the following:

1. Respecting the thinking of others.
2. Wanting to take a position on content acquired.
3. Appreciating opportunities to remain informed in the current affairs.
4. Developing interest in current events and current issues.
5. Desiring to use content from current affairs items to solve problems.
6. Valuing contributions made by others in attempting to keep citizens informed of what is current in terms of local, state, national and international happenings.

Learning Centers and the Current Affairs Curriculum

Open space education and learning centers harmonize well with concepts pertaining to a good current affairs curriculum. Learning centers such as the following may be appropriate in an updated current events and issues program:

1. ***A map center.*** A world map can be placed on a bulletin board. Pupils bring new clippings to school and place them around this map. The clippings should be attached with colored string or yarn to where the event took place. Content from this center needs to be discussed with pupils. A task card must be placed at the learning center containing tasks for pupils which provide for individual differences.

2. ***A speaking center.*** Here, pupils using a cassette recorder may practice presenting news items important on the local, state, national, and international levels. Pupils evaluate their newscasts in terms of agreed upon standards.
3. ***A reference center.*** Pupils read current content from reputable newspapers and newsmagazines. They summarize their ideas in notebook form. Pictures may be drawn or collected directly relating to the written content.
4. ***A listening center.*** Pupils at this learning center may listen to selected newscasts on radio or television. They may select the manner in which they wish to reveal comprehension of content such as in doing art work or engaging in constructing models and objects.
5. ***A writing center.*** Pupils write creative prose and poetry based on current affairs items. Pictures of current issues and events could provide background content for writing creative prose and poetry. A discussion of current affairs items could also provide background information for pupils in creative writing.

Evaluating Achievement in the Current Affairs

The teacher needs to engage in self evaluation to determine how well pupils have achieved in the current affairs. Questions such as the following should be answered by the teacher pertaining to teaching-learning situations:

1. How well did pupils achieve the desired objectives?
2. How well did the learning experiences help pupils to achieve stated objectives?
3. Were learners interested in ongoing learning activities?
4. Did pupils perceive meaning in learning activities participated in?
5. Did each pupil experience success?
6. Were inquiry approaches utilized adequately in teaching-learning situations?
7. Did pupils have adequate opportunities to engage in problem solving, critical thinking, and creative thinking?
8. Did pupils achieve structural ideas as identified by historians, geographers, political scientists, economists, sociologists, and anthropologists?
9. Were learning experiences utilized which helped each pupil develop to his/her optimum.
10. Were valid and reliable assessment procedures utilized to determine pupil achievement?
11. Were the evaluation procedures utilized to assess pupil achievement in harmony with child growth and development characteristics?

In Summary

Public school pupils must experience a quality current affairs program to keep the social studies curriculum updated. A study of current affairs items by the teacher reveals why the current issues curriculum needs to be kept up-to-date. Teachers must select relevant objectives for pupils to achieve. Relevant learning activities should be selected to help pupils achieve desired ends. Open space education and learning centers can harmonize well with a good current affairs program. The teacher must frequently engage in self evaluation to determine if high quality objectives were selected for pupils to achieve. Further evaluation by the teacher pertains to the quality of learning activities for pupils, as well as appropriate evaluation techniques utilized to assess learner achievement.

Kaltsounis wrote the following statements on the value of current affairs instruction:

1. They are a source for meaningful issues.
2. They bring textbook materials up to date.
3. They convey the changing nature of society as well as the persistence of some issues.
4. They enhance the children's ability to judge and distinguish between fact and opinion.
5. They help children become knowledgeable about their world—a valuable characteristic of citizenship.

REFERENCES

Ediger, Marlow. *Social Studies Curriculum in the Elementary School*. Simpson Publishing Company, 1982, chapter eight.

Ellis, Arthur. *Teaching and Learning Social Studies*. Boston: Allyn and Bacon, 1981.

Jarolimek, John. *Social Studies in Elementary Education*. New York: The Macmillan Company, 1986, chapter thirteen.

Kaltsounis, Theodore. *Teaching Social Studies in the Elementary School*. Second edition. Englewood Cliffs, New Jersey: Prentice-Hall, Inc., 1987, page 227.

Michaelis, John U. *Social Studies for Children in a Democracy*. Fifth edition. Englewood Cliffs: Prentice-Hall, Inc., 1972 chapter eight.

Sowards, G. Wesley, and Mary-Margaret Scobey. *The Changing Curriculum and the Elementary Teacher*. Second Edition. Belmont, California: Wadsworth Publishing Company, 1968.

30

Assessing the Social Studies Curriculum

The social studies curriculum needs to be assessed continuously in order to bring in the latest research, trends, and recommendations into teaching/learning situations. A survey of teachers, school administrators, parents, and lay persons may be conducted to notice preferences. A study first needs to be made of *what is* to *what should* be in the social studies. The *what should be* needs to be inherent in the questionnaire sent to respondents. Each item should be written with clarity and be meaningful to the receivers of the questionnaire. Peers need to review the items to make sure that relevancy and meaning is involved in the questionnaire. If the involved numbers are small, all may respond to the questionnaire. If it is a large group, a random sampling of respondents may be chosen. Which items may then appear on the questionnaire?

Questionnaire Items

After a thorough review if the literature on the teaching of social studies, the following are suggested for inclusion in a questionnaire and can be rated on a five point Likert scale by respondents:

1. A study of history should receive major emphasis in the social studies.

Generally on state mandated tests, history is of primary importance in terms of total test items appearing thereon from the social studies. The question arises as to, should there be rational balance among the social science disciplines appearing on the state mandated test? There are a few states which do not emphasize testing in the social studies. Does this indicate that the social studies is of lesser values as compared to reading and mathematics.

2. Geography should receive equal attention in the curriculum as compared to history.

Probably next to history, geography, receives secondary emphasis with the total number of test items on state mandated tests. History and geography are interrelated in that historical events occur within a geographical region. It would be extremely difficult to separate history from geography (Ediger, 1995, 7-10).

3. Government or political science receives third most emphasis in state social studies mandated tests.

A study of local, state, and federal levels of government are then to be emphasized in the social studies. All civilized societies have some form of government with its rules, regulations, and laws.

4. A study of culture (anthropology and sociology) should be strongly stressed in the social studies.

Nations and subgroups may differ much from each other in terms of languages spoken, foods eaten, clothing worn, shelter provided, laws in existence, and farming techniques used.

5. Economics understandings are salient in the social studies since individuals buy goods and services continually in society.
6. Democracy as a way of life should provide major learnings for students.

Here, students would learn about and practice respect for others, human rights, working for the common good, and fairness in life for all in class and in school.

7. Problem solving should be practiced in the social studies.

Students need to seek solutions to personal and social problems. They need to identify and seek solutions for these societal problems such as social inequalities among human beings, racism, poverty, crimes against human beings and property, terrorism, hate crimes, and unfair situations.

8. A good current events program needs to be implemented.

Staying updated in news items and happenings is at the heart of a democratic society. Being informed provides possibilities to make quality decisions personally and in the societal arena.

9. Skills should receive major emphasis in teaching and learning situations (Ediger, 2000, 30-37).

How to do something is more important then subject matter to be learned. Skills are needed to develop and use in being able to think clearly and effectively, using reasoning and logic, as well as to do critical and creative thinking.

10. Attitudes are very valuable to develop within students toward the social studies as well as in life itself.

Good attitudes toward the self, toward others, and toward society, can make for successful living. Negative attitudes could hinder personal and social development (Ediger, 2001, Chapter One).

The responses, after tabulation, can be separated in terms of how many teachers, administrators, parents, and the lay public gave the highest rating and going on down to the lowest, sequentially, for each of the ten categories listed above. The category receiving the highest numerical average rating from respondents might conceivably receive the most emphasis in teaching and learning situations. The other categories would also be stressed in the social studies curriculum, according to average ratings received. In item number one above it was stated that state mandated tests could give higher priority to the teaching of history. Respondents may then take into consideration what is stressed in state mandated tests and what is desired in the local school curriculum. What is desired then may well provide the *scope* of the social studies in the classroom setting. Scope answers the question of *what* should be taught in the social studies.

One important way of determining scope is to look at the social science disciples which provide content for the social studies. Involved social science disciplines providing subject matter for the social studies then include history, geography, political science, anthropology, sociology, and economics Psychology and literature might also be brought in, as needed, in teaching the social studies. It is difficult for the social studies teacher to have adequate knowledge of each of these social science disciplines. By working in committees, the social studies teacher may learn from others in evaluating subject matter more thoroughly in terms of which social science discipline is involved when planning and implementing instruction. Perhaps, an historian or other social scientist may meet with the committee at a designated time (Ediger, 1995, 23-28).

During the 1960s, Bruner's writings (Bruner, 1960) were emphasized strongly in the educational literature. His hypothesis stressed "Any subject matter can be learned by any child at any stage of development in some honest intellectual form." Bruner strongly stressed the importance of students learning structural ideas. These key ideas would then be identified by academicians in the social sciences for use in the social studies. Thus from each academic discipline such as in history, in geography, in political science, in sociology, in anthropology, and in economics, academicians would select, after much deliberation, the structure of knowledge from each social science area. These structural ideas would then be available to teachers for use teaching students. Key ideas, not trivia, would then be provided teachers for teaching/learning situations in the social studies. Even very young children could be taught structural ideas on his/her understanding level. For example, young children could learn about the economic concept of *goods* by actually seeing, feeling, tasting, hearing, and touching what is known as goods. Thus, a purchased toy is representative of the category *goods* and can be seen, felt, heard when shaken, and touched. Not all senses may be used such as tested in this case. But the young child may still learn about the category of goods in the concrete. Structural ideas, identified by social scientists may then be achieved at any age level in some honest, intellectual form. Social scientists should be heavily involved in determining content for students to learn in the social studies. Bruner also placed a heavy emphasis upon students learning content using methodology of the social scientist (Ediger, 1977, Chapter Eleven).

Obtaining subject matter from social scientists for each academic discipline may seem unrealistic. However, those public schools near the universities may attempt to have their teachers work with professors from each/some of the social science disciplines. This may be a definite possibility in having some ideas for teaching social studies come directly from the academic disciplines. The writer has known social scientists who are very willing to work with public school teachers. In fact, they welcome the idea!

A second approach in determining scope or what should be taught in the social studies might well stress the ten themes identified by the National Council for the Social Studies (NCSS, 2001):

1. Culture
2. Time, Continuity, and Change
3. People, Places and Environments
4. Individual identity and Development
5. Individuals, Groups, and Institutions
6. Power, Authority, and Governance
7. Production, Distribution, and Consumption
8. Science, Technology, and Society
9. Global Connections and Interdependence
10. Civic Ideals and Practice

Social studies teachers must discuss the meaning of each theme in depth. With a thorough discussion involving active participation of each social studies teacher, participants might well attach meaning to the different themes. An NCSS web site provides much information pertaining to each of the ten above enumerated themes: http://www.org/links/home.html. This provides further content for teacher understanding and use in the discussion. Informally, teachers may evaluate and rate each of these topics in terms of worth for classroom use. In this way, the social studies teacher may take the initiative in implementing that which has perceived value. The author recommends strongly that teachers do take these ten themes seriously for implementation in social studies lessons and units of study.

A third approach in determining scope in the social studies is in the very careful selection of basal textbooks and expanding therein what is necessary to emphasize relevancy for student learning. The ten themes from the above named NCSS publication is one vital suggestion. Other suggested inclusions are the following:

1. A quality current events program using up-to-date, salient news items and events.
2. Audio-visual aids which assist students to understand and elaborate in a meaningful way that which is contained in the basal text.
3. Library books and other developmental reading materials which emphasize enrichment learning.
4. Student/teacher planning of a project directly relating to the ongoing social studies unit of study.
5. Contract systems whereby the learner agrees to complete selected activities by a certain due date, signed by the involved student and the teacher (Ediger, 2001, 17-19).

Using a carefully chosen basal social studies textbook has its pros and cons, but much of he criticisms given can be changed by the teacher in that

1. Individual differences need adequate provision. One size does not fit all. The basal text needs to be adapted to individual needs and interests.
2. Careful attention needs to be given to the new vocabulary introduced in the basal. The teacher needs to be certain that students, with adequate background information, individually can identify each new word correctly and attach related meanings.
3. Enrichment activities provide expanded meanings to the content contained in the text.
4. Purpose for learning needs to be developed within learners to achieve, grow, and develop.
5. Quality sequence for student learning needs to be in the offing (Ediger, 2001, 79-83).

The unit titles have already been chosen when basals are used in teaching social studies. There is an accompanying manual which provides suggestions for the teacher to use in teaching students in terms of objectives, learning opportunities, and assessment procedures.

Objectives in the Social Studies

After the scope of the social studies has been decided upon, teachers need to select objectives for student attainment. It is good to involve students in the selection of objectives. There are three categories of objectives, basically, for learners to achieve.

Knowledge categories need discreet identification. Vital facts, concepts, and generalizations chosen provide the framework of what students are to achieve in any specific social studies unit. Time and deliberation need to be given in the selection of knowledge ends. Trivia and the insignificant must be avoided. Adequate evaluation of each objectives needs to be given by the individual teacher as well as within group endeavours.

Second, skills objectives need to be chosen for students to achieve in the social studies. Skills pertain to students using acquired knowledge in ongoing lessons and units of study. Knowledge might be used in the following situations:

1. To solve problems
2. To assess the worth of what is being accomplished.
3. To enable the student to pursue the next project or activity.
4. To provide background information for reading a given selection.
5. To identify and pursue a project in the social studies.
6. To do a written learning opportunity.
7. To engage in critical and creative thinking.
8. To apply what has been learned.
9. To comprehend ideas in depth.
10. To assess the value of ideas presented such as in brain storming (Ediger, 1979, 23-25).

The social studies teacher needs to emphasize balance, among knowledge and skills objectives, as well as in the third category to be discussed, namely attitudinal ends. If students develop quality attitudes, the chances are good that knowledge and skills objectives will be attained. The following attitudinal ends are worthy of consideration by social studies teachers:

1. Wanting to learn more about the social studies and its use in society.
2. Developing positive attitudes toward having a variety of learning opportunities in the social studies.
3. Having good human relations with other students.
4. Respecting the thinking of classmates and others in society.
5. Developing interest in learning social studies content.

6. Perceiving reasons for learning subject matter and skills in the social studies.
7. Volunteering to do extra work in ongoing lessons and units of study.
8. Assisting others as needed in the curriculum.
9. Developing feelings of being a part of a community of learners.
10. Desiring become a life long learner in social studies as well as in the larger social and natural environment (Ediger, 1994, 26-28).

From the above named ten attitudinal objectives, it is quite evident that each is very important in developing knowledgeable individuals who can do well as citizens in society.

Evaluation of Student Achievement

A variety of evaluation techniques need to be used to find out what students have learned. These must be valid to assess what has been taught. Reliability is a further valuable consideration when appraising student achievement be it test/retest, split half, or alternate forms. The following have been used to ascertain student achievement in the social studies:

1. State mandated tests.
2. Classroom tests.
3. Teacher observation.
4. Self evaluation by the student.
5. Student evaluation of their own committee endeavours and progress therein.
6. Checklists and rating scales.
7. Student choice of how to reveal achievement and progress (Gardner, 1993).
8. Noticing environmental conditions to enhance learning (Searson and Dunn, 2001).

Each student needs to achieve as optimally as possible in the social studies. It is important to assess each facet of the social studies in its development and maintenance. The social studies is not static but subject to continuous modification and change based on rational thinking.

REFERENCES

Bruner, Jerome (1960), The Process of Education. Cambridge, Massachusetts: Harvard University Press, p. 33.

Ediger, Marlow (1995), "Concerns in the Geography Curriculum, Perspectives, 27 (2), 7-10.

Ediger, Marlow and D. Bhaskara Rao, (2001), *Teaching Social Studies Successfully*. New Delhi: Discovery Publishing House, Chapter One.

Ediger, Marlow (1977), "Scope and Sequence in the Curriculum," *The Elementary Curriculum—A Handbook*. Kirksville, Missouri: Simpson Publishing Company, Chapter Eleven.

Ediger, Marlow (2000), "Social Studies Children's Literature," *College Student Journal*, 34 (10), 30-37.

Ediger, Marlow (1995), "Leadership in Curriculum", *Education Magazine*, nr. 113, pp. 23-27. Published by the Qatar National Commission for Education—The Middle East.

Ediger, Marlow (2001), "A Project Method," In Focus, 30 (1) 17-19.

Ediger, Marlow (2001), "The School Principal: State Standards Versus Creativity," *Journal of Instructional Psychology*, 28 (2), 79-83.

Ediger, Marlow (1979), "The Middle East and Unit Teaching," *The Intermediate Teacher*, 18 (1), 23-25.

Ediger, Marlow (1994), "Human Relations Amidst Change," The Progress of Education, 69 (2), 26-28. Published in India.

Gardner, Howard (1993), *Multiple Intelligences: Theory into Practice*. New York: Basic Books.

National Council for the Social Studies (2001), *The Curriculum Standards for Social Studies*. Washington, DC: NCSS.

Searson, Robert, and Rita Dunn (2001), *"The Learning Styles Teaching Model," Science and Children*, 38 (5), 22-26.

31

Computers in Social Studies

Computers are common in the school setting. Too frequently, they are not utilized adequately The computers are there, but they need to be used optimally in the classroom setting.

In society computers and computer service abound. Computers are common then in all types and kinds of businesses, including supermarkets, banks, and hardware stores, among others. School and society should not be separated. Since computers are fully in evidence in society, students in the school curriculum need to become proficient in utilizing that which is positive, efficient, and beneficial to people. The intent of computer use, as well as its consequences, will assist in determining its positive utilization.

Principles of Learning and the Computer

There are selected principles of learning applicable to computer and software use. These principles have stood the test of time and should be used flexibly in selecting objectives, learning activities, and appraisal procedures. In computer and software use, students need to attach meaning to ongoing learning opportunities. If learners experience meaningful activities, they understand what has been learned. Opposite of meaningful content are those experiences not understood and not making sense. Software then needs to be on the present achievement level of the involved student. Based on the present achievement level of the student, new learnings are to be attained by students. The new content must be meaningful and achievable. Frustration and failure set in if students do not perceive meaning in what is being learned.

Secondly, students need to experience quality sequence in computer and software use. With proper and appropriate sequential learning, success in learning may well be in offing for the involved student. Success in learning assists in developing an improved self concept. Positive self concepts aid students to improve and to achieve in the social studies. Thus, it is necessary that software components possess sequential steps in learning. If the steps in learning are too far apart within the software components, the student may experience failure. Rather, software must be tried out in pilot studies to take the weak spots out of its program.

Thirdly, quality software must contain purposeful content. If learnings are purposeful, students perceive values in acquiring the content, skills, and attitudes. Teachers must assist students to perceive purpose in utilizing computers and software programs. To develop purpose within students inductively, the teacher may ask selected questions covering content in the software to guide learners intrinsically to understand reasons for participation in and interacting with the computer program(s). To stress deduction, the teacher may clearly and concisely explain to learners values of the software program to be utilized. If students perceive purpose in learning, an increased desire to attain and to achieve should be in evidence.

Interest in learning is important. Software use should capture learner interest. If students perceive interest in learning, effort is involved in achieving objectives in the social studies. Too frequently, the student lacks interest in the ongoing learning opportunity, thus achievement is at a rather low level. Rather interest and effort need to become one and not dual in nature. With a high degree of interest in the software program, the student should apply continuous effort in learning.

Motivation is important in achieving vital ends in computerized instruction. With proper motivation, the learner has an increased energy level for learning. Stimuli from the software content then provides for a higher level of motivation. An eager learner desires to achieve and is motivated to attain definite objectives.

Balance among objectives is significant in emphasizing software and computer instruction. Generally cognitive (intellectual domain) objectives are stressed. This emphasis needs to be balanced with affective and psychomotor goals. Affective objectives stress a love for learning. Life itself consists of continuous, sequential learning. Psychomotor objectives reflect the use of the large and fine muscles. Learning opportunities can be developed, psychomotor in nature, which correlate with the software presentation. These activities may include construction experiences, model making, pantomimes, creative dramatics, as well as art tasks. Cognitive objectives should stress critical and creative thinking, problem solving as well as making inferences and predictions.

To summarize guidelines to be utilized in using software and computers, students need to experience meaningful learnings, sequential activities, purposeful tasks, interest in lessons, motivation and stimulation, as well as balance among objectives.

To summarize guidelines to be utilized in using software and computers, students need to experience meaningful learnings, sequential activities, purposeful tasks, interest in lessons, motivation and stimulation, as well as balance among objectives.

Kinds of Software Programs

Software selected for students in the social studies depends upon the purpose involved. Goals are to be achieved by students when using computers in the curriculum. Software programs should not be utilized for the sake of doing so, but rather definite reasons are inherent for the utilization of a specific learning opportunity.

Selected students may need to experience software emphasizing drill and practice. There are definite knowledge items important to learn, and yet these students have not done so and need drill and practice learning opportunities. Software emphasizing drill and practice in the social studies must stress that which is salient and important. The software should also emphasize subject matter necessary to be learned in the social studies unit being taught. The drill and practice opportunities need to capture student interests. Being interested in the content will assist learners to master the needed subject matter. Drill and practice experiences have frequently been boring to learners. Routine procedures of subject matter acquisition have been utilized. Software and computer use provide another media for students to learn through drill and practice.

Drill and practice activities should be sequential to the students own unique perception. Students need to interact very frequently to content presented on the monitor. A oneway street of communication in lecture form from what is on the monitor to the student is to be frowned upon. Rather, the learner must make frequent responses to answers wanted to questions presented on the monitor. Learners need to receive frequent feedback from responses made. Thus, for each question presented, the student makes a response. Based on the response, feedback is provided on the monitor to let the learner know of the adequacy of his/her response. If a correct response was made, a reward should be presented on the screen. Excessive time should not be given to show the reward. Rather, the reward clearly shows the involved student the correctness of the response made. Incorrect responses are remediated.

A second type of software stresses tutorial experiences for students in social studies. Tutorial software emphasizes new subject matter for student attainment. New content must be related to previously developed facts, concepts, and generalizations. Tutorials then need to emphasize proper order of experiences for students. Learners need to interact frequently to questions related to content presentation in the tutorial. Active participation, not passive recipients, is important in tutorials. These programs provide opportunities for optimal growth. Debugging of software is a must. Thus, the content contains no spelling, punctuation, and capitalization errors. Adequate pilot studies of the software have taken out in inherent weaknesses. The subject matter is sequential. With successful experiences, students may develop quality attitudes. Related learning to the software tutorial can emphasize psychomotor learnings, such as creative art endeavours. New subject matter is to be learned by the students in the tutorial, and the learner is motivated toward achieving definite objectives.

A third type of software in the social studies stresses diagnosis and remediation. To diagnose, specific errors are pointed out on the monitor pertaining to objectives being emphasized. After diagnosis, a program on a disc provides for remediation endeavours. Diagnosis could emphasize at which point a student cannot locate an entry in an encyclopaedia or dictionary. Remediation would emphasize tasks, sequential, to take care of the difficulties.

Software with a diagnostic remediation emphasis must truly pinpoint learner difficulty. Very precisely, the problematic error must be located. Equally salient is that the remediation endeavours assist the learner in taking care of the problem area. A direct relationship must exist between the diagnosis and the remedial concepts.

Too frequently, software has not been effective in identifying specific problems in learning faced by a student. A further problem exists when the remediation work stressed in the software fails to do its specific task. Quality software identifies and remediates problematic situations.

A fourth kind of software in social studies stresses simulations. A simulation emphasizes role playing. A real life-like series of situations are presented. Problem solving is in emphasis in that students make sequential choices from dilemma situations presented on the monitor. For each choice made, the student receives feedback, prior to the next decision to be made.

Simulations should not present artificial situations for students. The programmer must develop reality into the software program. Low risk decision-making is involved to the learner. Thus, a student does not personally experience the negative when responses are made. In life itself, incorrect decisions can be quite defeating to the chooser. The consequences of a choice can indeed be harmful to the student in the actual, societal arena. In simulations, the situations are reality based and as much as possible society based; however, the consequences of each decision is unreal in terms of negative choices made from among alternatives presented on the monitor or screen. The student is then shielded from the harsh realities of life.

Simulations place high value on students learning to make choices and decisions. The choices and decisions are based on reality and realness, rather than the fanciful and the absurd. Feedback is provided to each student based on the command typed into the computer. The learner can then judge the adequacy of his/her response. Problem solving is in evidence when a decision needs to be made based on alternatives. Several students can be involved in a simulation learning opportunity.

A fifth kind of software stresses the playing of games. Several students will be involved in the playing of a game. Each attempts to be the winner. Thus, a student may select, from among alternatives, whether to play for five, ten, fifteen, or twenty points in attempting to answer a question pertaining to social studies. The lower the point value, the easier it is to answer that question The student then may play it safer by attempting to answer an easier question. Or, more risk may be stressed by attempting to answer a question correctly with each having a higher point value, including twenty points received for answering a single question correctly. At the end of the game, the student with the highest total score is the winner of the game.

Games tend to motivate students to achieve. Play has long been advocated as an important means of learning. Games emphasize the play concept. Since play is enjoyable to students, it can be a significant vehicle to encourage learner progress and achievement. Software game development must emphasize student interest. Interest in an activity makes for effort. Each student needs to be challenged to attain optimally in games. The games help students to achieve definite objectives. Much learning of facts, concepts, and generalizations can come from gaming software. The games, if possible, should relate to ongoing lessons and units in the social studies.

Philosophy of Education and the Computer

There are definite philosophies, different from each other, which may well be utilized with software and computers. One philosophy, namely experimentalism, stresses that students identify and solve life-like problems in the environment. The problems need to come from society. School and society should be integrated, not separated from each other.

Flexible steps are involved in emphasizing problem solving in the classroom. First of all, a problem needs identification and selection. The problem must be clearly stated. A variety of learning opportunities need to be provided so that learners are stimulated to select a problem. Next, data or information needs gathering in answer to the problem. Computer databases can assist in securing the needed contents. A hypothesis is then developed. The hypothesis is tentative, not absolute, and is subject to testing.

What is to be learned has utilitarian values in the social studies. Databases and computer use provide solutions to problems which are life-like in the societal arena. Subject matter is not learned for its own sake, but it is used in problem solving situations. Simulations work well in decision-making situations involving the solving of problems.

Simulations emphasize reality with reduced levels of personal risk taking. Vicarious experiences are then involved for students. Experimentalism likes to go one step further in emphasizing the identification solutions of real problems existing in the societal arena.

Idealism, as a second philosophy, stresses an idea centered social studies curriculum. Vital subject matter may well be learned for its own sake. When using quality tutorials, vital facts, concepts, and generalizations can be acquired by learners. The major objective in idealism, as a philosophy of education, is to assist students to achieve content. In addition to software assisting learners to secure worthwhile subject matter, textbooks, workbook, worksheets, and selected audio-visual materials provide worthwhile experiences for students. The learning of subject matter can guide students in the future to become good citizens in society. Education is preparation for life, that is to interact with others in society.

The teacher as an idealist is well qualified and prepared to teach subject matter. This teacher needs to be highly knowledgeable of software which will assist students to achieve important facts, concepts, and generalizations. The intellectual facet of a student's development must receive primary emphasis in teaching and learning. Thus, the mind or mental development needs to receive primary stress in guiding students to achieve objectives. Mind is real and needs stimulation through a variety of worthwhile learning activities stressing an idea centered curriculum.

Idealism emphasizes definite ideals or moral standards for all students. Immanuel Kart (1724-1804), a leading idealist, advocated the Categorical Imperative for learner acquisition. The Categorical Imperative stated the people should be treated as end and not as means to an end. The means to an end would stress using individuals as stepping stones to achieve objectives. The Categorical Imperative is similar to the Golden Rule—"Do unto others as you would have others do unto you."

From software and computer instruction, students may acquire vital ideas. A subject centered curriculum is then in evidence. Tutorials, as a type of software, would especially be relevant in presenting content sequentially to learners.

Realism, as a third philosophy of education, advocates that one can know the real world and reality as it truly is, in whole or in part. A blue print or duplicate of the natural and social environment is then received. Since the real world can be known, in whole or in part, specifics or measurably stated objectives can be emphasized in the social studies. With precise ends, the learner has either been or not been successful in goal attainment. Diverse types of software programs offer objectives. Relevant objectives need to be in the offing. Thus, drill and practice, tutorials, diagnostic and remediation, simulations, and games stress specific goals. When responding, for example, to a drill and practice item, a learner is either right or wrong. Feedback to the learner is provided for each response he/she has made. At the end of a program, the student knows what per cent of the total items he/she responded correctly to.

Objectivity is important to a realist. In scoring results to test items in a software program, there are no subjective evaluations. The student responds correctly or incorrectly to sequential test items covering content read on the monitor. Thus, there is an objective world, outside the framework of the observer. This objective, outside world needs to be known in whole or in part by the student as he/she attains sequential objectives.

Existentialism emphasizes decision-making by students in terms of objectives, learning opportunities, and appraisal procedures. To make choices is to be human. Permitting others to make decisions for the self demands the latter. Software and computers can provide learners with opportunities to make choices. Simulations emphasize the making of decisions from among alternatives. Which decisions to make in a simulation are the perogative of the student. There could also be decisions made as to which simulations to pursue sequentially and which to omit.

A learning centers philosophy may harmonize well with existentialism as a philosophy of education. The student may then select which kinds of software to pursue pertaining to an ongoing social studies unit. Adequate software packages need to be available for sequential choices. Students need to select those learning opportunities which stress perceived purpose interest, and meaning. Other kinds of teaching materials may also provide activities as experiences at the diverse learning centers in the classroom setting. These include reading and audio-visual aid activities.

To advocate existentialism in the social studies, the individual learner chooses whether to work by the self or with others in a committee setting. Knowledge is subjective, not objective, to the decision-maker. Each social science discipline may provide content in the social studies which stresses the subjective in terms of knowledge, values, and beliefs. Ultimately in life, the decision-maker can make choices, among alternatives, which are truly awe inspiring.

Microcomputer Use and the Psychology of Learning

Behaviourism, as a psychology of learning, advocates the utilization of behaviourally stated objectives. These objectives are arranged in ascending order of complexity. The teacher selects learning opportunities for students to attain the ordered objectives. Only those stimuli stressed in the objective should be contained in the learning activity or experience. After instruction, the teacher can measure if a learner has or has not been successful in goal attainment. If the objectives has been achieved, the student is ready to attain the next sequential end. Students may do their own pacing to achieve optimally within the framework of sequentially stated objectives. If a learner does not achieve an end, a different teaching strategy needs to be in the offing. Measurably stated objectives and observable results are wanted from students after the learning opportunity has been implemented. Drill and practice, tutorial, diagnostic, and remedial software, in particular, emphasizes the thinking of behaviourists, when emphasizing a specific teaching strategy.

Humanism, as a psychology of learning, emphasizes concepts, such as student-teacher planning, student decision-making, as well as an open curriculum. Students with teacher guidance might then select software packages which meet the formers own personal needs. Interests, and purposes. Goals reside within the learner in choosing sequentially what to learn, according to humanism. A psychological curriculum is then in evidence. In comparison, behaviourism stresses a logical curriculum in that the teacher sequences objectives for students to attain.

In Summary

The classroom teacher must emphasize definite principles of learning when software and computers are utilized in the curriculum. These principles of learning when implemented in teaching-learning situations assist students to achieve more optimally in the social studies.

Diverse kinds of software programs need to be utilized in ongoing lessons and units. Drill and practice, tutorial, diagnosis and remediation, simulations, and games are different from each other in terms of objectives stressed. The kind of software selected for student use must reflect definite goals in the social studies.

Philosophy of education has much to say as to how software and microcomputers will be utilized in the classroom. Diverse philosophies such as experimentalism, idealism, realism, and existentialism may be utilized wisely in the classroom setting. An eclectic philosophy may be an end result.

Classroom teachers need to be clear on behaviourism and humanism as psychologies of learning. Psychologies used must help student's to achieve optimally.

REFERENCES

Bitter, G.G. and Camuse, R.A. *Using a Microcomputer in the Classroom*. Reston, Virginia: Reston Publishing Company, 1984.

Bozeman, W.C. *Computers and Computing in Education*. Scottsdale, Arizona: Gorsuch Scarisbrick, 1985.

Flake, J.L., et. al. *Fundamentals of Computer Education*. Belmont, California: Wadsworth, 1985.

Hofmeister, A. *Microcomputer Applications in the Classroom*. New York: Holt, Rinehart and Winston, 1984.

Lockyard, James, et. al. *Microcomputers for Education*. Boston: Little, Brown and Company, 1987.

Reidesel, C.A., and Clements, D.H. *Coping with Computers in the Elementary and Middle Schools*. Englewood Cliffs, New Jersey: Prentice-Hall, Inc., 1985.

Seigel, M.A., and Davis, D.M. *Understanding Computer-Based Education*. New York: Random House, 1986.

Wright, E.B., and Forcier, R.C. *The Computer: A Tool for the Teacher*. Belmont, California: Wadsworth, 1985.

32

Philosophy and Psychology of Teaching Science

Science teaching must reflect change within a curriculum that stresses assisting pupils to attain optimally. Objectives, learning opportunities, and appraisal procedures in science need to be relevant and updated in incorporate National and state standards. Units of instruction in science should stress inquiry, motivate pupils, and encourage high levels of interest. Educational philosophies and psychologies used in teaching-learning situations by the teacher must guide pupils to develop an inward desire to learn.

Philosophy of Science Teaching

The science teacher needs to have a wide repertoire or means of assisting pupils to achieve optimally. There are diverse educational philosophies for teachers to use that encourage optimal learner achievement.

First, a problem solving approach may be used. Inquiry learning is highly salient here. Ideally, pupils with teacher guidance need to identify a problem with the framework of an ongoing science unit of study. The problem must be clearly stated. Learners might then brain storm possible answers to the problem. Value judgments should not be made on responses given by pupils. The consequences or results of each brainstormed answer must be evaluated after the brainstorming session has been completed. A variety of manipulative, pictorial, and abstract materials should be used here. Science experiments may be at the heart of testing each response or hypothesis. Responses are then modified changed, or refuted as a result of the tests. John Dewey and other experimentalists emphasised problem solving strongly in their philosophy of experimentalism. Committee endeavours and cooperative learning are stressed in the problem solving science curriculum.

Experimentalists believe the science curriculum should be as closely related to the real world of society as possible. School and society are not separate but integrated entities. To emphasise problem solving, the science teacher must provide a learning environment that is stimulating and arouses pupil interests. Hopefully, the interests of learners will lead to problem identification. The goal of the science teacher is to have learners select relevant problems. The teacher becomes a resource person, guide, and helper, rather than one who lectures and presents content deductively to pupils. Thus learners need assistance in brain storming, locating reference sources, and attaining hypotheses as means of inquiry learning.

With pupils being heavily involved in selecting problems and strategies to solve each problem, a psychological curriculum is in evidence since each learner is heavily involved in sequencing or ordering his/her own experiences. The learner himself/herself tends to order experiences in a problem solving approach of teaching, according to educational psychologists. Pertaining to John Dewey's philosophy of experimentalism, Meyer (1949) wrote the following:

All this, of course, depends in no small way upon thinking. For Dewey, however, thinking becomes significant only when applied to life's situations. It is, he has said, "as instrumentality used by man is adjusting himself to the practical situations in life." Or to phrase it more simply, human beings think in order to live. Because to this stimulus, which has its basis in biology and sociology, it is impossible—it is absurd—to interpret life in a systematic and abstract way. Since, moreover, Dewey holds that life is in constant flux, it is impossible to solve problems with any degree of finality for the problems of tomorrow will be different from those of today.

As for the problem of knowledge, Dewey believes that knowledge is experience and that true experience is functional. What is this thing for? What is its use? Is a coal mine a physical deposit or does it have function? And if so, what is it? Such are the questions that help give meaning to one's experience; but such questions cannot be answered without antecedent action. Action must precede knowledge. Whatever knowledge we possess has resulted from our activities, our efforts to survive, to obtain food, shelter, and clothing. Only that which has been organised into our disposition so as to enable us to adapt our environment to our needs and to adapt our aims and desires to the situations in which we exist is really knowledge.

A second philosophy of education to stress is a subject centered science curriculum. Here, the science teacher must select and teach vital facts, concepts, and generalisations to pupils. Inquiry learning emphasising critical and creative thinking, explanations, and vital discussions are methods of instruction used to teacher learners. Intellectual development is a major objective of science instruction. Mind is real and needs challenging subject matter to encourage mental development. Cognitive objectives should be emphasised primarily. However, affective goals are also salient as they assist pupils to attain cognitive ends of science instruction. It is important to secure pupils interest in science, but each learner must also will to learn. Tasks in life are interesting as well as those that do not stress interest. Thus, the pupil must develop a will to achieve, attain, and develop well intellectually.

Subject centered approaches in teaching science emphasise the abstract instead of the concrete and semi-concrete facets of learning. The concrete (use of real objects, excursions, realia, and experiments), and the semi-concrete (illustrations, videotapes, videodiscs, computers with diverse capabilities, among other audio visual aids) should be used as learning opportunities to assist pupils to achieve the abstract. Thus objectives in teaching science need to stress the abstract in subject matter to be acquired as well as higher levels of cognition in ongoing units of study in science. The teacher largely determines which objectives and learning activities pupils are to pursue sequentially. Thus a logical science curriculum is being emphasised, according to educational psychologists. Ediger (1995) wrote:

Idealists are very academic and rigorous in the teaching of subject matter. They emphasise cognitive objectives much more so than affective (attitudinal) or psychomotor (use of muscles and eye-hand coordination) in teaching-learning situations. Meaning, understanding, and depth learning of subject matter are important to idealists. Vital subject matter, carefully selected, needs to be taught to students. The student in acquiring subject matter in ongoing lessons is to move form the finite (limited) to the infinite. Being. Ideas are important to attain in an idealist's curriculum. The ideal is also salient to achieve in terms of moral standards and values.

The teacher emphasising idealism as a philosophy of education stresses the selection of subject matter for student achievement which assists forming vital concepts and generalisations. Objectives of instruction need to reflect worthwhile concepts and generalisations. Depth teaching of specifics assists students to form and develop universal ideas. The use of behaviourally stated objectives for instruction would be frowned upon by the idealist teacher. Content would become too fragmented with the realist's position of testing and measuring reflecting measurably stated objectives. Rather, the idealist in emphasising an idea centered curriculum desires that students relate subject matter acquired so that intense learning transpires. Thus if students are studying causes of World War II, each cause would be studied thoroughly and not merely listed. Causes come in sequence and are complex to appraise. Viewing and analysing each cause takes time. After analysing, relating, or synthesising leads take time in order to emphasise intensity not survey teaching. Students are to be evaluated in progress as to how much vital subject matter has been acquired.

The use of the mind or intellect is salient for students to utilise in analysing and synthesising subject matter knowledge. Mental development is stressed as students learn, achieve, and develop.

Implications from idealism as a philosophy of education for the curriculum include the following:

1. intellectual, not attitudinal, nor psychomotor, goals come first in teaching-learning situations;
2. quality textbooks, workbooks, and selected audio-visual materials which aid in intellectual development should be used as learning activities to achieve stated goals for students;
3. evaluation techniques should stress appraisal of vital subject matter acquired by students;
4. depth teaching of subject matter is salient of guide learners to attain vital facts, concepts, and generalisations. Survey approaches are not acceptable;
5. the will of the student is needed to attain worthwhile subject matter. Interest of students, alone, is not adequate for students to achieve, attain, and develop well. Students must want to learn;
6. students need to achieve vital subject matter to prepare for the future life of an adult. Education is preparation for adult responsibilities, not present day situations in being a child;
7. learners need to develop from a finite (limited) being toward the Absolute or the Infinite (unlimited being). The Absolute may also be referred to as God;
8. a quality general education programme, consisting of vital content from major academic disciplines, is a must for all students;

A third philosophy of teaching emphasises pupils being heavily involved in decision making in terms of choosing objectives, learning opportunities, as well as evaluation procedures. The science teacher needs to set up more stations with quality tasks than what any one pupil can complete. The pupil may then select sequential tasks to complete. Those tasks not having perceived purpose may be omitted by the learner. The teacher must choose relevant learning opportunities for pupils to select. Inquiry, problem solving, as well as critical and creative thinking, tasks, are vital learning activities for pupils at each station. Careful consideration must be given to the worth of each station and task. The interests of pupils need to be cultivated in the science curriculum. The pupil is the chooser of which tasks to pursue and complete. The science teacher is a guide and stimulator but not a disappear of information.

The attitudinal dimension is very important to develop within pupils when they select that which is vital to attain. Learners need to learn to make choices and decisions. Life itself consists of making choices within the framework of being open-ended and possessing freedom. In the science curriculum, pupils too need to make choices in which coercion is kept to a minimum. A decision making philosophy stress the learner being responsible for choices and completions made. Decision making is a skill and an attitude that pupils should learn due to its tremendous value presently and in the future for pupils.

With pupils being heavily involved in choosing sequential tasks to complete, a psychological curriculum is then in evidence due to pupils sequencing their very own activities in the science curriculum.

Pertaining to existentialism and pupil choices in the curriculum. Ozman and Craver (1990) wrote:

It is interesting that most existentialists and phenomenologial philosophers have had lengthy and rigorous educations... . Most of them taught at one time or another, usually in a university setting. They have been primarily concerned with the humanities and have written exclusively in the genre. Through the humanities the existentialists have tried to awaken modern individuals to the dangers of being swallowed by the megalopolis and runaway technology. This seems to have taken place because the humanities contain greater potential for introspection and the development of self-meaning than other studies.

The humanities loom large in an existentialists curriculum because they deal with the essential aspects of human existence such as the happy, the absurdities as well as meaning. In short, existentialists want to see humankind in its totality—perverted well as the exalted, the mundane as well as the glorious, the despairing as well as the hopeful, and they feel that the humanities and the arts do this better than the sciences. Existentialists, however, do not have any definite rules about what should comprise the curriculum. They believe that the student-in-situation making a choice should be the deciding factor.

Although existential phenomenologists have been interested in understanding the lived experience of the learner than in the specific content to be learned, some of them have given attention to curriculum organisation and content. The tendency, however, is to view curriculum from the standpoint of the learner rather than as a collection of discrete subject matter.

A fourth philosophy of education for science teachers to follow is a criterion referenced (CRT) procedure of instruction. Here the teacher needs to write measurably stated objectives for pupil attainment. These objectives are always written prior to teaching pupils. Each objectives is written in as precise a manner as possible. Ideally there is no leeway in interpreting what will be taught when examining any one measurably stated objective. The science teacher can measure after instruction if a learner has or has not achieved a measurably stated objective. The CRT measures against the measurably stated objectives to ascertain pupil achievement.

Science teachers may even announce to pupils what they are to learn as a result of instruction. Learners then might possess security in terms of what they are expected to achieve as a result of teaching and learning. Learning activities selected by the teacher to assist pupils to achieve must be aligned with the measurably stated objectives. These activities must be selected on the basis of guiding each pupil to achieve objectives. A logical curriculum is in evidence if the teacher chooses sequential objectives for pupil attainment as well as learning opportunities that are sequentially arranged so that pupils can experience success in learning.

Since teachers determine the sequence of objectives and learning opportunities for pupils of pursue, a definite logical curriculum is being stressed by science teachers. The teacher then attempts to arrange the order of objectives and activities to guide optimal pupil achievement. Pertaining to realism, Bowyer (1970) wrote the following:

We have noted that there are different forms of naturalism and of idealism. The same is true of realism, which makes it difficult to define the realist point of view. One element that the various forms of realism do have in common is a rejection of the idealist theory of knowledge that the various qualities of experience depend upon a knower for their existence. Realists believe the universe is composed of real entities that exist in themselves. These entities can be known, and their existence is not dependent upon a knower or perceiver. Although realists can agree on this point, they do not all agree when they attempt to build a metaphysical system. Here, their views range from pluralism to dualism to monism.

The realist epistemological views include epistemological monism where it is held that objects are presented in consciousness, and epistemological dualism where objects are thought to be represented. The monist defines mind as a relation between the organism and an object, while the dualists identify mind more closely with the organisms. Realists do have a tendency to view the world as the mechanism described by the physical sciences and they generally believe in determinism, in orderliness in the universe, and the objectivity of science. The unifying thesis of realism is that knowledge is thought to have a universal character and comes to man through his sensory capacity. The realists have a confidence in their assertions about reality and value which is most discerning to pragmatists.

Recent Psychologies of Learning

B.F. Skinner (1904-1990) was very instrumental in emphasising S-R theory of instruction. With S-R theory in teaching science, Skinner advocated programmed learning for pupils. Programmed learning can take place either in textbook or computer/software form. Here, pupils move forward very slowly from the simple to that which is gradually more complex. Pupils then respond to a logical sequence developed by the programmer. Thus, the pupil reads a small amount of content, responds to a completion item, and check his/her response with that provided by the programmer. If the pupil responded correctly, he/she moves on to the next sequential item. If the learner responded incorrectly, he/she tries a different response. If correct, the learner also moves on to the next sequential item. The sequence is the same each time with read, respond, and check. If the learner is correct, he/she is rewarded and reinforced for giving the correct answer to the completion item as provided by the programmer. Skinner believes that a programmer can always put in another item should the pupil taking the programme in the pilot study miss out in a sequential item. A quality programme should make for a ninety per cent correct pupil response per item for each in the pilot study. The pilot study involves conducting experiments to find out where weaknesses lie in the programme. If too many learners, miss an item, perhaps an additional step needs to be put in where these pupils responded incorrectly. Poorly written items are taken out or modified so that responses can be made based on clarity within that step of learning. I have observed selected well written programmes in science units of study which reflect the thinking of B.F. Skinner. Pertaining to programmed learning, Harris and Sipay (1985) wrote the following:

Programmed materials are designed so that the user (1) encounters a series of small steps on which success is very likely (2) is involved in the learning process through actively responding (3) receives immediate feedback as to the correctness of each response. In theory, programmed material should greatly facilitate individualised instruction because they allow each student to work almost independently with material suitable for his or her needs, proceeding at a pace commensurate with ability and interest.

Ediger (1997) wrote the following pertaining to programmed instruction:

The programmer decides upon the objectives for each programme. Also, the sequential activities and appraisal procedures are determined by the programmer. There is basically no input for pupils or from teachers in terms of objectives, learning activities, and evaluation procedures when utilising programmed materials.

Advantages given for using programmed learning include the following:

1. each learner may pace his/her own optimal speed of learning. No two pupils need to be at the same or similar level of achievement;
2. learners know immediately if they are right or wrong in responses made;
3. rarely do learners make mistakes in quality programmed materials. The error rate is five to ten per cent in field tested programmes;
4. reinforcement is possible in field tested programmed items. Thus an involved learner might experience rather continual progress;
5. sequential progress is made in small steps rather than covering content in terms of a large scope at a time.

Disadvantages given in emphasising programmed with learning include:

1. programmed learning may not harmonise with learning styles of selected pupils;
2. step by step learning—read, respond, and check—does not harmonise with expectations of life in society. Life in society is not programmed;

3. programmed materials tend to deemphasise the utilisation of the concrete (reality), and semi-concrete (pictorial form) materials. Abstract content tends to be rather heavily emphasised in programmed materials;
4. selected pupils may not perceive interest and purpose in the programmer choosing objectives, learning activities and evaluation procedures;
5. small sequential steps in learning may be too finite or limited to meet personal needs of gifted and talented learners.

The influence of programmed learning and the thinking of B.F. Skinner has had wide influence in educational thought. There still are programmed books available on many topics in book form as well as in computer packages. Perhaps, the strongest influence of Dr. Skinner is in the use of behaviourally stated objectives in teaching. These objectives are very precise and are written prior to instruction. A pupil as a result of instruction either does or does not achieve any single objective. Thus, it is possible to measure if a pupil has been successful in goal attainment. Learning activities selected by the teacher align with the stated objectives. The evaluation procedures also are aligned with the measurably stated objectives. Objectives results from pupils are in evidence from instruction, regardless of who does the evaluating. Relating B.F. Skinner's thinking and that of the behaviourally stated objectives movement, the following writing will assist in clarifying the two (Morris and Pai, 1976):

As Skinner pointed out several times, the most important task of the teacher is to arrange the conditions under which desired learning can occur. Considering the fact that teachers are expected to bring about changes in extremely complex behaviour, they should be specialists in human behaviour. Effective and efficient manipulation of the multitude of variables affecting children's intellectual and social behaviours cannot be accomplished by trial and error alone, nor should such work be based solely on the personal experiences of the teacher, since this covers only a limited range of circumstances. Consequently, a scientific study of human behaviour is vital in the improvement of teaching, because it provides us with accurate and reliable knowledge about learning and leads us to the development of new instructional materials, methods, and techniques. Similarly, an empirical analysis of the teaching process is essential, for it clarifies the teacher's responsibility through a series of small and progressive approximations. Thus facilitating a more effective evaluation.

The measurably stated objectives movement also called behaviourism as a psychology of learning, emphasises a rather closed system of instruction. The objectives are predetermined and may be announced to pupils for each end to be stressed, as the need progresses. The learning activities and the evaluation techniques harmonise or align. Many educators believe that this alignment optimalise learner achievement in teaching and learning situations.

With this close alignment, little room is left for pupils to raise questions that they deem to be relevant and vital.

Humanism in the Science Curriculum

Toward the other end of the continuum, humanism, as a psychology of learning stresses heavy pupil involvement in selecting objectives, learning opportunities, and appraisal procedures, the pupil here is the focal point of instruction. Learners are to involved in sequencing their own experiences; this emphasises a psychological science curriculum whereas the behaviourally stated objectives psychology advocated a logical sequence for pupils whereby the teacher orders objectives for pupil attainment. Pertaining to humanism and existentialism, Ediger (1996) wrote:

Existentialists believe that one exists and then purposes need to be found or developed. The individual self then determines his/her own goals in life. There are no absolutes or guidelines in life to choose what is right and what is good. Each person must select and make decisions. To avoid making decisions is to lack being human. The choice then is to go along with the crowd. However, to be human involves making decisions.

The only broad criterion for existentialists to follow in choosing is to make moral decisions in a complete atmosphere of freedom. Others should definitely not decide one's destiny. One did not ask to be born and yet each person must make authentic decisions.

Moral decisions are difficult to make. An environment of awe exists in making authentic decisions.

Which objectives, learning activities, and evaluation procedures should be inherent in an existentialist curriculum? Existentialists believe in each person choosing objectives. In the school setting, the goals may be selected by learners with teacher guidance within the framework of an open-ended curriculum. The teacher needs to select ends, means, and evaluation procedures, which stress the importance of pupils becoming increasingly responsible for personal freedom. The teacher should definitely not be a policeman. Rather, teachers realise their role as providing for an open environment in order that the learner may select sequential experiences... .

Each decision made in life involves personal decisions in reaching a goal or goals... . Each person makes or breaks himself or herself. No other person or being is responsible for consequences of decisions made. Blaming others for what happened in life is meaningless, according to existentialists. Each person needs to learn to accept responsibilities for thoughts, deeds, and actions.

The humanist existentialist science curriculum may be implemented in several ways. One approach is to use learning centers in the school/classroom setting. We have observed the following learning centers pertaining to the science unit "The Changing Surface of the Earth," from which pupils may select sequential tasks to complete:

1. a reading center;
2. an art center;
3. a drama center;
4. a writing center;
5. an audio-visual center;
6. a computer and software center;
7. a music center;
8. a model making center;
9. a problem solving center;
10. an experiment center.

Each pupil in a classroom may select which center and which task to work on. There are more tasks at each center than what any one child can complete. Learners may then choose what to work on and what to omit in a humanistic science curriculum. The individual pupils determines sequence or order of which tasks to pursue and which to omit. Purpose for learning then reside within the pupil. Examples of which materials will be at a learning center and the kinds of tasks or learning activities that will be in evidence may be illustrated with the first center mentioned above—a reading center. Here, a variety of library books on the unit title and on diverse reading levels need to be in evidence. A pupil chooses a book to read and may complete as many of the following tasks at this center as individual purpose dictates:

1. write a summary covering content read;
2. make a model of inherent subject matter read, such as a model volcano;
3. draw a picture of folding and faulting;
4. write an additional page for the library book read;
5. identify a problem dealing with changes on the earth's surface and use various reference sources to locate information for solving the problem.

Pupils individually make choices sequentially as to what to learn and the means of learning. Tasks can relate to choosing to work by the self or with others. If too many work at one center, the teacher may make a rule as to the optimal number of pupils that may work at any one center. The science teacher here is a guide or motivator of pupils to stay on task and complete satisfactorily what has been selected as learning activities. The pupil may even plan with the teacher what to work on if greater purpose is perceived in working on something else than what is at any of the centers.

Humanists advocate that pupils reveal authentic behaviour, not facades, to be authentic, the pupil needs to reveal more of the real self. Trust in communicating with others is important. Humans have tremendous worth and value. Being authentic and trusting others in a positive relationship is relevant to humanists.

Many studies currently made stress the importance of multiple intelligences. Sternberg (1997) emphasises that a Yale University study, intelligence has analytical, creative, and practical aspects. He presets the following model for science in four categories:

Memory—name the four types of bacteria;

Analysis—analyse the means the immune system uses to fight bacterial infections;

Creativity—suggest ways to cope with the increasing immunity bacteria are showing to antibiotic drugs;

Practicality—suggest three steps that individuals might take to reduce the likelihood of bacterial infections.

In any lesson and unit of study, the science teacher may emphasise these four categories of instruction. Pupils need to achieve at higher levels of cognition than the memory level. Learners will then reveal in different ways what has been learned in the analysis, creativity, and practicality levels. Intelligence then is not a single score nor a single way of indicating what has been learned. Sternberg (1997) goes on to say:

By exposing students to instruction emphasising each type of ability, we enable them to capitalise on their strengths while developing and improving new skills. This approach is also important because students need to learn that the world cannot always provide them with activities that suit their preferences. At the same time, if students are never presented with activities that suit them, they will never experience a sense of success and accomplishment. As a result, they may tune out and never achieve their full potential... .

Success in today's job market often requires creativity, flexibility, and a readiness to see things in new ways. Furthermore, students who graduate with A's but cannot apply what they have learned may find themselves failing on the job.

Creativity, in particular, has become even more important over time, just as other abilities have become less valuable. For example, with the advent of computers and calculators, both penmanship and arithmetic skills have diminished in importance. Some standardised ability tests, such as the SAT, even allow students to use calculators. With the increasing availability of massive, rapid data retrieval systems, the ability to memorise information will become even less important... .

This is not to say that that memory and analytical abilities are not important. Students need to learn and remember the core content of the curriculum, and they need to be able to analyse—to think critically about—the material. But the importance of these abilities should not be allowed to obfuscate what else is important.

In a pluralistic society, we cannot afford to have a monolithic conception of intelligence and schooling, it's simply a waste of talent. And as I unexpectedly found in my study; it's no random waste. The more we teach and assess students based on a broader set of abilities, the more racially, ethnically, and socio-economically diverse our achievers will be. We can easily change our closed system—and we should. We must take a more balanced approach to education to reach all of our students.

Sternberg believes strongly that pupils individually are not permitted to indicate what has been learned in diverse ways. It is true that pupils so often are asked to show achievement through testing, generally through pupils taking multiple choice tests. Thus verbal approaches are used to ascertain what pupils individually have learned. This is limiting in that there are many other means of revealing achievement. Howard Gardner (1995) has determined there are at least seven intelligences, according to his research; these are verbal-linguistic, interpersonal, intrapersonal, musical, spatial, bodily-kinesthetic, and logical mathematics. Pupils may show similar strengths, but not necessarily in the same ways or to the same extent over time. With multiple intelligences, pupils learn in diverse ways and are interested in different subject matter in the academic arena. Learners then reveal their strengths and weaknesses in what has been learned in a variety of ways, not one way only such as in verbal testing using multiple choice items. Thus, the pupil who is strong in the verbal arena will reveal differently what has been learned as compared to the one endowed with musical intelligence. Too frequently, the emphasis has been upon verbal approaches to assessing pupil achievement and yet there are numerous other ways to indicate intelligence, as Gardner has indicated in multiple intelligence theory. Hatch (1997) wrote:

Such a view of intelligence is reflected in programmes and practices that seek to determine which areas young children show the greatest strengths. Children who do well on tasks in a particular area—story telling or reporting, athletics or dance, drawing or building—are broadly labeled as having strengths in linguistics, bodily-kinesthetic, or spatial realms, respectively.

Such an approach, however, implies that children have a reservoir of talent in a variety of activities, shown consistently over a period of time. It suggests that there are more intelligences but does not necessarily call into question assumptions about the nature, display, and development of intelligence.

In Conclusion

Science teachers need to develop a philosophy and psychology of instruction that optimalise learner attainment. Pupils differ from each other in many ways including methods and procedures of acquiring relevant facts, concepts, and generalisations. A careful study and implementation of a worthwhile philosophy and psychology of learning might well assist each pupil to learn as much as possible.

To stress science as inquiry in harmony with National Standards, the writer emphasises what he believes to be best from each school of thought discussed above. These are:

1. a problem solving science curriculum in which pupils with teacher guidance identify and solve relevant life-like problems;
2. a subject centered science curriculum emphasising pupils attaining higher levels of cognition in achieving salient facts, concepts, and generalisations;
3. pupil selection from among alternatives of takes perceived to be purposeful. Tasks at different stations should reflect science as inquiry;
4. measurably stated objectives which reflect National Standards in a predetermined science curriculum. Precise objectives are then selected prior to instruction for learner attainment. A carefully designed science curriculum may then be in evidence. The content obtained should be inherent in science as inquiry teaching and learning.

Pertaining to the psychology of learning in science, pupils should achieve quality sequence. Interests, purpose, and meaning are important concepts to stress in teaching science in ongoing lesson plans and units of study.

With multiple intelligence theory, pupils do learn in different ways and through diverse methods of instruction. Learners individually do possesses their favourite means of learning and achieving. There are numerous methods of revealing what has been learned.

The science teacher then needs to have pupils participate in a variety of learning opportunities and have them indicate achievement using diverse procedures to provide for different learning styles possessed. The following learning opportunities are available for pupils in the science curriculum:

1. hands on approaches in learning;
2. experiments and demonstrations;
3. field trips and excursions;
4. problems solving experiences;
5. reading from basal texts, library books, and science encyclopaedias;
6. viewing video tapes, video disks, films, and filmstrips;
7. Discussing, interviewing, dramatizing, and pantomiming;
8. writing poems, plays, outlines, summaries, diary entries, log entries, journal entries, and stories;
9. making dioramas, colleges, bulletin board displays, murals, models, and equipment for science experiments;
10. using technology such as computer packages, the word processor, internet and world wide web, and calculators.

REFERENCES

Bowyer, Carlton (1970), *Philosophical Perspectives for Education*, Glenview, Illinois: Scott, Foresman and Company, page 17.

Ediger, Marlow (1995), *Philosophy in Curriculum Development*. Kirksville Missouri: Simpson Publishing Company, pages 22 and 23.

Ediger, Marlow (1997). *The Modern Elementary School*. Kirksville, Missouri. Simpson Publishing Company, pages 110 and 111.

Ediger, Marlow (1996), *Essays in School Administration*. Kirksville, Missouri: Simpson Publishing Company, pages 58 and 59.

Ediger, Marlow and D. Bhaskara Rao (2000), *Teaching Mathematics Successfully*. New Delhi, India: Discovery Publishing House.

Gardner, Howard, (1995), "Reflections on Multiple Intelligences: Myths and Messages, *Phi Delta Kappan* 77, 3:200-203, 206-209.

Harris, Albert J., and Edward R. Sipay (1985), *How to increase Reading Ability*. White Plains, New York: Longman, Page 71.

Hatch, Thomas (1997), "Getting Specific about Multiple Intelligences," *Educational Leadership*, 54, 6:26.

Meyer, Adolph (1949), *The Development of Education in the Twentieth Century*. Englewood Cliffs, New Jersey: Prentice-Hall, Inc., pages 42-43.

Morris, Van Cleve, and Young Pai (1976), *Philosophy and the American School*. Boston: Houghton Mifflin Company, page 340.

Ozman, Howard A., and Samuel M. Craver (1990) *Philosophical Foundations of Education* Columbus, Ohio: Merrill Publishing Company, page 257.

Rao, Digumarti Bhaskara (2000), *Teacher and Education*. Guntur, India: Nagarjuna Publishers (in Telugu language).

Sternberg, Robert J. (1997), "What Does It Mean to be Smart? *Educational Leadership*, 22-24.

Vijaya Bharathi, D. and D. Bhaskara Rao (2000), *Educational Philosophies of Swami Vivekanand and John Dewey*. New Delhi, India: APH Publishing Corporation.

33

Objectives in the Science Curriculum

Careful attention must be given in selecting educational objectives for pupils to attain in elementary school science. Teachers, supervisors, and principals should cooperatively identify relevant educational goals for learners in the science curriculum. Objectives for pupils to acquire must be

(a) Attainable on the part of learners.

(b) Balanced among understandings, skills, and attitudinal ends.

(c) Clearly stated. Vague, excessively board objectives must be eliminated from the science curriculum.

(d) Acceptable to pupils, teachers, and parents.

(e) Used as guidelines to select appropriate learning experiences for each learner.

(f) Stated so that adequate provision may be made for slow learners, average achievers, and fast learners.

(g) Used as guidelines to appraise pupil achievement.

General Objectives

General objectives are broad in nature and are long-term ends for pupils to achieve.

One category of general objectives for pupils to achieve pertains to skills. Skills objectives emphasize doing something with increased refinement as indicated in the stated goals or ends. There are definite skills that pupils need to develop in elementary school science.

1. Observing. It is important for pupils to become increasingly proficient in observing.

   (a) What is happening in an ongoing science experiment.

   (b) What is seen in the natural environment during an excursion.

(*c*) What is viewed in terms of content from slides, films, filmstrips, and other audio. visual materials.

Pupils learn much science content through careful observation of what exists in their immediate environment.

2. Identifying problems. Learners generally reveal much curiosity by identifying problems and questions in ongoing learning activities. These problems and questions may be identified in a variety of situations involving learning activities such as
   (*a*) Reading and viewing content from diverse audio-visual aids.
   (*b*) Taking field trips with teacher guidance.
   (*c*) Observing and taking part in experimentation and demonstrations.
   (*d*) Interviewing individuals who specialize in a given area of knowledge.
   (*e*) Dramatizing selected content where additional information is needed.
   (*f*) Doing field work in science as homework.
   (*g*) Participating in a seminar related to an ongoing unit of study in science.
   (*h*) Working in a committee to complete a project in elementary school science.

To engage in problem-solving activities, the pupil must experience a stimulating learning environment from which problems and questions may be identified. Following the identification of a problem or problems in an ongoing unit of study in science, the pupil individually or in a committee may gather information from a variety of sources to obtain related content. Adequate time must be given to obtain enough data relevant to the solving of the identified problem or problems. Ultimately, the learner (or learners) should be ready to develop a hypothesis (or hypotheses) relating to the problem. With further study, the original hypothesis may need to be revised or modified.

3. Classifying knowledge. Pupils need to develop skill pertaining to classifying acquired facts, concepts, and generalizations. Thus, for example, a pupil studying a unit on "The Changing Surface of the Earth" should ultimately be able to classify rocks as being igenous, sedimentary, and metamorphic. Further divisions of these classifications include the following:

Igneous	Sedimentary	Metamorphic
a. basalt	a. shale	a. slate
b. obsidian	b. sandstone	b. marble
c. pumice	c. conglomerate	c. anthracite coal
d. granite	d. coal	d. quartzite

Pupils must be guided to develop skills pertaining to classifying knowledge. Facts, concepts, and generalizations become vague and excessive unless there is a means to bring order out of a highly relevant societal trend dealing with the explosion of knowledge. A first grade pupil studying a unit on "Seasons of the Year" ultimately should be able to classify the seasons in terms of:

(a)	Fall	*(b)*	Winter
(c)	Spring	*(d)*	Summer

Or, if learners are studying a unit on "Prehistoric Life," periods of time may be classified in terms of

(a) The paleozoic era
(b) The mesozoic era
(c) The cenozoic era

Knowledge acquired becomes anarchic in nature unless each pupil can classify content into appropriate and meaningful category systems.

4. Communicating ideas. It is highly important that each pupil be able to communicate content accurately and effectively to others. In oral and written communication, pupils need to be able to present the following kinds of content:
   (a) Outcomes of an experiment or demonstration, *e.g.*, what happens to selected liquids, solids, and gases when heated.
   (b) A report, *e.g.*, dinosaurs in their natural environment during prehistoric years.
   (c) A summary covering ideas presented in a film or filmstrip, *e.g.*, food chains and food webs.
   (d) A book review, *e.g.*, the main organs comprising the digestive system—mouth and salivary glands, the esophagus, stomach and liver, gall bladder and pancreas, large and small intestines, and the rectum.
   (e) Main ideas gained during a field trip, for example, pertaining to sheet erosion, gully erosion, strip-cropping, terraces, and cover crops.

Thus, in communicating ideas in oral and written form, each pupil must present content accurately

(a) Using appropriate sequence.
(b) In an interesting, enthusiastic, and pleasing manner.
(c) Using related pictures and other audio-visual aids effectively.
(d) Emphasizing meaningful learnings to the receiver.

5. Being able to use concepts pertaining to measurement. There are many occasions in which pupils need to present information to others using quantitative data.

(a) In a unit on "How Weather Affects Us", pupils record temperature readings at a selected time during each of the days the unit is in progress. Both fahrenheit and centigrade readings may be recorded. A bar or line graph should be developed to show temperature readings on each of these days. Pupils may also record the amount of rainfall during a specific interval as is indicated by the amount contained in the rain gauge on the school grounds. Air pressure also needs to be recorded on a daily basis as in indicated on a class-made or commercial barometer.

(b) In a unit on "Prehistoric Life", pupils with teacher direction might develop a related chart on the history of important plants and animals: On historic times such as the Precambrian era (approximately 5,000 + millions of years ago to 600 million years ago), Paleozoic era (approximately 600 million years ago to 230 million years ago), Mesozoic era (230 million years ago to 60 million years ago), and the Cenozoic Era (60 million years ago to the present). Pictures pertaining to selected plants and animals for each of these eras should be drawn on this chart by committees of learners.

(c) If pupils are studying a unit on "The Solar System", meaningful learnings must be attached to distances of planets in sequential order from the sun. Pupils may notice differences in miles of planets from each other as well as the diameter of each planet in miles.

		Approximate Diameter of Planet of Miles	Approximate Distance from Sun in Miles
Mercury	—	3,000	36,000,000
Venus	—	8,000	67,000,000
Earth	—	8,000	93,000,000
Mars	—	4,000	140,000,000
Jupiter	—	89,000	480,000,000
Saturn	—	75,000	890,000,000
Uranus	—	31,000	1,800,000,000
Neptune	—	33,000	2,800,000,000
Pluto	—	4,000	3,700,000,000

6. Developing inferences. It is significant for pupils to develop inferences from completed observations. Learners ultimately need to be able to develop generalizations pertaining to numerical data, direct observations made of natural phenomena, content read, recorded factual information, information presented on charts and tables, as well as from

other reference sources. The ability or skill to develop inferences is a highly valuable goal for individuals to acquire. This skill aids learners in being able to accurately summarize or generalize on a large amount of content acquired from a variety of learning activities. The pupil individually must be able to develop meaningful inferences from a mass of data. Unless inferences can be made, learners may feel and think that irrelevant, isolated content is being learned.

If a pupil is viewing population figures on a tabulation chart pertaining to the United States, Mexico, Great Britain, India, Pakistan, and Peoples Republic of China covering the intervals of time 1920, 1930, 1940, 1950, 1960, 1970, and 1980, certain conclusions and main ideas should be an end result. Looking at individual population figures with no attempts being made to see trends in population growth or to attach meaning to what is being read makes for fragmented, unrelated, and meaningless learnings. Pupils must study the population trends and develop possible inferences as to their meaning. An important skill then for pupils to develop in elementary school science is the ability to infer meaning from what appears to be a mass amount of information.

7. Thinking scientifically. Objective and unbiased thinking as objectives for pupils to acquire in ongoing units of study need much attention in the science curriculum. In a unit pertaining to "Plants in Our Environment", pupils identify and study diverse variables that are inherent in plant growth. These variables may be controlled when conducting experiments pertaining to what plants need in order to grow. Pupils with teacher guidance may identify variables such as
   (a) The type or kind of soil.
   (b) The quality of plants involved in the experiment.
   (c) The amount of moisture available for each plant.
   (d) The amount and quality of fertilizer used.
   (e) The amount of sunlight available.

Pupils may first wish to test how the amount of sunlight affects two potted plants. These plants contain similar quality stock, soil, moisture, and fertilizer. One potted plant has a box placed over it, while the second potted plant, located nearby, has access to the usual amount of sunlight. At selected intervals, pupils notice the effect of sunlight on plants. On variable was tested in this experiment—the effect of sunlight on plants. One potted plant being covered with a box may be classified as being in the experimental group. Whereas, the second plant receiving normal amounts of sunshine is in the control group. This experiment may be repeated several times so that pupils observe consistency in results.

Following this experiment, all conditions must be kept constant using two similar potted plants but varying the amount or quality of moisture, fertilizer, and then soil.

8. Using needed reference sources. Pupils develop needed skills pertaining to the use of reference materials. Only then can reference sources be utilized as learning activities involving problem-solving activities to check conclusions previously realized. Each elementary classroom where science instruction is involved must have access to an adequate number of quality reference materials. Reference materials must relate directly to diverse units of study in science. Pupils must have available up-to-date reference sources pertaining to
   (a) Science equipment for experimentation and demonstration.
   (b) General encyclopaedias as well as science encyclopaedias.
   (c) Filmstrips, slides, films, pictures, video tapes, and study prints relating to diverse units of study in science.
   (d) Cassettes, tapes, records, and a radio.
   (e) Library books, pamphlets, and monographs.
   (f) Newspapers, magazines, and periodicals written for pupils.
   (g) Maps pertaining to diverse projections and globes containing different kinds of information. Included should be a globe representing the moon.
   (h) Models, *e.g.*, the solar system, the human body, and animals (vertebrates and invertebrates).
   (i) A terrarium, an aquarium, potted plants, and a place for a small garden on the school grounds.
   (j) Diverse art media, *e.g.*, crayons, water color, colored chalk, colored pencils, finger paints, and different kinds of paper for presenting ideas.
   (k) An overhead projector and transparencies, an opaque projector, and a video disc player.

In addition to skills objectives, pupils should also achieve attitudinal goals. Desirable attitudes (the effective dimension of the human being) guide learners in achieving to their optimum in terms of skills and understandings objectives. Which are selected attitudinal ends which pupils should continually gain in elementary school science?

1. Being open-minded. It is highly important for pupils to continually gather and weigh evidence pertaining to developing concepts, facts, main ideas, and generalizations. A closed mind generally does not desire information to modify

or refute what is believed presently. Individuals of this caliber do not grow in achieving relevant understandings, skills, and attitudes. An open-minded individual wishes to learn more and obtain the most accurate information possible. To develop accurately hypotheses in problem-solving activities, an open mind is certainly desired. Closed minds have a tendency to generalize on an inadequate amount of information as well as jump to hasty conclusions.

2. Being curious. To acquire optimal development in achieving understandings, skills, and attitudinal objectives in science, curiosity on the part of pupils toward the natural environment is very important. There are numerous methods which the classroom teacher may utilize to continually arouse pupil curiosity in science.

   (a) Have a science corner in the class setting. Pupils bring to the science corner leaves of different colors, sizes and shapes during the early fall months. Further items to bring include an empty bird's nest, acorns, chestnuts, walnuts, twigs, rocks, minerals, and insects in appropriate containers. Pupils individually or in committees may carefully inspect and discuss these items at the science corner. The teacher guides learners in developing facts, concepts, main ideas, and generalizations in greater depth for each item at the science corner through the use of problem-solving activities. Pupils may be encouraged to ask questions such as the following:

   How do birds build and form their nests?

   How do trees produce acorns, walnuts, or chestnuts?

   (b) Take pupils on a excursion on the school grounds or near to the school grounds to observe science phenomena. Pupils may observe during the early fall months diverse kinds of birds, trees, grass, flowers, clouds, and changes in weather. Learners should feel free to discuss observations made as well as identify new problems and questions.

3. Appreciating the methods of science. Too frequently, pupils do not appreciate the opportunities to identify problems or gather relevant information for the solving of problems. Further weaknesses pertaining to pupils' thinking deal with inadequate hypotheses developed as well as inferior methods of testing these hypotheses. Learners too frequently want to

jump to hasty conclusions when gathering information to solve problems.

When pupils engage in problem-solving activities in ongoing units of study in science, each flexible step in this method of learning must receive its share of attention. When gathering related data to solve problems, the pupil must critically and creatively appraise acquired content. Related hypotheses must also be evaluated thoroughly. The pupil must be guided to appreciate and utilize flexible steps involved in problem-solving situations.

Which approaches in teaching-learning situations may help pupils to appreciate the methods of science as a means of acquiring relevant content?

(a) Provide a stimulating learning environment which guides pupils to identify problems of their very own choosing rather than the teacher determining specific questions for pupils to answer.

(b) Explain to pupils why scientific thinking is important. Guide pupils in using critical and creative thinking when appraising content related directly to problems and questions.

(c) Have materials available for use by pupils which stimulate curiosity in learning.

4. Wanting to learn more about a unit of study. Satisfactory methods should be utilized to

   (a) Initiate or introduce a new science unit. With these initiating activities, pupils should develop interest, sense of purpose, and perceive meaning in learnings acquired. Learners should also be stimulated to identify questions and problems. Learning activities must be selected by the teacher which will serve as appropriate initiating experiences for pupils.

   (b) Develop learnings in greater depth within pupils. Developmental learning experiences should help pupils to continually perceive interest, purpose, and meaning in learning as well as develop concepts, facts, generalizations, and main ideas in greater depth as compared to the initiating or introductory activities.

   (c) Culminate or end a unit. In culminating learning activities interest, purpose, and meaningful experiences are as important for pupils as ever. It is sad when pupils have "turned off" on a specific science unit sometime ago and yet additional days of teaching are still left before the allotted time for a unit is ended. Culminating activities should draw a unit of study to a successful

conclusion. Pupils need to have ample opportunities to review learnings previously gained as well as to identify new problem areas.

To guide pupils in wanting to learn more about a unit of study in science, the teacher must utilize appropriate teaching strategies to successfully.

(*a*) Initiate each unit.

(*b*) Select appropriate developmental activities.

(*c*) Culminate or end a unit.

What destroys pupils interest in desiring to learn new content in science?

(*a*) Excessive emphasis placed on reading as a means of acquiring information.

(*b*) The same methods and materials used in teaching science.

(*c*) Too much stress placed upon rote learning and memorization of content.

(*d*) Much emphasis placed upon explaining and lecturing by the teacher.

(*e*) Pupils required to be passive learners in a formal, rigid classroom setting.

(*f*) The teacher exclusively determining objectives, learning activities, and evaluation procedures for pupils.

(*g*) Facts being emphasized rather exclusively in teaching to the exclusion of problem-solving experiences, critical thinking, and creative thinking.

(*h*) The teacher requiring pupils to give "right" answers to questions rather than more open-ended approaches to teaching and learning.

(*i*) All pupils in the class setting participating in the same learning activity at the same time.

(*j*) The teacher emphasizing the importance of achieving present grade level standards for all pupils in the class setting.

(*k*) Sequence in learning for each pupil being strictly determined by the teacher.

(*l*) Large group instruction being stressed rather continuously to the exclusion of committee work and individual projects and study.

5. Appreciating the contributions of science which has helped improve standards of living in the following ways:

(*a*) Increasing the life span of human beings.

(*b*) Having modern conveniences in the home such as centralized heating and air conditioning, automatic clothes washers and driers, refrigerators, and electric lights.

(c) Experiencing fast and efficient means of transportation, *e.g.*, jet plane, car, bus and train.

(d) Possessing good means of communication, *e.g.*, telephone, television, radio, and mail service.

(e) Increasing production of farm crops and livestock on farms to provide a more adequate supply of food products.

(f) Experiencing increased production of goods and services in the economy.

(g) Providing more years of formal schooling for most people.

(h) Having more leisure time available presently as compared to past times.

It is important to guide pupils in developing ample appreciation for contributions made in science toward improved living conditions for human beings on the planet Earth.

Understandings objectives are also important for pupils to acquire. Relevant concepts, main ideas, generalizations, and facts should be gained by pupils. Understandings objectives must be selected in terms of specific units that are taught. In a unit entitled "Our Earth and Its Surface", pupils may achieve the following understandings objectives:

To develop within the pupil an understanding that

(a) Approximately seventy per cent of the earth's surface is covered by oceans, rivers, lakes and other bodies of water.

(b) Mountains change in shape as they mature in age.

(c) The earth continually undergoes change, such as the occurrence of earthquakes, volcanic eruptions, and erosion.

(d) There are three kinds of rocks—igneous, metamorphic, and sedimentary. Each of these kinds of rocks is formed in a different way.

(e) The study of the oceans has become increasingly important to human beings. Oceans will provide a greater supply of food, water, and minerals to human beings in the future.

(f) The breaking up of rock ultimately makes for topsoil.

(g) The history of the earth can be studied by examining rocks from diverse periods of time.

(h) One or more kinds of minerals comprise a rock.

(i) Both the surface of the earth and the ocean floor contain diverse geographical features such as mountain ranges and depressions.

Relevant understandings objectives must be identified for each specific unit of study in science. These kinds of objectives generally do not cut across all units of study in elementary school science as is true of many skills and attitudinal objectives.

Specific Objectives

There are teachers, principals, and supervisors who wish to write specific objectives for pupils to attain in science units. The specific objectives follow criteria such as the following:

1. It can be measured if learners have or have not acquired these desired ends.
2. The teacher can observe if pupils have achieved each stated specific objectives.
3. Specific objectives are written in terms of what the pupil will learn as a result of teaching.
   (a) Cognitive objectives (the use of the intellect in thinking processes).
   (b) Affective objectives (the attitudinal and feeling dimension of the human being).
   (c) Psychomotor objectives (the use of neuromuscular skills or use of the muscles of the human being).

First of all, cognitive objectives in science units of study will be discussed. The following are examples of cognitive objectives written at different levels of complexity relating to a specific unit of study:

1. The pupil will make a drawing of stars comprising the constellation Ursa Major (the Big Dipper). To achieve this goal, pupils would need adequate background information.
2. The pupil will reveal understandings gained about planets in our solar system by writing a sixty-word paragraph on a planet of his/her own choosing. Comprehension of content is stressed in this objective.
3. The pupils will write an essay on our solar system. (Learners need to utilize related previously gained learnings to complete the essay).
4. The pupil will read a science fiction story of his/her own choosing and analyze future possibilities for realistic space feats from the contents. (The student is to separate content read into categories of future possibilities as compared to fantasies in space travel).
5. The pupil, based on research, will present three hypotheses pertaining to possible new findings or discoveries on each of

these planets—Mercury, Venus, Mars, and Jupiter. (Thus, pupils need to gather data from a variety of reference sources in order to solve problems pertaining to "what will be" on each of the previously named planets).

6. The pupil will appraise a completed model solar system (see statement three above) in terms of agreed upon standards developed through teacher-pupil planning.

Psychomotor objectives (the use of the muscles or neuromuscular skills) also need to be stressed amply in ongoing units of study. The following psychomotor objectives may be emphasized in diverse elementary school science units:

1. The pupil will make a model dinosaur of his own choosing using clay. (After instruction, it can be determined if a pupil can or cannot complete a model dinosaur).
2. Three pupils in a committee will complete a diorama on a selected scene from prehistoric times. It can be determined, as a result of a variety of learning experiences, if learners can or cannot complete a diorama or prehistoric life).
3. A committee of pupils will complete a mural or either the Precambrian, Paleozoic, Mesozoic, or the Cenozoic era of time.

Each of the above named objectives stresses the use of the muscles in teaching-learning situations involving science in the elementary school. Each of these objectives is precisely written. Pupils and teachers can measure if learners have attained these desired ends.

Affective objectives (attitudinal dimension) are more difficult to write or compared to cognitive and psychomotor domain goals. However, affective objectives are highly important for learners to acquire. Thus, general attitudinal objectives such as the following are important for pupils to achieve.

1. The pupil will develop feelings of an adequate self-concept.
2. The learner will develop positive attitudes toward others.
3. The pupil will develop an inward desire to learn.

Each of the above attitudinal or affective objectives is important for pupils to achieve. None of them, however, are stated in measurable terms. Thus, in objective number one, it does not state how much of an adequate self-concept the pupil needs to develop. In objective two, vagueness exists in terms of how positive the learner's attitude needs to be toward others. Nor does it state in objective number three how much of an inward desire to learn is to be developed within the pupil.

It is difficult indeed to write measurable objectives pertaining to the attitudinal dimension. It is very difficult to write each of the previously discussed attitudinal objectives in terms of being measurable. It is recommended that each of these objectives be left as general objectives and be thoroughly emphasized in teaching-learning situations. These are indeed worthwhile objectives to emphasize in teaching-learning situations. If pupils would develop adequate self-concepts, positive attitudes toward others, and an inward desire to learn, higher achievement would then be an end result in acquiring cognitive and psychomotor objectives.

Specific measurable objectives in the affective domain could include the following:

1. The pupil will voluntarily read a library book on Space Travel and report his/her findings to three peers in a committee setting. (It can be measured if a learner has attained this specific objective).
2. The learner will volunteer to construct a hygrometer, a wind vane, or an anemometer. (In a related unit of study, the teacher can measure, after specific intervals of instruction, if pupils become instrinsically motivated to construct each of the objects mentioned previously).
3. The pupil will volunteer to write a two hundred word research paper on dinosaurs of prehistoric times.
4. Four pupils in a committee will volunteer to develop a creative dramatization on "Famous Scientists—Past and Present".

In each of the previously named specific objectives, the effective or attitudinal dimension is stated in pupils engaging in an act voluntarily. To stimulate pupils in wishing to achieve each of these objectives, the teacher needs to utilize appropriate readiness experiences. Thus, to stimulate pupils to achieve each objective numbered above, the teacher could

1. Show interesting illustrations and tell a little about the content of selected library books on space travel.
2. Show pictures of and discuss the purposes of hygrometers, wind vanes, and anemometers.
3. Show and discuss content of a filmstrip pertaining to dinosaurs in prehistoric times.
4. Guide pupils to read about and discuss important happenings in the lives of famous scientists, such as Albert Einstein and Louis Pasteur.

In Summary

Objectives for learners to achieve must be carefully selected and clearly stated. Important general objectives for pupils to acquire include

1. Being a good observer.
2. Being able to identify questions and problems.
3. classifying knowledge appropriately.
4. Communicating content clearly.
5. Measuring natural phenomena accurately.
6. Developing reliable inferences.
7. Thinking scientifically.
8. Using reliable reference sources.
9. Being open-minded.
10. Being curious.
11. Appreciating the methods of science.
12. Wanting to learn more about ongoing units of study in science.
13. Appreciating the contributions of science.

Specific objectives may also be written for teaching-learning situations. These kinds of goals may be divided into

1. Cognitive objective (use of the mind or intellect).
2. Affective objectives (attitudinal and feeling part of the human being).
3. Psychomotor objectives (use of neuromuscular skills).

REFERENCES

Cruickshank, Donald R. *Teaching is Tough*. Englewood Cliffs, New Jersey: Prentice-Hall, Inc., 1980.

Esler, William K. *Teaching Elementary Science*. Belmont, California: Wadsworth Publishing Company, Inc., 1973.

Ediger, Marlow and D. Bhaskara Rao. Science Curriculum. New Delhi, India: Discovery Publishing House, 1996.

Friedl, Alfred E. *Teaching Science to Children: The Inquiry Approach Applied*. New York: Random House, Inc., 1972.

Henson, Kenneth T. *Secondary Teaching Methods*. Lexington, Massachusetts: D.C. Heath and Company, 1981.

Joyce, Bruce, and Marsha Weil. *Models of Teaching*. Third Edition. Englewood Cliffs, New Jersey: Prentice-Hall, Inc., 1986.

Joyce, Bruce, et. al., *The Structure of School Improvement*. New York: Longmans, 1983.

National Society for the Study of Education. *The Humanities in Precollegiate Education*, Part II, Chicago, Illinois: The Society, 1984.

National Society for the Study of Education. *Staff Development*, Part II. Chicago, Illinois: The Society, 1983.

National Society for the Study of Education. *Becoming Readers in a Complex Society,* Part I. Chicago, Illinois: The Society, 1984.

National Society for the Study of Education. *Education in School and Nonschool Settings.* Part I. Chicago, Illinois: The Society, 1985.

National Society for the Study of Education. *The Ecology of School Renewal,* Part I. Chicago, Illinois: The Society, 1987.

National Society for the Study of Education. *Society as Education in an Age of Transition,* Part II, Chicago, Illinois: The Society, 1987.

Rowe, Mary Budd. *Teaching Science as a Continuous Inquiry.* New York: McGraw Hill Book Company, 1978.

Victor, Edward. *Science for the Elementary School.* Fourth Edition. New York: The Macmillan Publishing Company, Inc., 1980.

Washton, Nathan S. *Teaching Science in Elementary and Middle Schools.* New York: David McKay Company, Inc., 1974.

34

Learning Opportunities for Pupils in Science

There are numerous quality learning opportunities that may be provided for learners in ongoing science lessons and units of study. These opportunities need to provide for individual differences in the classroom, such as pupils with diverse levels of achievement. Each learner needs to achieve optimally. The science teacher needs to provide activities and experiences for pupils that are:

1. purposeful to have pupils perceive reasons for participating actively;
2. interesting in that the attention of pupils is secured so each may learn, achieve, and grow;
3. meaningful so that pupils individually may make sense of and comprehend that which is taught;
4. goal centered in order to achieve motivated individuals;
5. reflective in nature so that pupils individually ponder over what has been taught.

Learning opportunities chosen need to guide pupils to achieve objectives in ongoing lessons and units of study. Thematic units help pupils to focus upon the centrality of what is being emphasised and stressed in the science curriculum. A variety of leaning opportunities need to be in the offing so that multiple intelligences theory (Gardner, 1993) is in the offing. Thus, the following are intelligences for pupils to reveal what has been learned in science thematic units:

1. scientific—emphasising objective thought pertaining to the natural environment;
2. verbal/linguistic—stressing the use of reading, writing, speaking, and listening. The latter four skills are indeed relevant in science teaching;

3. logical/mathematics—indicating numeral and logical thinking abilities. Mathematics tends to be the language of science in that numerals are applied to quantities and qualities in science;
4. musical—revealing talents in lyrics and musical notation. Science content acquired may be written in terms of musical content by selected learners. Then too, music has vibration, pitch, stress, accent, and other items pertaining to the quality of sound that relates directly to the world of science;
5. bodily/kinesthetic—possessing neuromuscular skills, relevant in handling and using science equipment, as well as in a hands on approaches in learning;
6. interpersonal—pertaining to achieving well in committee and group endeavours when pupils work collaboratively in science;
7. intrapersonal—being able to achieve at a high level in individual tasks and responsibilities, such as in the project method of learning;
8. visual/spatial—abilities in art work, architecture, and geometry. Here, pupils may make and develop art products, collages, murals, dioramas, movie sets, and video-tapes of group or individual work. Creative and formal dramatics when studying the lives of famous scientists may also be pictured in video or snapshot forms.

Using Experiments and Demonstrations

Experiments and demonstrations should be the heart of the science curriculum. Scientists in a laboratory setting conduct research in controlled settings; pupils should also be involved in these kinds of learning opportunities, among other activities, directly related to an ongoing unit in science in the classroom setting.

In a thematic unit on air pressure, learners with teacher guidance may be actively involved in performing the following experiments:

1. using the classroom aquarium, a glass tumbler may be used together with a piece of tissue paper. Pupils may hypothesise what happens to the dry tissue paper when the glass tumbler is placed upside down inside the aquarium which is filled with water. Pupils should feel that the tissue paper is completely dry and give hypotheses freely. Each pupil's response needs to be accepted, respected, and written down on a transparency using the overhead projector. Unless, this experiment has been conducted previously or remembered as

to its outcomes, learners are fascinated with the results! Selected experiments should be performed/demonstrated again due to their relevance to what is being studied;

2. the egg in the bottle is a good experiments to show the force of air pressure. By taking a gallon glass milk jug and placing a piece of tissue paper at the bottom, pupils may watch as a hard boiled egg with the shell taken off is placed at the opening of the container. Learners then might hypothesise what will happen as the tissue paper is lit at the bottom of the gallon glass milk, jug and the boiled egg placed snugly at the opening. Pupils are to be helped in thinking scientifically and logically. Pupils are fascinated to notice the loud noise made as the boiled egg is 'pushed' through the narrow opening of the milk jug. With the tissue paper using the oxygen at the bottom of the jug and the air pressure at the top pushing the egg through the narrow opening, pupils understand what the concept of 'air pressure' means. Learners through research may also learn that at sea level there are fourteen pounds of air pressure per square inch;
3. pupils need to observe a tumbler filled with tap water placed on a table for all to observe clearly. Next, with pupils observing, the science teacher should place an ice cube inside the tumbler. Pupils will notice a thin film of water on the surface of the glass tumbler. Learners then should hypothesise as to why this happened. Recorded hypotheses should be checked against a reputable sources of information, such as from a science textbook, science encyclopaedia, and/or internet source;
4. the water level in an aquarium may be marked with pupils closely watching where the recorded line is located. A day later, the total water the aquarium should be marked and compared with the previous day's level. Successive day's markings may also be observed and noticed. Occurrences may be hypothesised for their happenings. Each hypothesis needs to be discussed in an atmosphere of respect. Pupils have given the following hypotheses for the successive lower water levels:
   (a) the fish drank the water;
   (b) the aquarium leaks;
   (c) water was dipped out of the aquarium;
   (d) fish needed the water to keep their skin soft;
   (e) the water evaporated.
5. a large cube of ice may be placed in a glass clear plastic dish. Learners may hypothesise what the state of matter is when referring to an ice cube. As the solid turns to water, pupils

need to hypothesise what the state of matter is then called. The liquid is then placed on a hot plate and pupils notice what happens when the water changes to steam. The causes for the physical changes need to be understood meaningfully by pupils when a solid changes to a liquid and then to a gas through evaporation. These three states of matter become a structural set of ideas for pupils to attach meaning and understanding. In many cases, matter can change from a solid to a liquid and then to a gas. Exceptions may be noticed later in sequence.

There are many experiments and demonstrations that may be conducted and performed in any science unit of study. The teacher needs to have qualified resource personnel, science textbooks and teacher education texts available as a ready source of information pertaining to using experimentation as a leading approach to learning in ongoing science units of study. Criteria to follow in using science experiments and demonstrations are the following:

1. make certain that pupils can observe the activity as well as the results clearly within each experiment;
2. have pupils, if possible, participate in planning and doing the science experiences;
3. be certain safety is stressed in each experiment and demonstration;
4. emphasise that the learning opportunity assist pupils to achieve worthwhile goals in ongoing science lessons and units of study;
5. relate the learning opportunity to a problem identified by learners;
6. do something with the findings, such as pupils' writing up the sequential steps in doing the experiment. Variety needs to be stressed as follow up activities;
7. stress sequence in learning opportunities so that pupils may build upon what has been learned previously;
8. obtain the attention of pupils;
9. invite questions from pupils before, during, and after each experiment;
10. identify additional problems within the ongoing experiment or demonstration.

Using Video-Tapes in Teaching Science

The science teacher and the school librarian should have access to videotapes housed in the library Videos should be rented and purchased from school moneys with adequately financing. The video tapes are directly related to the objectives of instruction within a science unit of study. A strategy needs to be developed whereby the teacher successfully initiates the videotape by stimulating learner interest, developing necessary background information so that each pupil may understand its contents, achieving sequential learnings with the previous learning opportunity, and having follow up experiences pertaining to the video-tape.

Video-tape content makes it possible for pupils to experience the semi-concrete in a meaningful way. It integrates with what a learner already knows. Scaffolding is an important concept for the science teacher to use in teaching. Scaffolding pertains to the zone of proximal distance. The zone of proximal distance may be thought of as the gap between where a pupil is presently in goal achievement and what is left to learn to satisfactorily achieve the desired end. The science teacher may use the videotape, or other learning opportunity to discuss subject matter with pupils to close this gap.

Pupils need to posses readiness to benefit from the video-tape. Readiness experiences include those that motivate learners in wanting to learn from the videotape, such as securing information in answer to questions and problems selected prior to implementing the showing of the video-tape. Which content might a videotape emphasise pertaining to a thematic unit in science?

1. celestial location and celestial distance of stars in the night sky;
2. origin and brightness of stars;
3. temperature of stars as well as the life of a star;
4. the Milky Way Galaxy, as well a the life of a galaxy;
5. the geocentric versus the heliocentric model of the solar system;
6. the planets, asteroids, comets, meteors, and meteorites.

The science teacher needs to choose a videotape that is on the understanding level of pupils and does not contain too many concepts. An excessive number of concepts covered in a videotape can make for a lack of meaningful learning. Vital concepts chosen need to be taught in depth such as # 1 above 'celestial location.' With depth teaching, pupils experience many examples and a variety of learning opportunities on content pertaining to one concept such as 'celestial location.' Survey teaching must be avoided. Survey teaching stresses shallow learning of each concept by pupils.

Using Slides, Filmstrips, and Transparencies

As compared to videotapes—slides, filmstrips, and transparencies contain no movement and motion in their inherent presentations. The science teacher, too, may use all the time needed on one frame in the slide or filmstrip, as well as the transparency. For example, in a sequential series of frames or transparencies, pupils with teacher direction may learn about each of the following, using as much time as is needed for meaningful concept learning:

1. air mass, arid, and climate;
2. cold front and continental air mass;
3. cyclone, hail, and hurricane;
4. polar air mass, precipitation, and stationary front;
5. tornado, tropical air mass, and typhoon.

There are concepts that are easier to understand due to being more concrete in nature and less abstract. Selected learners may also possess more background information on some concepts as compared to others. There are concepts, too, that are used more often in every day conversation as compared to others. Science teachers need to appraise rather continuously if a pupil understands a concept, rather than trying to memorise subject matter only. For example, a pupil may reveal understandings pertaining to air mass (number one above) if he/she can

1. give numerous examples;
2. explain the meaning of this concept;
3. make a drawing to indicate meaning;
4. use illustrations to explain and reveal comprehension;
5. raise related questions pertaining to the concept being studied.

Using Films in Teaching Science

Films have motion as do videotapes. There are selected pupils who learn more from an audiovisual aid that has inherent motion and movement as compared to those that do not. Generally, films are older devices in use as compared to videotapes. Still, many schools have films that have quality up-to-date content to be used in teaching science. In observing a student teacher and cooperating teacher teach, the following content was contained in a filmstrip:

1. continental shelf and continental slope;
2. an aquifer and an artesian well;
3. long shore current and ocean currents;
4. a sea and a pond in terms of surface water;
5. a water table.

For each of the above, the illustrations and explanations were very clear. Learners were very attentive when observing the contents in the film. This was indicated by excellent questions which were raised after the presentation. Thus for example, pupils indicated clarification when receiving additional comments on the differences between a sea and a pond as related to surface water, item number 4 above.

Using Daily Newspapers and Newsmagazines in Teaching Science

A good current events programme can do much to guide pupils to stay abreast with present day happenings in the world of science (for children's magazines see 'Current Science' and 'Ranger Rick' (addresses in the Reference section). For example, we are looking at additional finding in a newspaper pertaining to the dinosaur debate. Children find dinosaurs to be fascinating and pay considerable attention to the following debated items by scientists:

1. were all or some dinosaurs warm or cold blooded?
2. what caused the age of dinosaurs to become extinct?

Learners are eager to search for information, from a variety of reference sources, to locate necessary data in relationship to each of the above named questions. Pupils have then learned to use the following concepts pertaining to the age of dinosaurs in ongoing discussions:

1. Mesozoic era, as well as its subdivisions—triassic, jurassic, cretaceous in terms of time frames;
2. Meat eaters (carnivorous) versus plant eaters (herbivorous);
3. tyrannosaurus rex, stegasaurus, brontosaurus, diplodocus, triceratops, and duck billed dinosaurs, among others;
4. fossils, paleontologists, carbon dating, climatic changes, and meteorites;
5. mastodons and woolly mammoths—these animals were located in reference sources as a by product of pursing information on dinosaurs.

In looking at the above five numbered items, it is salient to notice that pupils can learn to use and attach meaning to very complex terms if interest is there in the learning opportunities. Interest tends to lead to motivation whereby pupils hardly look at their watches to notice the amount of time left for a lesson to end. Then too, learner can learn to read difficult words if the desire is there to do so.

When coming back to science being in the news, it appears that any issue of a newspaper or newsmagazine contains content pertaining to the scientific world, such as earthquakes, hurricanes, tornadoes, floods, mud slides, avalanches, drought, hail, blizzards, and snow storms. A teachable moment might well be when learners ask for the causes of any of these events, such as earthquakes. The teacher might then guide pupils to attach meaning as to why this phenomenon occurs.

When supervising student teachers and cooperating teachers in the public schools, we have observed radios and television being used to keep children abreast on current events that deal with science, such as viewing a sequential lift off for a relevant space feat on television. Pupils exhibit much curiosity in happenings such as these and have an inward desire to learn more about the following: space probes, space satellites, space shuttles, space stations, space labs, the Hubble telescope, the Voyager, the Magellan, and the Galileo.

For each news item to be read, make certain that each pupil has related necessary subject matter in his/her possession to understand that which is to be read and discussed in terms of scientific happenings. Assist learners with identifying unknown words in the reading selection. Ask questions in sequence which guides pupils to move from factual subject matter to that or critical and creative thought, as well as problem identification.

Using Technology in Teaching Science

The science teacher needs to be well versed with what exists in computer technology and teaching materials in order to provide for individual differences in the classroom. The school librarian also must be highly knowledgeable about what is available in computer and software materials. The following kinds of software need to be available that harmonise with ongoing science lessons and/or units of study:

1. tutorials that present new subject matter to learners;
2. simulation which provides lifelike situations involving problem solving;
3. drill and practice whereby pupils have opportunities to review and summarise what has been learned in an ongoing unit of study;
4. gaming which gives learners an opportunity to enjoy play activities that stress science subject matter;
5. diagnosis and remediation whereby the software programme detects an error and assists pupils to overcome the identified weakness.

Things for science teachers to notice when implementing technology into the science curriculum are the following:

1. Does the software assist pupils to achieve vital objectives of instruction?
2. Are the programmes sequential in nature whereby each package has new content within, that relates directly to the previous step of learning subject matter?
3. Do pupils feel they are actively engaged in each software programme?
4. Do pupils feel successful in learning?

5. Are pupils able to use what has been learned in new situations involving other kinds of learning opportunities?

Programmed learning moves forward very slowly in a step by step sequence. Thus, a learner reads a very small amount of content, such as a short paragraph, responds to a multiple choice item, and receives immediate feedback on what has been learned. The immediate feedback is there to guide pupils to avoid making errors in obtaining subject matter. Commercial software generally has been tried out in pilot studies in order to remedy weak sequences in the programme. Some programmes claim a ninety-five per cent correct rate of responses as given by pupils. Being right 95 per cent of the time is quite a record. Usually, software programmes do not stress critical and creative thinking as well as problem solving. Simulation programmes would come closest to stressing these kinds of objectives in science.

All pupils in sequence should learn to use the word processor. With using the word processor, the following learnings may be typed into the computer:

1. steps followed and conclusions found in doing a science experiment or demonstration;
2. an outline of an oral report to be given to learners in the classroom;
3. journal writing that pertains to completed science lessons;
4. diary entries kept on a day to day basis on learning opportunities pursued in class;
5. logs which summarise the diary entries, on a weekly or monthly basis;
6. summaries of science content read, directly related to the ongoing unit of study;
7. poems and stories written from science content studied;
8. letters written to order free science materials of instruction;
9. science subject matter acquired to be shared with pen pals. E-mail messages may also be sent;
10. experience charts may be typed to indicate specific activities and opportunities focused upon.

When using technology in the curriculum, much emphasis may be placed upon pupils engaging in doing research for a science project. Along with traditional quality methods of gathering data from print discourse and audio-visual materials, technology may stress using internet sources, CD ROMS, applicable software, World Wide Web, and the word processor. Information desired may be retrieved quickly and accurately for a research study.

Using Cassette Recorders in the Science Curriculum

There are numerous uses that may be made, as learning opportunities, of cassette recorders in science teaching. Cassette recording of subject matter from basal texts can be wisely used by pupils who do not read well. The recording may be listened to by slow readers as they read along in their textbook. These learners then comprehend better and become improved readers as a result of having the subject matter read. Selected library books may also be cassette recorded for pupils having difficulty in word recognition and comprehension. These readers may also enjoy reading content to achieve objectives as well as improve reading skills and possess increased knowledge. Additional ways to use cassette recording ongoing science units and lessons are the following:

1. having a committee record peer interactions in meeting quality standards for doing collaborative work;
2. recording a creative or formal dramatics activity in the classroom;
3. engaging pupils in giving individual or committee book reports;
4. explaining a college, a montage, a bulletin board display, and/or a diorama as each relate to a thematic science unit of study;
5. evaluating involved processes in doing a classroom science newspaper.

Science teachers should continually find new and better methods of instruction to guide increased levels of pupils achievement. Additional methods of teaching are found in time and newer procedures are in the offing in changing school and societal arena. Using Basals, Library Books, and Writing Activities in Teaching Science

A carefully chosen science textbook can do much to improve the curriculum if

1. it becomes a part of, but does not dominate the science curriculum;
2. it guides pupils to achieve vital objectives of instruction;
3. it can be used to initiate, develop, and culminate a science unit of study;
4. it supplements experiments and demonstrations as a knowledge source of pupils;
5. it helps pupils in developing a rich science vocabulary;
6. it assists pupils to increase reading and writing skills, necessary to communicate ideas clearly and effectively in thematic science units;

7. it is used as a source for objectives, learning opportunities, and appraisal procedures from the teacher's manual section;
8. it varies learning opportunities in order to stimulate and motivate pupil interest in science;
9. it makes for increased meaning and understanding in the science curriculum;
10. it increases pupil skills in word recognition and comprehension.

There is much that the science teacher may do the help pupils in word recognition and comprehension of subject matter. Thus, in word recognition, the science teacher may assist pupils in using phonics to unlock unknown words, in developing syllabication skills, in attaining context clues to determine new words in reading, in recognising a given set of useful sight words in science, and in application of background knowledge to subject matter being read.

To comprehend science subject matter being read, the teacher may assist pupils in reading for vital facts, concepts, main ideas, and generalisations. Learners also need to analyse subject matter read, synthesise ideas, evaluate content acquired, and use what has been learned in a new situation.

Library books may be used to enrich, to extend information, to develop ideas in greater depth, to achieve objectives in science, to develop interest in a topic, to use spare time wisely, and to enjoy the world of scientific endeavours.

Pupils, basically, should select their very own library books to read. The titles and topics in science should be broad in scope so that a learner may locate what is truly on his/her reading level (not the frustration level) as well as provide for the respective interests possessed by learners. Library books may be used to provide content for an oral/written report in a science unit of study, as a basis for small or large group unit discussion, as a method of instruction whereby the teacher reads stimulating sections aloud to pupils, and as a way for learners to appreciate quality literature in science.

Reading and writing are complementary in science in that each skill assists further competency in the other. There are many quality writing experiences for pupils in ongoing science lessons and units of study. Among others, the following salient writing activities:

1. diary entries and logs to record specific activities engaged in within sequential lessons in science;
2. journal writing to indicate content learned and that which is left to learn in unit teaching;
3. summarise and conclusions of content read from basal texts;

4. book reports and formal dramatisations written from that contained in relevant sections of library books;
5. steps involved in performing a science experiment and/or demonstration;
6. creative writings such as poetry or prose directly related to subject matter being studied in science;
7. letters written to order free and inexpensive science materials (See entry—Environmental Protection Agency Public Information Center and Library—in References section when writing for free and inexpensive science materials.

Using and Making Charts in Science

The science teacher should use charts in teaching pupils (Ediger, 1998, 36-38) Learners may also be actively engaged in chart construction. A chart, clearly visible to all learners in the classroom, may contain the following in a science unit on rocks and minerals:

Classification of Rocks

	Igneous		*Sedimentary*		*Metamorphic*
(a)	basalt	*(a)*	shale	*(a)*	slate
(b)	pumice	*(b)*	sandstone	*(c)*	marble
(c)	obsidian	*(c)*	conglomerate	*(c)*	anthracite coal
(d)	granite	*(d)*	coal	*(d)*	quartzite

The following chart on Prehistoric Life leaves space for pupils to fill in the needed subdivisions for each era:

The Precambrian Era
The Paleozoic Era
The Mesozoic Era
The Cenozoic Era

As the above named eras are studied by pupils, they may add information to each, such as the kinds of plant and animals in the Mesozoic Era included the age of dinosaurs. The chart might be quite extensive when illustrations are drawn directly related to a type of animal or plant.

In a science unit of study on The Solar System, pupils with teacher guidance may make a chart containing the names of the planets—Mercury, Venus, Earth, Mars, Jupiter, Saturn, Uranus, Neptune, and Pluto. Data on the diameter of each planet, as well as the approximate distance from the sun, may be filled in by learners as they are being studied in sequence. The chart may become quite large in size as learners write in major generalisations for each planet.

Why use charts in teaching science?

1. content shown pertains to one topic and focuses on classification of rocks only, for example, as these learnings are being taught;
2. the content is and should be large enough for all to see clearly in the classroom, or within a committee, as a related discussion pertaining to the involved subject matter is ongoing;
3. active involvement by learners is important in helping to make or in constructing a chart individually or collaboratively with teacher assistance;
4. charts vary the kind of learning activity used in the classroom to stimulate learner interest in science;
5. psychomotor skills and emphasised when pupils construct diverse kinds of charts for teaching and learning.

Science Equipment for Experiments and Demonstrations

Classrooms need to have the latest of equipment and materials for teaching science. Up-to-date subject matter must be in the offing for each pupil, as a result of science experiments and demonstrations. Too frequently, the science teacher must furnish all the materials of instruction. Instead, it is recommendable that pupils as well as the teacher bring selected materials for science experiments and demonstrations; however, many other materials need to be at the finger tips of teacher for ease of use. The following are recommended as available materials of instruction so that the teacher does not need to spend too much time in searching and locating: hand lens, a variety of kinds of magnets, iron filings, a telescope, an aquarium, beakers, calculators, a hot plate, aluminium foil, balance and standard masses, candles, rock samples (igneous, metamorphic, and sedimentary), balloons of diverse sizes, a barometer, dry cell batteries of different volts, copper wire, small bulbs in electrical sockets, bird book guides (to check bird migration, appearance, feeding habits, and geographical environments), graduated cylinders, compasses, a mineral collection accompanied by an identification book, litmus paper, maps and globes, microscope, prisms, a hygrometer, pulleys, levers, axles, wheels, graphic paper, mirrors, stop watch, metric measurement units (liters, centimeter tape, meter stick and scales and tables of metric measurements), thermometers, test tubes, as well as science encyclopaedias and other necessary reference books.

How might a few of the above named materials be used in unit teaching? For example the item listed first, a hand lens or magnifying glass, may be used by pupils to make observations from examining the enlarged sedimentary, igneous, and metamorphic rocks. Contrasts and comparisons may be recorded in journal form. Item second in the above listing were a variety of kinds of magnets. Here, pupils may learn that opposite poles attract and like poles repel. Iron filing may be placed on a sheet of paper directly above a magnet to notice magnetic forces. Science is a fascinating curriculum area and there are many experiments and demonstrations that capture pupil purpose and interest.

Pupils and the science teacher also may bring materials for instruction pertaining to experiments and demonstrations. Thus the following might be brought: seeds of different kinds to show rate of germinations as well as growth rates, cameras and film, cooking oil and corks, dishes and paper, feathers, flashlights, food colouring, lemon juice, measuring spoons and cups, masking tape clay, potting soil, different kinds of soil (loam, sandy, and clay), potholders, salt, metric, scales, a shell collection, sugar, sponges, a terrarium, vinegar, and dry yeast.

Pupils with teacher guidance can and do make excellent equipment in science to understand vital facts, concepts, and generalisations better than otherwise would be the case. In making magnets, for example, pupils may stroke steel needles in one direction on a magnet. The steel magnetised needle may be put on a cork and placed in a pan with water. Pupils will notice how the magnetised needle will take position according to the north/south pole orientation of like poles repel and opposite poles attract. Or, as a further example, pupils may develop a collection of and examine bird feathers with the use of a microscope. Observations made and discussed may be used to ascertain how feathers contribute to the ability of birds to engage in flight.

Pupils with teacher guidance may also make a barometer, an hygrometer, anemometer, and wind vane, among others, depending upon individual reediness factors.

In Conclusion

There are a variety of kinds of learning opportunities available for teachers to use in teaching and learning situations. Science teachers always need to be on the lookout for additional and new learning activities in order to guide more and increased pupil learning. Pupils learn in diverse ways and have unique intelligences as well as different style of learning. Science teachers need to study each pupil and assist him/her to learn a optimally as possible. It is vital to stimulate and maintain learner interest in science. Pupils need to become motivated and encouraged in ongoing science achievement. Learning is a continuous process and needs to be lifelong. Most pupils are fascinated with science phenomenon and have an inward desire to learn. Individual and collaborative endeavours need to be in the offing. Heterogeneous and homogeneous experiences need to be provided to harmonise with a pupil's talents, hobbies, and interests.

Inservice experiences need to be provided to assist teachers to stay abreast of the latest knowledge, skills, and attitudinal objectives. Learning opportunities need to be noticed and applied that guide pupils in goal attainment. Accepted technology needs incorporating into science units that truly inspires and challenges learner progress in science. The focal point of instruction should always be the learner and his/her achievement and progress in science.

REFERENCES

Current Science, Xerox Educational Publications, 5555 Parkcenter Circle, Suite 300, Dublin, Ohio 43017.

Environmental Protection Agency Public Information Center and Library, 401 M. Street, SW, Washington, DC 20460.

Ediger, Marlow (1995), 'Designing Science Units of Study', *School Science,* 33 (1), 14-15. Published in India by the National Council for Educational Research and Training.

Gardner, Howard (1993), *Multiple Intelligences: Theory Into Practice.* New York: Basic Books.

Ediger, Marlow (1997), *Teaching Science in the Elementary School,* Kirksville, Missouri: Simpson Publishing Company, Chapter One.

Ediger, Marlow and D. Bhaskara Rao (1996), *Science Curriculum.* New Delhi, India: Discovery Publishing House, Chapters Five and Six.

Ediger, Marlow (1995), 'Demonstration Teaching in the Schools,' *Education,* 114 (4), 371-372.

Ediger, Marlow (1995), 'Early field Experiences in Teacher Education, *College Student Journal.* 28 (3), 302-306.

Ediger, Marlow (1999), 'Issues in Curriculum Development,' *The Educational Review,* 105 (5), 90-92.

Ediger, Marlow (1998), 'Computers in the Science Curriculum', *School Science,* 36 (4), 62-71.

Ediger, Marlow (1998), 'Affective Objectives in the Science Curriculum,' *Spectrum.* 24 (2) 24-26.

Ediger, Marlow (1999), 'Objectives in the Science Curriculum,' *Exchange,* 22 (2), 24-26.

Ediger, Marlow (1995), *Philosophy in Curriculum Development,* Kirksville, Missouri: Simpson Publishing Company, Chapter Five.

Ediger, Marlow (1999), 'Attitudinal Objectives in the Chemistry Curriculum', *NEACT* Journal, 17 (2), 15-17.

Ediger, Marlow (1998), The Pupil and Writing in Science,' *School Science,* 36 (3), 36-38.

Ediger, Marlow (1998), 'Teaching Science As Inquiry,' *Resources in Education,* ERIC, SE 06/846.

Ediger, Marlow (1998), 'Use of Research Results in Teaching,' *School Science.* 36 (1), 35-43.

Ediger, Marlow (1996), 'Slogans in Education and in Society, *Journal of Educational Psychology*, 24 (1), 37-41.

Ediger, Marlow and D. Bhaskara Rao (2001), *Teaching Social Studies Successfully*. New Delhi, India: Discovery Publishing House.

Ediger, Marlow and D. Bhaskara Rao (2000), *Teaching Mathematics Successfully*. New Delhi, India: Discovery Publishing House.

Mehlinger, Howard (1996), 'School Reform in the Information Age', *Phi Delta Kappan*, 77 (6), 405-406.

Ranger Rick. National Wildlife Federation, 1412 Sixteenth Street, NW, Washington, DC 20036-2266.

35

Problems in Teaching Science

The science teacher has highly important tasks in implementing vital trends in the curriculum. In a rapidly changing society, the science curriculum needs to be assessed and updated where necessary. Changes should not be made for the sake of doing so, but rather due to meeting personal needs of pupils in a world of science. Pupils tend to be curious and interested in science as young learners. Sometimes, this curiosity and interest wears down as pupils progress through diverse levels of schooling. The teacher then has major responsibilities in helping pupils to be attentive in achieving vital objectives in ongoing lessons and units of study.

Thematic units provide a focal point for pupils to be actively involved in attaining objectives. Learning opportunities should guide learners to attain the objectives of instruction. These learning opportunities need to challenge pupils, but not be unduly complex whereby optimal achievement is not possible.

Objectives in Science

Objectives for pupil attainment should stress vital knowledge goals as one of three types of objectives. Securing knowledge emphasises pupils acquiring facts, concepts, main ideas, and generalisations. A second type stresses application ends. Here, a pupil is assisted to apply what has been achieved in terms of knowledge objectives. Ample opportunities need to be given for pupils collaboratively and individually to use what has been attained in the knowledge domain. With use, less forgetting occurs and, then too, learners might perceive value in learning that which is beneficial.

To be useful as objectives in science instruction, pupils need to have ample chances to engage in solving real problems identified in context. These problems require deliberation and thought in their solving, including the use of critical and creative thinking. Problem solving as well as critical and creative thinking, no doubt, will always be important in school and in society. Many trends and emphases in science teaching may come and go, but these three application skills are indeed worthy to stress presently as well as in the future.

A third kind of objectives to stress continuously is good attitudes of pupils towards the science curriculum. Mental health goals emphasise pupils achieving well in the affective dimension. Wholesome attitudes toward the self and others as well as toward acquiring knowledge and application skills in science are indeed worthy for all.

Sequencing Science Objectives

Sequencing objectives for pupil achievement is an important facet of teaching. The ordered objectives, then, should be arranged so that pupils experience new knowledge and skills based upon previously acquired learnings. A seamless web of achievement might then be in the offing. A logical sequence emphasises the teacher arranging to objectives so that success in pupil learning is increasingly possible. With a psychological sequence, the science teacher assists pupils to identify questions, problems and solutions they deem to be relevant. A combination of these two approaches is probably the most feasible and acceptable. Pupils differ on the kind of sequence they feel is the most worthwhile. Success in learning is salient for each pupil. Readiness for learning and achieving of new objectives depends much upon what the pupil has already learned and blends in with the new objectives of instruction. The learner should be guided to access what has been learned as well as relate his/her own experiences with the objectives to be realised.

Science Learning Opportunities

To achieve objectives, pupils need learning opportunities which capture and maintain learner attention. Unless pupil interest is being accessed, the chances are learning will not accrue as it should. Thus, to establish set, the science teacher needs to provide initiating experiences which engage the learner actively. It is important for pupils to attend to what is being presented for more optimal learning to occur.

Learning opportunities should contain concrete materials (objects, items, realia, excursions, and hands on approaches), semiconcrete, materials in teaching science (illustrations, videotapes, CD, ROMS, films, filmstrips, drawings, diagrams, graphs, charts, software packages, and multi-media presentations in general), and abstract (Reading, writing, listening, and speaking) experiences.

The materials of instruction may well provide content for science experiments and demonstrations which should be the heart of the science curriculum. Methods of teaching may also include problem solving, inductive and deductive activities, projects, pupil/teacher planning in ongoing lessons and units of study, unit teaching and thematic approaches, teacher directed experiences, peer teaching and collaborative endeavours, learning centers and constructivism as a philosophy of instruction, as well as sustained silent reading involving pupil choice of trade books in science.

Organisations of the Science Curriculum

Too frequently in the science curriculum, there are recommendations to use one approach in organising the science curriculum. We recommend multiple approaches of organising the science curriculum to provide for individual differences of and in pupil achievement. The separate subjects approach stresses using only one science academic discipline in ongoing units of study. There are times when only a single subject matter area should be taught. Why Depth learning is important in assisting pupils to acquire vital concepts and generalisations. This procedure tends to fragment learnings for pupils, if used exclusively. An other approach is to correlate two academic disciplines in science. An improved chance is then in the offing for pupils to perceive relationships in knowledge so that comprehension and retention are more likely to occur. In many situations, all science academic disciplines, as these are relevant, need to be implemented in teaching and learning in an integrated science curriculum. Pupils then have more chances to perceive how knowledge may be integrated. They may sense fusion of ideas and attach increased meaning to content in science experiences.

Going beyond the separate subjects, correlated, and integrated approaches to organise the curriculum, a teacher may stress interdisciplinary procedures. In inter-disciplinary procedures, the language arts (diverse reading materials and various purposes for writing, oral communication criteria in speaking experiences, and standards for quality listening), mathematics as the language of science, and social studies (the history of science, geographical influences on science, as well as economics, political science, anthropology, and sociology) may provide content for ongoing lessons and units of study as they are deemed significant to aid pupil interest and meaning in learning. Vital knowledge and skills need to be chosen to stress as objectives of instruction. Pupils need to be assisted to achieve these significant ends.

The Psychology of Instruction

To do better with increased engagement in learning opportunities, pupils need to experience principles of learning from educational psychology (Ediger, 1998, 203-208), there are selected principles which do pay off well when used in teaching science. First, the science teacher needs to secure the interests of pupils in ongoing lessons and units of study. Here, learning opportunities, need to be chosen which will interest learners. The manner of presentation should be such that the pupil has an inward desire to learn and achieve. Pupils need to ask questions pertaining to curiosities felt in these experiences. The questions identified might well become problems areas to be solved. A learning center containing items and objects stressing the new unit in science might well serve as an area of engagement in learning for pupils. The teacher needs to allow ample time for pupils to become fascinated with the items and objects at the learning center. Once problems have been identified, committees may be formed in using a variety of materials to work toward solutions. A committee of four members may serve on each committee. Ideally, learners should volunteer to serve on the committee of their choice. If a special committee needs to be formed to meet interest needs of pupils, this should be emphasised with implementation. Individual problem areas also need to be considered. Needs of each pupil should be met in ongoing science units of study.

Meaning must be stressed as a second vital principle of learning in teaching pupils. For meaning to occur, pupils need to understand that which is being taught. Comprehension on different cognitive levels should be emphasised in each science lesson. If pupils do not attach meaning to what has been learned, the chances are the subject matter and skills being taught will soon be forgotten.

A third principle of learning emphasises pupils perceiving purpose in learning. To sense purpose, the pupil needs to feel that there are valid reasons for achieving and developing. Thus, each pupil with purpose perceives one or more important reasons for active engagement in ongoing learning opportunities.

Fourth, individual differences need to be provided for in the science curriculum. To provide for individual differences, the teacher needs to provide for the learning styles of learners (Dunn and Dunn, 1979). Some pupils, for example, like to work on individual endeavours while others prefer committee work. Multiple Intelligences Theory stresses pupils using their unique intelligence(s) to indicate what has been learned (Gardner, 1993). Here, the following means are available to have learners indicate achievement: scientific, verbal/linguistic, logical/mathematical, visual/spatial, musical, bodily/kinesthetic, interpersonal, and intrapersonal.

Fifth, pupils need to become motivated individuals in studying science. To motivate, the teacher should show enthusiasm for reading science content as well as doing scientific endeavours. The high energy level for teaching science should then be reflected in pupil interest and achievement.

Learners individually should also be assisted to develop a good self concept for learning. Thus, the teacher needs to help each pupil to be successful in making progress in the science curriculum. Success in achieving objectives in science in a must! Recognition needs of individuals also must be met. Each pupil should be identified for doing well in facets of science regardless of ability levels. It behooves the teacher to observe where esteem needs should be rewarded in ongoing lessons.

Assessment of Pupil Achievement

A variety of assessment techniques need to be used to appraise achievement in science. Teacher observation of learner progress in context is important. Better sequence in pupil learning might well be an end result when the teacher uses quality standards to assess when observational methods are used. In addition, the following, among others, need to be used to assess and improve the science curriculum for pupils:

1. portfolios and pupil journal writing;
2. diary entries and logs written individually or collaboratively by learners;
3. pupil participation in discussions;
4. project methods of instruction and evaluating their processes and products;
5. art work, written reports, and dramatic experiences as each relates directly to a science lesson or unit of study;
6. tutorial results from software packages, using microcomputers.

The following may be used diagnostically with positive attempts made to remedy vital deficiencies:

1. teacher written tests;
2. standardised, norm referenced tests;
3. criterion referenced tests.

In Conclusion

The science teacher has vital responsibilities in providing the best science curriculum possible to guide optimal pupil progress.

The objectives need to represent salient knowledge, skills, and attitudes for learner attainment. Proper sequence of the objectives assists pupils to achieve in a more optimal manner. The learning opportunities need to help pupils achieve the desired ends. Principles of learning from educational psychology used in teaching provide for motivated learners. Quality assessment techniques need to be used to appraise what pupils have learned. What has not been learned needs diagnosis and remediation with excellent learning opportunities.

REFERENCES

Bhaskara Rao, Digumarti, ed. (2000), *International Encyclopaedia of Science and Technology Education*, 11 Vols. New Delhi, India: Discovery Publishing House.

Dunn, Rita, and Kenneth Dunn (1979), 'Learning Styles/Teaching Styles,' *Educational Leadership*, 36 (4), 238-244.

Ediger, Marlow (1997), *Teaching Science in the Elementary School*. Kirksville, Missouri: Simpson Publishing Company, Chapter Six.

Ediger, Marlow (1998), 'Change and the School Administrator,' *Education*, 118 (4), 541-548.

Ediger, Marlow and D. Bhaskara Rao (1996), *Science Curriculum*. New Delhi, India: Discovery Publishing House, Chapter Four.

Ediger, Marlow (1996), 'Evaluation of Pupil Achievement,' *Education Magazine*, Published by the Qatar National Commission for Education—The Middle East.

Ediger, Marlow (1998), 'Sequence in Primary Grade Mathematics', *Journal of Instructional Psychology*, 26 (3), 203-208.

Gardner, Howard (1993), *Multiple Intelligences: Theory into Practice*. New York: Basic Books.

Rao, D. Bhaskara Rao, and Marlow Ediger (1996), *Scientific Attitude Vis-A-Vis Scientific Aptitude*. New Delhi, India: Discovery Publishing House, Chapter Two.

Rathaiah, L., D. Bhaskara Rao and P.K. Rao (1997). *Correlates of Achievement*. New Delhi, India: Discovery Publishing House.

Veena Kumari, B. and D. Bhaskara Rao (2000), *Psycho-social Correlates of Achievement*. New Delhi, India: Discovery Publishing House.

36

Improving the Teaching of Science

Science teachers need to stay abreast of recent trends in teaching science. They need to study, analyse, and appraise new developments in the teaching of science. We will indicate selected trends and discuss related comments. Each School might then appraise their very own science curriculum to make necessary changes. The science curriculum needs to be brought up to date frequently. Modification of the present science curriculum is necessary so that pupils achieve as much as possible in each unit of study.

Recommended Trends in Teaching Science

First, the science teacher needs to develop thematic units of study which provide for individual differences. In the science unit, there needs to be a carefully thought through set of objectives. These objectives should emphasise vital subject matter, skills, and attitudinal objectives. Subject matter for the objectives section should be based upon structural ideas identified by university professors in science, public school teachers, and school administrators. Structural ideas represent key concepts and generalisations in each unit of study. These concepts and generalisations represent important and relevant content in science. The skills objectives section should stress, among others, critical thought whereby pupils separate the accurate from the inaccurate, the relevant from the irrelevant as well as the important from the unimportant ideas in science content.

Generally with critical thinking, the content chosen will fit into the solving of problems in science. Pupils with teacher guidance need to identify problems in ongoing units of study in science. Each problem is adequately delimited and salient. Information is then needed to secure content as an answer to the problem(s) identified. Creative thinking, as a further skill, is necessary so that pupils come up with unique, novel solutions to problem areas. Tried and true solutions may not work. Therefore originality in pupil skills is needed so that problems are identified and solved. After adequate data has been secured, the pupil needs to test the solution in a lifelike situation. Should the solution work the hypothesis (tentative answer to the problem) is accepted. If the answer to the problem does not work, a new solution needs to be found with further collecting of information.

In addition to subject matter and skills objectives, a third kind of objective for the science teacher to stress is attitudinal objectives. Attitudinal objectives include developing pupil interest in science, establishing diverse purposes for learning, wanting to learn more science, and wishing to use science content in everyday life.

A second trend in teaching science emphasises relating subject matter acquired in ongoing lessons and units of study. If pupils learn to correlate and integrate subject matter, the chances are less forgetting will occur. Why? A pupils who thinks of content being related will find that one idea recalled triggers other ideas to the level of consciousness. The process is continuous in that each idea recalled will assist in the recollection of others. Thus, the areas of biology, chemistry, geology, astronomy, physics, and geology may be taught as being interrelated.

Third, inservice education is necessary so that teachers keep abreast of modern methods of instruction. The workshop and faculty meeting approaches need to stress what teachers deem to be of help in the instructional arena. Teachers need to have much input into the development of inservice education programmes. Ideas gleaned from inservice education need to be applied in teaching and learning situations. Feedback to participants need to be given at the inservice education meeting so that others may try new ideas in teaching to assist each pupil to achieve as optimally as possible.

Fourth, teachers need to appraise pupils more so within the actual engagement of learning, rather than external factors. What are these external situations? Testing in their diverse dimensions tend to be outside the actual specific act of learning. Rather, evaluating a pupil within the framework of being involved in performing science experiments in ongoing lessons and units of study stresses the constructivist philosophy. With constructivism as a philosophy of evaluation, the pupil is evaluated within the framework of teaching and learning, not outside of it. Thus, within science experiments, demonstrations, viewing audio-visual materials, reading science content, giving a book report, making a diagram, constructing a graph, and doing an art project related to the thematic unit being studied, pupils reveal achievement and progress. Evaluation may then be continuous. Diagnosis and remediation are possible in constructivism as a philosophy of evaluation.

Fifth, pupils need to indicate progress to teachers, parents, and school administrators through the development of the portfolio. A portfolio contains a collection of relevant materials of pupil achievement in ongoing units of study. A representative sampling of pupil work needs to be a part of the portfolio. To organise the portfolio properly, the pupil with teacher guidance needs to select those products and processes that reveal learner progress. A table of contents is needed as well as a selection of listed worthwhile objectives to achieve. The objectives need to guide pupil achievement in selecting what goes into a portfolio. Items for a portfolio might include written work, art products, construction endeavours, snapshots of pupil work, videotapes of collaborative endeavours, and drawings, as well as statistical data in the form of graphs and tables. The completed portfolio may be shown to parents and others who are responsibly involved in evaluating pupil achievement. The philosophy of constructivism is involved in that pupil work reflects what was done within different ongoing lessons and units of study. What about test results? By all means, these should be a part of the portfolio contents. However, they are a part of the portfolio and should not dominate the contents therein. The portfolio should not become unwieldy, but represents what a pupil has completed in terms of being a representative sampling.

Sixth, there should be ample input into thematic science units of study form the pupil. The pupil needs to be actively engaged in learning and therefore needs to have input in terms of objectives, learning activities, and evaluation procedures to be stressed in the science unit of study. For this kind of pupil input, we would suggest a set of learning centers as being the heart of the thematic unit of study in science.

With learning centers as the heart of the thematic science unit of study, pupils individually may choose which center and which tasks to pursue sequentially. The tasks need to have learner appeal and inherent interest. The learner might then order his/her own tasks to pursue as learning opportunities. Ideally, there should be more tasks than what a pupil can complete so that omissions can be made. Time on tasks is very important for each pupil so learners achieve as much as possible. A psychological sequence is involved when pupils individually choose the order of their very own tasks to complete.

The learning centers may also be used for enrichment activities. Here, a more limited number of learning centers are available for pupils to choose from, but these tasks are used to supplement pupils' work from other kinds of learning activities not found at the learning centers. When spare time is available, a pupil may work at the enrichment centers to achieve additional objectives in the thematic science unit of study. The teacher then selects most of the objectives, learning opportunities, and evaluation procedures in the regular science curriculum with a logical sequence being in evidence. Why is this a logical sequence? The science teacher orders which activities come first, second, third, and so on in teaching and learning. These activities are selected on the basis of being meaningful and purposeful to involved learners.

Seventh, the psychology of pupil learning needs to be selected based on how pupils individually and collaboratively may achieve as much as possible. Behaviourism stresses stating objectives in science in measurable terms prior to instruction. The teacher develops and orders the objectives for pupils to attain. Learning activities are chosen by the teacher on the basis of having pupils achieve the objectives. With precise objectives of instruction, a pupil either does or does not achieve the stated objectives as a result of instruction. If a pupil fails to attain an objective, he/she may experience a different teaching strategy. Criterion referenced tests (CRTS) are a major way to determine pupil achievement. These tests are aligned with the stated objectives so that validity and reliability in testing is in evidence.

In addition to behaviourism as a psychology of learning being emphasised in teaching, a somewhat opposite approach stresses pupil/teacher, planning of objectives, learning opportunities, and evaluation procedures. Here, the pupil may have opportunities to plan with the teacher the objectives of instruction as well as the learning opportunities to achieve the objectives. Evaluation procedures to ascertain what has been learned might also be planned cooperatively with the science teacher. Planning together involving the pupil with teacher assistance is a difficult method of instruction. However, the end result is that pupils have a better chance of experiencing unit teaching that meets personal needs and interests.

In between points of view may be stressed in ongoing units of study such as having some teacher determined facets of the science curriculum, such as in behaviourism, as well as emphasising pupil input into the curriculum, such as in the pupil teacher planning model of unit teaching in science. What determines which plans to implement in teaching pupils?

1. Under which conditions does the pupil do best in learning?
2. Under which plan are pupil's needs and interests met best?
3. Under which plan of instruction does the teacher do the best job of professional teaching?
4. Under which plan might the psychological needs of pupils and teachers be met best?
5. Under which conditions can the methods of science be taught so that pupils experience excitement and optimal achievement in a positive learning environment?

Eighth, the philosophy of education needs to be considered in designing the science curriculum. There are diverse philosophies which assist pupils to achieve more optimally. A problem solving philosophy certainly does harmonise well with objectives to be stressed in science. Science educators seemingly agree that problem solving should be at or near the apex of objectives for pupils to achieve in ongoing lessons and units of thematic study. To be involved in problem solving, pupils also need to think critically when data is gathered in answer to the problem. Creative thought is needed when unique solutions are necessary for answers to problem solving.

A second philosophy stresses an idea centered science curriculum. Here, the teacher guides pupils to achieve objectives in science which stress the abstract in concept development and achievement of generalisations. The abstract is prized more highly in teaching science as compared to the concrete and semi-concrete learning activities. However, the concrete and semi-concrete are valued as learning experiences that assist pupils to achieve abstractions in science lessons and units of study.

A third philosophy stresses pupils attaining measurable results in the science curriculum. Thus, a pupil can pinpoint an exact level of achievement in science such as the fiftieth percentile or being one standard deviation above the mean. With quality tests that are valid and reliable, the teacher may pinpoint the exact achievement level of the involved learner. Here, the precise objectives are stated prior to instruction. The learning opportunities guide pupils to achieve each measurably stated objectives in ongoing science lessons and units of study. Test results indicate how well a pupil is doing in science.

A fourth philosophy of education in teaching science emphasises a decision making model. Here, the learner is actively involved in planning the objectives, learning activities, and evaluation procedures in teaching and learning. The pupil with teacher assistance is to be a responsible person in selecting what to learn in the science curriculum. What is learned in science units may stress problem solving, an idea centered approach, and/or achieving measurably stated objectives. The decision making model emphasises pupils being accountable for goal attainment in the science curriculum. In deciding upon which philosophy of science teaching to stress, the teacher will need to appraise his/her strengths in the instructional arena as well as appraise learner progress involving to teaching and learning in the science curriculum. The choice(s) zero in upon pupils needing to attain as optimally as possible in science instruction.

Principles of Learning

There are specific principles of learning that are recommended to be used to teaching pupils on science. These principles of learning are advocated by educational psychologists in the teaching arena:

1. set establishment is important. If pupils are to learn and achieve, their attention must be secured in ongoing learning experiences. A definite strategy needs to be formulated by the science teacher to obtain pupil attention for teaching and learning situations. Pupils who do not attend to the ongoing lesson do not attain as much as they should;
2. pupils need to possess reasons for achieving stated objectives in science. The science teacher may use an inductive approach in guiding pupils to establish reasons for learning. Here, the teacher asks questions of learners in class on why it is salient to master what is contained in the stated objectives. Or a deductive procedure may be emphasised in that the teacher might explain to pupils why it is important to learn that which is contained in the listed objectives on the chalkboard or overheard projector. Teachers advocating extrinsic rewards may announce prizes/awards for pupils who attain a certain precise level of achievement in science. Pupils need to be clear on what to learn so that the prize/award is obtained;
3. pupils need to perceive relationships of the new subject matter to be taught with the previous content emphasised and mastered. Quality sequence is an end result;
4. time on task is relevant. Here, pupils perceive as worthwhile that which is being presented as learning opportunities to achieve objectives;
5. motivation for learning is in evidence in that each pupil is revealing a higher energy level for accomplishment in sequential units of study in science;
6. learners attach meaning to content presented. Understanding and comprehension of ideas gleaned make for meaningful learning.

National Science Education Standards

Voluntary standards for science teachers to emphasise in teaching have been developed and published in the volume National Science Education Standards (NSES). There are excellent objectives here for teachers to stress in teaching and learning situations. The Science as Inquiry Standards section states the following (NSES, 1996):

Scientific inquiry refers to the diverse ways in which scientists study the natural world and propose explanations based on evidence derived from their work. Inquiry also refers to the activities of students in which they develop knowledge and understanding of scientific ideas as well as an understanding of how scientists study the natural world...

The Teaching Standard for all K-4 students emphasise the following, as an example:

In guiding and facilitating science instruction, teachers should:

1. Focus and support inquiries while interacting with students;
2. Orchestrate discourse among students about scientific ideas;
3. Challenge students to accept and share responsibility for their own learning;
4. Recognise and respond to diversity and encourage all students to participate fully in science learning;
5. Encourage and model the skills of scientific inquiry, as well as the curiosity, openness to new ideas and data, and skepticism that characterises science.

In Conclusion

The science teacher needs to use diverse ingredients in teaching and learning which guide optimal progress. The structure of knowledge, the psychology of learning, the philosophy of education, and vital principles of learning need to be used to determine and organise a purposeful set of sequential units in science instruction. Subject matter, skills, and attitudinal objectives must reflect careful planning by the science teacher. Learning opportunities should guide pupils to achieve objectives. Evaluation of achievement needs to indicate the kinds of progress made by pupils in ongoing lessons and units of study. Diverse evaluation procedures need to be used to acquire information pertaining to each pupil's progress in science. The information obtained should be used to plan further sequential units of instruction.

REFERENCES

Ediger, Marlow (1997), *Teaching Science in the Elementary School*, Kirksville, Missouri: Simpson Publishing Company, pp. 1-7.

Ediger, Marlow (1994), 'Shared Leadership in the Curriculum; *Education Magazine*. Qatar National Commission for Education, (23): 110, pp. 11-15.

Ediger, Marlow (1996), *Elementary Education*. Kirksville, Missouri: Simpson Publishing Company, pp. 10-24.

Ediger, Marlow (1995), *Philosophy in Curriculum Development*, Kirksville, Missouri: Simpson Publishing Company, p. 1-18.

National Science Education Standards (1996), published by the National Research Council. Washington, DC: National Academy Press.

Marja, Talvi and Digumarti Bhaskara Rao, eds. (1996), *Educational Leadership and Social Changes*. New Delhi, India: Discovery Publishing House.

37

Quality in the Science Curriculum

Each person lives in a world of science. The natural environment affects all of us. It operates in terms of scientific theories, principles, and laws. Pupils in the public school setting need to achieve relevant goals in science. These goals should be attainable, meaningful, and possess purpose for the learner. *The Show Me Standards* (1996) list the following science objectives for pupil achievement in Missouri schools:

In science, students in Missouri public schools will acquire a solid foundation which includes knowledge of

1. properties and principles of matter and energy;
2. properties and principles of force and motion;
3. characteristics and interactions of living organisms;
4. changes in eco-systems and interactions of organisms with their environment;
5. processes (such as plate movement, water cycle, air flow) and interactions of Earth's biosphere, atmosphere, lithosphere, and hydrosphere;
6. composition and structure of the universe and the motions of objectives within it;
7. processes of scientific inquiry (such as formulating and testing hypotheses);
8. impact of science, technology and human activity on resources and the environment.

Each of the above named objectives should be emphasised within a related, designated unit of study. The objectives might also be written more precisely, if desired so that it can be measured if a pupil has/has not achieve each stated end of instruction. There are states in the United States that mandate measurably stated objectives. Other states have a more open-ended approach in allowing leeway in writing objectives. We recommend that objectives not be written so precisely that facts only are emphasised on tests to appraise pupil achievement. The following objective stresses memorising facts: the pupil will list in writing the names of ten arthropods. Then too, objectives can be so broadly stated that they become meaningless such as 'The pupil will learn science.' This objectives certainly lacks clarity in terms of what will be taught and evaluated to determine pupil achievement.

To improve the quality of life for each person, a problem solving approach should be emphasised in ongoing lessons and units in science. With problem solving, change occurs from what is to what should be in science.

Diverse schools of philosophical thought will be discussed and how each might relate to improve the science curriculum.

Realism in the Science Curriculum

A science teacher who is a realist emphasises that one can know the real world, in whole or in part, as it truly is. The mind then does not modify or change what is being perceived. Tillman, Berofsky, and O'Connor (1971) wrote, "Most people when they think about the objects of perception, would say that they perceive a world of objects which is external to them and which exists independently of their perception of it. This view is called realism."

Since the external world is perceived the way it is in actuality, specific objective of instruction can be determined by scientists and science educators for pupils to achieve. Each objective must be relevant and is a part of the whole that can be known by the learner. Thus in geology, biology, chemistry, physics, and astronomy, among other academic disciplines, measurably stated objectives of instruction need to be emphasised in teaching and learning in the science curriculum. With quality learning opportunities selected by the science teacher, pupils either achieve or do not achieve the specific objective(s) as the result of instruction. Measuring pupil achievement in learning stresses what pupils have learned what was stated in each objectives. Realists desire observable results in learning from pupils. The results are verifiable regardless of which teacher is appraising learner progress. The verification principle is very important to teacher of science who adhere to realism as a philosophy of instruction.

Skinner (1979) was a leading advocate in stressing precise objectives for pupil attainment. Reinforcement is emphasised to reward correct/good responses in learning. Observable, measurable results are obtained from what pupils have achieved. Guesswork is not involved, but per cents, standard deviations, quartile deviations, grade equivalents, and percentile ranks emphasise how well each pupil is doing in the area of science instruction. Numerical results of pupil achievement in science is wanted by the realist teacher. Scores from tests; objective evaluations of science experiments and demonstrations performed by pupils; ratings given to learner performance as well as responses to questions, oral reports, portfolios and related papers written in which interobserver reliability is in evidence, present data as to how well pupils are achieving. These procedures qualify as objective means of appraising learner progress.

Mager (1972) stressed the importance of writing objectives so they are operationalised. Objectives are then specific and clear to teachers, pupils, and other interested persons. Learning opportunities may be chosen and aligned with the stated objectives. Appraisal procedures used to determine pupil achievement are also aligned with the objectives. Quality validity and reliability are then in the offing. A pupil reveals if he/she attained or did not attain a stated objective. The realist science teacher wishes to know if pupils individually are or are not achieving objectives of instruction. The results may then be reported to parents in a very precise way.

Prior to instruction, the teachers may announce to pupils which objectives will be emphasised in the science lesson or unit. The pupil knows exactly what will be expected in terms of knowledge or skills to be obtained. The involved pupil should have more confidence in learning when realising what the instructor's expectations are. The science teacher might desire to arrange the objectives in an ascending order of complexity. A logical sequence follows since the teacher sequences objectives in science for the pupil to achieve.

Advantages given for emphasising realism as a philosophy of instruction are the following:

1. teachers may realise how successful they are in teaching since results form pupil learning are clear and observable;
2. objectives, learning activities, and evaluation procedures are interrelated in that the learning activities and the evaluation procedures must harmonise with the stated objectives. Thus, for example, it becomes easier to choose learning activities than otherwise would be the case due to the harmony needed between these activities and the stated objectives;
3. effective schools research states that pupil achieve better if there is a clear relationship between the learning activities and the evaluation procedures with that of the objectives of science instruction (Edmonds, 1982).

Disadvantages given for emphasising realism as a philosophy of education stress the fragmented knowledge that pupils may learn since each objective achieved emphasises parts of a whole. The teacher controls the science curriculum since he/she determines the objectives, learning opportunities, and evaluation procedures; pupils are not involved here in decision making. The products of instruction in science are emphasised, leaving little room for processes such as abstract thinking which is rather difficult to measure.

Examples of precise objectives for pupils to achieve in science are the following:

1. The pupil will write a paragraph indicating seven animals involved in a food chain;
2. The pupil will make a drawing showing ten animals in a forest food web and their interactions;
3. The pupil will list in writing the names of five parasites and their respective hosts;
4. The pupil will define each of the following; producers, consumers, decomposers, symbiosis, and an aquatic—land community.

Experimentalism in the Science Curriculum

Experimentalists stress a problem solving approach in the curriculum. They emphasise that individuals cannot know the real world as it truly is. Individuals, however, obtain experiences of this reality. With experiences, changes occur in one's thinking and believing. A changing world makes for problematic situations. Problems need identification and solutions sought. In the science curriculum, pupils with teacher guidance select a problem within an ongoing lesson or unit of study. The problem needs to be adequately delimited so that meaning and understanding is involved. An hypothesis is developed directly related to the stated problem. Information from a variety of sources is used by learners to arrive at a tentative solution. Experimentalists believe all knowledge to be tentative, not absolute. The result might well involve changing and modifying the original hypotheses. The new hypothesis is then tried out in a concrete situation (Geiger, 1955). Problem solving may be used in all curriculum areas and in life itself. Knowledge here is used to solve problems and is not an end in and of itself. The practical and the utilitarian are emphasised within the framework of problem solving: knowledge secured from a variety of sources has an application dimension. Knowledge then is useful to solve problems in changing world, science included.

Experimentalists emphasise that school and society are one, not separate entities. Since groups in society select and solve problems, pupils in committees also need to be involved in cooperative learning stressing problem solving. School and society are one, not separate entities. Dewey (1915) is still very widely recognised as a leading advocate of experimentalism in teaching and learning. In integrating the learner with the self as well as with the societal arena, he advocated four characteristics of pupils which have wide implications for the teaching of science. These are that pupils posses the social impulse in that they desire to work together with others in the curriculum; the constructive impulse in which learners like to learn by doing, not being passive individuals; the investigative and experimentation inclination whereby pupils desire to learn by discovery rather than being told and lectured; and the creative or expressive impulse, rather then have rigid formal expectations for achievement.

Advantages given in emphasising experimentalism as a philosophy of teaching science are the following:

1. pupil interest in science becomes paramount when they with teacher assistance identify problem areas. Interest in learning makes for effort in achieving;
2. very young pupils in early primary grades may be involved in problem solving experiences;
3. problem solving is useful in all curriculum areas and in life itself when problems are selected and solutions sought.

Disadvantages of using experimentalism as a philosophy of education included problem selection being too difficult as well as problem solving may not be a favourite style and way of learning for a few pupils. Also motivation may be lacking for some pupils to identify and solve problems.

The following are examples of possible problems for pupils to solve:

1. How do animals adapt to their natural environment?
2. How do cells differ in size and shape to fulfill their unique functions? How are cells similar in features possessed?
3. How do unicellular and multicellular organisms differ from each other?
4. Which life processes do all living things perform?

Pertaining to John Dewey's philosophy of experimentalism, Meyer (1949) wrote:

All of this, of course, depends upon in no small way on thinking. For Dewey, however, thinking becomes significant only when applied to life situations. It is, he has said, 'an instrumentality used by man in adjusting himself to the practical situations in life.' Or to phrase it more simply, human beings think in order to live. Because of this stimulus, which has its basis in biology and sociology, it is impossible—it is absurd—to interpret life in a systematic and abstract way. Since, moreover, Dewey holds that life is in constant flux, it is impossible to solve problems with any degree of finally for the problems of tomorrow will be different from those of today.

As for the problem of knowledge, Dewey believes that knowledge and true experience is functional. What is this thing for? What is its use? Is a coal mine a physical deposit or does it have function? And if so, what is it? Such are the questions that help to give meaning to one's experience; but such questions cannot be answered without antecedent action. Action must precede knowledge. Whatever knowledge we possess has resulted from our activities, our efforts to survive, to obtain, food, shelter, and clothing. Only that which has been organised into our disposition so as to enable us to adapt to our environment to meet our needs and to adapt our aims and desires to the situation in which we exist is really knowledge.

Idealism in the Science Curriculum

Idealists believe that one can receive ideas about the real world only. Thus one cannot know the real world as it truly is independent of the observer. Mental development in idealism becomés of utmost importance since an idea centered world is in evidence. Mind is real and needs development. As a leading idealist still quoted widely presently, Horne (1932) stressed the importance of the use of reason and rational thought in arriving at truth. Concepts and generalisations or universals such as justice, truth, goodness, ethics, and beauty have always existed and can be discovered by human beings. These universals are a priori, to an idealist, in that they have existed prior to human experience.

A subject centered curriculum in science is of paramount importance. In science lessons and units of study, pupils should achieve vital concepts, and generalisations. Depth teaching is needed to cultivate the intellect in guiding pupils achievement in science. A multimedia approach in learning is needed to assist pupils to achieve abstract ideas in science. The abstract to an idealist is superior to the concrete and semiconcrete in learning. The concrete and semiconcrete facets of learning in science are salient to the degree that learners attain the abstract such as vital facts, concepts, and generalisations in ongoing lessons and units of study. Since reading and writing, in particular, stress abstract learnings, they should not be minimised in the science curriculum.

To emphasise a subject centered curriculum as idealists recommend, an academically inclined teacher needs to teach in a scholarly way so that objectives stressing intellectual goals are attained by pupils. Blanchard (1964) wrote:

The aim of thought from its very beginning, we saw, was at understanding. To understand anything meant to apprehend it in a system that rendered it necessary. The ideal of complete understanding would be achieved only when the system that rendered it necessary was not a system that itself was fragmentary and therefore contingent, but one that was all—inclusive and so organised internally that every part was linked to every other by intelligible necessity.

Advantages given for emphasising idealism as a philosophy of teaching science include the following:

1. pupils are to achieve significant subject matter. Idealism emphasises the acquisition of vital content in science that pupils need to attain. Uses made of knowledge in science need to emphasise what is just too all, what is truthful, what is good in its application, what will truly stress ethical dimensions, and that which has beauty in its esthetical areas;
2. many pupils may be motivated to learn when an academic approach to learn science is stressed. This might be especially appealing to the gifted and talented learners in science. All pupils need motivation to achieve and learn in science;
3. the abstract in idealism is preferred to the concrete and semiconcrete; relevant concepts, and generalisations, and other universals emphasise abstract goals in science teaching. Idealist advocate wholeness in knowledge, not fragmentation. Knowledge is related in all of its manifestations.

Disadvantages given for idealism as a philosophy in teaching and learning include minimising a hands on approach in learning science since the focal point of teaching is to have pupils develop well intellectually; placing emphasis upon universals much more so than specifics—the latter is salient in pupils arriving at conclusions such as in science experiments; and integrating of knowledge to the point where science as a discipline is not as clearly defined as ti might be. Idealists tend to stress that which goes beyond the five senses. Thus metaphysics and the a priori are salient to an idealist.

Quality sequences in science might be slighted when abstract phases of learning are more prized more highly than the concrete and semiconcrete. Most educators, presently recommend a sequence of concrete, semiconcrete, to the abstract in teaching-learning situations. Quite similar is sequence, Bruner (1968) advocated using manipulative materials such as objects and items; followed by iconic materials such as audio-visual materials which are one step removed from the manipulative phase; and then symbolic activities which stresses the abstract including reading and writing.

Objective in science, according to idealism as a philosophy of education, might well stress the following universal topics:

1. monerans such as bacteria and blue green algae. Monerans are prokaryotes in that they have no true nucleus. They consist of producers, consumers, and decomposers. A few move around whereas others are stationary;
2. protists, such as paramecium, euglenas, diatoms, and cribaria. Protists are unicellular and have a true nucleus. With a true nucleus, protists are eukaryotes, and are producers as well as consumers;
3. fungi, such as mushrooms and bread molds. Most fungi are multicellular. Since fungi do not contain chlorophyll, most are decomposers with a few being consumers;
4. plants, such as mosses, liverworts, ferns, and seed plants. Plants are eukaryotes and producers. Plants do not move from one place to another.

Pertaining to idealism, Bigge (1982) wrote:

The heart of idealism is the belief that basic reality consists of ideas, thoughts, minds, or substantive selves, not physical matter. Since priority is given to minds, minds have bodies, but bodies do not have minds. Idealism carries with its view the idea of subsistence (the superexistence) of God, who also is basically mind or self. The universe is an expression of intelligence and will; its order is due to an eternal, spiritual reality. For idealists, people are good-active substantive minds; they are absolutely real selves endowed with free will or genuine moral choice. This philosophy has ancient roots; it dates back to Socrates (469-399 BC) and Plato (427-347 BC).

Idealism really is idea-ism. The source of this title is based on Platonic thought. For Plato, ideas only are genuinely real; they consisted of immaterial essences. That which people perceive is a shadow of reality; each thing that they perceive gets its existence from its Thingness; and idea. A book is a book because of its being more or less an imperfect replica of Bookness. A woman is a woman because she is a replica of Womanness. Plato's assumed world of 'eternal verities' consisted of the True, the Good, and the Beautiful.

We can trace the development of idealism by listing some of the leading philosophers who have contributed to this position and stating a leading idea that each has contributed to this philosophy. Socrates believed that children are born with knowledge already in their minds, but they needed help to recall this innate knowledge. Plato contributed to the idea of ideas, which are the universal forms of all existing things and are the essence of reality. St. Augustine (350-430) held a dualistic (mind-body) force of goodness.

Existentialism and the Science Curriculum

Existentialists believe that one exists first and then finds his/her purposes in life; there are no standards to guide human beings other than those developed by the human race. Most existentialists advocate that people are condemned to be free with no a priori standards in life. Individuals then make or break themselves due to the kind of society wanted. Each person chooses and makes choices continually. To be human is to choose. If a person permits the self to have someone else makes one's own decisions, then the individual ceases to be human.

Combs (1972) stresses that the way individuals perceive a situation will assist in determining how the individual will behave. Perception in unique to the individual. Each person decides upon what is true, judges what is good, and decides upon plans of action. The science curriculum then must provide opportunities for pupils individually to decide what to learn, that is the objectives of instruction. The pupil needs to be heavily involved in selecting learning opportunities as well as methods of determining progress. The teacher is a guide and encourages pupil learning. The teacher, however, does not lecture nor determine the science curriculum for the individual pupil. A learning centers approach in teaching science may then be emphasised. Here, there are an adequate number of centers with quality tasks for learners at each center. There needs to be more tasks than what a pupil can complete so that individual sequential choices may truly be made. A psychological, not logical, science curriculum is then in evidence. Each pupil may select tasks based on personal needs, interests, and purposes. The choice to be made is up to the individual pupil. If tasks do not meet personal needs of the involved learner, he/she might plan with the teacher what has merit and value to the pupil. A contract system might also be implemented in which the pupil with teacher guidance selects tasks to put into a contract for completion. The learner himself/herself is responsible for choices made. The individual perceives what is good and has quality. Knowledge is subjective, not objective to the existentialist. For example, in a values clarification session, the pupil determines what is moral in terms of uses made of science and technology; the teacher has a difficult position as a stimulator and of one who encourages pupil learning. Being humane in an absurd environment is a major goal for pupil achievement in existentialist thought and thinking.

Within an existentialist science curriculum, through pupil/teacher planning a learner may select topics such as the following to pursue:

1. How do pesticides and herbicides help or hinder the natural environment? This question pertains to curbing insects and weed growth for the raising of farm crops versus possible contamination of soil and water;
2. How does one deal with animals in a humane way? This question stresses what to do with surplus dogs and cats roaming an area, as well as using animals for food and for scientific experiments;
3. How can the natural environment be used for development so that adequate numbers of jobs are available for workers versus the destruction of natural habitats for wildlife?
4. How can the needs of individuals be met as well as those in the societal arenas? This raises the question of the individual versus the larger group in a community, state, nation, and the world.

Alston and Brandt (1978) write the following direct quote of Jean Paul Sartre, a late leading existentialist:

Man is nothing else but what he makes of himself. Such is the first principle of existentialism. It is also what is called subjectivity, the name we are labeled with when charges are brought against us. But what do we mean by this, if not that man has a greater dignity than a stone or table? For we mean that man fist exists, that is, that man first of all is the being who hurls himself into the future and who is conscious of imagining himself being in the future. Man is at the start a plan which is aware of itself, rather than a patch of moss, a piece of garbage, or a cauliflower; nothing exists prior to this plan; there is nothing in heaven; man will be what he will have planned to be. Not what he will want to be. Because by the word 'will' we generally mean a conscious decision, which is subsequent to what we have made for ourselves. I may want to belong to a political party, write a book, get married; but all that is only a manifestation of an earlier, more spontaneous choice that is called 'will'. But if existence really precedes essence, man is responsible for what he is. Thus, existentialism's first move is too make every man aware of what he is and to make the full responsibility of his existence rest upon him. And when we say that a man is responsible for individually, but that he is responsible for all men.

The Psychology of Education

Principles of learning from the psychology of learning give direction to the science teacher in teaching-learning situations in ongoing lessons and units of study. Ediger (1994) lists the following criteria upon which educational psychologists agree should be followed by teachers:

1. meaningful learning experiences should be provided pupils in the curriculum;
2. interesting content and skills should be offered in lessons and units of study;
3. purpose needs to be established within pupils for learning;
4. quality sequence for pupil learning is a must;
5. rational balance among knowledge, skills, and attitudinal objectives is important in the instructional arena.

In Conclusion

Science teachers need to select tenets form the philosophy of education which stress pupils attaining vital content, abilities and attitudes. In reviewing the different philosophies of education discussed in this paper, the following is salient from each philosophy:

1. clarity in objectives of science instruction, carefully selected, as recommended by realists. However, it is important to avoid fragmenting knowledge obtained by pupils;
2. problem solving procedures as recommended by 50 experimentalists. Life in society emphasises the importance of being able to solve personal and social problems;
3. major concepts and generalisations, an universals in science, advocated by idealists;
4. decision making opportunities in science as recommended by existentialists. Each person needs to learn to make decisions.

We believe that a problem solving philosophy encompasses the other three philosophies. We recommended problem solving as a major philosophy of education to emphasise in teaching science due to its relevance in the curriculum and in life itself. Problems abound and need solutions. Knowledge acquired then is instrumental or useful in problems to be solved which are selected by pupils with teacher guidance.

Ediger and Rao (1996) wrote the following in summarising different psychologies of teaching:

Comparisons were made among the following models in teaching science:

1. problem solving with teacher guidance;
2. behaviourism with its pre-determined precise objectives for student attainment;
3. humanism and its emphasis upon students selecting sequential activities from among alternatives;
4. the structure of knowledge with key concepts and generalisations identified by academicians in their respective areas of specialisation. Science teachers assist students to achieve these structural ideas inductively using methods and procedures of scientists in a science laboratory setting;
5. stimulus—response learning of students in which a specific response is associated with a precise stimulus.

The writers advocate a problem solving approach be utilised in teaching science. From a stimulating learning environment in science, students with teacher guidance identify and solve vital problems. Problem solving skills are useful in all academic areas, as well as in the societal arena. Behaviourism, humanism, the structure of knowledge, and stimulus—response learning may be emphasised within the framework of problem solving situations. Subject matter in science may then be utilised in the problem solving science curriculum.

REFERENCES

Alston, William P., and Richard W. Brandt (1978), *The Problems of Philosophy*, third edition. Boston: Allyn and Bacon, Inc. pages 257-258.

Bigge, Morris (1982), *Educational Philosophies for Teachers*. Columbus, Ohio: Charles E. Merril Publishing Company, pages 25-26.

Blanchard, Brand (1964). *The Nature of Thought*. New York: Humanities Press, 492-517.

Bruner, Jerome (1968), *Toward A Theory of Instruction*. Cambridge, Massachusetts: Harvard University Press.

Combs, Arthur (1972), *Educational Objectives: Beyond Behavioural Objectives*. Washington, DC: Association for Supervision and Curriculum Development.

Dewey, John (1915), *School and Society*, Chicago: University of Chicago Press.

Ediger, Marlow (1999), 'Teacher Education and the Public Schools', *The Progress of Education*. 73 (12) 278-279, published in India.

Ediger, Marlow (1998), 'Objectives in the Science Curriculum,' *Spectrum*, 24 (2), 24-27.

Ediger, Marlow (1995), 'Demonstration Teaching in the Schools'. *Education*, 114, 371-372.

Ediger, Marlow (1994), Mathematics, Problem Solving, and the Young Learner. *The Primary Teacher*, 19, 34-37.

Ediger, Marlow (1997), 'Excellence in the Science Curriculum', ERIC # Ed 406144.

Ediger, Marlow, Early Field Experiences in Teacher Education. *College Student Journal*. 28, 302-306.

Ediger, Marlow, and D. Bhaskara Rao. *Science Curriculum*. New Delhi, India: Discovery Publishing House, page 117.

Ediger, Marlow and Digumarti Bhaskara Rao (2000), *Teaching Mathematics Successfully*. New Delhi, India: Discovery Publishing House.

Edmonds, Ron (1982), Programmes of School Improvement: An Overview. *Educational Leadership*. December, Volume 4.

Geiger, George W. (1955), An Experimentalists Approach to Education. *Modern Philosophies and Education*. Chicago, Illinois: National Society for the Study of Education, 54, 137-174.

Horne, Herman Herrell (1932), *The Democratic Philosophy of Education*. New York: The Macmillan Company, 325-340.

Mager, Robert F. (1972), *Goal Analysis*. Belmont, California: Fearon Publishers.

Missouri Department of Elementary and Secondary Education (1996), *Show Me Standards*. Jefferson City, Missouri.

Meyer, Adolph E. (1949), *The Development of Education in the Twentieth Century*. Englewood Cliffs, New Jersey: Prentice-Hall, Inc., pages 42-43.

Skinner, B.F. (1979), Beyond Freedom and Dignity. New York: Alfred Knopf. Inc.

Tillman, Frank A., and others (1971), *Introductory Philosophy*. New York: Harper and Row, page 550.

38

Evaluation of Achievement in Science

There are numerous approachs utilized to appraise pupil achievement in the elementary science curriculum. A variety of techniques should be utilized to evaluate learner progress. Each technique can provide different data pertaining to a pupil's achievement in science. Thus, a specific assessment technique such as the use of teacher observation provides information about a pupil's progress that the results of standardized tests may not reveal. Also, the same facet of a pupil's progress is not measured by all appraisal techniques. For example, results from the use of sociometric evaluation techniques do not appraise learner progress in intellectual development. They do give data pertaining to social development of learners. Pupils' progress should be appraised in intellectual, social, emotional, and physical development.

Teacher Observation

The use of teacher observation can be an effective method to appraise pupil achievement. The teacher must possess appropriate understandings, skills, and attitudes pertaining to modern trends in teaching elementary science in order to appraise pupil progress comprehensively. What are selected facets of a learner's achievement that may be appraised with the use of teacher observation?

1. How effectively pupils utilize science equipment in conducting experiments in ongoing units of study.
2. How skilled learners are in identifying problems and working toward solving these problems in science.
3. How well pupils are able to use reading, audio-visual aids, and other reference materials in teaching-learning situations.
4. How proficient pupils are becoming in working within committee settings, such as making science equipment in a related unit of study.

Discussions

In a discussion setting, feedback from learners is obtained in terms of relevant concepts and generalizations gained in a specific unit. Thus, learners may reveal the following understandings in a discussion:

1. What causes earthquakes, cyclones, and hurricanes.
2. What causes diverse kinds of whether on the earth's surface.
3. How gasoline and electric engines operate in terms of involved scientific principles.

Using discussions as a technique to appraise learner achievement, pupils also indicate

1. If they stay on the topic being pursued.
2. If they communicate ideas orally in an effective manner.
3. If they respect the thinking of others.

Oral Reports

Be listening to selected oral reports given by pupils, the teacher notices learner growth in the following ways:

1. Has the report been carefully planned and prepared?
2. Is there appropriate sequence of content being presented?
3. Does the reporter really understand the content being presented to listeners? Thus, if a learner is reporting on cirrus clouds, does he/she understand how these clouds are formed as well as well as have accurate perceptions on their physical appearance?
4. Does the learner speak clearly enough so listeners can understand the contents being presented?

Written Products of Pupils

A folder for each individual learner should be kept to retain personal written products. Each written product should be dated and thus pupils individually may contrast present with earlier papers to notice progress and achievement.

The following may be appraised in pupils' written work:

1. Unity in content within each paragraph.
2. Sequence of paragraphs.
3. Depth of ideas presented.
4. Legible handwriting.
5. Appropriate capitalization, punctuation, and usage.
6. Pupils on their appropriate stage of readiness and development may write content on the following topics relating to ongoing units of study:

1. Past and present progress in space travel.
2. Medical science achievement in selected diseases such as diabetes, cancer, and heart attacks.

3. Air transportation, including the supersonic transport plane.
4. Approved methods of controlling air, land, noise, and water pollution.
5. Sources for a more adequate supply of food.

Art Products of Pupils

Completed art products of pupils can be saved in individual folders in the same way as was stated previously for written products. Pupils reveal achievement in science units through ongoing and completed art work. Thus, in a mural, frieze, or individual illustration, pupils reveal the following in related ongoing units of study:

1. Molecules and atoms.
2. Selected plant and animal cells.
3. Hibernation and migration of specific animals.

Prior to developing these drawings, pupils need to get adequate background information. Ultimately, learnings gained can be shown by pupils in completing related murals, friezes, and individual illustrations. Comparisons for each learner may be made of present with earlier achievement levels.

Conferences with Pupils

The teacher may conduct conferences with pupils individually or in a group setting. If a pupil has completed reading a library book directly related to an ongoing unit of study, the teacher may conduct an informal conference to determine comprehension and attitudes of the involved learner. The teacher may conduct a conference with a small group of pupils who have read the same or related library books. Thus, learners may read library books on the following topics relating to the unit presently being studied in science:

1. The Seasons, Plants and Animals.
2. Plants and Animals of Prehistoric Times.
3. The Uses of Nuclear Energy.
4. Uses of Magnets and Electricity.
5. Wishing to engage in reading for recreational purposes.

Self-Appraisal by Pupils

Pupils with instructor guidance need to have ample opportunities to appraise their own progress. Thus, with appropriate guidance from the teacher, pupils develop criteria or standards against which they evaluate their own achievement. Objectives may then be cooperatively developed with teacher and pupil involvement for the latter to attain. The following objectives may be cooperatively developed pertaining to a unit, "Animals with Backbones—A study of Vertebrates".

1. The pupil will name four characteristics of fish.
2. Each learner will write five differences between amphibians and reptiles.
3. The pupil in a committee of three will complete a diorama on either fish, amphibians, or reptiles.
4. The pupil will write a sixty-word paragraph on birds.
5. The learner will voluntarily read a library book on birds and report findings to classmates.
6. Each pupil will identify a problem area pertaining to vertebrates and gather related content from a variety of reference sources.
7. The pupil will develop a timeline pertaining to when selected vertebrates originated in geological time.
8. Three pupils in a committee will select a specific mammal and gather data on their selection.

Pupils with teacher guidance evaluate how well each of the objectives have been achieved.

Teacher Prepared Tests

Essay items may be written by the teacher to appraise learner achievement in a specific unit of study in science. Learners need to have an adequately developed writing vocabulary to respond proficientiy to essay test items. In a unit entitled, "The Seasons and How They Affect Us", the teacher may write essay items such as the following to evaluate pupil progress:

1. Explain how the concept of 'latitude' affects temperature readings in a specific geographical area.
2. Select a specific field-grown agricultural product and describe the kind of climate needed for optimal growth and production of the selection made.
3. Write a paragraph on how climate affects everyday activities of human beings.

True-false items may also be written to evaluate selected learnings acquired by learners. The following could be appropriate true-false items written by the teacher to appraise pupil achievement:

1. Degrees north or south of the equator refer to longitude.
2. The southern hemisphere has more land than does the northern hemisphere.
3. Much plant growth occurs in equatorial areas.

Multiple choice items which may measure learner progress in a given unit of study could be the following:

1. Which of the following is not true of the category of vertebrates known as fish?

   (a) They breathe oxygen through the use of gills.
   (b) Scales may cover all or part of their bodies.
   (c) The young hatch from eggs.
   (d) The body temperature of fish remains the same throughout the year.

2. Amphibians
   (a) Spend part of their lifetime in water and part time on land.
   (b) Include animals such as frogs, turtles, and snakes.
   (c) Have the same body temperature throughout the year.
   (d) Do not hibernate during cold winter months.

Other kinds of teacher-written test items which may be utilized to appraise pupil achievement include.

1. Completion tests.
2. Matching tests.

Teacher-written test items should adhere to the following criteria:

1. Items should be clearly written. Vague items should be omitted from testing situations.
2. Each test item should be written on the understanding level of learners.
3. Learners should have an adequately developed writing vocabulary prior to the use of essay items as a means of appraising progress.
4. Test items should cover what learners have had opportunities to learn. Thus, valid test items are in evidence.

Standardized Tests

Standardized achievement tests may be utilized to appraise learner progress in elementary school science. Standardized tests utilized in the school testing program should be

1. Valid, *e.g.*, measure pupil achievement in terms of the school's objectives in science.
2. Reliable, *e.g.*, consistency of test results is in evidence for each pupil in consecutive testing situations.

Ideally, standardized tests should measure pupil achievement in:

1. Problem-solving skills.
2. Analytical and creative thinking.
3. Positive attitudes developed toward science and scientific methods of thinking.
4. Ability to work together well with others.
5. Relevant concepts and generalizations developed.
6. The ability to manipulate and utilize science equipment.

Too frequently, standardized achievement tests measure pupil gains in recall of factual information. There are relevant facts for pupils to acquire. There are higher levels of thinking or cognition that pupils should also develop. Thus, pupils need to go beyond the recall level of facts and

1. Understand what has been recalled.
2. Utilize acquired learnings.
3. Analyze content learned.
4. Develop hypotheses directly related to problem areas.
5. Appraise content in terms of criteria or standards.

Results from standardized achievement tests may be utilized, along with other data-gathering techniques, to appraise pupil progress in the science curriculum.

Other Appraisal Techniques

There are numerous other techniques which may be utilized to appraise learner progress. These techniques include

1. Diary entries and summaries written by pupils covering learnings gained in units of study in science.
2. Dramatizations performed by learners.
3. Voluntary assignments completed by selected pupils.
4. Use of sociometric devices and personality tests.

In Summary

The teacher of elementary school science must use a variety of appraisal techniques to evaluate pupil progress. Thus, assessment procedures such as the following may be utilized to evaluate learner achievement:

1. Observation by the teacher of pupil progress.
2. Pupil participation in discussions.
3. Written work of learners.
4. Pupil's art products.
5. Informal conferences conducted with pupils.
6. Pupils evaluating their own achievement.
7. Teacher-developed tests.
8. Use of standardized tests.

No appraisal technique is a perfect device to assess achievement. Thus, several techniques should be utilized collectively to evaluate total growth of learners in

1. Intellectual growth.
2. Social development.
3. Emotional growth.
4. Physical development.
5. Moral achievement.

REFERENCES

Bernard, Harold W. *Psychology of Teaching and Learning*. Second Edition. New York: McGraw-Hill Book Company, 1965.

Blough, Glenn O., and Julius Schwartz. *Elementary School Science and How To Teach It*. Seventh Edition, New York: Holt, Rinehart and Winston, Inc., 1984.

DeVito, Alfred, and Gerald H. Krockover. *Creative Science, A Practical Approach*. Boston: Little, Brown and Company, 1976.

Dewey, John. *Democracy and Education*. New York: The Macmillan Company, 1916.

Ebel, Robert, and David A. Frisbie. *Essentials of Educational Measurement*. Fourth Edition. Englewood Cliffs, New Jersey: Prentice-Hall, 1986.

Ediger, Marlow and D. Bhaskara Rao. *Teaching Science Successfully*. New Delhi, India: Discovery Publishing House, 2001.

Gronlund, Norman E. *Measurement and Evaluation in Teaching*. New York: Macmillan, 1985.

Kilpatrick, W.H. *Philosophy of Education*. New York: The Macmillan Company, 1951.

MacDonald, John. *A Philosophy of Education*. Atlanta: Scott, Foresman, and Company, 1965.

Morris, VanCleve, and Young Pai. *Philosophy and the American School*. Second Edition. Boston: Houghton-Mifflin Company, 1976.

Thomas R. Murray. *Judging Student Progress*. Second Edition. New York: David McKay Company, Inc., 1960.

39

Teaching Elementary School Mathematics

Teachers, supervisors, and principals need to study, appraise, and implement selected innovative trends in the elementary school mathematics curriculum. Trends in mathematics that are ultimately implemented should follow these criteria:

1. Pupils should be successful in learning.
2. Learners need to understand and attach meaning to what is being learned.
3. Pupils should perceive reasons for learning new content.
4. Individual differences among learners are provided for in elementary school mathematics.
5. Pupils need adequate background content in order to achieve new objectives.
6. Balance between and among understandings, skills, and attitudinal objectives must be in evidence.
7. Teachers, principals, and supervisors need to understand and accept innovative ideas.
8. Adequate emphasis must be placed upon pupils being able to use new learnings in class as well as in society.

Innovations in the Mathematics Curriculum

There are many recommended trends in the elementary school mathematics curriculum. Literature in the field abounds with relevant innovative ideas which may be implemented in the school and class setting.

1. Pupils should have ample opportunities to develop learnings inductively. In teaching-learning situations involving inductive learning, pupils *(a)* have ample opportunities to discover answers to questions and problems, *(b)* are guided by the teacher to arrive at their own conclusions, *(c)* are actively

involved in learning, *(d)* need to engage in higher levels of thinking to come up with needed solutions to problems and questions, and *(e)* should be encouraged to think critically and creatively in ongoing units of study.

Inductive approaches in learning do not stress *(a)* lecture methods being used by the teacher in the class setting, *(b)* the teacher doing much explaining to pupils of processes and procedures to use in problem solving, and *(c)* the use of programed materials at the time that learning by discovery is being emphasized in ongoing units of study.

When discussing inductive approaches as a method of learning by pupils, the following criteria should be followed:

(a) There needs to be rational balance between learning by discovery and deductive learning by pupils. Pupils could spend much time in developing a specific learning if inductive approaches are utilized exclusively.

(b) Selected pupils may learn more using deductive approaches or a combination of inductive and deductive procedures as compared to utilizing the learning by discovery approach alone.

(c) Pupils may develop much interest in and attach meaning to learnings obtained stressing deductive methods of teaching and learning.

The following steps in sequence with a specific lesson may well stress pupils learning by discovery or inductively:

(a) The teacher—"How many blocks do we have in the set that I am pointing to?" A pupil—"I counted five." The teacher—"Let's count them together to see if we are correct." The teacher points to each block as pupils engage in rational counting. (The teacher praises pupils for giving correct responses.)

(b) The teacher—"How many blocks are there in the second set?" A pupil—"four." The teacher—"Let's count the blocks." With the use of rational counting, pupils realize there are more than four blocks in the set. The teacher—"How many blocks then do you see in this set?" A pupil—"five." The teacher—"Do you all agree?" (Pupils as a whole agree.)

(c) The teacher—"Now let's put the blocks together from the two sets to form one set only. Now how many do we have?" Several pupils respond—"Ten". The teacher may wish to have pupils engage in rational counting to determine the number of members to the new set.

(d) A child may write the numerals on the chalkboard telling how many members there were in each of the two sets.

The plus sign may need to be written by the teacher and explained to pupils depending on their present level of achievement. Thus, learners see the number sentence present "5 + 5 = 10" written on the chalkboard to correspond with the materials used in teaching, *e.g.*, the two sets of blocks.

(e) Other materials utilized in teaching basic addition facts include corn and bean seeds, pencils, beads, and checkers.

Pupils may also attach meaning to and find interest in ultimately developing abstracts learnings through deductive approaches.

(a) The teacher places five blocks in a set which all pupils in the class setting may view clearly. The teacher points to each member using rational counting to show to the class what is involved in deciding upon the number of members in a set. The teacher follows the same procedure using a second set of five blocks. The abstract numeral "5" should be written on the chalkboard to show the corresponding value of each set.

(b) The two sets of blocks each consisting of five members are placed into one group. The teacher points to each member using rational counting simultaneously and indicates a set of ten members in the new group. The teacher writes on the chalkboard the number sentence "5 + 5 = 10" to relate the abstract to the concrete situation involving the use of blocks.

(c) Each child could now be asked by the teacher to place five corn seeds in a set on his/her desk. The teacher may quickly observe if each of the pupils is doing this correctly. Guidance must be given to learners needing help in placing five corn seeds in a set. The teacher next asks each pupil to put five corn seeds in the second set. The teacher diagnoses which pupils individually need help in a given learning experience. Pupils can then join two sets together and indicate how many members there are in the new set.

(d) Other materials such as pencils, crayons, chalk, beads, and books may be utilized to guide pupils in understanding that five members in each of two sets may be combined to form a new set of ten members.

2. Pupils should attach meaning to what is being learned. If learners, for example, are to understand the number sentence "5 – 3 = 2," the teacher may utilize the following procedure:

(*a*) Place five pencils in a set which are clearly visible to all in the class setting. Pupils should respond to the number of pencils in the group.
(*b*) The teacher removes three pencils and asks learners how many remain on the desk.
(*c*) A pupil comes to the chalkboard to write the number sentence "5 – 3 = 2" which corresponds to the concrete situation involving the use of pencils.

It is important for pupils to understand what is being taught. If pupils do not attach meaning to ongoing experiences in mathematics, the following may result:

(*a*) Pupils memorize content for a test.
(*b*) Learners withdraw mentally from the learning situation.
(*c*) A lack of interest follows on the part of selected learners.
(*d*) Discipline problems are an end result.
(*e*) Pupils may be lost in achieving future related learnings in mathematics due to not understanding prerequisite tasks.

3. Pupils should develop relevant concepts. There are major concepts that pupils need to acquire. The concepts include *(a)* the commutative property of addition and multiplication, *(b)* the associative property of addition and multiplication, *(c)* the distributive property of multiplication over addition, *(d)* the property of closure, among others.

If pupils, for example, are to learn that an odd number plus an even number equals an odd number, the following experiences provide needed understandings:

(*a*) Have pupils observe two red checkers and tell how many members there are in the set.
(*b*) Let pupils notice three black checkers and indicate the number of members in this set.
(*c*) Finally, have learners combine the two sets and tell how many members exist in the new set.
(*d*) Have a pupil take the five checkers and divide the members of this set between two classmates to each has an equal number of checkers. Observers in the class setting will notice that each pupil gets two checkers with one left over. Thus, learners inductively understand that five is an odd number. A pupil should also take the two red checkers (the original addend) as well as the three black checkers (second original addend) and divide each set between two classmates. Pupils in the class setting will notice that the two red checkers can be divided equally between two classmates; however, one checker

is left over when the three black checkers are divided between two learners. Thus, "three" is an uneven number (representing the second addend) and "five" is an uneven number representing the sum.

(*e*) Different materials and aids need to be utilized to help pupils understand that an even number plus an odd number equals and odd number, such as using beads, seeds, sticks, chalk, clothes pins, and paper clips. Pupils should experience other addition facts than the one mentioned previously (2 + 3 = 5) to understand that an even number plus an odd number equals an odd number, such as 4 + 3 = 7, 2 + 5 = 7, 8 + 1 = 9, and others.

4. Pupils should have ample opportunities to experience the mathematics laboratory concept of working. The mathematics laboratory emphasizes tenets of teaching and learning such as the following:
   (*a*) Pupils are actively involved in ongoing learning activities.
   (*b*) A variety of experiences is in evidence so that pupils may select materials and aids necessary for problem solving.
   (*c*) Practical experiences are experienced for learners in that they actually measure the length, width, and/or height of selected people and things; weigh real objects and record their findings; find the volume of important containers; as well as determine areas of selected geometrical figures.
   (*d*) Pupils become interested in mathematics due to reality being involved in ongoing learning activities.
   (*e*) Provision is made for individual differences since there are a variety of learning opportunities for pupils.
   (*f*) Meaning is attached to what is being learned since pupils individually and in committees work on tasks adjusted to their present achievement levels.
5. Pupils should experience balance in the mathematics curriculum in terms of learnings obtained from the areas of arithmetic, algebra, probability, statistics, and geometry. Prior to the 1960's pupils largely experienced learnings pertaining to arithmetic. Geometry and algebra were then greatly deemphasized in the mathematics curriculum. A modern program of elementary school mathematics stresses balance among the curriculum areas of arithmetic, algebra, probability, statistics, and geometry. Thus, it is important that pupils develop proficiency in addition, subtraction, multiplication, and division of whole numbers as they progress through the

elementary school years. Pupils should also experience the following as readiness permits:

(*a*) Addition, subtraction, multiplication, and division of fractions, as well as using decimals and per cents.
(*b*) The Roman and Egyptian systems of numeration.
(*c*) Other bases, such as base five and base two.
(*d*) Solve problems in everyday living involving the use of mathematics.
(*e*) Use ratio and proportion.
(*f*) Diverse units and topics in geometry including geometric shapes, lines, points, curves, and planes; topology and Euclidean geometry as well as coordinates.
(*g*) Measure to find perimeters, areas, volumes, and temperature readings.
(*h*) An adequate number of instructional units of study on the metric system.
(*i*) Functional use of probability and statistics.

Learners should develop positive attitudes toward the mathematics curriculum in the elementary school. Positive attitudes can be developed if pupils

(*a*) Are successful in learning.
(*b*) Experience interest in ongoing units of study.
(*c*) Perceive purpose or reasons for acquiring selected concepts, generalizations, and structural ideas in mathematics.
(*d*) Understand new learnings obtained in mathematics.
(*e*) Have adequate background information to benefit from new learnings.
(*f*) Have personal needs met in experiencing proper sequence in ongoing learning opportunities.

When pupils are guided in developing positive attitudes toward the curriculum area of mathematics, learners generally achieve to their optimum.

6. Pupils may experience management systems of learning in the mathematics curriculum.

There are numerous management systems of mathematics programs available on the market. These programs of instruction generally emphasize the following:

(*a*) The objectives, learnings activities, and appraisal techniques have been developed by writers for a commercial company producing educational materials or by teachers and supervisors in instructional management systems (IMS).

(*b*) A pretest is given to pupils to determine where each is to start within a specific unit of study involving the adopted management system of instruction. The pretest covers the specific objectives in a unit.

(*c*) Prescriptions (learning activities) are chosen by the teacher or teachers for pupils as is indicated by appraisal results.

(*d*) Pupils work in the direction of achieving a measurable objectives, are appraised, and if successful in achieving the desired goal, begin to attain the next objective in sequence.

(*e*) Aides help in checking completed products of pupils in mathematics, thus freeing the teacher to diagnose student difficulties in learning and prescribe needed activities for pupils.

(*f*) Pupil achievement is evaluated continuously in ongoing units of study using management systems of instruction.

Teachers may develop their own program of instruction in elementary school mathematics using the model (or models) advocated by writers of management systems of instruction. Thus, for example, in utilizing a reputable elementary school mathematics textbook (or textbooks) of recent copyright, the teacher may

(*a*) pretest pupils to place each learner within a unit of study that harmonizes with his/her present level of achievement.

(*b*) Have pupils engage in learning experiences within the unit being studied based on pretest results.

(*c*) Guide and stimulate each pupil to achieve optimal development during the time that learning activities are being experienced within an ongoing unit of study.

(*d*) Continually evaluate pupil achievement at each step along the way.

(*e*) Prescribe learning activities to individual pupils based on diagnosed needs.

(*f*) Record pupils' results to notice gains as each learner progresses in achieving desired objectives.

7. Pupils may experience relevant learning centers in the mathematics curriculum. Tasks or learning experiences for pupils should be carefully determined and may be written on task cards for pupils at each learning center. Thus, pupils, for example, experience the following kinds of centers in elementary school mathematics:

(*a*) A practice center. A pupil may work with another child to practice responding to basic addition, subtraction, multiplication, and division facts using flash cards. Thus, a learner may show flash cards pertaining to basic number pairs in addition with the second learner giving, responses to 6 + 3 = —, 3 + 6 = —, 4 + 5 = —, 5 + 4 = —. A "fishing pond" may also be utilized to provide practice to pupils.

1. Designs of fish may be cut out of different colours of construction paper.
2. A paper clip should be attached to the mouth of each fish.
3. Basic number pairs should be neatly printed on each fish, such as 2 x 8 = —, 8 x 2 = —, 3 x 5 = —, 5 x 3 = — (depending upon what a child needs in terms of review of previous learnings).
4. A stick with an attached string and a magnet may be utilized to catch fish.
5. The child must respond correctly to the number pair to be able to keep the fish. Otherwise, it is thrown back into the water.

(*b*) A measurement center. Pupils could work at tasks involving measuring height of individuals as well as the length and width of selected objects. Learners should also experience ample opportunities to weigh relevant items. The area and perimeter of selected squares, triangles, rectangles, parallelograms, and circles could be found by pupils.

(*c*) A game center. At this learning center, pupils could play games pertaining to the Olympics. A discuss throw involving the use of round paper plates could be conducted. A meter stick may be utilized to measure the distance a discuss was thrown. Paper straws could be used to represent javelins. Each pupil throws the javelin with peers measuring the involved distance. Pupil ingenuity with teacher guidance can aid in identifying other facets of the "Olympics" and how distances are to be recorded, including the use of line, bar, and picture graphs.

(*d*) A problem solving center. Pupils select and work photocopied papers dealing with word problems stressing the problem-solving approach. These problems should be life-like, interesting, and challenging to learners.

(*e*) Other learning centers could include a metric system center, an art center involving the making of geometrical models, a music center using content dealing with mathematics, and a dramatization center. All pupils should experience sequential learnings from a reputable series of elementary school mathematics textbooks.

8. Pupils may experience contracts in mathematics. The learner, together with the teacher, determines which goals the former is to achieve within a specific period of time. For example, the pupils with teacher guidance may work on completing the following contract which must be on the achievement level of the involved individual:

Name______________________________ Date__________

1. Work pages, 30, 31, and 32 from our mathematics textbook with 90 per cent accuracy.
2. Make a geoboard and show the following using a rubber band:
   (a) Square, rectangle, and triangle.
   (b) Trapezoid, rhombus, and parallelogram.
3. Give correct definitions for a square, rectangle, and triangle.
4. Give five examples in architecture where there are *(a)* circles, *(b)* squares, and *(c)* rectangles.

______________________________ due date__________
(signature)

It is good teaching procedure periodically to involve parents in developing contracts. Standards for designing contracts include the following:

(a) Pupils experience success in achieving the objectives.

(b) A variety of objectives should be stressed in the contract such as cognitive (use of the mind or intellect), psychomotor (use of the muscles or eye-hand coordination), and affective (attitudinal dimension).

(c) Tasks in the contract emphasize the interests of the learner as well as meaning and purpose being inherent in ongoing learning experiences.

(d) The pupil should meet the deadline date for completing requirements. If the contents of the contract later appear to be unreasonable, proper adjustments of the complexity level need to be made.

(e) Pupils definitely should not be forced to complete that which is unrealistic.

(f) Each learner needs to experience continuous success.

9. Pupils with teacher guidance need to diagnose their own errors and work in the direction of remedying these deficiencies. The learner must know why an answer to a

problem is incorrect. If a teacher merely reads correct answers to pupils and the involved learner or a peer checks answers to word problems, the pupils whose work is being evaluated would not be able to improve in performance due to not knowing why selected content was incorrect.

$$\begin{array}{r} 24 \\ +17 \\ \hline 31 \end{array} \qquad \begin{array}{r} 25 \\ +17 \\ \hline 43 \end{array} \qquad \begin{array}{r} 34 \\ +18 \\ \hline 53 \end{array}$$

It is obvious that the learner in the above completed addition problems has difficulty with

(a) Regrouping and renaming.

(b) Selected addition facts.

Thus, in these three addition problems, the learner is not able to regroup the sum of the units column in terms of ones and tens value. In the first addition problem (7 + 4) = 11, the pupil must develop understandings pertaining to 11 = 1 ten and 1 one. The one ten must be added to the tens column; 2 tens + 1 ten + 1 ten = four tens. 24 + 17 = 41. In the second problem, the pupil evidently experiences difficulty in responding correctly to 7 + 5 = 12 in the units column. The pupil may need to use markers such as checkers, beans, sticks, and the like to attach meaning to 7 + 5 = 12. Seven markers may be placed in one set and five markers in the second set resulting in a new set of twelve members when joined together.

In any unit of study, pupils with teacher guidance need to diagnose why specific kinds or errors were made an attempt to remedy identified deficiencies.

There are many reasons as to why pupils exhibit errors in mathematics. The following are relevant reasons:

(a) The pupil lacks understanding of new processes to be developed.

(b) The learner is careless and hasty in completing necessary work.

(c) A lack of readiness or background information is inherent on the part of the learner.

(d) The pupil is bored and lacks challenge in ongoing learning experiences.

(e) The teacher is not providing adequate guidance and direction in the mathematics curriculum.

(f) The learner possess an inadequate self-concept.

(g) Negative attitudes on the part of the learner hinder achievement in elementary school mathematics.

(h) The content being studied is too complex for learner.

(i) Understandings, skills, and attitudes developed by the learner lack appropriate sequence.

(j) The pupil lacks interest in mathematics.

10. Pupils in the class setting must experience an adequate number of units pertaining to the metric system. Understandings objectives in units of study pertaining to the metric system should reflect interesting, meaningful, and purposeful experiences for learners. Pupils should experience relevant learnings pertaining to metric system units of measure.

Length	Weight
10 millimeters = 1 centimeter	10 milligrams = 1 centigram
10 centimeters = 1 decimeter	10 centigrams = 1 decigram
10 decimeters = 1 meter	10 decigrams = 1 gram
10 meters = 1 decameter	10 grams = 1 decagram
10 decameters = 1 hectometer	10 decagrams = 1 hectogram
10 hectometers = 1 kilometer	10 hectograms = 1 kilogram

Volume
10 milliliters = 1 centiliter
10 centiliters = 1 deciliter
10 deciliters = 1 liter
10 liters - 1 decaliter
10 decaliters = 1 hectoliter
10 hectoliters = 1 kiloliter

The metric system is easier for learners to understand as compared to the English system of measurement. The metric system has a based value of 10. In measuring length of an object, 10 millimeters equal 1 centimeter; 10 centimeters equal 1 decimeter; 10 decimeters equal 1 meter; and so on. The prefixes are the same when comparing units of measurement dealing with length, weight, and volume, *e.g.*, millicenti-, deci-, (meter, gram, and liter are root words); deca-, hecto-, and kilo-. The prefixes come in this sequence for measuring length (meter is the root word used here); weight (gram is the root word used here); and volume (liter is the root word).

The English system of measurement stresses the following units:

Length	Weight
12 inches = 1 foot	2000 pounds = 1 ton
3 feet = 1 yard	16 ounces = 1 pound
5½ yards = 1 rod	

Volume
2 cups = 1 pint
2 pints = 1 quart
4 quarts = 1 gallon

It is quite obvious that the English system of measurement lacks patterns in moving from a smaller unit of measurement to a larger unit such as 12 inches = 1 foot, 3 feet = 1 yard, and 5½ yards = 1 rod. The English system of measurement lacks the base ten consistency inherent in the metric system, *e.g.*, 10 millimeters = 1 centimeter, 10 centimeters = 1 decimeter, 10 decimeters - 1 meter, and so on. As was mentioned previously, the metric system contains consistent prefixes when moving from smaller to larger units of measurement, (or *vice versa*): milli-, centi, deci-, the root words—meter (for length), gram (for weight), and liter (for volume), deca-, hecto-, kilo-. There is no consistency in words used for measuring length, weight, and volume in the English system when moving from smallest to larger units of measurements, *e.g.*, inches, feet, yards, and rods in measuring length.

In Summary

Teachers, principals, and supervisors need to study, evaluate, and implement recommended trends in the elementary school mathematics curriculum. The following, among others, should be considered by educators in the school setting to update the mathematics curriculum:

1. Inductive learning by pupils.
2. Meaningful learnings developed by learners.
3. Relevant concepts acquired in mathematics.
4. Use of mathematics in society.
5. Balance in the mathematics curriculum.
6. Management systems of instruction.
7. Learning centers in the mathematics curriculum.
8. The contract system.
9. Diagnosis in the mathematics curriculum.
10. The metric system.

Decision-making is one of the most important skills for pupils to develop in mathematics. Bley and Thornton wrote:

> All problem solving involves making decisions. Even in the broader context, as students begin working with larger numbers and more complex situations, they are required to make decisions. Very young children make a decision when they tell whether the symbol in front of them is two or three. As they progress and learn more skills, decision making continues to enter their daily work in mathematics. Does that sign mean to multiply or divide? Do I carry? How can I add two fractions with different denominators? Should I use a decimal or a fraction to find the per cent of that number? What do I do first to solve that problem?
>
> The decision-making process is a complex one. It involves strong abstract reasoning ability. It requires that a student be able both

to receive and express words in a meaningful way. It requires the ability to draw on previously learned concepts and skills, to distinguish among them, and to choose the one that is appropriate in a given situation.

REFERENCES

Ashlock, Robert B., *Error Patterns in Computation*. Columbus, Ohio: Charles E. Merrill Publishing Company, 1982.

Bley, Nancy S., and Carol A. Thornton. *Teaching Mathematics to the Learning Disabled*. Rockville, Maryland: An Aspen Publication, 1981.

Ballew, Hunter. *Teaching Children Mathematics*. Columbus: Charles E. Merrill Publishing Company, 1973.

Cawley, John F. *Cognitive Strategies and Mathematics for the Learning Disabled*. Rockville, Maryland: An Aspen Publication, 1985.

Fehr, Howard F., and Jo McKeeby Phillips. *Teaching Modern Mathematics in the Elementary School*. Second Edition. Reading, Massachusetts: Addison-Wesley, 1972.

Higley, Joan. *Activities Deskbook for Teaching Arithmetic Skills*. West Nyack, New York: Parker Publishing Company, 1983.

Jenson, Rosalie. *Exploring Mathematical Concepts and Skills in the Elementary School*. Columbus: Charles E. Merrill Publishing Company, 1973.

Kennedy, Larry G. *Guiding Children's Learning of Mathematics*. Fourth Edition. Belmont, California: Wadsworth Publishing Company, 1984, Chapter One.

Lesh, Richard, and Marshall Landau (Editors). *Acquisition of Mathematics Concepts and Processes*. New York: Academic Press, 1983.

Stern, Catherine, and Margaret B. Stern. *Children Discover Arithmetic*. New York: Harper and Row, 1971.

40

Objectives in the Mathematics Curriculum

Teachers, supervisors, and principles need to select relevant objectives for pupils to achieve. A recommended philosophy in the teaching of mathematics is needed prior to the time that these important goals are to be chosen. With much study and thought pertaining to teaching mathematics, educators may develop a philosophy of teaching containing the following strands of thought:

1. Each pupil in the school setting must achieve to his/her optimum in the elementary school mathematics curriculum.
2. Diverse learning opportunities should be provided to allow for different learning styles which pupils individually possess.
3. Critical thinking, creative thinking, and problem solving must be stressed in the mathematics curriculum.
4. Pupils should be guided to develop well socially in all curriculum areas in the elementary school.
5. Ample opportunities must be given to aid pupils in learning using both inductive and deductive approaches.
6. Experiences obtained by pupils should be interesting, and meaningful, as well as purposeful.
7. Each child should have feelings of success in the mathematics curriculum.
8. Pupils with teacher guidance should diagnose learner difficulties in the mathematics curriculum and work toward remedying these identified deficiencies.
9. There should be rational balance among understandings, skills, and attitudinal objectives which pupils are to achieve.

10. The total development of the child should be emphasized such as physical, social, academic, and emotional in ongoing units of study in mathematics.
11. The mathematics curriculum must frequently be appraised by teachers, principals, and supervisors to keep this curriculum area updated. Faculty meetings, workshops, and departmental meetings become important in modifying and revising the elementary school mathematics curriculum.
12. Learners should experience realistic situations in ongoing units of study.

Objectives and Mathematics

After careful study and thought, the elementary teacher may identify and implement general understandings objectives such as the following in elementary school mathematics for pupils to attain:

1. The commutative property of multiplication and addition.
2. The associative property of multiplication and addition.
3. The distributive property of multiplication over addition.
4. The identity elements for addition and multiplication.
5. The property of closure for addition and multiplication.
6. The inverse operations of subtraction and division.
7. Relationships among operations such as multiplication pertains to repeated addition, and division refers to repeated subtraction, of equal amounts.
8. The problem solving method.
9. Reference sources available to solve problems in elementary school mathematics.
10. Methods used to have pupils evaluate their own achievement.

It would not be adequate to have pupils achieve relevant understandings objectives in the mathematics curriculum only. Pupils also need ample opportunities to acquire important skills objectives. Thus, learners may attain skills such as the following as they progress through the elementary school years:

1. Perform addition, subtraction, multiplication, and division operations meaningfully and accurately.
2. Identify and diagnose difficulties in performing these basic operations and attempt to remedy these deficiencies.
3. Identify and draw accurately squares, circles, rectangles, triangles, and other important geometrical figures.
4. Draw and measure angles accurately in geometry.
5. Use the number line when applicable to get needed content to solve problems.

6. Become proficient in thinking critically and creatively in the mathematics curriculum.
7. Use appropriate algorithms which harmonize with one's own style of learning in solving problems in the area of mathematics.
8. Use a variety of learning aids and activities to aid in achieving optimal development in the area of mathematics.
9. Analyze and obtain needed content to solve word problems.
10. Use software and computers effectively.

Kennedy identifies four questions pertaining to computer hardware and software, as follows:

1. Collect information about input devices. Include pictures of keypunch, phone modem, keyboard, and other devices. Prepare a display of disks and tapes, keypunch cards, test-answer sheets, and other input paraphernalia.
2. Collect information about storage devices. How does a primary storage unit work? How is the capacity of a computer determined? Collect examples of secondary storage paraphernalia, such as keypunch cards, magnetic tape, disks, and Braille and other printouts.
3. How do central processing units work? Learn about the CPU's arithmetic-logic control and its memory units.
4. Investigate different programming languages. Why have different languages been developed? Which language are most suitable for children? For teachers?

Another kind of objective that is important to emphasize in teaching-learning situations is attitudinal, or effective objectives. If pupils achieve attitudinal, or affective objectives, they will do better in acquiring needed understandings and skills. Teachers, principals, and supervisors need to carefully select attitudinal goals which learners are to achieve. These may include:

(*a*) Respecting the thinking of other learners.
(*b*) Wanting to compute mathematics content accurately.
(*c*) Desiring to participate effectively in committee work.
(*d*) Appreciating the orderliness of the Hindu-Arabic system of numeration.
(*e*) Appreciating, among others, the contributions of the Egyptian, Roman, and Mayan systems of numeration.
(*f*) Desiring to work to one's own optimal level of achievement in mathematics.
(*g*) Appreciating the contributions of mathematics in the arithmetic, algebra, and geometry curriculum.
(*h*) Wanting to think creatively and critically in problem solving activities.

(i) Developing an appreciation for working in bases other than base ten in arithmetic, such as performing operations in base two, base five, and base eight.

(j) Contributing fully in the selection of objectives, learning experiences, and evaluation procedures when teacher-pupil planning is utilized in the class setting.

(k) Wanting to use computers in the mathematics curriculum.

Specific Objectives in the Mathematics Curriculum

Selected teachers, principals, and supervisors emphasize that objectives which pupils are to achieve should be stated in a specific manner. Thus, specific objectives in mathematics may follow the following criteria:

1. It can be measured if pupils have or have not attain the desired objectives.
2. Learning activities may be selected which guide learners in achieving these precisely stated objectives.
3. Pupils and the teacher can observe if the former have achieved the desired criteria or objectives.

The following are examples of specific objectives in the mathematics curriculum.

1. The pupil will add correctly the basic number pairs of 4 + 4 = □; 3 + 6 = □; 2 + 5 = □; 6 + 3 = □; and 5 + 2 = □.

2. The pupil will utilize two algorithms in solving each of these problems:

24	32	52	34	41
x 42	x 23	x 22	x 22	x 22

3. The pupil will solve correctly 90 per cent of the addition problems on page 87 of his/her textbook.
4. The pupil will solve correctly four out of five word problems on page 90 of the textbook.
5. The pupil will write five word problems and include in each an irrelevant item not needed in working toward desired solutions.

In analyzing each of the previously stated objectives, the first specific objective involves recall of content in giving sums to each basic number pair in addition. The second objective deals with a higher level of cognition other than recall of content. Pupils need to use more than one method to solve each problem. The third objective is not clear in and of itself as to what pupils are to achieve. The reader of this objective would need to look at the mathematics textbook being utilized in the class setting to determine the level of achievement being stressed in teaching-learning situations. The fourth objective could involve complex problem-solving activities when encountering the solving of word problems. The fifth objective could stress creative writing on the part of each pupil in the writing of word problems. Irrelevant content would also need to be written in each word problem. Thus, the reader may notice that objectives in mathematics may be written to emphasize.

(*a*) Recall of content.

(*b*) Comprehension of information to solve problems.

(*c*) Problem solving.

(*d*) Creative thinking as well as critical thinking.

It behooves the elementary school mathematics teacher to have pupils achieve at a higher level of thinking than the recall level. Thus, critical thinking, creative thinking, and problem solving must be stressed in teaching-learning situations in the mathematics curriculum.

Grossnickle, *et. al* list the following four components in a quality mathematics curriculum:

1. A component designed to assist children in discovering meanings, through the use of manipulative materials. A mathematics laboratory stocked with carefully selected instructional materials provides children with many opportunities to explore basic number ideas.
2. A component designed to assist children in developing and understanding of mathematical structure, through the use of pictures, drawings, structural aids, mathematical notations, and the like. Emphasis is on using number patterns created at the concrete level and recorded at the picture and symbolic levels of learning. The knowledge that children acquire encompasses ideas from arithmetic, geometry, and metrics.
3. A component designed to assist children in developing an intelligent mastery of computational skills. This is a different type of knowledge from that of components 1 and 2, though it stems from experiences provided by these two components.
4. A component designed to assist children in developing problem-solving skills, as well as on understanding and appreciation of the application and uses of mathematics in various real-life problem settings, including measurement.

In Summary

Teachers, principals, and supervisors need to develop a philosophy of teaching elementary school mathematics which makes ample provision for each individual pupil to realize his/her optimal achievement.

A relevant philosophy pertaining to the teaching of elementary school mathematics will stress the importance of pupils achieving important understandings, skills, and attitudinal objectives. Each objective that pupils are to achieve should be weighed against alternative goals in making the final selection so that learners truly learn what is important in the school and class setting.

Selected teachers, supervisors, and principals may wish to emphasize the use of general objectives in teaching-learning situations. Other educators may rather desire to use specific, measurable objectives. What is of utmost importance in teaching and learning is that pupils attain quality objectives which emphasize higher levels of cognition such as critical thinking, creative thinking, and problem solving. Thus, the dichotomy between general versus specific objectives may be resolved by selecting those objectives which will guide a learner in becoming a fully functioning member of society.

REFERENCES

Bitter, Gary G., et. al. *Activities Handbook for Teaching the Metric System*. Boston: Allyn and Bacon, Inc., 1976.

Ediger, Marlow. *Essays in Teaching Mathematics*, Kirksville, Missouri: Stenographic Office, Northeast Missouri State University, 1987.

Grossnickle, Foster E., et. al. *Discovering Meanings in Elementary School Mathematics*. Seventh Edition. New York: Holt, Rinehart and Winston, Inc., 1983, Chapter One.

Kennedy, Leonard M. *Guiding Children's Learning of Mathematics*. Fourth Edition, Belmont, California: Wadsworth Publishing Company, 1984.

Marks, John L., et. al., *Teaching Elementary School Mathematics for Understanding*. Fourth Edition. New York: McGraw-Hill Book Company, 1975. Chapter One.

Riedesel, C. Alan. *Guiding Discovery in Elementary School Mathematics*. Second Edition. New York: Appleton-Century-Crofts, 1973. Chapter One—Four.

41

Designing the Mathematics Curriculum

Teachers, principals, and supervisors need to study, evaluate and implement in the public school setting accepted ideas pertaining to an effective design in elementary school mathematics. Concepts such as scope and sequence become important when an appropriate design is developed for a relevant curriculum.

Scope in the Mathematics Curriculum

The question frequently arises as to "what should be taught in elementary school mathematics." Which understandings, skills, and attitudes must pupils develop to become proficient and contributing members of society? There are no clear-cut, easy answers to this question. There are, however, selected individuals and groups whose studies and/or statements of thought and philosophy provide relevant guidelines.

1. Writers of reputable mathematics textbooks provide a guide in determining "what" (scope) pupils are to learn in an up-to-date curriculum. There are advantages as well as disadvantages in using this approach rather exclusively. Advantages are the following:
   - *(a)* Recognized writers and involved publishing companies in the field have spent much time and money in developing and evaluating content contained in mathematics textbooks for pupils.
   - *(b)* The teacher's manual related to the mathematics textbook for pupils can have excellent teaching suggestions to utilize in ongoing units of study.
   - *(c)* The textbook for pupils on any grade level clearly indicates the inherent unit titles for learners in teaching-learning situations.

(d) Learning activities for pupils within each unit of study and sequentially presented from the author's unique perception.

(e) The contents of the textbook can be utilized to provide for individual differences in the class setting by having pupils work at different presented achievement levels.

(f) Much of the work of the teacher has been done in developing the mathematics curriculum when utilizing a reputable textbook to select objectives, learning experiences, and appraisal techniques.

(g) Pupil interest and purpose can be developed within specific units of study when effectively utilizing a relevant series of textbooks. Carefully selected experiences for pupils can aid in stimulating interest and purpose for learning.

Disadvantages in using mathematics textbooks rather exclusively would be the following:

(a) Sameness in kinds of learning experiences provided for pupils may become rather boring. Pupils generally like to experience a variety of experiences including the use of reputable mathematics textbooks.

(b) The heavy use of textbooks in the mathematics curriculum does not meet the needs, interests and abilities of selected pupils.

(c) Pupils differ from each other in terms of learning styles possessed. Thus, the learning style of a few pupils may not harmonize with the heavy use of textbooks in providing content for the mathematics curriculum.

(d) Teachers need to be creative in selecting objectives, learning activities, and appraisal techniques. Heavy use of mathematics textbooks in teaching-learning situations can deemphasize creative efforts of teachers.

(e) There is a tendency to keep an entire class of pupils together at the same place at the same time when textbooks are used in teaching-learning situations. Thus, individual differences are not adequately provided for in the class setting.

(f) Units of study in a series of mathematics textbooks may over-emphasize selected facts, concepts, and generalizations and deemphasize other relevant learnings for pupils. For example, the structure of mathematics may be overly stressed to the point where computation skills are deemphasized.

It appears desirable to utilize reputable mathematics textbooks along with other carefully chosen learning activities to provide for the needs, interest, and abilities of individual learners.

Emphasis upon the use of mathematics textbooks to determine the scope (what is taught) in ongoing units of study for a specific school year may reveal the following content for the fifth grade level:

(a) Sets, Numeration, and Number.
(b) Properties and Patterns of Addition and Subtraction.
(c) Properties of Multiplication and Division.
(d) Fractional Numbers and Their Operations.
(e) Decimals, Ratio, and Proportion.
(f) Nonmetric Geometry.
(g) The Metric System.
(h) Metric Geometry-Finding Perimeter, Area, and Volume.
(i) Measurement in Today's Society.
(j) Line, Bar, and Picture Graphs. Probability.
(k) Numeration Systems (other than base ten).

In utilizing reputable textbooks as a basis for providing content in teaching-learning situations, the following would be viable criteria to follow:

(a) Use a variety of learning activities-such as markers of different kinds, films, filmstrips, transparencies, video tapes, and the overhead projector-to enrich experiences of pupils and to provide for individual differences.
(b) Preassess pupils to determine where each should begin at the beginning of a specific school year within a given unit of study, and guide each learner to experience continuous progress.
(c) The scope of the mathematics curriculum should include those learning experiences which guide learners to become contributing members in society.

2. The teacher may write measurable behaviourally stated objectives when determining scope in the elementary school mathematics curriculum. The following are examples of behaviourally stated objectives in a unit on "Addition and Subtraction of Whole Numbers."

   (a) The pupil will add correctly nine out of ten problems; each addition problem containing two one-digit addends.
   (b) The pupil will subtract correctly nine out of ten problems containing a one-digit minuend and a one-digit subtrahend.

(*c*) The pupil will solve correctly five out of six word problems containing two one-digit addends to be added.

(*d*) The pupil will subtract correctly in five out of six word problems containing a one-digit minuend and a one-digit subtrahend.

For each of the above behaviourally stated objectives, the teacher needs to select interesting, purposeful, and meaningful learning experiences in order that learners may achieve these desired ends sequentially. Pupil achievement may then be measured to determine if each objective has or has not been attained. If an objective is not realized by a learner, the teacher diagnoses to determine the cause or causes for this happening. Additional learning experiences need to be provided so that pupils may be successful in attaining stated measurable objectives.

Thus, behaviourally stated objectives written by the teacher (or teachers) pertaining to diverse units of study in mathematics can pertain to what is taught or the scope of that curriculum area. Knowledge needs to be perceived as related and not as isolated bits of information.

3. Pupils should achieve structural ideas in elementary school mathematics. Jerome Bruner, psychologist from Harvard University, has been very instrumental in stressing the importance of pupils perceiving properties or the structure of a curriculum area. Pupils would continually understand these structural ideas in greater, depth as they progress through the public school years. Jerome Bruner in the book, *The Process of Education*, writes the following:

   We begin with the hypothesis that any subject can be taught effectively in some intellectually honest form to any child at any stage of development (page 33).

   Important structural idea that pupils may achieve in mathematics could include the following:

   (*a*) The commutative property of addition and multiplication.

   (*b*) The associative property of addition and multiplication.

   (*c*) The distributive property of multiplication over addition.

   (*d*) The identity elements for addition and multiplication.

   (*e*) The property of closure for addition and multiplication.

   Jerome Bruner would stress the importance of pupils developing structural ideas inductively. Thus, the teacher must

   (*a*) Select relevant learning experiences which would guide pupils to discover structural ideas in mathematics. The teacher definitely would not lecture or present long explanations to pupils on the meaning or meanings attached to these key ideas.

(*b*) Assist learners to continually discover these structural ideas as they progress through the public school years. (These key ideas cannot be mastered on any one grade level in the elementary school).

(*c*) Guide pupils to realize these structural or key ideas on increased levels of complexity as learners achieve continuous progress in the school and class setting. (For example, on the first grade level, most pupils learn that "5 + 7 = 7 + 5." On higher grade levels pupils learn that "13 + 18 = 18 + 13; 145 + 258 = 258 + 145; 3296 + 1835 = 1835 + 3296," and so on—the commutative property of addition.)

Reasons for emphasizing the structure of knowledge in teaching pupils include the following:

(*a*) Subject matter specialists can do a better job of selecting what is important for pupils to learn as compared to teachers, principals, and supervisors in the class setting.

(*b*) It is the teacher's role to choose learning experiences which guide pupils to achieve inductively the identified structural or key ideas as determined by content specialists.

(*c*) Subject matter specialists and educators must work together to improve the public school curriculum.

(*d*) Public school public utilize methods of study emphasized by subject matter specialists such as that used by mathematicians.

4. Pupils may experience the use of programmed learning in the mathematics curriculum.

Programmed learning follows selected ideas pertaining to how pupils learn. The following are major generalizations pertaining to programmed learning:

(*a*) Pupils progress in very small steps in learning.

(*b*) Each small step of learning is sequentially arranged.

(*c*) In the use of programmed materials, the pupil generally looks at a picture, reads related content, responds to an item, and then checks the correctness of the response. The first step of learning indicated above (looking at a picture) may be omitted in some programmed materials. The sequence of these steps in learning is repeated again and again as far as pupils learning is concerned.

(*d*) The learner knows immediately if he/she is right or wrong in terms of responses given. If the pupil was correct in the response given, reinforcement in learning is involved. If an incorrect response was given by the learner, he/she knows the correct answer after checking with the correct answer indicated by the programmer.

(*e*) The pupil may progress at his own optimal rate of learning when programmed materials are used.

(*f*) Rarely does a learner respond incorrectly to an item in sequence since the progressive steps in learning are small enough to prevent incorrect responses.

Disadvantages in utilizing programmed materials include the following:

(*a*) Problem solving is not stressed in programmed materials.

(*b*) The sequential steps in learning may be too small for certain pupils. Gifted and talented pupils may not need these small sequential steps in learning to be successful achievers.

(*c*) If programmed materials were used exclusively in learning, boredom may set in on the part of individual learners. Human beings seemingly crave a variety of experiences in the school and class setting as well as in life.

(*d*) The learning styles of selected pupils may not harmonize with the philosophy inherent in programmed learning in the class setting.

Programmed materials emphasize the Stimulus-Response school of thought in terms of how pupils learn. Thus, pupils in the mathematics curriculum using programmed materials must experience a Stimulus, such as seeing a picture of three boys and being asked to tell how many members are in this set. The pupil gives a Response to this item by writing the numeral "3" or the word "three." Next, the learner may check the correctness of his response with the answer given by the programmer in the programmed mathematics textbook. Similar, small sequential steps in learning then follow for the individual pupil utilizing programmed materials.

The teacher of mathematics could program content for pupils pertaining to arithmetic, algebra, and geometry. These resulting materials must

(*a*) Present learnings in small steps to pupils (Stimulus).

(*b*) Give pupils an opportunity to respond to each item (Response).

(*c*) Be arranged sequentially to insure pupil success in responding to each item (Reinforcement).

(*d*) Give learners an opportunity to check the correctness of each response made before going on to the next sequentially developed item (Feedback to students).

5. Pupils should experience problem-solving activities in the class and school setting. The Gestalt school of thought in terms of how pupils learn emphasizes the following conditions for pupils:
   (*a*) The whole child is involved in learning such as the emotional, intellectual, social, and physical facets of an individual's development.
   (*b*) The pupils perceives situations as wholes first rather than parts.
   (*c*) The wholeness of a situation can be analyzed in terms of parts.

Pupils in a stimulating learning environment should have ample opportunities to identify problem areas. Learners, for example, identify problem areas in the mathematics curriculum from the following learning activities:

(*a*) Viewing a bulletin board display emphasizing four cookies to be divided among eight pupils. Division of a counting number by a counting number resulting in a fraction may be emphasized in an ongoing unit of study. A pupil may think of related situations in life that he/she is facing, a situation whereby a counting number is to be divided by a counting number resulting in a fractional value.

(*b*) Viewing a filmstrip on sets. The pupil is noticing in this presentation how two sets which are disjoint may be joined together to form a new set. An involved pupil may have wanted to find out how many marbles he/she now has after originally having a set of eight, and six additional marbles were added to the set as a gift from a peer.

(*c*) Watching a demonstration by the teacher using markers to show the meaning of a subtraction problem involving a single digit minuend and a single digit subtrahend. The involved learner thinks of a related problem in subtraction which needs solving as far as his/her own personal experiences in everyday living are concerned.

(*d*) Noticing situations in the class setting which require problem-solving skills. From the class and school environment, pupils notice a problem or problems which need solving pertaining to the use of arithmetic, algebra, and geometry. Pupils then measure, weigh, or find the volume of a container in a real life situation. Selected pupils may need to find out how many cups are in a pint when following directions in developing a food product in the class setting.

In daily situations outside the school and class setting, pupils, of course, detect problems needing solutions involving the use of mathematics:

An eight year old has saved $6.75 from allowance money received; the desire is to buy a baseball glove costing $12.98. The child attempts to determine how much more money is needed to make the purchase. The eight year old thinks about different approaches to use in coming up with a solution to the problem. The child brings to bear related knowledge in attempting to solve the problem. Ultimately, the eight year old may count by fives or tens from $6.75 to $12.98 to determine how much additional money will be needed to buy the baseball glove.

The Gestalt approach in learning emphasizes

(a) Wholistic situations in life from which a problem or problem areas are identified.

(b) Previously gained related knowledge is brought to bear upon the situation of the problem.

(c) Insight is gained by individuals in obtaining a needed solution.

(d) Solutions to problems are held tentative. Thus, new problems are identified from existing situations.

In Summary

There are numerous schools of thought in psychology and philosophy attempting to explain how individuals learn. Teachers, principals, and supervisors must study and appraise diverse schools of thought in education pertaining to how human beings learn. Ultimately, educators in the public school setting must develop a philosophy and psychology of their own to implement in teaching-learning situations. Teachers, principals, and supervisors may develop a rather consistent school of thought such as Stimulus-Response or the Gestalt approach. Other public school educators may be eclectic in teaching-learning situations selecting that which is deemed relevant and viable from diverse schools of thought explaining how individuals learn.

Whichever school of thought is selected, the following principles of learning should be accepted by all teachers, principals, and supervisors in the school setting pertaining to teaching mathematics and other curriculum areas:

1. Learning activities must capture the interests of pupils.
2. Pupils must understand what is learned.
3. Balance among understandings, skills, and attitudinal goals must be emphasized in ongoing units of study.

4. Good sequence in learning must be inherent on the part of learners.
5. Pupils need to feel successful in learning.
6. Learners must develop feelings of an adequate self-concept.
7. Each pupil must experience adequate readiness activities prior to experiencing new learnings.
8. A variety of learning experiences must be provided for learners.

Barlow quoted the summarized research by Kyriacow and Sutcliffe on factors that contribute to teacher stress. These are

1. Excessive clerical work
2. Supervisory duties
3. Inadequate salary
4. Negative student attitudes
5. Required discipline curtailed teaching time
6. Poor staff relations
7. Inadequate or unsupportive administration
8. Inadequate buildings and equipment
9. Overload; large classes
10. Inadequate training
11. Low status of the profession in society
12. Conflicting demands
13. Lack of parental cooperation

Many of the stresses listed above if eliminated or minimized would definitely assist students to achieve more optimally.

REFERENCES

Barlow, Daniel L. *Educational Psychology*. Chicago: Moody Press, 1985.

Duke, Daniel Linden and Adrienne Maravich Meckel, *Teacher's Guide To Classroom Management*. New York: Random House, 1984.

Ediger, Marlow and D. Bhaskara Rao. *Teaching Mathematics Successfully*. New Delhi, India: Discovery Publishing House, 2000.

Kramer, Klaas. *Teaching Elementary School Mathematics*. Second Edition. Boston: Allyn and Bacon, Inc., 1970.

Mahaffey, Michael L., and Alex F. Perrodin. *Teaching Elementary School Mathematics*. Itasco, Illinois: F.E. Peacock Publishers, Inc., 1973.

Miller, John P. *The Educational Spectrum*. New York: Longman, 1983.

Schminke, C.W. et. al. *Teaching the Child Mathematics*. Hinsdale, Illinois: The Dryden Press, Inc., 1973.

42

Learning Activities in the Mathematics Curriculum

Mathematics teachers in the elementary school need to select relevant objectives for pupils to achieve. These objectives should emphasize rational balance among understandings, skills, and attitudinal objectives. After these aims have been chosen, the teacher must guide pupils in attaining objectives through learning opportunities that are

(a) Challenging and interesting.
(b) Rewarding and satisfying.
(c) Purposeful and meaningful.
(d) Individualized and provide for each learner.
(e) Sequential from the learner's point of view.
(f) Inquiry oriented, and yet deductive learning is also emphasized.
(g) Characterized by child growth and development tenets.
(h) Geared to continuous progress on the part of each learner.

Specific Learning Activities to Attain Objectives

The teacher of elementary school mathematics must select learning opportunities which guide each pupil to achieve optimal development in arithmetic, geometry, probability and statistics, as well as algebra. Possible learning experiences for pupils will now be discussed.

Utilizing the Textbook

Reputable mathematics textbooks can and do provide valuable experiences for pupils in the school and class setting. Textbooks ultimately selected for adoption in teaching mathematics should follow criteria such as the following:

1. Proper order of learning for pupils is in evidence.
2. Adequate illustrations and diagrams are inherent to help pupils understand mathematical concepts, facts, and generalizations.
3. The textbook captures pupil interest and appeal.
4. Key structural ideas are emphasized such as the commutative property of addition and multiplication, the associative property of addition and multiplication, identity elements for addition and multiplication, and the distributive property of multiplication over addition.
5. The teacher's manual section presents ample suggestions for teaching-learning situations such as objectives or goals, learning activities, and appraisal procedures.
6. The authors are reputable from the point of identifying relevant learnings for pupils to achieve in mathematics.
7. Adequate attention is given to guide pupils to develop proficiency in problem solving and using various algorithms in computation.
8. Opportunities are given for pupils to utilize what has been learned previously.

Too frequently, all pupils are on the same page at the same time when textbooks are utilized in teaching-learning situations. The teacher needs to individualize instruction. Thus pupils are assessed to determine their individual present level of achievement within the confines of the adopted textbooks. Each pupil may then be working at a different achievement level as compared to other learners in the class setting. For example, in a fifth grade class, a few learners may need to use third or fourth grade textbooks in order to work at their present levels of continuous progress. As further examples, pupils A, B, and C as revealed by the pre-assessment may begin on pages 15, 80, and 100 respectively in the fifth grade mathematics textbook. A few selected learners may need to utilize sixth and seventh grade texts in teaching-learning situations since this is their present achievement level. Once each child's present achievement level in mathematics has been determined at the beginning of a school year, the teacher then needs to guide pupils to experience continuous progress. The teacher, during the time devoted to mathematics instruction, would teach, stimulate, and supervise each child to achieve optimal growth and development.

Utilizing the Flannel Board

Primary grade pupils, in particular, may develop many learnings in elementary school mathematics through the use of a flannel board as a learning activity. The teacher on the first grade level, for example, may place two triangles in one set and three triangles in another set. These cutouts may be made of flannel or felt. Pupils may be asked how many members there are in the first set. After responding correctly to this question, learners are asked to give the number being represented in the second set. The two sets may then be combined with pupils stating the number of members making up the new set. The order of presenting the two previously named sets may then be changed. Pupils realize that 2 + 3 = 3 + 2. Children are realizing in these learning experiences that the order of addends considered in adding does not affect the sum (commutative property of addition).

If pupils are not ready for addition of two one-digit addends, the following learnings must come in prior sequence:

1. rote counting. Here pupils say the counting numbers in their proper order such as "one", "two", "three", "four", "five", and so on.
2. Rational counting. A child points to a first object like a crayon and says "one", points to a second crayong and says "two", the third crayon and says "three", and so on. Rational counting is more complex for learners as compared to being able to count in a rote manner. Objectives must be arranged in proper order or sequence so they can be achieved by pupils.

Cutouts made of flannel or felt for the flannel board should vary in terms of the following:

1. Color of cutouts. Pupils desire variety in learning experiences; Thus appealing red, blue, yellow, orange, and green cutouts should be utilized.
2. Geometric form of cutouts. Triangles, circles, squares, rectangles, and parallelograms should be available for use in teaching-learning situations.

Cutouts of diverse pictures may be used with the flannel board. These pictures may be used in helping pupils understand the operation of addition (two jet planes in one set and three jet planes in the second set make a total of how many?) Thus, pictures of animals, cars, trucks, buses, boats, and people may be used in the ongoing units of study. Each picture should have a small piece of sandpaper pasted on the back so that it will stay attached when placed on the flannel board.

Utilizing Markers

An ample supply of markers should be available to help pupils achieve optimal development in mathematics. Markers such as the following may then be utilized in providing interesting, meaningful, and purposeful experiences.

1. Bean, pea, and corn seeds.
2. Beads and buttons.
3. Crayons, chalk, and pencils.
4. Pop caps and tongue-depressor sticks.

These markers may be utilized in the following ways:

1. Have pupils count the number of markers in a set.
2. Have pupils write numerals that relate to the number of markers in each set in addition. The operations of subtraction, multiplication, and division may also be taught using selected markers.
3. Have pupils place the number of markers in a set as specified by the teacher in a given learning experience.
4. Guide pupils understanding the process of regrouping and renaming with the use of these markers. If pupils are to understand the meaning of 22 – 13 = □, appropriate experiences should be provided. Since three markers cannot be taken from two markers in the units column, a set of ten markers may be regrouped from the two tens column and joined with the two ones. The result is a set of twelve markers in the ones column. Pupils now take three markers from the twelve markers in the units column. Nine markers are left in the ones column. If a set of ten is taken from a set of ten markers in the tens column, none is left. Thus, 22 – 13 = 9.

Using Place Value Charts

Place value charts may be made very inexpensively in the class setting. Construction paper may be utilized here. Separate pockets hold congruent slips o construction paper. These pockets hold the slips of paper in the ones, tens, and hundreds pockets. Thus, if paper strips for the value of twenty-three are to be represented in the place value chart, the learner may place three pieces in the ones pocket. Two sets each containing ten pieces with a rubber band around each set may be placed in the tens column.

Uses for the place value chart may be the following:

1. Have pupils develop meaningful pertaining to addition. If pupils are to add 25 + 16, five single congruent strips of paper may be placed in the ones pocket; two sets of ten each enclosed with a rubber band may be placed in the tens pocket. The number 25 has been represented with two tens and five ones. Next, six congruent slips of paper are placed into the ones pocket and a set of ten fastened with a rubber band placed in the tens pocket. Five ones and six ones may be joined together to represent one set of ten with a rubber band placed around this set and placed in the tens pocket. In the unit pocket then

there will be one member. In the tens pocket, there will now be two tens plus one ten plus one ten. The final sum is then 41, or four tens and one 1.

2. Guide pupils in attaching meaning to subtraction. If learners are to attach understanding to 35 – 16, five congruent slips may be placed in the ones pocket. Three sets of ten with congruent slips in each may be put into the tens pocket (each set should have a rubber band around it). The pupil notices he cannot take six from five ones in the problem 35 – 16. He may take one set of ten from the tens pocket and place these into the ones pocket. The problem now results in the minuend containing two tens and fifteen ones. Now the pupil can take six ones from fifteen ones resulting in a difference of nine. Also, one ten taken away form two tens leaves one ten. Thus, 35 – 16 = 19.
3. Have pupils achieve basic understandings pertaining to multiplication. For example, if pupils are working on a problem such as 3 x 23, three congruent slips of paper may be placed into the ones pocket and two sets of ten each placed in the tens pocket. Next, two sets of three each may be placed into the ones pocket and two sets of two tens may be put into the tens pocket. Thus, pupils understand that 3 x 3 = 9; this numeral would represent how many would be in the one column. Also, three sets, two tens in each set, would make six tens in the tens column. The final product of 3 x 23 = 69.
4. Guide pupils in attaining desired learnings in division. If pupils are developing understandings pertaining to the division problem 42 ÷ 2, the dividend of 42 may be represented by two congruent slips of paper being placed in the one's pocket and four sets, with ten members in each set, being placed in the tens pocket. To divide the child may now place one member in each of two sets to represent the ones column. Next, the four sets of ten each in the tens pocket may be separated into two equal sets. Thus, the answer to the division problem 42 ÷ 2 is 21.

The teacher should utilize place value charts to help pupils attach meaning to understandings objectives in ongoing units of study in elementary school mathematics.

Using Transparencies and the Overhead Projector

Overhead projectors may wisely be utilized in the class setting due to the following inherent factors:

1. The teacher faces pupils when utilizing transparencies in the class discussion.

2. Specific content that pupils are to learn only, may be put on a transparency. Irrelevant content then is not part of ongoing learning experiences.
3. Transparencies can be developed which are appealing and interesting to pupils.
4. The order of discussing content in several transparencies may be arranged sequentially from the point of view of the child's own unique perception.
5. Content should be added to any transparency as the need arises.

Transparencies and the overhead projector can be utilized in ways such as the following:

1. Pupils count how many members there are in a set as given in a specific transparency.
2. Learners tell how many members make a new set if two previously given sets are combined or joined together.
3. Pupils tell how many members are left if, for example, there were nine circle and two are taken away.
4. Pupils begin initial learnings in multiplication, *e.g.*, three sets of circles with four members in each set, 3 x 4 = □.
5. The inverse operation of multiplication (division) may be shown and discovered from the previous example, *e.g.*, twelve circles are to be divided equally into three different sets. Thus, four members are in each of these three sets.

Using Filmstrips

There are leading publishers of filmstrips who have excellent curriculum materials for teachers to utilize in elementary school mathematics. These filmstrips should exemplify criteria such as the following:

1. The content must capture interests of pupils.
2. The diverse frames must follow appropriate sequence.
3. Pupils should have ample opportunities to develop learnings inductively as well as deductively.
4. Problem-solving activities need to be stressed adequately.
5. A manual should accompany the filmstrips to give possible suggestions as to their use.

Filmstrips may be utilized in learning experiences such as the following:

1. To introduce a new unit. If pupils are to study addition of unit fractions with unlike denominators, a carefully selected filmstrip may give learners an overview of the new unit. Pupils can then see how knowledge of unit fractions with unlike denominators is useful in problem solving situations in class and in life outside of the school setting.

2. To develop learnings in greater depth. The content of filmstrips guides learners in attaching meaning to fractions such as ¼ + 1/6 = □, or 1/3 + 1/6 = □. Social situations stressed in the filmstrips presentation guide learners in perceiving practical application of abstract learnings. In the filmstrip presentation, numerous experiences would be provided pupils in understanding what is involved if unit fractions with unlike demonstrators are added.
3. To end or culminate a unit of study. In the filmstrip presentation, pupils should have ample opportunities to review what has been learned previously pertaining to adding unit fraction with unlike denominators. In reviewing what has been learned previously, pupils should have many opportunities to apply learnings that have been developed previously. If pupils can use that which has been learned previously within the framework of purposeful learning experiences, it will be possible to retain these understandings, skills, and attitudes for a longer period of time.

Content in the filmstrip should provide opportunities for pupils to

1. Respond to questions and problems.
2. Make practical application of what has been learned previously.
3. Arrive at relevant concepts and generalizations at their own unique rate of speed.
4. Assess their own achievement in learning.
5. Experience success and satisfaction in learning.
6. Branch out in the direction of new related learning.
7. Achieve understanding of selected structural ideas in mathematics, *e.g.*, commutative and associative properties of addition and multiplication.
8. Perceive diverse operations in mathematics as being related, *e.g.*, division undoes multiplication.

Using Graphs

Pupils in the elementary school should experience the making and using of graphs. Graphs developed by pupils with teacher guidance should

1. Emphasize content within the experiences of learners.
2. Present generalizations in a simplified manner.
3. Contain a heading to orientate viewers to inherent conclusions.
4. Provide interesting, meaningful, and purposeful learning experiences.

Kinds of graphs which may be developed by elementary pupils with teacher assistance include

1. Picture graphs. (Pictures graphs may be the easiest to read and develop on the part of the pupils.)
2. Line graphs.
3. Bar graphs.
4. Circle or pie graphs. (The teacher should develop and draw circle and pie graphs. Pupils can be guided in reading content from this kind or type of graph).

Situations involving the use of graphs may include

1. Recording the number of visitors during American Education Week. For example, if three visitors came to the class setting on Monday, three pictures in one to one correspondence can represent these guests. For Tuesday, if five visitors visited school, one picture should represent each of these guests individually in a picture graph. The graph should, of course, also show the visitors for Wednesday, Thursday, and Friday.
2. Showing population figures of selected countries being studied in a social studies unit. The result could be recorded in a picture, line, or bar graph. Thus, if pupils are studying a unit on Common Market Countries of Western Europe, each country such as West Germany, Italy, France, and other members must be represented on the graph. Pupils with teacher direction should determine how many people will be represented by a picture on a picture graph. Or, in using line and bar graphs, the size of interval must be determined in terms of how many people will be represented therein. Each interval should be congruent in size. Thus, for example, in a bar graph (horizontal and vertical bars), each one inch bar may represent five million people. Pupils may then see that situations involving reality may be put in graphic form.

If pupils are studying a unit on Weather, a line graph may be developed pertaining to temperature readings for each of the days of the week during the time the unit is being taught.

Using Songs

There are numerous recordings which can help pupils to develop increased proficiency in rote counting. Learning in the early primary grade years generally enjoy singing these selected songs. In learning to sing the song, "Ten Little Indians," pupils learn to use selected counting numbers in proper order or sequence. Thus, in singing "One little, two little, five little, three little Indians; four little, six little Indians; seven little, eight little, nine little Indians; ten little Indian boys," pupils are learning the correct order or sequence of counting numbers. Later on, pupils should attach meaning to rational counting; here, a learner points to an object and says "one," he points to a second object and says "two," Other sets of course, may also be counted in sequence such as "three," "four," "five," and so on.

Pupils with teacher guidance may develop songs dealing with saying the counting numbers in proper sequence.

Using Money

Real coins and play money should be utilized in teaching-learning situations to help pupils understand not only money values but other relevant learnings. Thus, real and play money may be used in the following ways:

1. Counting members given in a specific set, such as five coins pertaining to the cardinal number of five. Pupils may also develop learnings here pertaining to ordinal numbers, such as which coin is the third member in a specific set.
2. Joining two sets together to make a new set, such as a child spending fifteen cents for a candy bar and ten cents for a package of chewing gum. Thus, the learner can see practical application in the use of money when items and purchased.
3. Subtracting when regrouping is involved such as a child having thirty-two cents and spending fifteen cents on a candy bar. The learner can be guided in understanding that a set of ten needs to be taken from the tens column in the value of three tens. These ten pennies may then be added to the two ones making a total of twelve cents. Now the pupil may take five ones from the twelve ones leaving seven cents. One ten may be taken from the two tens and leaving one ten. The answer then to the problem 32 – 15 is 17.
4. Multiplying a factor times a factor. If a pupil, for example, had 10 cents and needed four times that amount to buy candy, the learner could be guided to think about four distinct sets, each having ten members. Thus, 4 x 10 = 40.
5. Dividing, such as twenty-five cents being divided among five boys. How many cents then would each receive?

In using real money as a learning activity in the mathematics curriculum, the following criteria should be followed:

1. Pupils should notice money can buy needed goods and services.
2. Learners should apply what has been learned previously.
3. Pupils need to attach meaning to ongoing learning activities involving the use of money. Thus, pupils, for example, may count the number of coins in a set emphasizing the one to one

correspondence concept. Learnings acquired by pupils must make sense and be comprehendable.

4. Learners need to be involved in determining learning experiences involving the use of money.

Using the Geoboard

In a modern program of elementary school mathematics, adequate emphasis must be given to the study of geometry. This would be true for the following reasons:

1. The world of geometry is all around us. Pupils may see squares (such as in a tile on the floor), rectangles (such as in doors and window panes), circles (such as in circular windows and circle drives), and triangles.
2. Geometry can be interesting to pupils. Many learning experiences involving creative endeavours may be provided for pupils such as developing geometrical designs.

The geoboard made by the teacher or purchased commercially can provide interesting learning experiences for pupils. The base of a geoboard may consist of plywood. The size of the base can vary; eighteen inches by eighteen inches provides a suitable size geoboard for teaching-learning situations. Small finish nails about a square inch apart may be driven into the geoboard. These nails should be driven in far enough to make for stability and yet protrude adequately. Rubber bands may be stretched around these nails as protrusions to form triangles, squares, rectangles, and other geometric forms.

Using Drill and Practice in Mathematics

Once pupils understand in a meaningful, purposeful, and interesting manner basic addition, subtraction, multiplication, and division facts, drill procedures may be utilized in teaching-learning situations. Varied procedures must be used to provide drill sessions for pupils pertaining to these basic facts. The interests of pupils must be developed and maintained in the elementary school mathematics curriculum. The following procedures may be utilized to fix basic addition, subtraction, multiplication, and division facts in the mind of the learner;

1. Flash cards (pupils are given the time they need to respond to facts such as the following, each on a three by five-inch card):

$$\begin{array}{r} 3 \\ +5 \\ \hline \end{array} \quad \begin{array}{r} 5 \\ +3 \\ \hline \end{array} \quad \begin{array}{r} 4 \\ +4 \\ \hline \end{array} \quad \begin{array}{r} 4 \\ +5 \\ \hline \end{array} \quad \begin{array}{r} 5 \\ +4 \\ \hline \end{array} \quad \begin{array}{r} 6 \\ +3 \\ \hline \end{array} \quad \begin{array}{r} 3 \\ +6 \\ \hline \end{array} \quad \begin{array}{r} 2 \\ +6 \\ \hline \end{array} \quad \begin{array}{r} 6 \\ +2 \\ \hline \end{array}$$

2. Games (these may be made by the teacher); pupils move forward a certain number of squares on a broad, as indicated by a spinner, if they respond correctly to a basic addition,

subtraction, multiplication, or division fact. The fact to be responded to would be on a small card, face down, drawn in order of players taking their turns playing the game. Penalties such as losing a turn or moving back a space or more may be inherent in the game.

3. Fishing for fish (small "fish" may be cut from different colors of construction paper—each fish has a paper clip in its mouth.) The child uses a "fishing pole" consisting of a stick, attached string, and a magnet to catch fish; each fish has a number pair printed on its such as

5	4	3	5	6	6	7
– 3	– 3	– 2	– 4	– 3	– 2	– 5

A child may keep the fish caught if he gives the correct answer to the number pair.

4. Slides and transparencies. The teacher may write basic number pairs on individual slides. Pupils may then respond to these number pairs by attempting to give the correct answers.

Practice would involve guiding pupils to use previously developed learnings in new situations. Learners must be aided to transfer learnings obtained from one situation to the next problematic area. Thus, if pupils have learned that 10 + 5 = 15 in a meaningful, purposeful, and interesting manner, they should be able to apply these learnings to a new situation such as determining the cost of items that cost 10 cents and 5 cents respectively. Thus, facts, concepts, main ideas, and generalizations that have been acquired may be utilized in functional situations. Content learned previously that is used in functional everyday life situations generally is not forgotten by pupils.

The following criteria should be followed by teachers of mathematics when teaching for a transfer of learning:

1. Have pupils attach meaning to new learnings being acquired.
2. Point out to learners or have them discover how previously attained learnings may be used in new situations.
3. Have pupils perceive reasons or purpose for learning content in elementary school mathematics.
4. Guide pupils in perceiving essential understandings when learning a new process.

In Summary

Teachers need to provide a variety of learning experiences for pupils in elementary school mathematics. This is necessary due to pupils

(a) Achieving at diverse levels of accomplishment in the mathematics curriculum.

(*b*) Individually possessing different learning styles in the class setting.

The following, among others, can be relevant learning activities to present to pupils:

1. Using a selected series of elementary school mathematics textbooks.
2. Utilizing the flannel board to guide individual pupil achievement in mathematics.
3. Helping pupils attach meaning to learning through the use of markers.
4. Guiding pupils in learning by using place value charts.
5. Aiding learner achievement through the use of transparencies and the overhead projector.
6. Stimulating learner interest in mathematics with the use of selected filmstrips.
7. Using graphs in functional situations.
8. Helping young pupils to develop interest in numbers by singing songs directly related to ongoing units of study in elementary school mathematics.
9. Using to geoboard to help pupils experience the world of geometry.
10. Providing drill and practice for pupils so that previously developed learnings will not be forgotten.

Jarolimek wrote:

1. Not all children learn in the same way; different media are able to appeal to the learning styles of different learners.
2. The reading ranges among children who are randomly selected to form elementary school classroom groups are great, averaging three to five years in the lower grades and five to ten years in the middle and upper grades.
3. Each of the media has peculiar strength and limitations in the way it conveys messages.
4. The impact of a message is likely to be stronger if more than one sensory system is involved in receiving it.
5. Material to be learned varies greatly in its abstractness and complexity.
6. The use of variety of media has motivating and interest-generated qualities.
7. Teaching modes that stress inquiry and problem solving require extensive information searches and sources.
8. Different sources may provide different insights on the same subject; there may be discrepancies or inaccuracies that go undetected if a single source is used.

REFERENCES

Ashlock, Robert B., et. al., *Guiding Each Child's Learning of Mathematics*. Columbus, Ohio: Charles E. Merrill Publishing Company, 1983.

Cawley, John F. *Cognitive Strategies and Mathematics for the Learning Disabled*. Rockville, Maryland: Aspen Systems Corporation, 1985.

Copeland, Richard. *Mathematics and the Elementary Teacher*. Fourth Edition, New York: MacMillan Publishing Company, Inc., 1974.

Copeland, Richard W. *How Children Learn Mathematics*. Second Edition. New York: MacMillan Publishing Company, Inc., 1974.

Copeland, Richard W. *Diagnostic and Learning Activities in Mathematics for Children*. New York: MacMillan Publishing Company, Inc., 1974.

Grossnickle, Foster E., et. al. *Discovering Meanings in Elementary School Mathematics*. Sixth edition. New York: Holt, Rinehart and Winston, Inc., 1973.

Hicks, William Vernon et. al. *The New Elementary School Curriculum*. New York: VanNostrand Reinhold Company, 1970. Chapter Three.

Jarolimek, John. *Social Studies in Elementary Education*. Seventh edition. New York: MacMillan Publishing Company, 1985.

Marks, John L., et. al. *Teaching Elementary School Mathematics for Understanding*. Fourth edition. New York: McGraw-Hill Book Company, 1975. Chapters Four—Eleven.

43

Providing for Individual Differences in the Mathematics Curriculum

Teachers, principals and supervisors need to become thoroughly familiar with individual differences among pupils and how to guide each learner to achieve optimal development. It is important to be highly knowledgeable about traits pertaining to slow learners, average achievers, as well as talented and gifted pupils.

The Slow Learner

Which traits and characteristics do slow learners possess? Generally, it can be said that slow learners may be described in the following ways:

1. They may come in the category of having IQ's or Intelligence Quotients ranging from 75 to 90.
2. Their achievement is lower than that of average achievers and will register lower than their present grade level expectancy.
3. The attention span of slow learners is shorter than that of higher achievers.
4. It takes more time for the slow learner to understand a new process in mathematics as well as to master basic addition, subtraction, multiplication, and division facts.
5. These learners need more of concrete and semi-concrete learning activities.
6. Slow learners need learning activities which provide proper sequence.
7. More supervision and direction need to be given to slow learners compared to pupils who achieve at a higher level.
8. A lack of opportunities to learn in the home setting may be the lot of many slow learners.

9. It is necessary for teachers to be patient and understanding in teaching pupils achieving at a slower rate of speed.
10. Slow learners generally ask fewer questions and may reveal less of curiosity in the school and class environment as compared to peers of similar age levels.

The Talented Pupils

Teachers, principals, and supervisors need to identify and provide adequately for talented learners in the class setting. Talented pupils reveal characteristics such as the following:

1. Having a rather lengthy attention span.
2. Possessing the ability to gain understandings and skills quickly.
3. Being able to retain learnings well.
4. Completing tasks more rapidly than others in the class setting.
5. Showing much curiosity in learning.
6. Revealing tendencies of being creative individuals.
7. Becoming more independent in learning.
8. Having a desire to complete additional work in the school and class setting.
9. Possessing knowledge and skills hopeful in the areas of problem solving.
10. Being able to engage in constructive learning activities when spare time is available in the school and class setting.

Comparing Talented Pupils and Slow Learners

There are always exceptions to statements made about human beings. However, in general the following comparisons may be made between talented pupils and slow learners:

1. Talented pupils retain learnings longer than do slow learners.
2. Talented learners possess more initiative and become increasingly independent in learning as compared to peers in the school and class setting.
3. Pupils with much ability acquire learnings sooner as compared to those with less capacity.

Learning Activities and Individual Differences

The teacher must select interesting, meaningful, and purposeful learning experiences to provide for individual differences in ongoing units of study in mathematics. Slow learners will need the following kinds of experiences:

1. Concrete phases of instruction need to emphasized adequately whereby pupils use bean and core seeds, checkers, crayons, beads, sticks, and other objects to clarify learnings in counting, addition, subtraction, multiplication, and division.

2. The teacher must explain new processes in mathematics thoroughly and patiently to slow learners. Adequate opportunities also must be given to aid these pupils in learning inductively.
3. Emphasis must be given to help slow learners develop sequential learnings. Too frequently, the teacher wants to "jump" too far ahead of these pupils in teaching-learning situations. Thus, selected slow learners have been taught addition involving regrouping and renaming (*e.g.*, 48 + 17 = —; 39 + 18 = —) whereas these learners need more practice and guidance in simple addition (*e.g.*, 32 + 13 = —; 43 + 13 = —).
4. The teacher needs to observe the attention span of slow learners in each learning activity. Slow learners need to experience a new learning activity in mathematics before the preceding experience becomes dull and boring.
5. Adequate supervision and guidance must be given to slow learners to aid in achieving optimal development in mathematics. The teacher needs to evaluate if these pupils have achieved a desired objective before the next sequential end is stressed in a new lesson or unit of study. Kindergarten and first grade pupils should be able to count to ten in a rote manner before counting the number of members in a set of ten.
6. There are many abstract symbols which may be emphasized in teaching-learning situations. These abstract symbols include + (plus), – (minus), X (times), ÷ (divided by), = (equals), and others. Pupils should be guided to attach meaning to these symbols in functional situations. Abstract symbols in mathematics should not be emphasized to the point where slow learners feel frustrated and lack feelings of success.
7. Slow learners may be less creative in finding diverse solutions to a problem as compared to faster learners in the class setting. Thus, for example, a slow learner may be able to find one solution to a problem such as
Other algorisms could include the following:

	(a)		(b)	
42		42		42
x 6		x 6		x 6
12		240		252
240		12		
252		252		

8. Slow learners need ample opportunities to engage in practice and drill activities involving previous learnings obtained. Slow learners need to experience new learning activities directly related to content mastered previously. If a pupil has

learned in a meaningful, interesting, and purposeful way that 8 + 4 = 12 and 4 + 8 = 12, he/she may practice related learnings in which these addition facts and contained in relevant word problems. Drill as a method of teaching could involve in the use of flash cards, games and the overhead projector to fix specific learnings in the minds of pupils. A pupil may need drill with the use of flash cards pertaining to the following:

$$\begin{array}{r}8\\+5\\\hline 13\end{array}\qquad\begin{array}{r}5\\+8\\\hline 13\end{array}\qquad\begin{array}{r}13\\-8\\\hline 5\end{array}\qquad\begin{array}{r}13\\-5\\\hline 8\end{array}$$

9. Slow learners need to experience objectives in mathematics which are attainable. Pretesting of slow learners before a new unit in mathematics is implemented aids in adjusting the new unit to the present achievement levels of these learners. Objectives for slow learners to attain should not be too difficult nor should they pertain to what these learners have already acquired. Thus, new learnings may be gained by slow learners when achieving desired objectives in mathematics and at the same time success can be inherent in these experiences.
10. Slow learners should be guided to develop feelings of an adequate self-concept. These learners too frequently have experienced failure in mathematics, as well as in other curriculum areas. Other pupils in the school and class setting may have minimized the worth and achievement of the slow learner. All pupils need to be respected for their intrinsic worth regardless of ability, socio-economic level, or creed.

Adequate provision needs to be made for the fast learner in the mathematics curriculum. These pupils need to experience the following:

1. There needs to be less emphasis upon the concrete stage of learning and more emphasis upon abstract learnings. The teacher, however, must observe if these students are ready for relevant abstract learnings and guide each to acquire optimal development.
2. The teacher generally needs to give less of explanation to these learners in terms of understanding new concepts and processes in the mathematics curriculum. Talented learners can become quite self-directed and independent in their work.
3. Fast learners gain concepts and generalizations readily. These learners with teacher guidance become relatively independent in sequencing their own learnings.

4. The talented pupil has a longer attention span as compared to the slow learner. Time devoted to the teaching of mathematics should harmonize with the attention span of gifted learners.
5. Less direct supervision in mathematics of talented and gifted pupils needs to be in evidence by the classroom teacher. These learners can be independent and responsible in ongoing units of study in mathematics.
6. Talented and gifted pupils may be highly fascinated and challenged when encountering abstract symbols and concepts in the mathematics curriculum. A stimulating environment with interesting, meaningful, and purposeful learning experiences will aid pupils in wanting to acquire relevant abstract content. Thus, for example, talented first grade pupils may attach meaning to abstract concepts, such as lines, line segments, points, and rays. With appropriate sequence in learning talented sixth graders, as a further example, can attach meaning to abstract concepts such as square root, complex, numbers, irrational numbers, and tolerance.
7. Talented and gifted pupils in the mathematics curriculum should be guided to become increasingly independent in their work. These learners should have ample opportunities to select what to learn, as well as methods of learning. With teacher guidance, talented pupils should be guided in evaluating their own achievement in ongoing units of study as well as with a specific problem or area of difficulty being experienced. Talented and gifted pupils with teacher leadership should assess their own progress in units of study dealing with the following:
   (a) Sets and mathematical sentences.
   (b) Structural ideas or properties in mathematics.
   (c) Basic addition, subtraction, multiplication, and division facts.
   (d) Algorisms for addition, subtraction, multiplication, and division using whole numbers.
   (e) Prime numbers, composite numbers, and integers.
   (f) Addition, subtraction, multiplication, and division using fractional numbers.
   (g) Addition, subtraction, multiplication, and division using decimals and per cents.
   (h) Metric and nonmetric geometry.
   (i) Other systems of numeration.
   (j) Uses for probability and statistics.
   (k) Functions in the mathematics curriculum.

8. Talented and gifted pupils should be guided to achieve to their optimum in individual endeavours as well as in committee work in the class setting. The teacher must guide learners to experience continuous progress in ongoing units of study in mathematics as well as to work together harmoniously with others. Too frequently, the mathematics teacher may emphasize individual efforts on the part of the pupil. Committee work on the part of pupils is greatly deemphasized. Certainly, there needs to be rational balance between pupils working on an individual basis as well as within a committee setting. Gifted and talented pupils may work together within a committee to understand a new process, check computations, and/or solve a problem in an ongoing unit of study in mathematics. There are several values inherent in a learning activity involving fast learners helping slow learners in mathematics.
   (a) Talented and gifted pupils may develop feelings of an adequate self concept by helping others who need assistance.
   (b) Fast learners may understand previously developed learnings more fully by explaining related content to pupils who learn at a slower rate.
   (c) Talented and gifted pupils may develop wholesome attitudes toward those who experience difficulty in learning.

Talented and gifted pupils as well as those learners who achieve at a slower rate need to develop feelings of being accepted by others, belonging to a group, having security and status, and being able to participate freely in ongoing learning experiences.

Specific Ways of Providing for Individual Differences

There are numerous ways available to provide for individual differences in mathematics. The following approaches, among others, can be utilized to provide for slow learners, average achievers, as well as talented and gifted pupils:

1. Using behaviourally stated objectives. Learners of different achievement levels would achieve the same measurable objectives. However, slow learners would attain each objective in sequence at a slower rate as compared to average achievers and fast learners.
2. Pretesting pupils to ascertain their own individual achievement level at the beginning of a new school year when using a series of reputable mathematics textbooks. Each pupil depending on his/her present achievement level would be

participating in learning activities directly related to pretest results based on content from mathematics textbooks. Thus, for example, a fourth grade pupil may be participating in learning experiences involving the use of the third grade textbook, while a talented and gifted peer may be involved in learning experiences using content from a fifth or sixth grade mathematics textbook.

3. Providing learning centers to enrich experiences for talented and gifted pupils who have completed assigned work in mathematics.
4. Grouping pupils within the class setting to provide for individual differences. Slow, average, and fast learners could be taught in separate groups in an atmosphere of respect. The curriculum would be adjusted to the present achievement level of each of these groups of learners.
5. Grouping pupils homogeneously for instruction on the intermediate grade levels. Thus, if feasible, fast learners could be taught in one class setting, average achievers in a different class setting, with slow learners comprising a third group.
6. Using a variety of materials and methods in the mathematics curriculum. The curriculum is adjusted to diverse learning styles exhibited by learners. Also, there are more complex learnings in mathematics available for fast learners as compared to other levels of achievement. With the use of concrete materials (real objects or replicas), differences between and among pupils in mathematics achievement may be more adequately provided for as compared to the use of abstract learnings. In using a meter stick (a concrete object) in a unit on "Measurement and the Metric System", slow learners may measure the height of selected objects such as a door, window, and desk. Talented learners may use a meter stick to find the area of the classroom or the volume of selected containers.

When abstract learnings are to be acquired in mathematics, it is much more difficult to provide for individual differences. For example, if pupils are to learn to divide the following as a new experience for all learners in a heterogeneously grouped classroom; 8478 ÷ 36, talented pupils generally develop new understandings much more rapidly as compared to peers of similar chronological age. If talented pupils are ready for developing learnings pertaining to the previously named division problem, slow learners and average achievers may not possess needed background knowledge.

7. Accelerating achievement of talented and gifted pupils in mathematics. In a nongraded program of mathematics

instruction, fast learners can be guided to experience continuous progress within the framework of a challenging and meaningful curriculum. For example, in a fourth grade class, selected talented learners may be acquiring relevant experiences based on criteria related to fifth, sixth and seventh grade level of attainment.

8. Organising a mathematics club to provide for individual differences. Selected pupils with teacher guidance may wish to organise a mathematics club as a means of enriching the curriculum as well as providing for individual differences. At selected intervals, meetings may be held involving members in the mathematics club. The members may
   (a) View and discuss content from filmstrips relating to stimulating topics in mathematics.
   (b) Identify topics, units, and specific problems in mathematics for discussion and evaluation.
   (c) Interact with a resource person (high school or university mathematics instructor) involving a challenging area of interest in mathematics.
   (d) Make models pertaining to learnings gained from ongoing units of study in geometry.

In Summary

Teachers, principals, and supervisors need to study, appraise, and implement research findings pertaining to helping slow, average, and fast achievers realize optimal development in the school and class setting. Educators in the public schools need to ask questions and attempt to arrive at solutions pertaining to the following problem areas:

1. How do slow learners differ from average achievers in intellectual, emotional, social, and physical development? How are slow learners different from fast learners in these same four facets of development?
2. How can educational objectives be selected which are attainable for slow, average, and fast achievers?
3. Which criteria should be utilized to select learning activities for all pupils in the school and class setting so that each may experience continuous progress in mathematics?
4. How can each child's progress in different curriculum areas be evaluated appropriately and help to insure the best quality learning experiences possible for each learner?

Burton wrote:

Positive teaching takes patience and a commitment to the idea that children learn differently from adults, that they need to build up their own mathematical ideas, and that ideas cannot be handed to or told to them. It assumes that children are active, willing learners and that teachers perceive learning mathematics as a joint and joyful adventure between teacher and child.

REFERENCES

Burton, Grace M. *Good Beginning*. Menlo Park, California, 1985.

Copeland, Richard W. *Mathematics and the Elementary Teacher*. Fourth edition. New York: The Macmillan Company, 1982, Chapter 13.

Joyce, Bruce R., and Berj Harootunian, *The Structure of Teaching*. Chicago: Science Research Associate, Inc., 1967.

Kidd, K., et. al., *The Laboratory Approach to Mathematics*. Chicago: Science Research Associates, Inc., 1970.

National Council of Teachers of Mathematics. *The Learning of Mathematics, It's Theory and Practice*. Washington, D.C.: Twenty-First Yearbook, 1953.

National Society for the Study of Education. *Mathematics Education*. Chicago: NSSE, Sixty-Ninth Yearbook, 1970.

Turnbull, A.P. and J.B. Schulz. *Mainstreaming Handicapped Students: A Guide for the Classroom Teacher*. Boston: Allyn and Bacon, Inc., 1979.

44

Parents, Teacher and Mathematics

To leave parents out of planning the mathematics curriculum is a mistake. Teachers need to work with parents in determining objectives, learning opportunities, and evaluation procedures in mathematics. Parents need to show a willingness to cooperate in working with the teacher in providing the best curriculum possible for learners. There are definite criteria that both teachers and parents need to follow to make for good human relations. Respect for others is an important criteria that works in most cases. There needs to be consideration and acceptance of diverse personalities. Wanting to work with others in a cooperative manner helps in developing a better working relationship. Good attitudes toward others are a must! Careful listening to what the other person is saying assists in communicating ideas. Content in communication needs to be clear and meaningful. The objective in teachers communicating with parents is to offer the best mathematics curriculum possible to pupils.

The Parent and Teacher Conference

Parent/teacher conferences are generally held once or twice a year. There is no reason why these conferences cannot be more frequent. Teachers may call parents by phone at any time before, during, and after the school day. Many parents are at work during the school day hours; however, a voice recorder may provide the needed message for the pupil. The phone call may deal with the need for the parent to stop in to discuss problems the pupil is experiencing in mathematics. Praise for the pupil in doing better in mathematics is also very appropriate to communicate via telephone. A chance to work together is then possible to assist the pupil to achieve at a more optimal rate. When parents come to school for the regular scheduled conference once or twice a year, there are important guidelines to follow:

1. The teacher needs to be well prepared for the conference and know the sequence of content that will be discussed. Doing one's homework here is very important. An unprepared teacher indicates a lack of sincerity and interest in having the conference.
2. The teacher should show as much completed pupil work in mathematics as possible. Parents should see first-hand how well the child is doing in mathematics. Thus, daily work using paper and pencil, computer printouts, projects completed or ongoing, and construction endeavours should be there for parents to see. Questions may be raised about how well the pupil is doing at any point in the ongoing unit of study.
3. Questions to be answered and problems to be discussed must emphasize politeness and consideration for others. There should be a "we-ness" in the conversation, not an "I-ness." *We* want to work together for the good of the child in mathematics instruction.
4. There needs to be an agreement as to what should done to assist the pupil to achieve at as an optimal rate as possible. Details should be spelled out as to how the parents can specifically help pupils in mathematics, if a second parent/teacher conference is held later in spring, comparisons may be made of the pupils achievement at the first as compared to the second conference. Definite achievement towards goals should be in evidence.
5. The more evidence that can be shown as to what a child has learned the more objective the results will be. The teacher needs to thank the parent for coming to the conference and invite future visitations and conferences. There should be an open door in having parents come to school.
6. The teacher should learn as much as possible about the child and his/her parents so that aspirations of the latter are held in high esteem, providing these are positive (Ediger, 1998).

The about six steps should be kept flexible and not as absolutes. Modifications should be made as the need arises. Teacher education classes should stress working with parents as a three semester hour class. The education literature abounds with articles involving parents in the school setting. There can be profitable as well as unprofitable situations involving parents in the school arena. Ways of positive involvement of parents in the schools should be emphasized so that teachers truly receive the cooperation and help that is deemed desirable.

There should be additional times that parents are definitely invited to school, in addition to parent teacher conferences as well as informally to visit the school setting and the child's classroom. Open house during late September is an ideal time for parents to meet the teacher. It might well be that the time here is too short for a thorough parent/teacher conference. At open house, the teacher may meet the parents of the child being taught. As much time as possible should be spent in talking about the child's progress to parents. Comments made should always be positive and friendly. The teacher is there to help and assist the child to do well in mathematics. Concerns of parents for children should be voiced openly. The principal of the school should introduce each teacher to parents at the introductory session of the open house. Refreshments need to be available to make for informality and cordiality at the open house. Every attempt should be made to have parents visit with the teacher of their child. Feelings of welcome and assistance for teaching children should be felt at open house. More optimal achievement of each pupil should be an end result (Ediger, 1997).

Parent/Teacher Organisation Meetings

Parent/teacher organisation meetings (PTO) are generally held monthly throughout the school year. These meetings provide opportunities for the parents to talk with to the teacher about the offspring's progress in school. Here, the teacher, in the limited time available, may discuss the child's progress in mathematics as well as things that parents may do to advance achievement in mathematics of the involved child.

It is important for each pupil to have a role in performing in a PTO meeting during the regular school year. The role need not be a major one, but it should provide the opportunity from the pupil to be recognized. Esteem or recognition needs should be met for each pupil. I have observed pupils being in roles such as the following in PTO meetings:

1. Telling about what was studied recently in mathematics and how the knowledge and skills may be used.
2. Showing mathematical models constructed in an ongoing unit of study by the committee.
3. Doing a team dramatization on a functional experience in mathematics.
4. Indicating how a mathematical problem was identified and solved in a collaborative setting.
5. Singing a chant, involving kindergarten children, when counting numbers are used in jumping rope.

6. Indicating and showing a completed art project pertaining to multiplication and division of fractions.
7. Revealing skills in computer use pertaining to simulation experiences in mathematics.
8. Writing experiences shown in emphasizing journal entries that relate to a present day unit being studied in mathematics.
9. Presenting oral book reports on mathematics library books.
10. Using a video-tape to show a classroom in action in mathematics instruction.

There are very valuable topics that speakers may cover on the teaching of mathematics at parent/teacher conferences. The following topics have been covered with parental questions as these have arisen during the presentation at PTO meetings:

1. Objectives of mathematics instruction.
2. Variety in learning opportunities used to provide for individual differences.
3. Evaluation procedures used to determine achievement in mathematics.
4. Peer learning in mathematics.
5. Learning by discovery and problem solving.
6. Reasoning and logical thinking in mathematics.
7. A hands on approach in teaching mathematics.
8. Innovations in teaching mathematics.
9. Integrating mathematics with other academic areas.
10. Team and collaborative learning in mathematics (Ediger, 1996).

Each presentation given at a PTO meeting should be brief and to the point. Salient ideas, only, should be presented. A clear speaking voice should be used with proper stress, pitch, and juncture. Objects and illustrations should be used where applicable. Presentations are aimed at the audience in which they may ask questions as needed.

The Learning Environment in Mathematics

Teachers and administrators need to think of ways to help children begin a new school year in a successful manner. For early primary grade pupils, in particular, it is important for learners to experience success and interest on the first days of school. The school environment should emphasize accepting of learners and caring for others. How might pupils learn to care for others? The objective of caring for others should be started early in the home setting. We will discuss how pupils may care for each other in the mathematics curriculum.

1. Learners need to assist each other to complete assignments in mathematics. Early in the primary grades, public should learn to communicate clearly and concisely to assist others in understanding and attaching meaning to ongoing assignments. Pupils should also help each other at enrichment centers so that quality sequence in learning is in evidence. If pupils do not understand a new process in mathematics, the new learnings may lack order or sequence. This hinders pupils in attaching meaning and understanding to attain relevant objectives in mathematics. By assisting others, a pupil has opportunities to review what was acquired previously as well as to notice if there are personal gaps in understanding facts, concepts, and generalizations in mathematics.
2. A pupil may read, orally, word problems in mathematics as others follow along in their textbooks. Those who have problems with word recognition and identification when reading word problems are helped here in reading as well as in problem solving in mathematics.
3. A learner may befriend a child who is an isolate and not doing well in mathematics. Sometimes, an individual does better in mathematics achievement when *belonging* needs are met and the former isolate feels he/she is a member of a group.
4. When unwholesome disagreements occur in collaborative endeavours, a pupil may assist in getting the group to work successfully on the problem area encountered in mathematics.
5. A pupil volunteers to orally record on cassette tapes so that those who do not comprehend well due to reading problems may follow along in their own textbooks as the recorded voice proceeds.

Each pupil has much worth and may need assistance at intervals in doing well in mathematics. It is important for a pupil to have his/her own mathematics curriculum to achieve as optimally as possible. There are times, too, when caring for others becomes important. Society depends upon individuals who care for each other in many ways. Otherwise human beings could not survive as a civilization. Achievement in learning, too, depends upon caring people who accept each other and assist others to do as well as possible in mathematics as well as in other subject matter areas.

Parents need to know the latest trends in teaching mathematics. Thus, parents in the home setting have a better chance to understand how to assist their children in learning to achieve vital objectives in mathematics.

A difficult task for numerous teachers, principals, and supervisors is to work effectively with parents. Certainly, the home and school need to work together to develop a quality mathematics curriculum for each pupil. If the home and school are at loggerheads pertaining to what and how pupils should learn, achievement for learners cannot be optimal. There needs to be flexible agreement upon objectives, learning opportunities, and evaluation procedures between the home and the school so that learners individually may achieve as much as possible. Open and amiable communication must be in the offing (Ediger, *School Science*, 1998).

The Psychology of Learning

An interesting learning environment needs to be in the offing so that pupils may learn vicariously from it. The bulletin board display may be used vicariously as well as for direct teaching. A mathematics environment should permeate the school setting to encourage pupil learning. When supervising student teachers and cooperating teachers in the public schools, one of us noticed a fascinating bulletin board display. Display related to the ongoing lesson/unit of study and was entitled, "Measuring in Square Units." There were one inch squares neatly tacked on to the side, and pupils were to determine how many one inch squares there were in a rectangle which was four inches long and three inches wide. The separate one inch squares could be used to determine the asked for area. Additional dimensions were given for the sizes of rectangles and learners were to determine the number of square units within each. Pupils could work individually or collaboratively in coming up with solutions. The bulletin board display emphasized pupils learning vicariously; however, almost all pupils in the classroom desired to work on finding the asked for answers.

In addition to the bulletin board display, there also was an enrichment center for pupils to learn from on their very own. Cup, pint, quart, and gallon containers were located at this center. Pupils might then find out in using sand, at the center, how many cups go into a pint or how many pints make a quart. The information was recorded on a chart nearby. There was much enthusiasm at the bulletin board display and at the enrichment center.

Bulletin board displays should capture pupil interest and attention. Thus, there is something to learn from when viewing the bulletin board contents. Enrichment centers should have fascinating materials for teaching mathematics. These materials need to be manipulated freely by pupils in an inviting atmosphere.

Pupils have a better chance of understanding what has been taught if concrete materials (realia, physical objects, and items) are used to clarify abstract learnings (numbers, numerals, and symbols). Thus, if meaning is attached to what has been learned, pupils might then attach understanding to ongoing activities and experiences.

Learners should have ample opportunities to practice what has been learn. The practice might involve problem solving. Through problem solving, pupils use what has been learned. With application, pupils truly can apply that which has been learned. Drill may be needed, at times, to fix addition, subtraction, multiplication, and division facts in the minds of pupils. But, this should be done only if pupils understand and attach meaning to ongoing learning opportunities involving these facts.

Pupils should feel that purpose is involved in learning. Thus, there are reasons for achieving each and every objective deemed salient in the mathematics curriculum. The teacher may explain the purpose to involved learners. The explanation should be brief and understandable to pupils. An inductive procedure might be used to vary methods used to have pupils perceive reasons for learning in mathematics. Here, the teacher needs to raise questions of pupils in terms of the worth perceived in the new content or skills to be attained. There are teachers who use extrinsic rewards to motivates pupils in the new lesson or unit. Thus, the teacher explains to pupils what needs to be achieved in order that a reward may be received. The award needs to be seen clearly by pupils in order to motivate achievement in mathematics. What pupils need to learn in order to obtain a reward needs to be explained with clarity so that pupils know with certainty what is to be learned. Extrinsic rewards are advocated by behaviourists as a means of stimulating pupils to achieve and attain more optimally in mathematics and other curriculum areas. Thus, prior to instruction, as an example, the mathematics teacher announces to pupils that if nine out of ten basic numbers pairs in addition are answered correctly, each will receive three M and M's. To receive the M and M's, pupils need to answer correctly nine out of ten basic number pairs in addition, as a minimum level of achievement.

We personally advocate that pupils feel motivated from within or intrinsically, rather that extrinsically. With mathematics teachers being well prepared for each day for teaching, pupils see this as a model to follow in that mathematics is important to learn. With careful planning, the teacher has in mind a certain order or sequence of learning opportunities for children to be successful in learning. Using a variety of fascinating learning opportunities on their understanding level assists pupils to become actively involved to learn in ongoing lessons and units of study. Evaluation of pupil achievement should result in using the data to improve instruction in mathematics. The teacher needs to obtain feedback from pupils to ascertain what should come next sequentially in instruction. Diagnosis of pupil achievement should result in remediation efforts in order that each pupil makes continuous progress in mathematics.

When teachers use the psychology of learning in teaching mathematics, it provides a model for parents to use in providing help at home to their offspring in the area of mathematics instruction. Parents also need to assist their children by having them perceive interest, purpose, meaning, and application in a hands on approach in learning mathematics. An open door policy needs to be in evidence whereby parents are truly invited to come to school and observe teaching during National Education Week as well as at other times during the ensuring school year (Ediger, *Education*, 541-548).

Teacher Education

The teacher education course should involve students actually working with parents in assisting the latter's offspring to achieve more optimally. The evaluation of working with parents should involve assessing if the child does better in mathematics as a result of teacher/parent interaction. Parents and teachers working together should not be merely for the sake of doing so, but rather to help children achieve at a higher level due to these conferences. Thus, in teacher education, the university student should engage in real experiences with parents. To be sure, students need to possess readiness in the three semester hour class in working with parents. Students should learn how to conduct parent/teacher conferences, as well as meet parents at open house, at parent's night, and at PTO meetings. Definite guidelines need to be in evidence for interacting with parents. Problems need to be identified in readiness experiences when teachers work with parents. The results should be positive, but as is true of many things, negative occurrences happen. Remediation of problem areas in these conferences need to be discussed in the teacher education class involving working with parents. The above readiness activities need to be studied involving students with professor assistance in a course which may be entitled "Working with Parents and the Child." The readiness facets of the course in teacher education must be followed by direct experiences in working with parents in diverse settings and situations. A major objective here is for the teacher to learn to be polite and accepting of parents in all situations. Teaching involves caring and nurturing children to achieve in mathematics and in all curriculum areas. What needs to be present as elements in a student teacher/parent interaction?

1. Have evidence available of pupil products in mathematics to discuss with parents.
2. Display pupil work in mathematics such as book reports on mathematics content, completed assignments, printouts from the word processor on word problems solved by learners, art and construction projects ongoing or completed by pupils, and show videotapes of pupils at work individually or in a committee in using hands on approaches in learning in mathematics.
3. Discuss problems faced by the pupil in mathematics with the parent.
4. Detail what the parent(s) can do to assist the learner to achieve more optimally in mathematics. It is important to agree upon a plan of action. Results recorded from later parent/teacher conferences may be compared with earlier ones to notice progress made by the pupil.
5. Conduct the conference in an atmosphere of respect and trust. Hostile statements and remarks have no role to play in a quality parent/teacher conference. Show a caring attitude toward the pupil's progress and toward his/her parents.
6. Be well prepared for the conference and adhere to time limits, if others also have come for a scheduled parent/teacher conference.
7. Get to know the goals parents have for their offspring. It is salient to notice how parents feel toward their child. The teacher should also notice what benefits the parents are able to provide for the child such as instrumental and vocal lessons as well as tutoring after school.
8. Observe if parents expect too much of the child as well as too little in terms of achievement in mathematics. Some parents have said they did not do well in mathematics and do not expect their offspring to achieve.

There should be an ample opportunities for university students to be involved in mock parent/teacher conferences as well as in actual situations. A framework needs to exist in conducting these conferences and we suggest using the above eight standards, as needed. Teachers and principals may serve as model parents in mock conferences. We have also observed where parents are willing to donate time for these simulations. Each conference should be evaluated in terms of desired criteria.

We have used both cooperating teacher/student teacher and ourselves, as supervisors, in cooperatively evaluating student teacher performance in the internship. We have also observed parent/teacher conferences with pupil involvement. These seem to work satisfactorily in most cases. Individual differences are involved here and selected pupils may not contribute positively in the parent/teacher conference.

In addition to assisting pupils with homework, there are numerous other approaches which parents may use to guide learner progress in mathematics:

1. Reading library books orally to pupils that contain content dealing with mathematics. For those who read well, these kinds of library books should be available for pupil reading in school and also in the home setting.
2. Taking pupils to the public library to check out books that have fascinating and interesting content on mathematics.
3. Assisting pupils who have difficulty in reading word problems as well as with abstract symbols and notation.
4. Taking pupils to the supermarket, or other kinds of stores, to notice prices of objects purchased, the total price, and the computer printout of the sale.
5. Letting pupils be actively involved in measuring ingredients that go into the making of a soup dish or other kind of food.
6. Parents realizing that the pupil needs to do the learning. Ready made answers to homework may not assist pupils in learning. Assistance given as needed is different than giving answers to pupils immediately in word recognition and drill/practice situations in mathematics. Pupils needs to become as independent as possible and lean upon the self in mathematics achievement.
7. Involving pupils in learning the cost of selection of an item, such as replacing a carpet in the home setting.
8. Implementing quality sequence in mathematics lessons and units of study tailored to the individual pupil is a key item in instruction. Teachers and parents need to study the concept of "sequence" to assist a pupil in developing sequential leanings in order to achieve as optimally as possible.

There are pupils who need to work very hard in mathematics to do well. Even then, diagnosis and remediation may be an end result. Pupils grow up in unfortunate home situations with abounding poverty. There may be crime ridden areas with mice and rats in the home and in the neighbourhood of these pupils. If pupils do poorly in mathematics after twelve years of schooling, the following questions need to be raised:

1. Did the involved pupil not try or was poor quality teaching involved.
2. Did parents assist the pupil in any way with homework? Was there encouragement for the learner from either parent?
3. What kind of home life did the pupil have?
4. Did the pupil miss many school days? Missing school days or being tardy frequently hinders the pupil from making sequential progress.
5. Why did the learner not learn mathematics on his/her own when it is so functional in society?

Teachers need to discuss ways of impressing pupils upon doing their utmost continuously to achieve well in mathematics. Time wasted by the learner cannot make for continuous progress. The pupils needs to take each day of instruction in mathematics seriously. There is much to learn in mathematics and in other curriculum areas. Pupils need to discipline themselves to achieve as well as possible. Parents need to set an example whereby the learner is motivated to achieve, grow, and learn. Among other things, parents need to indicate the many practical uses that can be made of mathematics. They should encourage the pupil to learn as much as possible. Never should the curriculum area of mathematics be minimized in the home setting, but rather it is a basic and is the third R in "reading, writing and arithmetic." Proficiency in mathematics is essential for successful living presently as well as at the work place. We live in a world of numbers whereby so many items are expressed numerically such as the goods and services purchased, checkbook balances, bank statements, allowances received and spent by children, page numbers in printed materials, and materials ordered from companies, among others.

Human Relations in the Mathematics Curriculum

The mathematics teacher needs to stress good human relations in the school setting. Why? Pupils very often work collaboratively on mathematics problems to be solved. Unless pupils respect and accept each other, there is little chance of committee work having positive effects upon learners. Teachers, too, need to work harmoniously with each other so that ideas for teaching mathematics are discussed and appraised. Teachers need to learn from each other in ways of improving instruction in mathematics. Parents need to be accepted as parents in mathematics education so that their offspring achieves as well as possible. We wish there were a two way street of acceptance in educating children between teachers and pupils, parents and teachers, teachers and teachers, and school administrators and teachers. If parents, for example are rude and crude, the teacher still needs to be polite and accepting of the child as well as of each parent. It would be better if all parents were kind and polite in dealings with the mathematics teacher. Let us look at some guidelines for the mathematics teacher to use in working with others in the school and societal setting:

1. Be a caring person who desires the best for each pupil in the mathematics curriculum.
2. Be a promoter in stressing quality mathematics instruction for all learners.
3. Be highly knowledgeable about mathematics content, skills, and attitude that pupils need to attain.
4. Be proficient in communicating ideas to others be it orally or in writing.
5. Be patient in dealing with human beings.

I believe good human relations and mathematics achievement for pupils being one, not separate categories.

In Conclusion

There are many avenues available for teachers and parents working together for the good of the child in mathematics achievement. These include the following:

1. Having quality parent/the conferences.
2. Meeting parents at PTO meetings.
3. Initiating an introduction to the New School Year time with parents.
4. Implementing an invigorating *Introduction to the New School Year* meeting.
5. Using the psychology of learning from educational psychology for parents to model in assisting offspring with homework.
6. Trying to initiate parental education classes in Teacher Education programs at colleges and universities.
7. Integrating human relations and curricular improvement into teaching and learning situations.

The concept of parent involvement is interrelated with parent and teacher efficacy/involvement. Parental efficacy of self image, locus of control, developmental status, and interpersonal support are linked in more effective parent involvement. Specific strategies in the areas of communication, shared learning, and guidance are specified as ways to nurture parental efficacy and strengthen parent-teacher relations (Swick and Broadway, 1997).

REFERENCES

Buday, Mary Catherine, and James A Kelley, "National Board Certification and the Teaching Profession's Commitment to Quality Assurance," *Phi Delta Kappan*, 78 (3), 215-219.

Ediger, Marlow (1998), "The Teacher, Reading, and Parents," *Teaching Reading Successfully in the Elementary School*. Kirksville Missouri: Simpson Publishing Company, 231-232.

Ediger, Marlow (1997), *Teaching Mathematics in the Elementary School*. Kirksville, Missouri: Simpson Publishing Company 18-19.

Ediger, Marlow (1996), "Goals in the Mathematics Curriculum," *Elementary Education*. Kirksville, Missouri: Simpson Publishing Company, 156-164.

Ediger, Marlow (1997), "Psychology in Teaching Mathematics," *School Science*, 35 (1), 1-14.

Ediger, Marlow (1998), "Philosophy of Teaching Mathematics, *School Science*, 36 (1), 39-53.

Ediger, Marlow (1998), "Change and the School Administrator," *Education*, 118 (4), 541-548.

Ediger, Marlow and D. Bhaskara Rao (2000), *Teaching Mathematics Successfully*. New Delhi: Discovery Publishing House.

Swick, Karen J., and Francis Broadway (1997), "Parental Efficacy and Successful Parental Involvement, *Journal of Instructional Psychology*, 24 (1), 69.

45

The Guidance Counselor and the Mathematics Curriculum

The guidance counselor is a vital person to involve in developing and improving the curriculum. With high stakes testing in the offing for students in 49 states, there is much coercion in having students do well in state mandated tests. Recent trends in state mandated testing have included the following:

1. Paying teachers salaries or bonuses based on student achievement in test results.
2. Rewarding schools financially whose students meet state standards through test results in academic achievement.
3. Having students receive high school diplomas who pass the exit exams of the state.

In the state of Georgia, the Governor is turning up the heat on school to show high academic achievement on test results. Results from the last state mandated criterion referenced test revealed that 35 per cent of the 4th graders did not meet state standards in reading and almost half of the eighth graders did not meet the standards in mathematics (See Education Week, May 2, 2001). Many other states have similar test results whereby a high number of students do not meet state standards in terms of test results.

Reading achievement, the first "r", cuts across all curriculum areas, including mathematics instruction. Writing, the 2nd "r", also is inherent and important in each curriculum area. Arithmetic (the 3rd "r" in reading, writing and arithmetic) is a strong member of the basics consisting of the 3rs.

With pressures for more optimal student achievement in school, the guidance counselor is in a good position to assist teachers to guide learners to achieve more optimally in the academics, as well as develop ways of coping with pressures to achieve and to attain. The purpose of this paper is indicate approaches for guidance counselors to use in assisting teachers to guide optimal student achievement in mathematics (See Ediger and Rao, 2000, Chapter Thirteen).

The Guidance Counselor and the Mathematics Curriculum

Many referrals by teachers of students to the guidance counselor involve academic problems. Discipline problems also may actually be masked in difficulties faced by students in the academic arenas. Mathematics is vital for each student to do well in since the subject matter therein is useful in school and in society. It is salient for students to be able to use mathematics in every day situations when buying and selling goods and services. Thus, mathematics is a very practical curriculum area which has high utilitarian values in the societal arena (Ediger, 1993, 7-12). Why do students have difficulties in achieving well in the mathematics curriculum? The guidance counselor may provide much assistance to teachers in making the needed diagnosis pertaining to the following problems areas:

1. Students lack interest in mathematics. If interest is lacking, the guidance counselor may discuss with teachers how to develop and maintain learner interests in mathematics (Ediger, 1993, 24-25). A variety of teaching materials should be used so that each student may be actively engaged in teaching and learning situations. Thus, concrete (objects and items), semi-concrete (illustrations, CD ROMS, filmstrips, films, video-tapes, place value charts, fraction charts, among others), and abstract (basal textbooks, workbooks, worksheets, chalkboard examples, word processor activities, software, and diagrams, among others) materials of instruction need to be used in teaching students. A workshop may be necessary here to assist teachers to use a variety of teaching material in the mathematics curriculum. The guidance counselor needs to take leadership role in working toward improving the curriculum through the workshop method. Problems faced by learners may well become a part of the workshop agenda to improve mathematics instruction.
2. Students lack purpose for learning. Here, the guidance counselor may guide teachers to help students perceive reasons or purpose for learning. Teachers then may use a few sentences to introduce an objective by stating why students need to learn selected subject matter in the ongoing lesson. A deductive procedure is used here in having students perceive

purpose or reasons for learning. A different approach would be to ask students why the content in the new lesson is relevant to learn. An inductive approach is being emphasized in this case. Taking time to stress purpose for learning is time spent well indeed. The guidance counselor may well play a vital role in assisting teachers to understand the importance of student purpose in learning and achieving.

3. Students do not attach meaning to ongoing subject matter being taught. Student then need to understand what is being learned in mathematics. Meaning theory is certainly of utmost importance in teaching and learning situations. Careful monitoring of the student's ongoing activities might well reveal what an individual does not understand. Depth teaching then is needed to help students understand the underlying principles involved in addition, for example. A student who does not understand the meaning of 6 + 3 = 9 may well need concrete experiences to show a set of 6 sticks and a set of 3 sticks. The two sets of sticks of markers then need to be combined to show a set of nine. Each set of concrete markers needs to be counted rationally with one to one correspondence so that understanding of addition is revealed. The chances are that a student who does not understand foundational learnings of the basic addition facts will later on have difficulties with more complex understandings. The teacher then needs to take time in depth teaching to stress meaning in ongoing learning opportunities. The guidance counselor is a necessary professional to take a lead in stressing with teachers the importance of assisting students to understand that which has been learned.

4. Students cannot show what has been learned in a unique way. There are a plethora of ways which students may use to indicate what has been learned. One ways is to use abstract numerals to reveal learnings obtained. Thus reality may be shown through writing in abstract numerals a selected value such as 6 + 3 = 9. Additional ways are the following:
   - *(a)* To make a drawing of the abstract such as six cats and three cats to indicate a combined set of nine in pictorial form.
   - *(b)* To dramatize a set of six children and three children coming to the front of the classroom and then combining the two sets to make a total of nine.
   - *(c)* To show objects nearby such as six pencils and three pencils having a value of nine when combined.

The guidance counselor is in an excellent position to assist teachers in guiding students to reveal what has been learned, according to their talents and abilities possessed (See Gardner, 1993).

5. Student classroom work is not diagnosed adequately to indicate the kinds of errors made. Once the kinds of errors made have been diagnosed, then remediation needs to be in the offing. If a student then does not answer correctly what six plus three are, the learner and the teacher need to find out why this error occurs. The following are possibilities:
   - *(a)* The student has difficulties in counting a set of six and/ or a set of three. The student may also not be able to join the two sets together to make a set of nine.
   - *(b)* The student cannot associate the abstract numerals with the concrete or semi-concrete markets.

Very early in the school life of the child, the teacher needs to diagnose and remedy problems faced by students in mathematics. This will prevent difficulties from arising in the future when addition, subtraction, multiplication, and division can become very complex or when geometry, algebra, and trigonometry become the curriculum in mathematics. The guidance counselor needs to impress upon teachers the need for continual diagnosis and remediation in mathematics (Ediger and Rao, 2000, Chapter Nine).

Reading in Mathematics

Sometimes mathematics has become a reading course. It is true that students do need to engage in much reading such as numerals, operations symbols (+, –, x, and divide) as well as content in word problems. However, mathematics education goes beyond being a reading class. Thus students need to engage in higher levels of thinking in mathematics such as in the following:

1. Critical thinking. Here, the learner must learn to separate the salient from the unimportant. Thus, in solving a word problem in mathematics the learner needs to sort out what will solve the problem from what will not do the job. Justification needs to be in the offing for selecting the necessary information. Sometimes, too, irrelevant information is put into a word problem to notice if a student is truly a good critical thinker.
2. Creative thinking. The learner needs to develop and possess a creative mind in which novel, unique ideas are considered. "Tried and true" ideas may not work. Originality is then needed. Creativity is always a good trait for individuals to possess in mathematics as well as in life itself!
3. Problem Solving. The student needs to be good problem solver in mathematics as well as solve problems in life's endeavours. To solve problems in mathematics, the learner with teacher

guidance needs to identify the problem with clarity, gather necessary information to use in solving the problem, develop an hypothesis or answer to the problem, and evaluate the correctness of the hypothesis.

4. Applying that which has been learned. Students need to make application of learnings acquired. A student who can use knowledge acquired in mathematics can apply school learnings in mathematics to everyday situations in life involving the use of number and mathematics in general.
5. Logical thought. Mathematics as a curriculum area certainly does make use of logical thinking. The if-then procedure of thought is used frequently such as "if A is larger than B, and B is larger than C, *therefore* A is larger than C." Logical reasoning is needed and necessary in ongoing lessons and units of study in mathematics as well as in the societal arena (Ediger, 1986, 27-29).

The guidance counselor is in a good position to be a leader in providing inservice education for teachers in order that students in the latter's care do engage in higher levels of cognition. Why should students participate in critical and creative thinking, problem solving making application of that which has been learned, as well as in logical thought? These levels of thinking are important in mathematics, but also in daily life's situations. Students are more likely to be able to cope with and live in a complex world when being abler to think things through and solve the many dilemmas that exist. The Educational Policies Commission (1962) of the National Education Association deliberated on the one major objective of education that would cut cross all curriculum areas and also be important is life and living. What was this objective? Developing within students the ability to think.

Providing for Individual Differences

Teachers should always provide for individual differences among students in the classroom. Why? Learners differ much from each other in many ways such as abilities, achievement, aptitude, interests, and purposes. Thus a developmental curriculum in mathematics needs to be in the offing for students. Objectives for students to achieve may then be achieved by learners at different rates of speed. Thus, selected students will need more time to achieve an objective as compared to others. Or different learning opportunities may need to be provided for particular students due to having diverse styles of learning. Searson and Dunn (2001), from their research, have indicated the following to be salient when providing for different styles of student learning:

1. Acceptable noise levels temperature readings, and informal versus formal seating arrangements.
2. Emotional elements such as conformity versus nonconformity, as well as preferences for structure versus choices in terms of what to learn.
3. Sociological factors such as studying alone or with others as well as preferring collegial versus a more authoritarian teacher.
4. Physiological factors such as using auditory, tactual, and/or kinesthetic ways of learning. Included too are moving around the room or sitting still as well as eating versus not eating while concentrating on the task involved.
5. Psychological factors such as analytic learners who focus on facts in a step by step fashion which lead to an understanding, as compared to global learners who desire to understand how what is to be learned relates to themselves before focusing on facts. Analytic students respond best to printed words whereas global learners respond better to pictures and illustrations.

There certainly is much that learning styles theory has to offer in terms of providing for individual differences. For example in #2 above, there are students who prefer structure in mathematics learning such as assigned work to be completed, whereas others prefer open ended choices such as in learning centers when choosing sequentially what to complete from among alternatives. Also, #3 above stresses the importance of students wishing to work by the self as compared to working with others in cooperative learning. The guidance counselor then needs to impress upon teachers that selected students do better in mathematics when working on assigned work as compared to wanting to choose what to learn from among alternative options, as well as those who desire to work individually on assignments as compared to those who like to work within committees when engaging in achieving objectives of instruction.

In Conclusion

The guidance counselor has salient responsibilities in working toward curriculum improvement. It is necessary to work toward an improved curriculum since it will assist students to develop a better self concept and be able to solve personal and social problems more effectively. Mathematical objectives emphasize numerous goals that cut across the entire curriculum. Thus, students need to reflect upon concepts and generalizations achieved. Ideas need to be communicated between and among peers and the teacher. An appreciation for the orderliness and patterns in mathematics should be a salient end result in achieving objectives of instruction. Reading, writing, listening, and speaking skills are vital to achieve in mathematics as well as in all curriculum areas. Guidance counselors need to work effectively with teachers too provide the best curriculum possible for each learner.

REFERENCES

Ediger, Marlow (1993), "Perspectives in Counseling," *Manitoba Journal of Counseling*. 19 (4), 24-25.

Ediger, Marlow (1993), "The Innovative Mathematics Curriculum," *Menemui Matematik*, 15 (1), 7-12. 27-29. Published by the Malaysian Mathematical Society.

Ediger, Marlow (1986), "La Resolution De Problemes Dans Le Program de Mathematique," *Instantanes Mathematiques*, 23 (2), 27-29. Published by The Quebec, Canada, Mathematics Society.

Ediger, Marlow, and D. Bhaskara Rao (2000), *Teaching Mathematics Successfully*. New Delhi, India: Discovery Publishing House, Chapter Nine.

Ediger, Marlow and D. Bhaskara Rao (2000), *Teaching Reading Successfully*. New Delhi, India: Discovery Publishing House, Chapter Thirteen.

Education Week (May 2, 2001), "Georgia Governor Acts Fast To Turn Up the Heat on Schools," p. 8.

Educational Policies Commission (1962), *The Central Purpose of American Education*. Washington, DC: The National Education Association.

Gardner, Howard (1993), *Multiple Intelligences: Theory into Practice*. New York: Basic Books.

Searson, Robert, and Rita Dunn (2001), "The Learning Styles Teaching Model," *Science and Children*, 38 (5), 22-26.

46

Evaluating Achievement in Mathematics

Pupil achievement in mathematics must be appraised in terms of objectives in ongoing units of study. In teaching-learning situations the teacher must select objectives carefully which learners are to attain. Secondly, learning activities must be chosen which guide pupils in achieving desired ends. Finally, the teacher must appraise pupils progress in terms of stated objectives.

Using Teacher Observation

The teacher through careful observation may evaluate pupil achievement. The teacher observers traits such as the following in the area of achievement in elementary school mathematics:

1. Pupils completing assigned work on time.
2. Interest learners reveal in mathematics.
3. Continuous progress made by pupils.
4. Specific errors pupils make in mathematics.
5. Pupils understanding new learnings.
6. Additional practice learners need in understanding a new process in mathematics.
7. How to group pupils for instruction.
8. The learning styles of individual pupils.

Thus, the classroom teacher can evaluate many facets of pupil achievement in mathematics using the technique of teacher observation.

Using Checklists

The classroom teacher may wish to utilize checklists to appraise pupil performance in mathematics. Many of the teacher's observations are forgotten unless recorded. With the use of a checklist the observations of the teacher can be recorded for each learner. The teacher in developing a checklist must write out the behaviours that learners are to be appraised in. The following is an example of a checklist containing relevant behaviours in a specific ongoing unit of study:

Name of pupil____________________Date__________

1. The pupil satisfactorily adds two one-digit addends.
2. The learner reproduces with markers values of two single-digit addends.
3. The pupil appears to enjoy working on addition problems containing two one-digit addends.
4. The learner is becoming increasingly independent in his/her school work.

The teacher should write the pupil's name and the date of appraisal on each checklist. Thus, the teacher notices specific weaknesses learners exhibit in an ongoing unit of study and attempts to remedy these deficiencies. Comparisons may be made of each learner's progress from past times to the present when checklist are used.

Using Teacher Made Tests

Teacher-made tests may be utilized to appraise pupil performance in the mathematics curriculum. Teacher-made tests should be valid. Thus, the test will attempt to measure what pupils have had opportunities to learn during class sessions devoted to mathematics instruction. The test should also be reliable. For example, if pupils took the same teacher-made test over again, results should be comparable from the first time to the second time. This would be true if circumstances were equivalent in taking the teacher-made test the second time. Consistency of results is important when thinking of the concept of reliability in testing.

The following are examples of terms which may be included in a teacher-made test providing pupils have opportunities to engage in previous practice of these learnings:

1. Simple computation of two one-digit addends — 9 + 5 = —, 8 + 7 = —, 4 + 8 = —, 5 + 9 = —, 7 + 8 = —, and 8 + 4 = —.
2. Word problems involving computations studied previously—John had nine marbles; he bought five more. How many marbles does he now have?
3. Multiple choice items — Which of the following is not true:
   (a) 17 + 18 = 18 + 17 *(b)* 35 – 17 = 35 – 18
   (c) 35 – 17 = 18 *(d)* 35 – 18 = 17

Teacher written test items must follow criteria recommended by specialists in the area of testing and measuring of pupil progress. Test items written by the teacher must be:

1. Valid and reliable.
2. Clearly written.
3. On the understanding level of pupils.
4. Properly ordered for pupils in ascending order of difficulty.

Essay items may also be written by the teacher to appraise pupil achievement in elementary school mathematics. Essay tests should only be utilized as an appraisal technique if

1. Pupils have an adequately developed writing vocabulary.
2. Learners possess an adequate reading vocabulary to comprehend the content of the test items.
3. Pupils have had ample learning experiences to respond effectively to essay items in the test.
4. The items are properly delimited and yet do not require factual recall of information. For example, an essay item requiring the following response would be too broad—Discuss mathematics. Certainly, the pupil is entitled to know what facet of mathematics learning he/she is to respond to. The following would be too narrow in scope to be called an essay item—Write a definition for the term "sum" as used in addition. Essay items should reflect pupils' skills in problem solving: How does knowledge of the distributive property of multiplication over addition help in solving related problems in mathematics?
5. Pupils can be evaluated in terms of selecting and organising major ideas when developing desired responses to the test question. The teacher may also wish to evaluate pupils in terms of the mechanics or writing such as
   (a) Spelling and handwriting.
   (b) Capitalization and punctuation.
   (c) Grammar and usage.

It is recommended by the writer that the mechanics of writing be assessed separately from ideas expressed by learners when responding to different essay items. Pupils, of course, can work on remedying a few deficiencies in the mechanics of writing at a given time. Objectives that pupils are to achieve should be attainable and not overwhelming.

Using Standardized Tests

Standardized tests which are valid and reliable may be utilized periodically to appraise pupil achievement in mathematics. Pupils' results from taking of standardized tests need to be evaluated in terms of the following questions:

1. Did the learner respond correctly to important concepts or word problems? If not, what remedial measures would be important to remedy identified deficiencies?

2. Were errors made in the area of computation? If so, specifically which kinds of errors were made? What provisions need to be made to correct these deficiencies on the part of learners?
3. Did it appear that pupils were interested and properly motivated in taking the test?

Pupils' results from standardized tests will generally be given in terms of the following results:

1. Grade equivalent score. For example, a pupil in the beginning of the fourth grade may obtain a raw score equivalent to the 5.7 grade level. A different fourth grade pupil may be achieving on the 2.9 grade level as indicated by results from the standardized test. Regardless of the present grade level of the pupil, the raw score obtained by learners from taking the standardized test is converted to a grade equivalent as indicated in the manual for administering the test.
2. Percentile ranks. A pupil, for example, in the fourth grade may have obtained a raw score of 65 (number of items responded to correctly) on a standardized mathematics test which is equivalent to the 45th percentile according to the manual for administering the test. Being on the 45th percentile would indicate that 45 per cent of the pupils on the fourth grade level would score lower on the test than the previously named pupil. Fifty-five per cent of the fourth graders taking the same standardized mathematics test would score higher. The 45 per cent and the 55 per cent figures mentioned previously would pertain to pupils whose test results were utilized as norms in developing the standardized test.

In utilizing standardized achievement tests to appraise pupil achievement in mathematics, the following facets of pupil growth are generally evaluated:

1. Computation in arithmetic. Thus, pupils respond to test items involving addition, subtraction, multiplication, and division.
2. Concepts in mathematics. The standardized test in mathematics may contain items pertaining to *(a)* the meaning of fractions, *(b)* inverse operations such as subtraction undoing addition, *(c)* place value in decimals, *(d)* the Roman system of numeration, *(e)* number systems, *(f)* estimating, *(g)* understanding place value in counting numbers and *(h)* geometric terms.
3. Word problems. Learners exhibit proficiency in analyzing which facts are needed in a problematic situation to obtain a needed solution.

A family on a vacation traveled 325 miles the first day, 460 miles the second day, and 411 miles the third day. How many miles were traveled in the three days?

In the above problem, learner must glean necessary content, such as adding 325 + 460 + 411, to be able to arrive at the correct answer. Word problems can contain content on different levels of complexity.

Standardized achievement tests provide different results pertaining to pupil's progress as compared to teacher-made tests.

1. The teacher may notice how learners in the class setting compare with pupils in the standardization group as indicated by results from the standardized achievement test. The manual of the standardized achievement test indicates the pupil population utilized in the developing norms for the test. The teacher may compare the achievement of his/her own pupils with that of the group used to develop norms for the standardized achievement test.
2. The teacher may also notice the spread of scores, from high to low, of pupils in the class setting as indicated by results from the standardized achievement test. The spread of scores in the class setting provides needed data to the teacher in providing adequately for each pupil in the mathematics curriculum. Each learner should, of course, be guided to achieve to his/her optimum in elementary school mathematics.
3. Specific kinds of errors that pupils reveal in elementary school mathematics, as indicated by standardized achievement test results, can provide relevant diagnostic data with the end result being to remediate deficiencies.
4. Pupil progress in mathematics may be noted as reliable and valid standardized mathematics achievement tests are given learners at selected intervals.

Using Anecdotal Records

The teacher must record an ample number of observations made about each pupil's achievement in mathematics. It is recommended that observations be recorded of each pupil's progress frequently enough to notice a pattern of behaviour. The teacher of mathematics may notice the following from recorded information (anecdotal records) about a particular child's progress:

1. The learner does not respond accurately to basic addition and subtraction facts, such as 9 + 8 = —, 8 + 9 = —, 17 − 8 = —, and 17 − 9 = —.
2. The pupil is slow in getting started on assigned work in mathematics.
3. The child is easily distracted from working in mathematics by happenings in the elementary school.
4. The pupil seemingly does not enjoy mathematics as much as other curriculum areas in the elementary school.

It is easy for a teacher to forget how each child is progressing in mathematics unless observations are recorded systematically. The recorded items or anecdotal records should be utilized to improve instruction for each child. Viewing the above numbered items, the teacher may remedy deficiencies by *(a)* giving the child meaningful practice in addition and subtraction facts which need mastering, *(b)* guiding the pupil to develop appropriate work study habits, *(c)* attempting to develop a learning environment conductive for pupils making continuous progress, and *(d)* providing interesting, understandable, and purposeful experiences for pupils in elementary school mathematics.

The results of anecdotal records should be utilized to guide pupils to achieve continuous progress in elementary school mathematics. Anecdotal records should not be used *(a)* to defame pupils, *(b)* for gossip purposes, or *(c)* as a threat to involved learners.

Using Work Samples

A manila folder containing work samples of each pupil in mathematics is highly recommendable. Within a manila folder for a particular child, the teacher may save representative samples of a child's work pertaining to elementary school mathematics.

The completed papers should be dated before being placed in the folder. Thus, comparisons can be made by the teacher as well as the pupil of the latter's present as compared to earlier achievement in mathematics? Too frequently, the teacher has felt that a specific child is not achieving well in mathematics until comparisons are made between and among earlier and later work in mathematics.

Pupils should evaluate their own achievement in mathematics using work samples. A child can appraise progress by noticing if he/she is doing better than formerly when comprising results from earlier times to the present. In adapting the mathematics curriculum to the present achievement level of each learner, the pupil individually can take pride in noticing achievement from earlier times to the present when appraising completed products in this curriculum area.

Using Parent-Teacher Conferences

The teacher may obtain valuable feedback from the parent or parents as to understandings, skills, and attitudes pupils have developed in elementary school mathematics. Criteria to follow in conducting parent-teacher conferences include *(a)* respecting the thinking of parents, *(b)* wishing to obtain information about a child's progress in mathematics, *(c)* working together with parents to develop a good mathematics curriculum for each learner, *(d)* using information obtained from parents as to future courses of action pertaining to a relevant mathematics curriculum for each pupil, and *(e)* revealing positive attitudes toward parent-teacher conferences.

Work samples of pupil's completed products in mathematics may be shown and discussed with parents in a conference. Thus, parents have opportunities to notice

(a) The present achievement level of the child.
(b) Kinds of errors made by the individual pupil.
(c) Rate of progress accomplished by an individual child.
(d) Neatness of work revealed by the learner.

Conducting a parent-teacher conference is not an end result in and of itself. The results of a parent-teacher conference should aid in developing a meaningful, purposeful, and interesting mathematics curriculum for each child. Individual differences must be provided for in a modern program of elementary school mathematics.

Using the Tape Recorder

A tape recorder can be wisely used in the class setting to appraise pupil achievement in mathematics. The following, among others, are major ways in which tape recorders may be utilized to appraise pupils performance:

1. Have pupils listen to a playback pertaining to their involvement in a discussion of a new process in elementary school mathematics.
2. Date and file tape recordings of pupil's discussions in learning a new process in elementary school mathematics. Periodically, pupils with teacher guidance may notice growth in mathematics achievement when comparing earlier with later recordings.
3. Have pupils discuss ways to improve the mathematics curriculum. Pupils may listen to a replay of the recording to evaluate criteria given. The teacher may obtain valuable feedback from the recording in terms of content for improving the mathematics curriculum.

Video taping of classroom discussions may well add the visual dimension in appraising student progress.

Diagnosing Pupil's Responses in Mathematics

The teacher must be a good diagnoser of pupil achievement in elementary school mathematics. Thus, the teacher identifies specific kinds of errors that pupils individually are exhibiting. If a pupil, for example, continually responds incorrectly to the sum of 6 + 5, the following reasons may be inherent:

1. The pupil may need to attach meaning to concepts pertaining to a set of six and a set of five. Crayons, beads, chalk, books, and bean and corn seeds, as well as buttons may be utilized to have pupils see and duplicate a set of six markers and a set of five markers. The two sets may then be joined together to form a new set of eleven markers.
2. The learner may need practice in committing the addition fact "6 + 5 = 11" to memory. A variety of experiences should be utilized in providing practice for pupils pertaining to selected learnings in elementary school mathematics. Dull, boring, and routine learning activities are to be avoided.
3. Pupils may even need to work on learnings in elementary school mathematics where they are at a less mature level than what is called for in rational counting. The teacher could help the individual pupil to utilize the concept of one-to-one correspondence when counting six members of a set. The proper counting number as it is said would then correspond with the object being counted in the set consisting of six members, *i.e.*, count "one" as the first object is being touched, "two" for the second object, "three" for the third object, and so forth, until all six members have been counted.

The teacher of elementary school mathematics must analyze specific difficulties that pupils face in ongoing units of study. Only then can remedial efforts be applied to guide pupils to overcome identified problems in the mathematics curriculum.

Using Conferences to Appraise Pupil Progress

The teacher may conduct conferences with elementary school pupils in order to evaluate achievement in mathematics. Criteria to follow in conducting these conferences include the following:

1. Respect the contributions of each pupil.
2. Permit free expression of ideas so that the teacher may obtain feedback from each pupil's thinking about ways to improve the curriculum.
3. Try to determine specific help that pupils need in order to achieve optimal development in mathematics.
4. Agree upon a plan of action to help each pupil achieve relevant understandings, skills, and attitudinal objectives in elementary school mathematics.

After the conference has been completed with a pupil, the teacher should *(a)* briefly record important ideas gained from the learner, and *(b)* determine how ideas gained from the conference can provide input for an improved mathematics curriculum for the involved learner.

The teacher may conduct a conference lasting, approximately, five to ten minutes for a pupil each day. It does not take long before all pupils in the class setting have been involved in a conference. For example, if there are 25 pupils in a class, the first conference could be completed for each pupils in five weeks' period of time. The conference approach can be one method, among others, utilized to appraise learner achievement.

In Summary

There are numerous techniques available to appraise pupil achievement in elementary school mathematics. The teacher must utilize a variety of approaches to assess pupil growth in the mathematics curriculum. Each evaluation technique has its strengths as well as weaknesses. Thus, a specific evaluation technique may be utilized as a check on other approaches to appraisal. Pupil achievement must be assessed in terms of stated relevant understandings, skills, and attitudinal objectives. It is not adequate to appraise pupil growth in terms of understandings objectives only. Pupils must also be assessed in terms of skills objectives. The understandings acquired by learners must be utilized; thus, skills objectives need to be stressed adequately in ongoing units of study in elementary school mathematics. Adequate emphasis also needs to be placed upon pupils achieving attitudinal goals. Desirable attitudes on the part of the learners aid in achieving understandings and skills objectives. A defensible program of evaluation would then stress that pupil achievement be adequately appraised in terms of understandings, skills, and attitudinal objectives.

Marks, Hiatt, and Neufeld wrote:

> Under what conditions can pupils learn most effectively? How can the teacher provide these conditions? Classroom teachers, as well as experts in learning theory, have studied these and similar questions for many years. One important fact that has emerged is that learning conditions must be related to desired outcomes. If information and simple mastery of operations are all that are desired from the mathematics class, then the mechanical learning process of memorize, drill, and test is wholly satisfactory.
>
> The outcomes sought in mathematics classes today are much broader and more significant than is mere mechanical mastery. An important new responsibility of the mathematics teacher is to encourage creativity by helping pupils discover the basic ideas, laws, and principles of mathematics. As a result of this focus on understanding as well as mastery of skills, many pupils discover

that the most interesting thing in the study of mathematics is mathematics itself. One of the most striking features in the teaching of mathematics today is thus the increasing attention given to development of ability to discover, verify, and generalize in the systematic study of mathematics. If pupils are to acquire these abilities, they must devote more attention to the development of concepts and gain a precision in vocabulary without which they cannot refine the concepts.

REFERENCES

Devine, Donald F., and Jerome E. Kaufymaun. *Elementary Mathematics for Teachers*. New York: John Wiley and Sons, 1983.

Grossnickle, Foster E. et. al., *Discovering Meanings in Elementary School Mathematics*. New York: Holt, Rinehart and Winston, Inc., 1983. Chapter Twenty and Twenty-One.

Kamii, Constance Kazuko. *Young Children Reinvent Arithmetic*. New York: Teacher's College Press, 1985.

Kennedy, Leonard M. *Guiding Children's Learning in Mathematics*. Fourth Edition. Belmont, California: Wadsworth Publishing Company, 1984.

Marks, John L., et. al. *Teaching Elementary School Mathematics for Understanding*. Fifth Edition. New York: McGraw-Hill Book Company, 1985.

McDonald, Frederick J. *Educational Psychology*. Second Edition. Belmont, California: Wadsworth Publishing Company, Inc., 1965. Chapters Fifteen—Seventeen.

Swenson, Esther J. *Teaching Mathematics to Children*. Second Edition. New York: The Macmillan Company, 1973.

47

Assessing State Mandated Tests

State mandated tests are being implemented rather rapidly in the public schools. The purpose of these tests is to

1. Notice and report pupil achievement.
2. Publish the results from these tests in the media.
3. Make comparisons among school districts and schools within the involved state.
4. Weed out low performing schools or give pupils in these schools a chance to transfer out, to a well performing school.
5. Provide diagnostic tools from test results to the classroom teacher of their pupils tested.
6. Provide teachers with a listing of state mandated objectives. The teacher may then align the local curriculum with the mandated objectives.
7. Establish inservice education programs for local teachers so that they may be able to assist pupils to achieve the state mandated objectives.
8. Develop within teachers the desire to have high expectations for pupil achievement.
9. Have teachers become conscious and motivated to achieve necessary skills to teach pupils to attain high standards of excellence in learning.
10. Help teachers to become conscious of the testing and measurement movement as a means of improving instruction (Ediger and Rao, 2000, Chapter Nine).

Comparing Differences Among Diverse State Standards

States differ much from each other as to the complexity level of their respective tests. Thus, the test results from the state's set of standards may be high as compared to a different state which has low pupil test results.

It is quite obvious that state standards are set arbitrarily. Perhaps, this is true of all state standards for pupils to achieve. Who is to decide which levels pupils should achieve in any academic discipline? In addition, the following questions are relevant to consider:

1. Should state pupil test results be compared with other states in the union when there is much variance in results in comparison with NAEP?
2. Should the difficulty level of each state's tests be reevaluated? This is crucial in high stakes testing whereby a pupil who fails may not receive a diploma for graduation.
3. Should the level of difficulty of state mandated tests be more realistic? It is one thing to desire a certain level of pupil achievement whereas pupils are not ready to perform at that level of complexity.
4. Should state objectives be more clearly written so that teachers may understand what might be covered in a mandated test?
5. Should test items on each state's assessment be reevaluated in terms of validity and reliability? There might well be test items which do not cover what has been taught in a classroom. Thus, validity is lacking. The tests may not measure consistently; reliability is then lacking.
6. Should each state mandated test be thoroughly pilot tested? In pilot studies, data may be obtained on test/retest, alternate forms, and/or split half reliability.
7. Should each state list the standard error of measurement for their tests? This is important in that the observer may then notice how much error in measurement there is on a state mandated test.
8. Should more faith be placed on alternatives to testing to notice pupil achievement? A single test score is hardly enough evidence to ascertain how well pupils are achieving.
9. Should state mandated tests be omitted and the NAEP take its place? Comparisons are made as to how state mandated tests differ from NAEP in terms of per cent passing each when making state by state comparisons.
10. Should a national curriculum be developed and implemented so that a nation wide mandated test may be given? This would tend to eliminate selected problems that exist when each state writes their very own tests (Ediger and Rao, 2001, Chapter Sixteen).

Thus, there are a plethora of questions which need answering, pertaining to state mandated testing. These are not easy questions to answer. It appears that for every action taken in state mandated testing, there is an opposite and equal reaction.

Alternative Forms of Pupil Evaluation

Educators looking for alternative forms of pupil evaluation have identified a portfolio replacement. Portfolios might also be used in addition to state testing and measurement. The two approaches differ form each other in philosophy involved.

The testing and measurement movement emphasizes a philosophy of realism. Realists stress a scientific approach in dealing with knowledge. Thus, the observer can know the real world in whole knowledge. Thus, the observer can know the real world in whole on in part, as it truly is. For example, chemists have identified 106-107 elements making up the planet earth. Elements can be combined to form molecules. Thus, for example, the formula for sugar is $C_6H_{12}O_6$. Six atoms of carbon, 12 atoms of hydrogen, and six atoms of oxygen is the formula for a molecule of sugar. Exactness and precision are then inherent in measurement. The behaviourally state objectives movement has it basis in realism in that

1. Each objective for pupils to achieve needs to be stated with precision.
2. The learning opportunities must be aligned for pupils to achieve these objectives.
3. Measurement and testing to ascertain if these objectives have been achieved is necessary to notice what pupils have learned.
4. The objectives of instruction need to be arranged in ascending order of complexity. Careful sequencing is wanted.
5. A numerical score provides the exact answer as to where a pupil is achieving. The numeral may be a percentile or a per cent (Ediger, 2002, pp 20-21).

Statewide testing omits pupil achievement reports from the every day work in class which learners do. The teacher has no input into test items content, times limits in giving the test, pilot study involvement, and/or modifications of the test. Portfolios take care of selected problems involved here. A portfolio then emphasizes constructivism/existentialism tenets in that the emphasizes constructivism/existentialism tenets in that the

1. The pupil with teacher guidance selects products/processes which should go into the personal portfolio to indicate that which has been learned.
2. A random sampling of items are then chosen for the portfolio.
3. Everyday classroom work is selected to be represented in portfolio content.
4. Parents and other responsible individuals might then view portfolio items to notice pupil achievement and progress.
5. Portfolios are to be assessed by professionals in the field of teaching and learning. The following are weaknesses in advocating portfolio use to appraise pupil achievement:

1. They are difficult to assess and cannot be machine scored. Since human evaluators need to assess the portfolio, much time is spent in the assessment process. If these are paid assessors, the expenses could be great, indeed, in the assessment program.
2. Interrater reliability could be low. Thus, two or more assessors for the same portfolio may come up with quite different results in its scoring.
3. It is difficult with the many entries for an evaluator to notice which products and processes pertain to any single objective of instruction.
4. Rubric use may cut down on some of the subjectivity in the assessment process. But, rubrics generally contain rather broad criteria to use in their evaluation by raters.
5. Too many entries in a portfolio make for a time consuming assessment activity (Ediger, 1994, 31-43).

Portfolio advocates need to view the above five named weaknesses and work in the direction of taking out kinks. Weaknesses identified in either the testing/measuring approach or in portfolio use, provide healthy suggestions in working toward overcoming these problem areas.

Suggestions for Developers of State Mandated Tests

Those in charge of developing state mandated tests should not become overly ambitious in establishing complex objectives for pupil attainment. The objectives should be challenging, but achievable. Each pupil needs to achieve as much as possible. What is desired by the state for pupils to achieve may not be possible in reality. Establishing state standards and objectives for pupils to attain is not a science, but an art. *People* choose which standards and objectives pupils are to achieve. They do the analyzing and writing. Truth is in the eye of the beholder.

What has been taught and learned meaningfully may be tested in order for validity to be present. The state, too, needs to be careful that adequate reliability is there when tests are adopted to evaluate pupil achievement. Thus, consistency of test results from any one pupil is important. From pilot studies, the standard error of measurement needs to be spelled out clearly by the state. If the standard error of measurement is large, then specific cut off points for high stakes testing should not be enforced.

States need to test meaningfully what pupils have had opportunities to learn, as listed in their objectives of instruction and these must be available to all teachers to use as guidelines for teaching. To use a single test for all pupils in a state violates the concept of providing for individual differences. Pupils differ from each other in a plethora of ways, one being the intelligences possessed. Testing emphasizes the use of verbal intelligences as in reading. Others may excel in music, art, physical skills as in athletics and dance, among others (Gardner, 1993). Pupils, too, differ from each other in abilities possessed. A single standard such as a state mandated test does not appear to provide or individual differences. The handicapped child may need accommodations such as having more time to complete test items (Searson and Dunn, 22-26).

There are numerous problems which need identification and solutions pertaining to testing and measuring pupil achievement, but it state mandated or other tests. High quality tests with desired validity and reliability data need to be in the offing.

REFERENCES

Ediger, Marlow (1994), "Philosophy in Teacher Education Programs," *The Journal of Teaching Practice,* 14 (2), 31-43.

Ediger, Marlow, and D. Bhaskara Rao (2001), *Teaching Social Studies Successfully.* New Delhi, India: Discovery Publishing House, Chapter Sixteen.

Ediger, Marlow, and D. Bhaskara Rao (2000), *Teaching Mathematics Successfully.* New Delhi, India: Discovery Publishing House, Chapter Nine.

Ediger, Marlow and D. Bhaskara Rao (2002), *Improving School Administration.* New Delhi, India: Discovery Publishing House.

Ediger, Marlow (2002), *"Writing Achievement in Technical Education,"* ATEA Journal, 29 (3), 20-21.

Gardner, Howard (1993), *Multiple intelligences: Theory Into Practice.* New York: Basic Books.

Olson, Lynn (February 20, 2002), "A Proficient Score Depends Upon Geography," *Education Week,* 21 (23), pp 1, 14, 15.

Searson, Robert, and Rita Dunn (2001), "The Learning Styles Teaching Model," *Science and Children,* 39 (5), 22-26.

Bibliography

Additional Reading

Bhaskara Rao, Digumarti (1994). *Scientific Aptitude*. New Delhi: Ashish Publishing House. pp: 100. Rs. 100. ISBN 81-7024-658-X.

Bhaskara Rao, Digumarti (1995). *Animal Kingdom*. New Delhi: Discovery Publishing House. pp: 135. Rs. 200. ISBN 81-7141-274-2.

Bhaskara Rao, Digumarti (1995). *Batracology*. New Delhi: Discovery Publishing House. pp: 174. Rs. 250. ISBN 81-7141-279-3.

Bhaskara Rao, Digumarti (1996). *Scientific Attitude vis-a-vis Scientific Aptitude*. New Delhi: Discovery Publishing House. pp: 143 Rs. 275. ISBN 81-7141-308-0.

Bhaskara Rao, Digumarti, ed. (1996). *Encyclopaedia of Education For All*, 5 vols. New Delhi: APH Publishing Corporation. pp: 1460. Rs. 3000. ISBN 81-7024-759-4. (set).

Vol. I *Education For All: The World Conference* pp: 440. ISBN 81-7024-760-8.

Vol. II *Education For All: The EPA—9 Summit*. pp: 340. ISBN 81-7024-761-6.

Vol. III *Education For All: Quality Education For All*. pp: 250. ISBN 81-7024-762-4.

Vol. IV *Education For All: Planning and Monitoring*. pp: 170. ISBN 81-7024-763-2.

Vol. V *Education For All: The Indian Scenario*. pp: 260. ISBN 81-7024-764-0.

Bhaskara Rao, Digumarti, ed. (1996). *Global Perceptions on Peace Education*, 3 Vols. New Delhi: Discovery Publishing House. pp: 980 Rs. 1800. ISBN 81-7141-319-6.

Bhaskara Rao, Digumarti, ed. (1996). *National Policy on Education*, 2 Vols. New Delhi: Anmol Publications Pvt. Ltd. pp: 710. Rs. 1000. ISBN 81-7488-323-1.

Bhaskara Rao, Digumarti, ed. (1997). *Care the Child*, 2 Vols. New Delhi: Discovery Publishing House. pp: 616. Rs. 1000. ISBN 81-7141-394-3.

Bhaskara Rao, Digumarti, ed. (1997). *Education for the 21st Century*. New Delhi: Discovery Publishing House. pp: 288. Rs. 500. ISBN 81-7141-389-7.

Bhaskara Rao, Digumarti, ed. (1997). *Reflections on Scientific Attitude*. New Delhi: Discovery Publishing House. pp: 310. Rs. 500. ISBN 81-7141-328-5.

Bhaskara Rao, Digumarti (1997). *Scientific Attitude*. New Delhi: Discovery Publishing House. pp: 120. Rs. 225. ISBN 81-7141-381-1.

Bhaskara Rao, Digumarti, ed. (1997). *Success Story of a Primary Education Project*. New Delhi: APH Publishing Corporation. pp: 260. Rs. 400. ISBN 81-7024-850-7.

Bhaskara Rao, Digumarti, ed. (1997) *World Food Summit*. New Delhi: Discovery Publishing House. pp: 153. Rs. 300. ISBN 81-7141-386-2.

Bhaskara Rao, Digumarti, ed. (1998). *Adolescence Education*. New Delhi: Discovery Publishing House. pp: 238. Rs. 350. ISBN 81-7141-432-X.

Bhaskara Rao, Digumarti, ed. (1998). *Community and School Nutrition Education*. New Delhi: Discovery Publishing House. pp: 425. Rs. 650. ISBN 81-7141-435-4.

Bhaskara Rao, Digumarti, ed. (1998). *District Primary Education Programme*. New Delhi: Discovery Publishing House. pp: 506. Rs. 650. ISBN 81-7141-396-X.

Bhaskara Rao, Digumarti, ed. (1998). *Earth Summit*, 2 Vols. New Delhi: Discovery Publishing House. pp: 930. Rs. 1500. ISBN 81-7141-435-4.

Bhaskara Rao, Digumarti, ed. (1998). *National Policy on Education: Towards an Enlightened and Humane Society*. New Delhi: Discovery Publishing House. pp: 542. Rs. 860. ISBN 81-7141-426-5.

Bhaskara Rao, Digumarti, ed. (1998). *Reforming School Education*. New Delhi: Discovery Publishing House. pp: 575. Rs. 750. ISBN 81-7141-403-6.

Bhaskara Rao, Digumarti, ed. (1998). *Teacher Education in India*. New Delhi: Discovery Publishing House. pp: 424. Rs. 600. ISBN 81-7141-406-0.

Bhaskara Rao, Digumarti, ed. (1998). *World Summit for Social Development*. New Delhi: Discovery Publishing House. pp: 278. Rs. 450. ISBN 81-7141-420-6.

Bhaskara Rao, Digumarti, ed. (2000). *Education For All: Achieving the Goal*. 3 Vols. New Delhi: APH Publishing Corporation. pp: 830. Rs. 2000. ISBN 81-7648-152-1.

Vol. I *The Global Consensus*. pp: 285. ISBN 81-7648-153-X.

Vol. II *Mid-Decade Review Reports of Regional Seminars*. pp: 198. ISBN 81-7648-154-8.

Vol. III *Issues and Trends*. pp: 346. ISBN 81-7648-155-6.

Bhaskara Rao, Digumarti, ed. (2000). *International Encyclopaedia of AIDS*, 11 Vols. in 13 parts. New Delhi: Discovery Publishing House. pp: 3676. Rs. 7500. ISBN 81-7141-465-6 (set).

Vol. 1 *Introduction to HIV/AIDS*. pp: 246. Rs. 500. ISBN 81-7141-523-7.

Vol. 2 *HIV/AIDS—Issues and Challenges*, 2 parts. pp: 805. Rs. 1700. ISBN 81-7141-524-5.

Vol. 3 *HIV/AIDS—Socio Economic Realities*. pp: 436. Rs. 900. ISBN 81-7141-525-3.

Vol. 4 *HIV/AIDS Law Ethics and Human Rights*, 2 parts. pp: 859. Rs. 1800. ISBN 81-7141-526-1.

Vol. 5 *AIDS and NGOs*. pp: 215. Rs. 450. ISBN 81-7141-527-X.

Vol. 6 *Aids and Home Care* pp: 183. Rs. 400. ISBN 81-7141-528-8.

Vol. 7 *STD Case Management* pp: 223. Rs. 475. ISBN 81-7141-529-6.

Vol. 8 *HIV Prevention and Care—Teaching Modules for Nurses and Midwives*. pp: 125. Rs. 275. ISBN 81-7141-530-X.

Vol. 9 *HIV/AIDS Prevention Education for Educational Institutions*. pp: 75. Rs. 150. ISBN 81-7141-531-8.

Vol. 10 *Instructional Modules for AIDS Education*. pp: 111. Rs. 250. ISBN 81-7141-532-6.

Vol. 11 *School Health Education to Prevent AIDS and STD—A Package for Curriculum Planners*. pp: 298. Rs. 600. ISBN 81-7141-533-4.

Bhaskara Rao, Digumarti, ed. (2000). *International Encyclopaedia of Science and Technology Education*. 11 Volumes. New Delhi: Discovery Publishing House. pp: 4892. Rs. 8500. ISBN 81-7141-548-2 (set).

Vol. 1 *Science and Technology Education*. pp: 557. Rs. 975. ISBN 81-7141-568-7.

Vol. 2 *Science Education in Developing Countries*. pp: 334. Rs. 600. ISBN 81-7141-570-9.

Vol. 3 *Organisational Structure of Science*. pp: 334. Rs. 600. ISBN 81-7141-570-9.

Vol. 4 *Science Education in Asia and the Pacific*. pp: 429. Rs. 750. ISBN 81-7141-571-7.

Vol. 5 *Science and Technology Education For All*. pp: 464. Rs. 800. ISBN 81-7141-572-5.

Vol. 6 *Values, Ethics, Talent and Girls in Science and Technology Education*. pp: 463. Rs. 800 ISBN 81-7141-573-3.

Vol. 7 *Popularization of Science and Technology Education*. pp. 334. Rs. 600. ISBN 81-7141-574-1.

Vol. 8 *Scientific, Power and Society*. pp: 357. Rs. 625. ISBN 81-7141-575-X.

Vol. 9 *Information Technology*. pp: 442. Rs. 775. ISBN 81-7141-576-8.

Vol. 10 *Teacher Training in Science and Technology Education*. pp: 536. Rs. 975. ISBN 81-7141-577-6.

Vol. 11 *Science, Technology and Society: A Curriculum Framework*. pp: 642. Rs. 1000. ISBN 81-7141-578-4.

Bhaskara Rao, Digumarti, ed. (2001). *Distance Education in Different Countries*. New Delhi: APH Publishing Corporation. pp: 574. Rs. 1500. ISBN 81-7648-229-3.

Bhaskara Rao, Digumarti, ed. (2001). *Decentralised Management of Education (Management of Education in Panchayati Raj and Municipal Bodies)*. New Delhi: Discovery Publishing House. pp: 116. Rs. 250. ISBN 81-7141-617-9.

Bhaskara Rao, Digumarti, ed. (2001). *Electrochemistry for Environmental Protection*. New Delhi: Discovery Publishing House. pp: 208. Rs. 400. ISBN 81-7141-619-5.

Bhaskara Rao, Digumarti, ed. (2001). *Global Educational Studies*. New Delhi: Discovery Publishing House. pp: 145. Rs. 300. ISBN 81-7141-616-0.

Bhaskara Rao, Digumarti, ed. (2001) *Global Synthesis of Educational Assessment*. New Delhi: Discovery Publishing House. pp: 152. Rs. 300. ISBN 81-7141-613-6.

Bhaskara Rao, Digumarti, ed. (2001). *International Encyclopaedia of Human Rights*, 7 Volumes in 13 Parts. New Delhi. Discovery Publishing House, pp: 6500 (Royal Size). Rs. 22000. ISBN 81-7141-567-9 (set).

Vol. 1 *International Instruments of Human Rights*, 2 Parts. Rs. 3500. ISBN 81-7141-595-4.
Vol. 2 *Regional Instruments of Human Rights*. Rs. 1500. ISBN 81-7141-604-7.
Vol. 3 *Human Rights and the United Nations*, 2 Parts. Rs. 2800. ISBN 81-7141-605-5.
Vol. 4 *Fact Files of Human Rights*, 2 Parts. Rs. 3000. ISBN 81-7141-606-3.
Vol. 5 *Study Stories of Human Rights*, 3 Parts. Rs. 5200. ISBN 81-7141-607-1.
Vol. 6 *International Meetings on Human Rights*, 2 Parts. Rs. 3800. ISBN 81-7141-608-X.
Vol. 7 *Professional Training in Human Rights*. Rs. 2200. ISBN 81-7141-609-8.

Bhaskara Rao, Digumarti, ed. (2001). *Jomtein Decade of Education*. New Delhi: Discovery Publishing House. pp: 106. Rs. 225. ISBN 81-7141-618-7.

Bhaskara Rao, Digumarti, ed. (2001). *Nuclear Materials: Issues and Concerns*, 2 Vols. New Delhi: Discovery Publishing House. pp: 1100. Rs. 2200. ISBN 81-7141-611-X.

Bhaskara Rao, Digumarti, ed. (2001). *World Conference on Education for All*. New Delhi: APH Publishing Corporation. pp: 380. Rs. 995. ISBN 81-7648-274-9.

Bhaskara Rao, Digumarti, ed. (2001). *World Conference on Higher Education*. New Delhi: Discovery Publishing House. pp: 306. Rs. 600. ISBN 81-7141-610-1.

Bhaskara Rao, Digumarti, ed. (2001). *World Conference on Science*. New Delhi: Discovery Publishing House. pp: 85. Rs. 200. ISBN 81-7141-612-8.

Bhaskara Rao, Digumarti, ed. (2002). *Chernobyl Never Again*. New Delhi: Discovery Publishing House.

Bhaskara Rao, Digumarti, ed. (2002). *Habitat Agenda*. New Delhi: Discovery Publishing House.

Bhaskara Rao, Digumarti, ed. (2002). *International Studies in Education*. New Delhi: Discovery Publishing House.

Bhaskara Rao, Digumarti, ed. (2002). *Inspiring Experiences in Teacher Education*. New Delhi. Discovery Publishing House.

Bhaskara Rao, Digumarti, ed. (2002). *Military Conversion: Impact on Science and Technology*. New Delhi. Discovery Publishing House.

Bhaskara Rao, Digumarti, ed. (2002). *Virology and Immunology*. New Delhi. Discovery Publishing House.

Bhaskara Rao, Digumarti, ed. (2002). *World Assembly on Aging*. New Delhi. Discovery Publishing House.

Bhaskara Rao, Digumarti, ed. (2002). *World Conference on Human Rights*. New Delhi. Discovery Publishing House.

Bhaskara Rao, Digumarti, ed. (2002) *World Education Forum*. New Delhi. Discovery Publishing House.

Bhaskara Rao, Digumarti, C.A.P. Swamy and B.S.V. Dutt (1997). *Self Evaluation in Student Teaching*. New Delhi: Discovery Publishing House. pp: 762. Rs. 150. ISBN 81-7141-374-9.

Bhaskara Rao, Digumarti, C. Sridevi and K. Vijaya (1995). *Achievement in*

Social Studies. New Delhi: Discovery Publishing House. pp: 102. Rs. 150. ISBN 81-7141-281-5.

Bhaskara Rao, Digumarti and Digumarti Pushpa Latha (1994). *Achievement in Biology*. New Delhi: Discovery Publishing House. pp: 102. Rs. 125. ISBN 81-7141-264-5.

Bhaskara Rao, Digumarti and Digumarti Pushpa Latha (1995). *Achievement in English*. New Delhi: Discovery Publishing House. pp: 214. Rs. 275. ISBN 81-7141-283-1.

Bhaskara Rao, Digumarti and Digumarti Pushpa Latha (1995). *Achievement in Science*. New Delhi: Discovery Publishing House. pp: 159. Rs. 225. ISBN 81-7141-280-7.

Bhaskara Rao, Digumarti and Digumarti Pushpa Latha (1995). *Achievement in Mathematics*. New Delhi: Discovery Publishing House. pp: 125. Rs. 175. ISBN 81-7141-278-5.

Bhaskara Rao, Digumarti and Digumarti Pushpa Latha, eds. (1998). *International Encyclopaedia of Women*, 5 Vols. New Delhi: Discovery Publishing House. pp: 2172. Rs. 4000. ISBN 81-7141-410-9.

Vol. 1 *Status of World's Women* pp: 427. Rs. 750. ISBN 81-7141-494-X.

Vol. 2 *Women, Education and Empowerment*. pp: 467. Rs. 875. ISBN 81-7141-498-2.

Vol. 3 *Women Challenges and Advancement*. pp: 354. Rs. 650. ISBN 81-7141-497-4.

Vol. 4 *Women and Family Health*. pp: 470. Rs. 875. ISBN 81-7141-497-4.

Vol. 5 *Women and International Action*. pp: 453. Rs. 850. ISBN 81-7141-498-2.

Bhaskara Rao, Digumarti, Digumarti Pushpa Latha and Digumarti Harshitha, eds. (2001). *Biological Warfare*. New Delhi: Discovery Publishing House. pp: 422. Rs. 800. ISBN 81-7141-597-0.

Bhaskara Rao, Digumarti, Digumarti Pushpa Latha and Digumarti Harshitha, eds. (2001). *Women as Educators*. New Delhi: Discovery Publishing House. pp: 112. Rs. 200. ISBN 81-7141-602-0.

Bhaskara Rao, Digumarti and Digumarti Harshitha (2000). *Education in India*. New Delhi: APH Publishing Corporation. pp: 280. Rs. 700. ISBN 81-7648-207-2.

Bhaskara Rao, Digumarti, and Digumarti Harshitha eds. (2001). *Assessing Learning Achievement*. New Delhi: Discovery Publishing House. pp: 128. Rs. 225. ISBN 81-7141-601-2.

Bhaskara Rao, Digumarti and Digumarti Harshita, eds. (2001). *Energy Security*. New Delhi: Discovery Publishing House. pp: 564. Rs. 1000. ISBN 81-7141-598-9.

Bhaskara Rao, Digumarti, D. Harshitha and K.R.S.S. Rao. eds. (1999). *Advanced Biotechnology*. New Delhi: Discovery Publishing House. pp: 335. Rs. 550. ISBN 81-7141-516-4.

Bhaskara Rao, Digumarti and D. Sridhar (2002). *Job Satisfaction of School Teachers*. New Delhi. Discovery Publishing House.

Bhaskara Rao, Digumarti and K.R.S. Sambasiva Rao, eds. (1996). *Current Trends in Indian Education*. New Delhi: Discovery Publishing House. pp: 234. Rs. 400. ISBN 81-7141-311-0.

Bhaskara Rao, Digumarti and K. Vijaya (1995). *A Text Book Evaluation*. Ambala Cantt: The Associated Publishers. pp: 100. Rs. 160.

Bhaskara Rao, Digumarti and N.V. Mohan Rao (2002). *Problem of Mentally Handicapped Children*. New Delhi. Discovery Publishing House.

Bhaskara Rao, Digumarti, V.V. Rao, V.V. Lakshmi and V.V. Krishna, eds. (2000). *Status and Advancement of Women*. New Delhi: APH Publishing Corporation. pp: 570. Rs. 1100. ISBN 81-7648-169-6.

Babu, P.C. and Digumarti Bhsakara Rao, ed. (2002). *Flowers of Wisdom*. New Delhi. Discovery Publishing House.

Bhagya Lakshmi, Lingineni and Digumarti Bhaskara Rao, ed. (2000). *Reading and Comprehension*. New Delhi: Discovery Publishing House. pp: 108. Rs. 175. ISBN 81-7141-543-1.

Bhuvaneswara Lakshmi, G. and Digumarti Bhaskara Rao, ed. (2000). *Attitude Towards Science*. New Delhi: Discovery Publishing House. pp: 128. Rs. 250. ISBN 81-7141-541-6.

Devraj, T.A.S. and Digumarti Bhaskara Rao, ed. (1997). *Trace Analysis of Uranium and Thorum*. New Delhi: Discovery Publishing House. pp: 195. Rs. 350. ISBN 81-7141-375-7.

Durgani Rani, K. and Digumarti Bhaskara Rao, ed. (2000). *Educational Aspirations and Scientific Attitudes*. New Delhi: Discovery Publishing House. pp: 130. Rs. 250. ISBN 81-7141-555-55.

Dutt, B.S.V. and Digumarti Bhaskara Rao (2001). *Empowering Primary Teachers*. New Delhi: Discovery Publishing House. pp. 283. Rs. 475. ISBN 81-7141-615-2.

Ediger, Marlow and Digumarti Bhaskara Rao (1996). *Science Curriculum*. New Delhi: Discovery Publishing House. pp: 309. Rs. 450. ISBN 81-7141-321-8.

Ediger, Marlow and Digumarti Bhaskara Rao (2000). *Teaching Mathematics Successfully*. New Delhi: Discovery Publishing House. pp: 279. Rs. 525. ISBN 81-7141-552-0.

Ediger, Marlow and Digumarti Bhaskara Rao (2000). *Teaching Reading Successfully*. New Delhi: Discovery Publishing House. pp: 386. Rs. 750. ISBN 81-7141-556-3.

Ediger Marlow and Digumarti Bhaskara Rao (2001). *Teaching Science Successfully*. New Delhi Discovery Publishing House. pp: 320. Rs. 600. ISBN 81-7141-600-4.

Ediger, Marlow and Digumarti Bhaskara Rao (2001). *Teaching Social Studies Successfully*. New Delhi: Discovery Publishing House. pp: 296. Rs. 575. ISBN 81-7141-596-2.

Ediger, Marlow and Digumarti Bhaskara Rao (2002). *Improving School Administration*. New Delhi. Discovery Publishing House. Rs. 500. ISBN 81-7141-633-0.

Ediger, Marlow and Digumarti Bhaskara Rao (2002). *Philosophy and Curriculum*. New Delhi. Discovery Publishing House. Rs. 450. ISBN 81-7141-631-4.

Ediger, Marlow and Digumarti Bhaskara Rao (2002). *Language Arts Curriculum*. New Delhi. Discovery Publishing House.

Ediger, Marlow and Digumarti Bhaskara Rao. *Teaching Language Arts Successfully*. New Delhi: Discovery Publishing House.

Jayasree, Kandi and Digumarti Bhaskara Rao, ed. (1999). *Correlates of Socialisation*. New Delhi: Discovery Publishing House. pp: 160. Rs. 375. ISBN 81-7141-517-2.

John Babu, Ch., T.J.R. Prasad, G.M. Madhukar and Digumarti Bhaskara Rao, eds. (2001). *Problem Solving in Mathematics*. New Delhi: APH Publishing Corporation. pp: 125. Rs. 250. ISBN 81-7648-273-0.

Kostiouk, Valery V. and Digumarti Bhaskara Rao, ed. (2002). *A Text Book of Cryogenics*. New Delhi. Discovery Publishing House. Rs. 575. ISBN 81-7141-642-X.

Koustiouk, Valery V. and Digumarti Bhaskara Rao, ed. (2002). *Refrigiration and Environment*. New Delhi. Discovery Publishing House.

Marja, Talvi and Digumarti Bhaskara Rao, eds. (1996). *Educational Leadership and Social Changes*. New Delhi: Discovery Publishing House. pp: 236. Rs. 400. ISBN 8-7141-320-X.

Nirmala, Jyothi and Digumarti Bhaskara Rao, ed. (2002). *Non-Detention System*. New Delhi. Discovery Publishing House.

Prabhakaram, K.S. and Digumarti Bhaskara Rao, ed. (1998). *Concept Attainment Model in Mathematics Teaching*. New Delhi: Discovery Publishing House. pp: 122. Rs. 200. ISBN 81-7141-424-9.

Prasanth Kumar, J. and Digumarti Bhaskara Rao, ed. (1998). *Effectiveness of Distance Education System*. New Delhi: Discovery Publishing. pp: 152. Rs. 275. ISBN 81-7141-437-0.

Prasanth Kumar, J., and Digumarti Bhaskara Rao and G. Sundara Rao, eds. (2000). *Open University Student Support Services*. New Delhi: Discovery Publishing House. pp: 100. Rs. 200. ISBN 81-7141-550-4.

Ramkumar Ratnam, M.V, and Digumarti Bhaskara Rao, ed. (2002). *Dukkha: Suffering in Early Buddhism*. New Delhi. Discovery Publishing House.

Rama Krishnaiah, D. and Digumarti Bhaskara Rao, ed. (1998). *Job Satisfaction of College Teachers*. New Delhi: Discovery Publishing House. pp: 251. Rs. 400. ISBN 81-7141-438-9.

Rama Tulasamma and Digumarti Bhaskara Rao, ed. (2002). *Job Satisfaction of Teacher Educators*. New Delhi. Discovery Publishing House.

Ramesh, Ganta and Digumarti Bhaskara Rao, eds. (1998). *Environmental Education: Problems and Prospects*. New Delhi: Discovery Publishing House. pp: 324. Rs. 525. ISBN 81-7141-423-0.

Rathaiah, L. and Digumarti Bhaskara Rao, eds. (1997). *International Innovations in Education*. New Delhi: Discovery Publishing House. pp: 514. Rs. 750. ISBN 81-7141-359-5.

Rathaiah, Lavu, Digumarti Bhaskara Rao and Paturi Koteswara Rao. (1997). *Achievement Correlates*. New Delhi: Discovery Publishing House. pp: 116. Rs. 225. ISBN 81-7141-385-4.

Sanjeeva Rao, P.C. and Digumarti Bhaskara Rao, ed. (1996). *A Text Book of Geology*. New Delhi: Discovery Publishing House. pp: 320. Rs. 525 ISBN 81-7141-313-7.

Satya Narayana, V. and Digumarti Bhaskara Rao, ed. (2001). *Physical Education, Social Attitudes and Leadership Qualities*. New Delhi: Discovery Publishing House. pp: 296. Rs. 575. ISBN 81-7141-593-8.

Srinivasulu Reddy, M., K.R.S. Sambasiva Rao and Digumarti Bhaskara Rao, ed. (1999). *A Text Book of Agriculture*. New Delhi: Discovery Publishing House. pp: 296. Rs. 525. ISBN 81-7141-482-6.

Sudhakara Reddy and Digumarti Bhaskara Rao, ed. (2002). *Creativity in Adolescents*. New Delhi. Discovery Publishing House.

Vanaja, M. and Digumarti Bhaskara Rao, ed. (1999). *Inquiry Training Model*. New Delhi: Discovery Publishing House. pp: 189. Rs. 325. ISBN 81-7141-515-6.

Veena Kumari, Balusu and Digumarti Bhaskara Rao (1996). *Operational Black Board*. New Delhi: APH Publishing Corporation. pp: 140. Rs. 200. ISBN 81-7024-711-X.

Veena Kumari, B. and Digumarti Bhaskara Rao, ed. (2000). *Psycho Social Correlates of Achievement*. New Delhi: Discovery Publishing House. pp: 136. Rs. 300. ISBN 81-7141-547-4.

Venkata Rao, P. and Digumarti Bhaskara Rao (1989). *A Text Book of Zoology—Junior Intermediate*. Guntur: Vignan Publishers. pp: 370. Rs. 57.

Venkata Rao, P. and Digumarti Bhaskara Rao (1989). *A Text Book of Zoology—Senior Intermediate*. Guntur: Vignan Publishers. pp: 480. Rs. 68.

Venugopala Rao, K. and Digumarti Bhaskara Rao, ed. (2000). *Teacher Morale in Secondary Schools*. New Delhi: Discovery Publishing House. pp: 300. Rs. 575. ISBN 81-7141-551-2.

Vidya, C. and Digumarti Bhaskara Rao, ed. (1996). *A Text Book of Nutrition*. New Delhi: Discovery Publishing House. pp: 438. Rs. 650. ISBN 81-7141-309-9.

Vijaya Bharathi, D. and Digumarti Bhaskara Rao, ed. (2000). *Educational Philosophies of Swami Vivekanand and John Dewey*. New Delhi: APH Publishing Corporation. pp: 200. Rs. 500. ISBN 81-7648-202-1.

Bhaskara Rao, Digumarti. (1986). *Dhrushya Sravana Bodhanapakaranalu* (Audio Visual Teaching Aids). Guntur: Nagarjuna Publishers.

Bhaskara Rao, Digumarti (1993). *Jeevasashtra Bodhana* (Teaching of Biology). Guntur: Nagarjuna Publishers.

Bhaskara Rao, Digumarti (1995). *Vignanasasthra Bodhana*. (Teaching of Science). Guntur: Nagarjuna Publishers.

Bhaskara Rao, Digumarti (1997). *Vidya Manovignana Sashtram*. (Educational Psychology). Guntur: Creative Press. pp. 434. Rs. 79.

Bhaskara Rao, Digumarti (1998). *DSC Study Material*. Guntur: Nagarjuna Publishers.

Bhaskara Rao, Digumarti (1998). *Upadhyayudu Vidya* (Teacher and Education). Guntur: Nagarjuna Publishers.

Bhaskara Rao, Digumarti (1998). *Vidya Dhrukpadhalu*. (Perspectives of Education). Guntur: Nagarjuna Publishers.

Bhaskara Rao, Digumarti (1999). *EdCET Teaching Aptitude*. Guntur: Nagarjuna Publishers.

Bhaskara Rao, Digumarti (2001). *Bharata Samajamulo Upadhayayudu Vidya*. (Teacher and Education in Emerging Indian Society). Guntur: Nagarjuna Publishers. pp: 256. Rs. 59.

Bhaskara Rao, Digumarti (2001). *Bhoutika Sastra Bodhana Padhatulu* (Methods of Teaching Physical Science). Guntur: Nagarjuna Publishers. pp: 324. Rs. 77.

Bhaskara Rao, Digumarti (2001). *Jeeva Sastra Bodhana Padhatulu* (Methods of Teaching Biological Science). Guntur: Nagarjuna Publishers. pp: 224. Rs. 59.

Bhaskara Rao, Digumarti (2001). *Vidya Manovignana Sastram* (Educational Psychology). Guntur: Nagarjuna Publishers. pp: 344. Rs. 77.